PULLING NO PUNCHES

PULLING NO PUNCHES

BARRY HALL

WITH MICHAEL COWLEY

Published in Australia in 2011 by Pier 9, an imprint of Murdoch Books Pty Limited

Murdoch Books Australia
Pier 8/9
23 Hickson Road
Millers Point NSW 2000
Phone: +61 (0) 2 8220 2000
Fax: +61 (0) 2 8220 2558
www.murdochbooks.com.au

Murdoch Books UK Limited
Erico House, 6th Floor
93–99 Upper Richmond Road
Putney, London SW15 2TG
Phone: +44 (0) 20 8785 5995
Fax: +44 (0) 20 8785 5985
www.murdochbooks.co.uk

For corporate orders and custom publishing contact Noel Hammond,
National Business Development Manager

Publishing director: Chris Rennie
Editor: Julian Welch
Project editor: Sarah Hazelton
Cover design: Blue Cork
Cover photography: Samantha Jarrett
Production: Joan Beal

Photographs in first section have been provided courtesy of the Hall family.
Photographs in second section provided by AFL Photos.

National Library of Australia Cataloguing-in-Publication entry
Author: Hall, Barry
Title: Pulling no punches / Barry Hall
ISBN: 978-1-74266-098-1 (pbk.)
Subjects: Hall, Barry
    Australian football players – Biography
    Football players – Australia – Biography
    Australian football – Biography
Dewey number: 796.336092

Printed by Hang Tai Printing Company Limited, China.

FOREWORD
BY RODNEY EADE

At times Australians suffer from tall poppy syndrome, looking to cut down those who have reached great heights in their chosen fields. But we do love an underdog, and cheer for those who attempt to battle back from adversity. Those who have made a mistake in their lives, whether it be one involving drugs or alcohol, or in sport. We support those who can take responsibility, admit they have done wrong, and then fight back, climbing out of where they have been to a better place. I think Barry Hall has done this.

I remember when I first met Barry, when I was coaching the Swans and we were looking at bringing him to Sydney from St Kilda. As a club, the Swans had been successful in transplanting players from Melbourne to Sydney, most notably Tony Lockett. With Tony retiring, the club was not only looking for a new forward, but a player who could be the face of the club. We saw Barry as that player.

Sure, I'd heard all the stories about Barry, but I tried not to pre-judge him. And after meeting him that first time, I could see I had done the right thing in giving him a chance. Barry is one of those colourful characters of football – larger than life to the fans who either love or loathe him. But there is so much more to Barry Hall than the on-field persona. He has a softer side to him that I learned about later by seeing him relate so well with people, especially kids.

In 2008, when he landed that blow on the chin of Brent Staker, I was both disappointed in him – that he'd done it, and disappointed for him – that he'd tarnished his image with an incident that would affect his reputation far into the future. What he did with Staker was really out of character. Sure, before that he'd been a physical player and had been suspended and reported, but he had never gone to that level, ever.

He's had quite a journey since then, and those incidents during his last two seasons in Sydney have left a shadow that will always hang over him. But I hope, through what Barry has done in the years since then, that people have seen another side of him. His work in the media has been very positive and has shown the public the sense of humour that those closer to him have always known. He can laugh at himself. More importantly, his conduct since has been exemplary in the way he presents himself, the way he speaks, and in his behaviour on the footy field.

I think, looking back, the bulk of what is said about him will be positive. He's put a lot of work into changing others' perceptions and opinions. People are often surprised when meeting Barry by just how humble he is, how hard he works and how generous with his time he is, especially with those in need. When it comes to Barry, he's more of a giver than a taker.

He's always put a lot of thought into his footy and been quite professional in the way he wanted to approach it. His thought process about the game is insightful, and being competitive has certainly helped. The thing, I believe, that dogged him in the years after our first meeting, and where he got into trouble, was that he could have a short fuse, which was made worse by the pressure of expectation he would often put on himself.

This was always a risk in signing Barry to the Western Bulldogs after he left the Swans in 2009, and he always said he couldn't promise anything. Barry is a very honest guy, there is no bull about him. What I knew through dealing with him was that if you're honest with him you will get it straight back. If you show some belief and trust, Barry will return it in spades.

Signing Barry was a community decision for the Bulldogs. As coach, I didn't make the decision alone. I pushed the idea forward and was positive about it, but we spoke to some players and the leadership group, then the management, the president, the CEO, and the football manager. Everyone had to be across it, and they were.

I was reasonably confident it would work out. I couldn't imagine he would play as well as he did in his first season – we certainly didn't expect him to come in and kick eighty goals in 2010. We really just wanted him to play his role in the team – and importantly, I thought he would fit into the environment at the Western Bulldogs pretty well.

And when it did work out for him, it wasn't about looking back or proving anyone who'd doubted him wrong – that wasn't a big issue for Barry. It was simply about living in the moment.

What I was most pleased about was that he got another shot after he left the Swans. If it hadn't been us at the Bulldogs, then I would still have liked to see him get a go somewhere else.

I think that's the point ... people generally want to see someone have a second shot. If a person has done wrong then to be able to rectify that, and to be able to show his or her true worth – as a sportsperson and as a human being, in this particular instance – well, everyone would want that chance.

Having the pleasure of knowing Barry, I think it would have been a shame if someone didn't actually give him that second chance. I'm glad we did, and I'm just as pleased for him that he grabbed it with both hands.

CHAPTER ONE

What was I like as a kid? No matter how many different ways I answer this question, I'm always greeted with a stunned look of disbelief – which is often followed by an accusation that I can't possibly be speaking the truth. Now, I consider myself a pretty honest guy, and I certainly have no reason to make up stories on this subject, yet I always find it hard to convince everyone what I was like.

People seem to think that Barry Hall the kid must have been a mini-version of Barry Hall the footballer. They imagine a big, imposing youngster, perhaps with a tattoo on his shoulder, a shaved head and a diamond stud in his ear. Most significantly, they picture a kid with a deeper-than-deep voice who used standover tactics on his schoolmates in the playground.

I'm going to have to shatter the myth. The youngster named Barry Hall who attended Broadford Primary School all those years ago was a skinny little kid with a high-pitched voice.

My voice has almost become a trademark now, and I suppose it fits in with my whole 'Big Bad Barry' persona, but it wasn't something I had as a kid. In fact, it didn't really start to get deeper until I was about sixteen or seventeen.

It can be quite funny nowadays. I might be making the simplest of statements to someone and they'll think I'm blowing up at them. But it's just my normal voice! It can work another way too. According to a few letters I have received from women over the years, my voice is pretty sexy and I should think about working on one of those live phone chat services. Hands up everyone who thought I would struggle for a career after football!

Anyway, back to the skinny kid with the squeaky voice. I was just a typical kid growing up in the country. Broadford, which is around ninety kilometres north of Melbourne, was a very quiet town of about 1500 people back then. It had a school footy oval, a couple of pubs and that was pretty much it. Like most small country towns, everyone knew everyone – and everyone knew everyone else's business, too.

We used to have a big bikie festival in Broadford each year, and as a result the town got a bit of a bad reputation as a rough and tumble sort of place. Admittedly, when you went to the pub you had to know how to hold your hands up, but for me Broadford was home and a good place.

I wasn't a straight-A student at school. I don't think I was terrible, although I did muck around a lot, but the problem was simple: I just didn't want to go. Like most kids, I had a bit of mischief in me, but really I was very shy and quiet. I loved the outdoors, and I'm told I loved kicking the footy from the moment I could walk. I remember early on I would get into trouble all the time because I would kick a rolled-up pair of socks around the house pretending I was a VFL player.

The only thing I ever really wanted when I was a kid was a good footy. I'm sure most people will probably know what I'm talking about when I say I owned one of those plastic footballs from Kmart. You know the ones – they're as hard as steel on the ends and soft in the middle, and once they got a hole in them, that was it, they were stuffed. But what do you expect from a two-dollar football? Anyway, that was all I had, and I made the most of it. Even if I do say so myself, I was pretty impressive in the back paddock with that ball, kicking plenty of after-the-siren, game-winning goals!

I was fanatical about footy. I didn't really have too many other interests, and there was certainly nothing I loved more than football. I'd been interested in cars since I was very young, and I had a motorbike. If I wasn't out kicking the footy I'd often be out in the garage watching Dad work on a car.

Dad worked in a quarry with explosives and things. Every evening, after he got home from work, he'd go straight out to the garage and work on his cars. I used to have a shower, get into my pyjamas and go out to the garage in the freezing cold so I could watch him build a motor or something like that. I don't know why, but it just mesmerised me – I'd sit there like a zombie, often for hours on end, watching him work.

But footy was the real passion for me as a kid, and everything else ran second to it. I'd ride my pushbike home from school every day, chuck my bag in my room, get changed and then head straight out into the back paddock on my own to play. I had goals set up and I'd play my own match out there, and even commentate it. That used to amuse Mum – she would sometimes peek over the fence, listen to my commentary and have a chuckle.

I was a Footscray supporter for as long as I can remember. It was a family tradition, and I was kind of brainwashed with it. My grandfather, my mother, my uncle: there were probably about five or six members of the family who barracked for the Bulldogs. My uncle Teddy used to take me down from time to time to watch a match at the Whitten Oval.

So I suppose it's hardly surprising that the results of my imaginary matches almost always finished in a win for my team, the Bulldogs. We would always find ourselves down by around ten or fifteen goals, but somehow we'd make a miraculous comeback. I would always pretend I was Simon Beasley, and during that final-quarter comeback – with a pretend Dougie Hawkins getting about thirty possessions – I'd always manage to get plenty of shots on goal, including that last kick, after the siren, from right on the boundary line, which I managed to kick more often than not! And when I'd miss, the umpire would sometimes call it back to give me another shot because someone had infringed. It's funny how things work out in a kid's world!

Back when I was growing up, one of the Hall family rituals was that, every Sunday, we'd have a roast dinner and then watch the game on TV. It was often a Sydney Swans game in fact, as their games in Sydney were usually played on Sunday afternoons and shown live in Melbourne. I could name every Swans player and all the players' numbers.

Back then, I never saw myself as being one of them. I played the game and kicked goals with my plastic footy in the paddock, but I never really thought that one day it might be me on TV playing in front of big crowds. I put those guys on a pedestal, and I never thought I could possibly be as good as any of them.

I wasn't one of those kids who dreamed of being a league footy player. Sure, like most kids, I would have loved to play for a living, but at no time during my childhood did I ever believe I had a realistic hope of making it to that level.

I moved from the back paddock to the footy field when I was eight and I started playing for the under-10s. It's a lot of years ago now, but I can still vividly remember my first game. It was pissing down with rain and there was mud everywhere. Mum and Dad took me to the game, and I can still hear Mum yelling out her encouragement to me. I think she was more excited about me being out there than I was.

In the young underage footy they pretty much put kids anywhere. I was thrown into the backline for my debut, but I didn't fancy staying there too long. I just kept following the ball around, like a bee to a honeypot, and the coach had to keep dragging me back to play on my man. I just had no idea what I was doing. I think I had one kick, and it was a kick off the ground. Hardly a memorable debut. I don't know why, but unlike in the back paddock, I just couldn't find Dougie Hawkins or Simon Beasley that afternoon.

Being an eight-year-old playing against older kids in the under-10s, and being one of the smaller ones as well, I quickly learned that I had to pull my weight in order to get anywhere. Even at training, competing against the bigger and older kids was difficult. If I sat back and didn't say anything, I knew I'd get walked all over. But it wasn't easy for me. At home, we'd been taught by Mum and Dad to be well-mannered. If we went out and visited people, us kids – my sister Amanda, who is three years older than me, my brother, David, who is nine years younger than me, and I – wouldn't speak up too much. We'd just sit there quietly. So it wasn't that I was too scared to speak up for myself in the footy team, it just wasn't the done thing.

We were pretty disciplined kids at home. We ate dinner at five o'clock every day, and we'd be there until we ate everything on our plates. If we didn't, we'd get the leftovers in the morning. That's not to say I didn't have some dinner-time tricks, like hiding the brussell sprouts in my sister's drink when she wasn't looking, or putting my peas in my pocket and flushing them down the toilet later.

But even though I was a shy eight-year-old, I learned fairly quickly that I couldn't just sit back when it came to footy. I needed to stand up, and the competitive streak came out in me. The next year I played fairly well. I started to learn more of the lurks and perks of the game – basically, I learned how to play footy – and I won the best and fairest.

In my final year in under-10s, I was tall, but from then until I was about sixteen I didn't grow very much. A mate of mine has kept a school photograph from when we were fourteen years old: I was about a foot shorter than everyone else, and as skinny as a rake.

Because I was small as a kid, I played on ball. My best attributes were that I was quick and could run long distances well – in fact, I was good enough to represent my school in athletics. I've no idea what happened to that ability!

When I tell people about how I was a short and skinny kid, I'm often asked whether I ever contemplated things like steroids to bulk up. The short answer is no – I never did and I never would.

And while I know there are players in the AFL who have tested positive to illicit drugs, I have honestly never seen drugs in any shape or form, not even marijuana, around any of the clubs I've been at. That may be because those who might have been using drugs knew how much I was against them, and so they never bothered offering them to me.

I've seen the effects drugs have had on people and I wouldn't want to go near them. With the exception of alcohol, I've never touched a drug; I've never even considered experimenting with them. Nor have I ever held a cigarette. Mum and Dad smoked and I hated it. My sister and my brother smoked as well. Why would you? It's disgusting.

I went camping once with my mates when I was younger. They were all sitting around the campfire smoking bongs and drinking beer. I had one beer and thought, 'You guys are dickheads – I'm not sitting around here with this bullshit.' I packed up my gear, jumped on my motorbike and went home. That was the last time I went camping with them.

CHAPTER TWO

While I was a bit of a timid kid, if push came to shove in the playground I made sure I shoved back. It wasn't that I ever went looking for a fight during my time at school, but somehow one or two managed to find me.

When I was about ten or eleven, my love of footy took a back seat. I started getting more involved in boxing, and particularly in martial arts. I learned a form called Zen Do Kai, then Ninjutsu, then karate, and after that I did Thai boxing, Muay Thai. My old man would take me and David down to Melbourne for it twice a week. I was right into it.

Because I was in the junior ranks, I wasn't allowed to fight full-contact. I won a couple of big all-styles tournaments, but I was also getting disqualified in others for head-high contact. It became a bit of a nightmare for me. The problem was that I had started training as a boxer, and so for me it was just instinctive to go for the head. Whenever I did that, I got disqualified, so my old man and I thought that the non-contact stuff wasn't much good for me. As the only full-contact sport for juniors was boxing, I began to get more involved in it.

I had always been interested in boxing. We had a Buffalo Sports yellow punching bag out in the garage. Every time I went out there, it looked so good that I always wanted to punch it. It was near the cars, though, and if it swung it would hit them, so I'd just tap it very lightly. Eventually, my old man said, 'Look, at night-time I'll back the cars out and you can give it a proper hit, and I'll teach you a little bit.' Gradually, with his coaching, I got better and better and better.

I played footy in the under-12s, but after that I quit and took up boxing full-time. The way I saw it, I could really only focus properly on one or the other, and I decided that it would be boxing.

I often wonder what might have been if I'd stuck with boxing and not got back into football, and that could easily have been the way it panned out. But in all honesty, I didn't really want to be a boxer. I did get quite good at it fairly quickly. It wasn't that Dad pushed me at all; he would just say, 'If you want to fight, we can get you a fight,' and things like that. I would say, 'Sure, no worries,' but I was doing it more to impress him than because I actively wanted to.

Dad put a lot of resources into my boxing. After a while, he transformed the garage into a gym for me – it was a pretty good gym too, and a lot of blokes who played in the seniors at the Broadford Footy Club would come around and use it. From the time I was twelve or thirteen, we'd go to Melbourne three times a week to train and spar. It was pretty full-on.

I don't know exactly how many fights I had during my career, but there were quite a few down in Melbourne – some at the Columbian Club, some at suburban RSL clubs or little pubs around the place. I lost one early on, but then I didn't lose one until my last fight, and I even managed to win a Victorian title – in the fifty-two-kilogram weight division – when I was fifteen.

The way it worked was you would get a phone call asking if you were keen on fighting this bloke or that bloke. I got a call asking if I wanted to fight for the state title and I accepted the offer.

While I got the win, it wasn't a dramatic knockout victory. In the fifty-two-kilo division there aren't too many knockouts. You have headgear on and the fights are just for three two-minute rounds. So it's a real sprint and you've got to be really fit. There isn't much power-punching going on. It's more of an accumulation of punches, trying to score points as quickly as you can because you don't have much time.

The feeling of winning that title isn't something that has stuck with me the way that winning an AFL premiership has. It felt okay at the time, but boxing is a bit like footy in that you don't linger too long on a win. You win a match and then you move on to the next one. This was a state title and it meant a bit more than the others I'd had, but if I lost my next fight then what would it mean? Nothing.

So there was no big hoopla or fanfare from me or my old man. We just went back to training and waited for the next fight.

Most amateur boxers start thinking about competing at the Olympics, and while it was in the back of my mind, it was never a goal for me. And I wasn't in the ring just to let out my aggression, either. I wasn't the sort of fighter who walked in and slugged it out. I relied more on my skill than my power. I was naturally competitive, but mainly I liked the fact that it was just me in there. In the ring I had no one else to rely on, and nowhere to hide. Amateur boxing has a lot to do with skill, and my dad and I believed that I was more skilful than most fighters I met.

When I was sixteen, I had a fight in Melbourne and lost. I was absolutely certain I had won, but politics played a part in it. I felt like I'd been completely ripped off. That was when I thought to myself, 'I'm working way too hard to be ripped off like this.' I decided that I needed a break from boxing.

I was training twice a day – before school and after school – and I was growing. I couldn't keep my weight down. I was doing my running training wearing a garbage bag, trying to strip off the weight, and I was starving myself. It was just a nightmare. And on top of that, my mates were starting to go to parties and hook up with girls, while I was sitting at home all the time thinking about getting my head punched in.

I was actually offered a fight for a national title, but I said no. I'd decided to take a break from boxing, but deep down I knew that meant I'd had enough. I just didn't have the guts to say I didn't want to do it anymore.

My old man's reaction wasn't good. He thought I had what it took to be a boxer, and I guess that's why he was so disappointed. But he didn't know how I really felt, or why I was boxing in the first place.

Before I told my old man I was quitting – when I was saying I was just taking a break – a guy I used to train with, Neville Williams, took me aside. He sat me down and said, 'You don't want to fight anymore, do you?' I said no, and he said, 'That's fine, and I don't expect you to tell your old man – your old man's pretty intense.' He made a phone call to my dad and told him I didn't want to fight anymore.

I stayed at Neville's house that night and then went home the next day. There wasn't too much talk at the dinner table that night. Dad had the shits with me really badly, and I knew he could hold a grudge. I understood why he was pissed off – I knew he'd invested a lot in my boxing.

A couple of days later, when I went out to watch him work on the cars, as he always did, he said, 'Get the hell out of my garage.' For about six months after that he didn't utter another word to me.

As a family, we lacked good communication skills. Nobody really knew how the others felt. The attitude was always: 'Harden up and move on.' When we tried to talk about things we usually blew up. My old man didn't know how I felt about boxing when I quit, or what my reasons were, or even why I'd got into boxing in the first place. We just never spoke about it, and hoped that time would heal things.

There were some pretty harsh times, then. I felt like my old man didn't want me around. All the stuff I had done as a kid – going out to the garage and watching him work on his cars – I couldn't do that stuff anymore. It was a really ordinary time for me.

There was no big event that started us talking again after those six months or so – it just gradually happened. But in all honesty, things were still not right between us. It was never the same as it used to be.

CHAPTER THREE

When I quit boxing at sixteen, it was 1993 and I hadn't played footy since about 1989. It wasn't as though I picked up a Sherrin straightaway and signed up to play again. The fact is that when I'd stopped playing footy back in the under-12s, I'd really never thought about playing again. It just wasn't on my radar at all, and I hadn't missed it one bit.

My life had been all about boxing and nothing else. I had felt like I would be betraying boxing if I tried to do both, and that I had to commit completely to one sport. If I was a boxer, I had to do it 100 per cent – fifty/fifty wouldn't do, and neither would ninety/ten. I knew that was how my old man wanted me to do it. It was all or nothing.

When I'd left footy and taken up boxing, for some reason or another I never saw myself playing the game again, which sounds a bit bizarre because I'd loved it so much as a younger kid. Back then, I couldn't think of anything better than booting the ball around our back paddock.

After boxing ended, for a year or so the only sport I was into was basketball. I played a fair bit of it with my mates and loved it. We were right into it, and we would play anywhere. This was when basketball was really big in Victoria and the National Basketball League was flying, and we got quite good at it. Darren Milburn, who ended up playing footy for Geelong, was on my team – he was also from Broadford and we were really good mates at school. By this time I had grown into a tall, skinny kid, which obviously helps in basketball. I couldn't shoot too well, so I just kept driving to the hoop.

I suppose most people have heard of Phil Cleary, the footballer, politician, author and commentator. Well, the man responsible for getting me back into football, and therefore the man responsible for kick-starting my AFL career, was Phil's brother, Paul Cleary.

I used to go to school with Paul Cleary's kids, Ben and Daniel. Out of the blue one day, they suggested I come and play with their under-18s team at Avenel. They were short of players and needed some kids to make up the numbers. Paul came around and convinced me to have a shot. He took me to training and it all started from there.

I was happy to go to training but I really wasn't planning to play, but Paul soon said, 'Come and play a practice match just for a bit of fun, and see how you go.'

I played that practice match and did pretty well. Afterwards, Paul said to me, 'Look, we're short on numbers this year and the team's going to struggle. Last season we came last, so we're not worried about winning the competition or anything too serious like that. Why don't you play with us this year?'

I thought about it for a while and decided I might as well. I had nothing else to do, I figured, so I played. After my big growth spurt, I was now a ruckman.

Avenel's in the middle of nowhere, really, so it wasn't as though we had football scouts coming along to see too many of our games. But our coach at Avenel, Ashley Pedder, and particularly Paul Cleary, would ring the Murray Bushrangers every week without fail, saying, 'Guys, you've got to come down and have a look at a few of these kids we've got.'

It took a while, but eventually they decided to make the trip and have a look at us towards the end of the year. Typically, I didn't have a great game that day. But Paul persisted, calling the Bushrangers back and telling them there was more to me, but the response wasn't good: 'Sorry,' they said, 'we just don't see what all the fuss is about.'

So, as determined as Paul was, it was left at that. Our team ended up being undefeated and won the flag. I managed to win the Inch Medal, the award for the best-and-fairest in the league, and one of Paul's sons, Daniel, won the goalkicking title. Paul was back on the phone to the Bushrangers again, saying, 'Look, you guys are kidding yourselves – you have to give these kids a shot.' Eventually – just to get Paul off their backs, I reckon – the Bushrangers invited both Ben Cleary and me to come and train with them.

The biggest problem I faced was that I was too old to come through the Bushrangers' development squad, which was their preferred route for their players. Realistically, I knew, I'd only be eligible to play one season with the team, so although I was offered a tryout, I didn't expect that they would think it was worth it for them to give me a go for that one season.

Anyway, at the end of our 1994 season, I went up to Wangaratta to do pre-season training with the Bushrangers squad. At one stage we did a full-ground drill, in which there was me and another guy leading out from full-forward. I was six-foot-four by this time and weighed in at eighty kilograms, and I was still quite mobile and athletic. I remember running at a couple of balls and jumping and plucking them out of the air pretty well. The coach, Kelly O'Donnell, came up to me after training and introduced himself. 'Who are you?' he asked. 'Where are you from, where have you been, and why weren't you here earlier?'

I was invited back, and over the next few weeks they started to cut the list back. Each time we did the full-ground drill, I was getting the centre half-forward job in front of the other guys. Within a month they had their final squad. While I made it, unfortunately Ben Cleary didn't.

Once the squad was finalised, Kelly O'Donnell came to me and said, 'We think you've got a heap of talent, and we want to build this team around you at centre half-forward.' It was crazy – in the space of a month I had gone from nothing, to getting a run at training, to being told by the coach I was a key figure in his plans.

It was a whirlwind for me. I'd been a ruckman for Avenel the previous season, and now I was to be a centre half-forward. I had no idea how to play centre half-forward. I was athletic and could run and jump. I could catch a football okay, and I felt I was a fairly good kick, but I knew I didn't have a good grasp of footy as a game, or the work required to be a better player. I realised that I faced a very sharp learning curve.

My transport situation also changed. Paul Cleary had been driving us up to the training sessions at Wangaratta, which was about an hour and a half from Broadford, but after they cut the list and his son Ben didn't make it, I could hardly expect him to keep driving me up there on my own, so I then had to start riding my motorbike up to training. Believe me, there were times when it was pouring down rain, or when trucks were roaring past me and nearly blowing me off my bike, that I was thinking, 'What the hell am I doing this for?'

Most of my family thought it was great that I'd made it into the Bushrangers squad, but I honestly don't know what my dad's feelings were. He might have thought it was good, but I guess if he had thought that, I would have sensed it a bit, and it didn't really come across that way to me.

While they were happy, the family, like me, weren't thinking about it leading to a career in the AFL. Our thoughts changed a little bit when I started playing: I got a few best-on-ground awards and was kicking six or seven goals a game.

But I only played about ten games that year, partly because of injury but also because I had a bit of a lackadaisical attitude. To be honest, sometimes I just couldn't be bothered training. From time to time I just rang up and said, 'Sorry, I'm not coming to training today,' and amazingly they'd just say, 'Okay.' I think I got away with a lot of crap because I was playing well. It wasn't that I thought I was so good that I could do whatever I wanted – not at all. In fact, it was probably the opposite – I just didn't care enough.

I guess I was just at that rebellious stage of life. I don't know if it had anything to do with what I'd gone through with my old man, but I just had the attitude that if I didn't want to do something, I wouldn't do it, no matter what it was or who wanted me to do it. If you fought against me, I'd just fight back even harder.

If the Bushrangers had said to me, 'Look, unless you turn up for training and give it your all, we're going to sack you,' then I probably would have said, 'Fine, nice knowing you, see ya later.' That's just how I was. When I think about it now, it sounds weird, but I really could easily have walked away then and gone to do something else. If I had, it probably would have been something to do with cars.

I had left school part of the way through 1994. I just didn't want to be there anymore. I wasn't the best student and I definitely wasn't there to learn, so I thought I should try to get a job instead. I was interested in cars and so I asked about getting an apprenticeship through a mate of a mate who knew a guy at Waterford Panels. Luckily, I was in the right place at the right time and they offered me the job.

My parents were okay with me leaving school. I think they were happy I had somewhere to go. If I'd had no job to go to then I'm sure they wouldn't have been too impressed, but it all worked out. I've never had any regrets about leaving school when I did.

My old man did give me a few bits of advice at the time – such as if I wasn't sure about things then I should make sure to ask. I guess the fact that he did take an interest in what I was doing showed me that he was pleased about it. At least, he was probably happy that I wasn't sitting on my backside doing nothing. And I reckon the fact that I had got into that sort of work with cars pleased him too, as it was something he was interested in.

As for the job itself ... Well, I wasn't too good at sweeping the dust off the floor!

I still hear from Paul Cleary every now and again. He's never reminded me about how he got me back into footy and how everything panned out, but I know he's always watched my career with interest. Of course, I'm extremely grateful for everything he did for me.

I look back on my life, as I guess everyone does, and see these little moments that have changed its course. For me, one such moment was when Paul Cleary convinced me to play footy again.

CHAPTER FOUR

I played only one season with the Bushrangers – 1995 – and late that year, about a month before the draft, I got a phone call from Kelly O'Donnell. He wanted to let me know that a few AFL clubs had been in contact with him and made enquiries about me. He told me the realistic feeling he got was that a club would pick me up and put me on their supplementary list. Typical of me at the time, I wasn't too excited. 'Oh, yeah?' I said. 'Whatever – to be honest, it doesn't bother me if they pick me or they don't.'

I was a pretty cynical young man back then, and so I didn't get too excited when some clubs started ringing Mum and Dad two weeks before the national draft. I started to take it a bit more seriously, though, when representatives from various clubs began making the trip up to Broadford. I remember guys from the Swans, Brisbane, Adelaide and St Kilda all coming to give us their spiel. As I saw it, they told us just what they thought we wanted to hear. Usually, at the end of these 'chats', they say something like: 'The first chance we get, we're going to grab you in the draft.' I guess that line is football's answer to 'I'll respect you in the morning'.

When the day of the draft arrived, I didn't really know what would happen and how it would pan out. I thought I was a chance to get picked by someone, but as to who and when, I was clueless. I was still pretty blasé about it all. If I got picked, great; if not, I'd keep going with my panelbeating apprenticeship.

One thing that made me a little more nervous, though, was that a television crew from Shepparton came to Broadford to film my family watching the draft on television, and to get our reactions when my name was – we hoped – called out.

It was pretty weird. We sat there watching the telecast, waiting and wondering if my name was going to be read out, and the crew had their camera focused on us the whole time, waiting for us to react.

After the first five picks, it was St Kilda's turn but they didn't choose me. Sydney had pick number eight and took Jared Crouch. Brisbane had pick twelve – still nothing. So much for those stories that they'd take me with the first chance they had. West Coast took a Murray Bushranger with pick fourteen, but it was Luke Trew, not Barry Hall. Adelaide had pick eighteen, but again it wasn't me. I could see the television crew getting a bit edgy.

But with the next selection, pick nineteen, St Kilda decided to use their second pick of the 1995 AFL draft to take a kid from Broadford named Hall. I don't think the television crew got the over-the-top, ecstatic reaction they'd hoped for, but I was still glad when my name was called. It would have been a bit ordinary and embarrassing – and boring television that night in Shepparton – if it hadn't been. I was happy, no question, but I was still a go-with-the-flow bloke, so there weren't any star-jumps or tears. It was pretty good when St Kilda coach Stan Alves rang me, though, to welcome me to the club.

There was a bit of excitement in the room when I got picked. My uncle Teddy and his wife, Mary, were there, and David (who was happy because now he'd have our bedroom to himself) and Amanda and Mum. I can't remember my old man being there. I don't know why, but when my name was called I jumped straight up and wanted to walk out of the room. My mum came over and hugged me and my aunty came over and kissed me, but with the television crew there I was a bit embarrassed and wanted to get out as soon as I could.

When the dust had settled, it hit me that this was actually real. I had a shot at becoming an AFL footballer. I was also happy later on in the draft when my basketball teammate and schoolmate Darren Milburn was taken by Geelong with pick forty-eight.

When I sat back to reflect on what it meant, though, I realised that I was hesitant about heading to Melbourne. To be honest, I didn't really like the place. I don't really know why, but I guess it was that I was a country kid. I thought the whole world was in Broadford, so why would I ever bother leaving?

St Kilda organised for me to move in with a host family – Jenny Jones, a single mum with a couple of boys – who lived in Cheltenham, just down the road from Moorabbin where we trained, and they were great. I still remember the first night I got there. I rocked up and Jenny wasn't home, but she had some house-sitters there – two young chicks – and they just happened to be having a party. The backyard was filled with about twenty people having a barbecue, and there was plenty of alcohol flowing. I thought to myself, 'What have I walked into here?'

Normally, I liked a party, but with my first training run the next morning, I realised it probably wasn't the best idea. So when one of them asked if I wanted a drink, I said, 'No, I'm alright, thanks,' and then I basically went to bed. It was about seven o'clock at night! I didn't have a car at that time, so it wasn't as if I could go anywhere. Welcome to Melbourne, Barry!

I was picked up early the next morning to go to training at Dendy Park. It was a boiling hot day and we ran our arses off. Back then, the young blokes weren't eased into it – we actually did more than everyone else because we had to get up to their standard. It was a bit of a shock to the system, but thankfully I could run okay back then. So, while it knocked us about a bit, it didn't bother me too much.

St Kilda had some pretty handy players – including Robert Harvey, Nathan Burke, Nicky Winmar, Stewie Loewe, Aussie Jones and Peter 'Spida' Everitt. But I didn't follow St Kilda at all, and so I wasn't starstruck when they were suddenly in front of me at training. The reality was that, apart from their best players, I didn't really know who many of them were.

What did intimidate me early on was how some of them

were built. I thought, 'What am I doing here?' I was a skinny eighty kilograms. Physically, I didn't feel I was in the same league as them.

I was a bit of a loner and hung around with the guys I'd been drafted with. Nowadays, there are mentoring systems set up at all the clubs – the older players take the younger guys under their wings, so to speak – but back then we certainly weren't inundated with advice and wisdom from the senior players. The culture was that the young blokes did their thing, and the older guys did theirs.

In fact, it was really very rare to even speak to the older guys. In those days, if your bag was in the wrong spot it would be tossed away, or if you sat in the wrong seat you would be told in no uncertain terms where to go.

One bloke I used to hate was Spida, who was a real smartarse. He used to hang crap on all the young blokes, and I used to think to myself, 'I'm going to whoop you one day.' I couldn't stand him. In my first year, 1996, he'd already been at the club for three or four years. He was a big, gangly bloke with dreadlocks, a larger-than-life character, loud as hell, who thought he was funny. The exact sort of person I hated.

Some years later, when I actually got to know Spida well, we got on okay. We spoke about it once. I said, 'Mate, I hated you, and I thought early on it was just a matter of time before I belted you.' He just laughed it off, not knowing how close I actually was to belting him. I guess we just got off on the wrong foot.

Naturally, footy back then wasn't anywhere near as professional as it is these days. We had three main training sessions a week, and we would also have weights in the morning if blokes wanted to do it. The main sessions were usually held in the evening because blokes had regular full-time jobs and were working during the day. I can't say that anything about the way an AFL team trained surprised me too much; it was more that the lifestyle change was a shock to me. I'd often catch myself thinking, 'I'm actually doing this for a living now.'

I was only earning around $16,000 a year in base payments in my first year, with a $2000 bonus for each senior game I played, so obviously I had to have another job to get by. I worked at a place that stored curtain fabric; in fact, I think I earned more money there than I did playing football that year.

It wasn't hard work. When the boss went away, I used to go for a sleep in the fabric stillages. When the boss came back, the other guys would bash on the steel bench out the front, and the noise would echo through the place. I'd instantly wake up, grab a roll of fabric, put it on my back and look like I was working. It was a good place to work and, as I said, the pay wasn't bad. I often did overtime, too, because early in my time at St Kilda I had nothing else to do outside of work and training.

I did get a tattoo at about this time. I often get asked about the significance of it now – 'Why do you have a big spider tattooed on your shoulder?' I was about eighteen when I got it done in Melbourne. A mate of mine was a tattooist, so it was just way too easy to get it done.

Actually, I already had a tattoo of a pair of boxing gloves on that shoulder, which I'd had done when I was younger. Some people get tattoos because they mean something special to them, or because they signify certain people or moments in their lives. As for mine, there really is no great significance: I had just asked my mate to 'draw something to cover those gloves up'. I haven't got a passion for eight-legged creatures. But I did have a major dose of stupidity at the time, and I now regret getting it done. I wish I could wash it off, actually.

Anyway, I was without a car in Melbourne for four or five months, which was tough. My car, an HR Holden, still had to be finished back at home in Broadford. It was my first car, and I'd been given it by my old man when I was nearly seventeen. It had been just sitting in the yard at home. My parents didn't have the sort of money to be buying cars for their kids, but my old man said to me, 'You can have that car sitting over there. As soon as you finish restoring it, that's your first car.'

I guess he also thought that if I put some work into restoring it, I might appreciate it more and take better care of it. It took me ages to finish it, though. For starters, I didn't really know what I was doing. I was learning as I went, but I'd also been working and then I got drafted. So as a result I was carless when I first hit Melbourne and had to manage by getting lifts everywhere. That was one of the reasons I found it hard to adjust to life in Melbourne.

Player-welfare management then wasn't what it is now. The family I stayed with was great, but I still got pretty homesick. I really struggled. When I was playing or training, I'd put everything into it, but I found it tough going during those other times.

When I did finally get my car finished and brought it down from home, I hated being in Melbourne so much that I started staying in Broadford whenever I could, and driving back and forth to Melbourne, which was an hour and three-quarters each way. I was still paying rent at my host family's home, but my car had been converted to gas so it was cheap to run. After a while, I moved back home altogether and continued commuting to the club in Melbourne.

About six weeks into the 1996 season I was getting closer to cracking it for a match with the senior team. For three weeks I'd been doing all the drills with the seniors, and I'd been named as an emergency, so I knew I was in the mix.

Back then, selection worked a bit differently. It wasn't all hush-hush like it is now, when the coach summons you into his office, locks the door, tells you that you're playing, and swears you to secrecy until the team is announced. I found out about my debut in the newspaper.

It was Round 9 and St Kilda was scheduled to play Carlton at Waverley Park. When I opened up the paper during the week, I saw a big picture of myself and a story announcing that 'Barry Hall has been selected to play his first senior game this weekend'. I thought, 'Oh! Wow, that's alright.' The next day at training, Stan Alves had a chat to me and congratulated me and that was it.

When word got out back home in Broadford that I was making my senior debut, most of the family – including my old man, somewhat surprisingly – decided they wanted to come and watch. So they hired a twenty-two-seater bus and all packed in, and away they went. It was a pretty big event for them.

Unfortunately, back then I didn't have any pull at the club. I was just a rookie on sixteen grand a year and couldn't get free tickets, so they all had to pay their own way.

Things were pretty different to how they are now. These days, if a young kid is making his debut, one of the senior players will have a few words to him to settle his nerves. Not back then. The attitude was: 'Do it your own way, young fella.' The older guys didn't really speak to the younger guys too much – saying hello was a good conversation, really – so nobody had any words of wisdom for me before the game. All I could do was get out there and do my best.

When I ran out onto Waverley Park that Sunday, I was feeling pretty nervous and a little strange, too. To be perfectly honest, I didn't really believe I should have been there at all. It was a long way away from kicking that plastic Kmart football around the back paddock.

I started on the interchange but got on the ground for the last five minutes of the first quarter. I was playing on Michael Sexton, a champion fullback who had won a premiership the year before. 'What the hell am I doing playing against guys like this?' I thought to myself. I never dreamed I'd be good enough to be matching it with players like him.

Then, all of a sudden, in the second quarter, it just hit me. I still remember it as clear as if it were this morning. I physically stopped in my tracks and stood there for a moment. 'This is just a game of footy,' I realised. 'What am I worried about? It's just a game of footy. Yeah, it's quicker and the guys are bigger and stronger, but it's the same game I've been playing for years.'

I decided then and there that I would not be intimidated by anyone. I would get on the front foot. A few of the Carlton players must have thought, 'Who the hell does this clown think he is?' Normally, it's the rookie who cops the push and shove and gets intimidated, but I was actually doing it to them. I finished the match by kicking the first goal of my career.

Unfortunately, we lost the game. While it would have been much nicer to have won, I certainly wasn't shattered by the result. From memory, I was just happy with the way I had gone, and on a bit of a high from that after the game. I couldn't wait to get out there and play my next match. I also remember seeing my picture in the paper the next day. The only problem was that it was a shot of Anthony Koutoufides taking a hanger on me!

My first game didn't pass without incident, though, as I suffered stress fractures to my foot. But I so desperately wanted to play the next week against Essendon that I pushed through it until I couldn't run anymore. When I took my boot off it was like I had a football on the end of my leg, which put me out for six or eight weeks.

Off the field, I never thought about any sort of recovery process straight after games like the players do now. It's bizarre, and, looking back, I can see what sort of idiot I was, but I always used to race home to Broadford – really speed to get home – get changed, and head to the local pub. Some of the locals found it a bit weird. They had not long ago watched or heard me playing on the TV or radio in Melbourne, and now I was sitting there having a beer.

Unlike today, when things are much more professional

and sensible, there were no curfews or alcohol bans on AFL players back then. We always used to drink after a game, win, lose or draw. During the week, if you felt like having a beer or two, you would. That doesn't happen these days. If it does, those players usually don't last too long.

The one thing I did concerning footy and the drink that I'm not proud of happened the following season. I was up in Broadford on the Friday night before our match against Essendon at the Melbourne Cricket Ground, and I got on the drink with my mates at the local pub. They were going to watch a band and I just couldn't miss it, so I went along with them and we drank reasonably solidly. The next day I drove to Melbourne, played the match and then drove back to Broadford and got back on the drink again.

I did alright in the game. Well, I started okay, but towards the end I definitely faded out. This made me realise I shouldn't try that again, and I never did.

My problem was that I just didn't think about what I as doing, and I didn't recognise that it was damaging my football career. I just never thought too far ahead. I used to think, 'Oh, I'll do this for now and see what happens later.' I wasn't driven to succeed at footy. At the same time, I wasn't going to quit; I didn't like being in Melbourne, but I didn't hate playing footy.

Don't get me wrong: when I got out on the ground I played my arse off. It wasn't like I didn't give my all, or that I was totally undisciplined or didn't try. I gave everything I could, and I trained harder than anyone. But I guess I was missing home and my mates, and the life I'd grown up with, and that was affecting me. If I had been called into the coach's office and told, 'That's it, it's over,' I wouldn't have been too worried about it.

I know a lot of guys just love to play and wish they didn't have to train, but I really enjoyed training. When I first got to the club, someone told me that I had to put on weight if I wanted to be a key forward. They said, 'Look at you compared to Stewie Loewe – you have a totally different body shape.' That really spurred me on at training.

We had a good friend of the family, Gary Stevenson, who was a body-builder, and I would do weights with him every chance I had – that was on top of what we were doing at St Kilda.

I was pretty much doing weights seven days a week: four sessions with Gary, and then three sessions with the club. Even during the season I was just drilling the weights, almost to the point of being a little obsessed by it. If I missed a session, I would be so filthy and think I had to do an extra one to catch up. I could see it was working. I was adding bulk and I could feel myself getting stronger and stronger.

But my lackadaisical attitude to life away from footy and training started to change when, late in my first season, I fell asleep at the wheel while driving home to Broadford one night. I ran off the road, hit an embankment and smashed my old HR Holden. While the car copped a bit of a hiding, it was tough as houses and was okay. Thankfully, so was I. If there had been a tree or a power pole there, though, I would have been stuffed. I was lucky that the club never found out about the crash.

It did prompt a chat with a mate of mine, Dave Allen, who told me to move back to Melbourne and give my footy career a real go. 'If it doesn't work out,' he said, 'come home, but you've got to have a go at it. We're not going anywhere – we'll still be here when you come back, and we'll still probably be doing the same things.'

I thought about what he'd said for a while but I stayed put in Broadford, still living at my parents' place. This wasn't something I discussed with my family. They just respected what I wanted to do and didn't argue with me about whether I was right or wrong.

The next year, though, Stan Alves came up to see me and told me that the club wanted all its players to be based in Melbourne from then on. At first I said no, that I wanted to stay in Broadford. Eventually, my uncle Teddy talked to me and gave me the same message that Dave had. 'What have you got to lose?' he said. 'You're not doing anything back here.'

Finally, I agreed that he was right, and I moved in again with Jenny Jones and her boys back in Cheltenham.

CHAPTER FIVE

Once I had made the commitment to move back to Melbourne and give the AFL a good shot, I was surprised by how well it worked out. It wasn't just the on-field stuff, but my life off the field was a lot better than when I was last living there.

Stewie Loewe had a pub called Lazy Moe's, and the team would go there after our matches and have a good time. I realised then that what the guys did in Melbourne was exactly what we were doing in Broadford. I thought, 'Geez, this is alright – why was I bothering to drive home all the time?' I wasn't well known at the time, so I didn't have to worry about people pestering me or wanting to fight me. I would still head back home to Broadford for a night here and there, but I began spending more and more time in Melbourne. I started to enjoy my life there, and my form on the field reflected that I was more settled off it.

And it had to. In the first year and a bit I was at St Kilda, I was very lucky not to be moved on. The fact was I had a bad attitude. I didn't see that I had been given a great opportunity to make a career out of football; I just thought it was something to do for the time being, and that when it ended, I would go on to something else. I wasn't going to push myself to make a success of things. If it worked, it worked.

I guess I still had a rebellious state of mind at this time. I don't know if it had anything to do with what was going on with my old man, but at that stage, if you fought against me, I would fight back twice as hard.

If there was a club function that I didn't want to attend, I wouldn't. There were a number of times when I was told, 'Hally, you've got to be here for this sponsor's function.' I'd say, 'I'm not going. Bad luck – I just don't want to do it.' To say I was difficult in those first couple of years is an understatement. I wasn't necessarily hard to coach, but I hated the other stuff we had to do off the field.

On the field I was having a few dramas too, but not because I wasn't pulling my weight. My bad attitude followed me onto the field and came out in my competitive streak. I hated anyone getting anything over me. It was obvious in contests – I'd try and crack the bloke just to let him know I was around. Looking back on it now, I can see it was all about ego.

I had always shown aggression on the footy field, and that hadn't stopped now that I had made it to the highest level. But in 1997 I was going too far, and our coach, Stan Alves, stepped in. His advice would turn out to have a big influence on my career.

The incident that prompted it had happened when I was playing in the reserves in Round 14. It was the only reserves game I played that year, and it was against North Melbourne. I was chasing my opponent, and North Melbourne's Sam McFarlane came in to shepherd me. I just let him have it and threw a punch, which broke his jaw. I was suspended for six matches.

I can see now that I had a real chip on my shoulder at the time. I don't know why – maybe it had something to do with the situation with my old man, maybe it was just how I was programmed. I'm still not sure, but I do know I just wanted to hurt people back then. Even when I was tackling or bumping them legally, I'd still make sure I put their heads in the turf. I didn't care if I gave away a free kick – it was just going to happen. I know how ridiculous it sounds now, but I wanted to make sure I hurt the opposition. They wouldn't forget me, I reasoned, and I'd be more likely to have something over them in the future.

Because it had happened in the reserves and I was still fairly unknown, the incident really didn't attract too much media attention, although it was brought up years later at another tribunal hearing to show what sort of character I was. And I guess back then, although it wasn't an acceptable thing, there were a lot more shots like that in the game – it was just the way it was. Nowadays it's different, of course.

It was my first time at the tribunal, so I didn't know what to expect. Because it was only a reserves' match, there hadn't been the publicity or scrutiny there would be if it had happened in a senior game. I went in there not having a clue what suspension I would be leaving with.

There was no real video evidence at all, which was probably why I only got six weeks. These days I would probably have copped fifteen weeks, but back then it was basically my word against his. My defence was that he ran in to shepherd me and I put my arm up and he ran into me.

Looking back on it now, I am remorseful about it, but at the time I wasn't thinking about remorse. I just thought that was all part of what goes on in footy. McFarlane was out of the game for quite a while. He came back to play the final two matches of the season but was then delisted. I hope I didn't ruin his career. I feel bad about it, but I can't do anything to change things now.

Even though it had happened in the reserves, Stan Alves had been watching. He was up-front with me and said, 'It looks like you enjoy hurting people, and I reckon you go way too far with it.' Stan pulled me aside and told me that he and the club thought I had enormous talent, and that I had the potential to be a ten-year player. 'But you have got to pull your head in a little bit,' he said. 'We love your aggression and your toughness, but all the other stuff is hurting you – we need to pull you into line.'

Stan told me that my problem was the opposite of his, when he was a young player. He said that, at times, he used to be terrified on the field. He told me he was timid and used to have boofheads trying to bash the crap out of him. He'd had to fight that fear, he said, and he told me his experiences and how he went about doing that.

It was huge of Stan to admit that to me, and I truly respected him for it. We spoke about what I should do to get the better of my on-field problem. He said we had to channel my aggression in the right way, so we could use it as a legitimate weapon. It wasn't that he wanted me to get it out of my game totally, but we had to use it in a positive way.

Contrary to what my tribunal record might say, I did tone it down a bit after that chat with Stan. Once I became a regular in the seniors, everything was scrutinised a whole lot more; I couldn't get away with the things I was used to getting away with in the reserves. And I reckon that, once I was in the sights of umpires for doing something stupid, I probably stayed there throughout my career.

Stan didn't want me to become some model, straight-laced footballer. I reckon everyone – the footy club, the fans, even the AFL – loved my aggression and the tough stuff, as long as it didn't cross the line. Unfortunately, however, it sometimes did.

I suppose I was a poster-boy for that rough-and-tough sort of thing, with my short hair, angry snarl, the big tattoo on my shoulder. And then came the nickname.

From what I gather, it was Sandy Roberts, a television commentator for Channel Seven, who kicked it off. The first I heard of it was at the Broadford pub. Even though I was living in Melbourne then and getting more used to the nightlife, I would still sometimes do my old thing of heading back home to Broadford straight after a game. After one match in late 1997, I had done just that. When I walked into the Broadford pub, all my mates immediately started calling me 'Big, Bad, Bustling Barry'. I had no idea what they were talking about.

They continued to give me heaps about it for quite a while. I always thought it was a bit corny and a bit silly, but

– as with most things like that – it stuck. I think I've almost shaken it now. I don't get called it as much nowadays – it's usually just 'Big, Bad Barry' rather than 'Big, Bad, Bustling Barry'. Sadly, however, I think I've managed to emphasise the 'Bad' a little too much throughout my career.

After the incident with Sam McFarlane, while I was serving my six weeks' suspension, it just so happened that a female marathon runner was training us at St Kilda. I did a lot of running with her and got myself super-fit. I can't remember being any fitter throughout my career. By this time I was 105 kilograms, and I was strong and could run well.

While the reasons for my enforced layoff weren't good, the work I did during those six weeks made me realise that if I did train fair-dinkum, it would pay off. That's a philosophy I've stuck with ever since.

My suspension finished after Round 20, just a couple of games before the finals. St Kilda had continued its good season without me, and we were sitting second on the ladder. Recognising my hard work and the improvements to my fitness, the match committee put me straight back into the seniors for Round 21 against Melbourne, and I kicked a couple of goals and was among our best. We won that game and then our final home-and-away game against Port Adelaide.

It had been a massive turnaround in my two seasons at St Kilda. The club had gone from missing the finals in 1996 to finishing on top of the ladder in 1997. We had been flogged by our fitness people in the 1997 pre-season and had all put in a lot of hard work, and now we were reaping the rewards.

It also really helped that our best players – Robert Harvey, Nathan Burke, Austinn Jones and a few others – were all injury-free and in great form. At the same time, quite a few younger blokes were stepping up and doing well.

The year before, we'd had talent but we'd had injuries, and as a team we weren't in the same sort of form. That's footy, though, and in 1997 there was a real buzz around the club. Our supporters, who had been waiting a long time for success, were getting pretty excited.

We played Brisbane out at Waverley Park in our first final – my first ever taste of AFL finals – and while they gave us a good run for our money for three quarters, we kicked away in the last and won by nearly eight goals. The big thing I noticed about finals footy was how the intensity really ramped up, compared to home-and-away games. It wasn't an elimination game for us, but Brisbane's season was on the line and they certainly stepped up the intensity.

Winning that first final was a pretty satisfying feeling, and I knew all my hard work had paid off. I didn't have a busload of twenty-two family members making the trek from Broadford this time, but a few had come down for the game.

My relationship with my old man was still a bit on the nose. He didn't make the trip for the game, and it wasn't as if we sat out the back with a beer and chatted about footy when I went home.

Our reward for beating Brisbane was that we got the week off before coming back to play a Preliminary Final against North Melbourne. While there had only been about 50,000 at Waverley for the Brisbane match, almost 80,000 turned up for the North Melbourne game at the MCG. At the time, that was by far the best atmosphere I had played in. We led all day and went on to win by thirty-one points, but I didn't play very well. In fact, I was dragged during the last quarter by Stan Alves, who shouted at me, 'Do you want to play in the fucking Grand Final or not?' He told me to get back out there and show them I wanted it. I was put back on for the last five minutes or so, and I managed to do a couple of good things.

I knew it was a bit touch-and-go whether I would be selected to play in the Grand Final the next week, so naturally I was relieved when I heard I had got the nod. But I was still a bit nonchalant about footy back then. Sure, my training had gone to a new level and I wanted to be successful when I was out on the field, giving 100 per cent every time, and of course I wanted to play in the Grand Final, but if I hadn't been picked then I wouldn't have been too fazed by it. That was just me back then.

Once I was picked, though, it was an exciting time. The build-up was huge, especially because we were playing the Adelaide Crows and so we had all of Melbourne and Victoria on our side. As exciting as it all was, it wasn't as though I couldn't sleep at night.

The day itself was surreal, and the atmosphere at the MCG was amazing. You can't explain what 100,000 people going crazy feels like. Being a Victorian team, it felt like we had eighty per cent of the crowd supporting us. It was just so loud – by far the loudest game I've ever been a part of. Every time we kicked a goal the roar was just deafening.

It lived up to all the expectations I'd had as a kid of what the MCG would be like on Grand Final day, but I caught myself wondering how on earth I'd ended up there. I learned a bit that day, too, about how everything can hinge on little actions in big games. There were turning points in the game that just passed me by; when I look back on it now, I can see that they were really important moments, and if we'd got them right we would have been more of a chance to win. But of course, you hardly dissect a game when you're twenty years old.

I played okay, I thought. I kicked three goals, but in the third quarter my man, Peter Caven, ran off me and kicked a goal. Stan was filthy about that. I got dragged and didn't play much of the last quarter. By that stage the Crows were running over the top of us; Darren Jarman kicked five goals in the final term and they won by thirty-one points.

It was disappointing to lose, but I wasn't shattered or devastated by it. There certainly weren't any tears from me in the rooms afterwards. In fact, all I was worried about was getting out of there for a decent drink.

I was young and naïve. It was my second season in AFL football and I'd played in the Grand Final. I took it all for granted, like many young blokes do in that situation, and I pretty much thought we'd be back next year. Of course, at the time I didn't know it would take me eight years to play in another one.

CHAPTER SIX

I got a lot of confidence out of the 1997 season, and I decided to really work my arse off during the off-season to get as fit as I possibly could so I could give it a real crack in 1998. It sounded great in theory, but in hindsight it turned out to be something I would pay for.

In my determination to get fitter than ever before, I over-trained. The result was that I injured my groin and got a case of osteitis pubis. It would not only disrupt and ultimately ruin my 1998 season, but it also became an injury that would hamper me for years.

Back then the football community didn't really know too much about osteitis pubis. The injury was recognised by our club doctors and physios, but they didn't really know how to rehabilitate it so I could get back to full fitness. It was like running with a weight jacket on. My mind would be telling me, 'Come on, run, you lazy bastard,' but my body just wouldn't do it. There were times that I literally couldn't move.

It's not an injury that hits you instantly. It comes gradually: you feel your groin tighten, and then, as you keep trying to run, you feel like you're carrying twice your body weight. The pain you get under your testicles ... well, let's just say it ensures you really can't run as you normally would.

It started with a pain in my groin area, and then I got a hernia, which felt like someone was digging their finger into my guts when I ran. I told the club doctors, and they said I'd be able to get through the season, although I would have to be needled up. At the end of the season, I'd be able to get some surgery done to fix it properly. But I was so restricted that I struggled with it for the whole season. In my career I would end up having six operations on my groin.

This was the first major injury I had suffered in football, and I didn't deal with it very well. Having had a good season in 1997, and having worked so hard during the off-season to make sure I was at peak fitness for the season, I was incredibly frustrated to be struck down by injury and unable to do anything to my full potential. Unfortunately, my frustration caused me to do some stupid things.

The season started in the worst way possible – I got suspended for three matches in the pre-season. I managed to play nine of the first eleven matches of the regular season but I was always struggling with injury. My frustration came out again later in the year and I got a four-match suspension. Both suspensions were truly just for dumb things, things brought about by frustration. By the end of the 1998 season, I was happy to see the back of it.

Injuries and suspension weren't my only problems around that time. My aggression on the field spilt off it on a number of occasions, and in one instance I ended up in real strife.

Some mates and I had been up at the footy club in Broadford having a few drinks one night, and I left and went home to Mum and Dad's place. I was standing at the window of the car, leaning over talking to my girlfriend, when I saw a car come down the road and swerve towards me.

I had no idea what the driver was thinking, but I reckon he was trying to scare me, and he literally missed me by inches. He continued up the road, chucked a U-turn and came back at us, and I grabbed a big branch from the side of the road and smashed it on his car as he drove past.

I knew the car and I knew who the driver was, and while I wasn't about to go after him then and there, the information was locked in my memory bank straightaway. That was a trait I had got from my old man. I could hold a grudge and never forget it.

About a month afterwards, two mates and I were in Seymour, driving to the pub. I was as sober as a judge. As we passed the pizza shop, I saw the bloke walking up the street. I shouted at my mate to pull over; I jumped out, caught up with the guy outside the Terminus Hotel, grabbed him and started pounding him.

I just belted the living crap out of him. I probably would have kept going if my mates hadn't dragged me off, shoved me in the car and got me the hell out of there. Who knows how it would have ended otherwise.

I knew I had made a mess of the guy, but I didn't know how badly. Word travels pretty quickly around a small country town, and I guess after someone saw him lying on the ground in a bad way, they jumped to the conclusion he was dead. It wasn't long before my aunt Yvonne rang my mum and told her I had killed the guy. For the next five or six hours at my parents' house I was thinking, 'Shit, I've killed a bloke.'

The really bizarre thing, though, was that while everyone in the family was walking around upset and wondering what the hell was going to happen to me, and facing the reality I would be going to jail, I wasn't thinking like that. I understood that had I killed the guy, that I would have to go to jail – and that I deserved to – but it wasn't as though it really bothered me. I didn't feel any nervousness or fear, or anything at all like that. My attitude was that he had deserved something for what he did to me, and that he'd got what he deserved.

I know how harsh that sounds now, but that was how I was thinking at the time. Looking back, though, I still sometimes think to myself, 'What was wrong with you?'

Was it that chip on my shoulder? Maybe. I don't know what I was trying to prove. To be perfectly honest, I don't think I knew what I was doing. These days, when I tell close friends – people who really know me – they tell me that they can't see that kind of behaviour in me. Frankly, as I am today, I can't see it in myself – but I have to acknowledge that it happened.

When I try to analyse it, I can see that I might have been trying to prove something to my old man. He had a reputation as a hard sort of a bloke, and while I don't really know exactly what I thought doing something like that would achieve, in some ways I was probably trying to prove to my old man how tough I was.

My relationship with my dad improved a little bit around this time. When I'd quit boxing we had six months of silence, but we were talking again. It was still pretty tense when we did, though. I always felt he was talking to me just for the sake of it, and that if he wanted to cut me off again, he would.

While Dad followed Essendon, he was never into footy in a big way. He never used to come and watch me play, even now that I'd made it to the AFL. Mum told me that he'd have the television on the footy watching my game, but that when she came into the room he would change the channel. Anyway, one night at around this time we had a real confrontation, and a lot of our anger came out.

A mate, Raymond Rowbotham, and I had got on the drink, and we grabbed a slab of beer and went back to my parents' joint in Broadford. My dad was out in the garage, and he had a few beers with us. When we were all pretty drunk, everything just came out.

Dad and Raymond were talking about my sister, Amanda. She was a bit of a lunatic and had done something at the time, and my old man said to Raymond that regardless of what she had done, the one thing he could rely on her and David for was to have his back at all times. Basically, it was a shot at me – he meant that I wouldn't have his back.

I was pretty full of drink and I'd never questioned my old man about anything – I'd been too scared. But now I was twenty-one or so, and things had changed. I thought, 'Bugger you – it's time to hit you between the eyes now.' I had some courage in me and I spoke up.

'What do you mean by that?' I said. 'What are you talking about there?' I don't know if it was beer courage, but it was the only time I ever had the guts to say what I really felt to him. I could see that Raymond was sitting there thinking, 'What have I walked into here?'

Dad said, 'Oh, well, I don't think you think I'm a good father, simple as that, and I guess you hate me.' He told me his feelings, which were totally different from what I thought – all this crap about being a bad father and so on.

We went at if for a while, but in the end, for some reason, instead of continuing on and having a real go at him and giving him both barrels, I consoled him. Looking back, maybe I just thought that was enough. Anyway, I said, 'Well, you being tough on me has probably made me better. I'm a tougher person from it now, and that taught me a lot about how to handle things that are difficult. It's given me a bit of a hard edge.' I had a bit of a go at him but not as much as I could have. I had no other option, really, when he poured everything out.

I can see now I should have told him at the time what I had been going through with boxing, but it's easy to say that now. I had been just a kid and I'd always been scared of him. He never hit me or anything like that, but I was still intimidated by him for some reason. He had a commanding voice and was pretty strict.

Our relationship had been very raw right up until that night. As I said earlier, he can be stubborn and hold onto things, and I can too. The next morning – apart from our hangover – things were totally different. It was like we had both got a big weight off our chests. We never spoke about that night again, but things were different straight away.

Anyway, after I'd attacked the bloke in Seymour, I went back to Mum and Dad's place. We found out that the bloke wasn't dead when we saw him on the television news that night walking out of hospital, but it wasn't too long before the police got a hold of me and I was charged with assault and battery. Luckily for me, St Kilda got their lawyers onto the case, and I managed to escape without a conviction. I was given a twelve-month good-behaviour bond and was required to attend anger-management classes.

To be honest, I thought the anger-management stuff was a load of crap. It wasn't that I didn't think I had a problem. I knew I had a temper problem but I thought there was nothing they could do to fix it. But the club wanted to help, and they also wanted to be seen to be putting me in the right direction. So I went along and did all they wanted, but really I just wasted my time there. I didn't believe I needed to change my behaviour. My family, mainly my old man and my sister, could be a bit fiery at times, and as a result they had a bit of a reputation around town for having short fuses, and so I suppose I half-thought that was okay. I know that's a slack excuse, but it was how I felt at the time.

All in all, 1998 was a nightmare season for me, but it was also pretty poor for St Kilda as a club. After showing such promise in 1997, we lost five of our last six home-and-away games, and then we bombed out of the finals with successive losses to Sydney and then Melbourne. At the end of the season, Stan Alves left the club.

CHAPTER SEVEN

Tim Watson was appointed coach of St Kilda for the 1999 season. While everyone knew and respected what Tim had done as a player at Essendon, there were a few queries as to whether he could be a great coach. By the end of his time at the club, which was just two seasons, his record would probably say coaching wasn't his caper. But I really liked Tim as a coach, and he truly helped me out.

Because of my injury and my troubles with getting reported and suspended, there had been quite a few rumours floating around that the club was looking to trade me. Stan Alves had been an ally for me and now he was gone. Perhaps the new coach might want to clear the decks and start afresh.

To hear these rumours was devastating to me, because by now I had finally committed myself to football. Although 1998 had been a disrupted and unsatisfying year, I felt that I had settled in as an AFL player. Now, I thought, 'Hell, I'm going to have to uproot and go somewhere else – or maybe I won't be able to find anywhere else ...'

But Tim went out of his way after he got the job to call me and say, 'No, we aren't going to trade you, Barry. I reckon you can really play.' When he arrived at the club, Tim told me he had a lot of faith in me and my ability, and that I was going to be his 'little pet project'. That was really good to hear, and I took a lot of motivation from it. I vowed that I would do everything I could to make sure I never had to fear for my future like that again.

Once again, I trained really, really hard throughout the season, and I definitely improved under Tim Watson's mentorship. We got along really well, and he spent a lot of time helping me out one-on-one. Although we missed the finals in 1999 for the first time in three years, I had a decent season. I was still battling with the osteitis pubis, but I managed to miss only the first and last games of the year. I kicked forty-one goals and was my club's leading goalkicker for the first time in my career. It was the year I really started to have some confidence in my ability at AFL level.

No game stands out in my memory, though, and I don't want to bore people or pump up my own tyres by going through it goal by goal. The main thing was that I was fairly happy with the way I played, and wasn't having dramas on the field. That was a good change.

Off the field, I made a couple of good mates at St Kilda. I was hanging around with Stevie Baker and Jason Traianidis, who I still get the odd text message from now and again.

I've spent a lot of time in football, but for some reason I never ended up with too many really close mates who I still stay in constant contact with. When I was at each of my clubs I had good mates – I would go out to lunch for or go for a drink with them and we would enjoy each other's company – but since I've left those clubs, they have just fallen off the radar. That's partly my own doing as well.

Sometimes I wonder if people maybe think they can't ring me. It's strange. I don't know whether they feel intimidated or something. I always got on well with the younger guys at the clubs, but maybe once we weren't playing together anymore they thought they couldn't get in touch. That said, I can call any of my mates I grew up with and feel comfortable talking to them.

By the 1999 season I had also moved out of the Jones' house and was living with my teammate Ben Thompson in Hampton, which was only about two minutes away from Moorabbin, where St Kilda trained. Benny was an easy-going bloke and a good guy to live with, but he wasn't the tidiest person, which was a bit of a problem for me. My mum was a clean freak and I was brought up that way, but Benny definitely wasn't. I wasn't keen on mess and we had words about it from time to time, but never any major dramas.

Things had also improved with my old man, since we'd had those words in the garage. We were talking, at least, and there wasn't the old tension whenever I headed home.

I wasn't going up to Broadford as regularly during the season as I had been previously, but my jet ski and motorbike were there. I would head up there at the end of the season and often spend a couple of weeks.

The following season, in 2000, I missed just three games – one through suspension for headbutting North Melbourne's

Adam Simpson (it wasn't a full-on headbutt or I would have got more than a week; I just sort of put my head against his and pushed) – and kicked thirty-seven goals.

In the last game of the season we played North Melbourne, and Tim told me early in the week that we were going to try something a little different against them. I was going to play at centre half-back on Wayne Carey.

I was happy to have a go at it. It was a good experience, but it was also a little daunting to play on one of the game's greats. I wasn't really that well equipped to be a backman. I had never played there before, and here I was trying to stop one of the best!

I did an okay job on him. It certainly could have been a lot worse, and I walked away from it pleased with the experience. But it didn't convince me I should be a backman rather than a forward.

As a club, we had a shocker that season. We finished with the wooden spoon with two wins, a draw and nineteen losses. Tim Watson resigned with a year still to run on his contract, and again a coach I had got on well with was gone.

It had been a pretty tough season for St Kilda. Wins were few and far between, and that becomes tough on everyone at a club, not just the players and coaches. The coaching staff threw everything at us to try to change our losing habits to winning ones, but nothing seemed to work.

Being part of a club in that position is strange. You get to the point where you accept your losses a lot more easily than you would if you were at a club that won all the time. You almost get used to losing, which is a sad thing to say, but unfortunately that was the way it was that season.

It's natural also to look at things on a personal level, but it wasn't as though I was thinking, 'Oh my God, I'm such a failure.' I think I was trying to survive at that stage.

I wasn't close to the leadership group at that time, but I never heard any banter about the problem being all about Tim Watson. There was no player revolt behind the scenes that I saw. All up, it was hard to know why the club wasn't performing.

Away from footy, things were still going alright for me. I had managed to stay out of trouble and I moved into a place in Mordialloc with my girlfriend, Kylie, who I had been with since I was about twenty. I sold my HR to a mate and updated to a VK Commodore Calais.

For the 2001 season, St Kilda spent a fortune to bring Malcolm Blight in as coach. It seemed like a fair decision, given the success he'd had in taking Geelong to several Grand Finals, and then winning the flag with Adelaide in 1997 and 1998.

I found out later that, when Malcolm had arrived, he'd wanted to trade me but was convinced not to. So instead he decided that he wanted to move me from centre half-forward to fullback. I thought he was crazy.

'Every good premiership team has got a good fullback,' he said to me. 'I reckon you can be our fullback – you've got the pace and size.'

I didn't want to play fullback, that was for sure, but I couldn't say that to my new coach. Malcolm had a bit of a reputation for not taking any rubbish from his players, so I bit my lip and played down back. I spent the whole pre-season playing fullback, and I actually went okay.

Unfortunately, though, off the field I found myself in some serious trouble. In our first game of the season, we caused a bit of an upset by holding on to beat the Western Bulldogs by five points. After the match, I went out with a few mates to the Metro nightclub, and by the end of the night I was in jail.

While I have definitely been in the wrong in many of my altercations, both on and off the field, on this occasion I wasn't. A friend and I were in the club when he accidentally spilt his drink on a girl. The girl's boyfriend came rushing over, carrying on, and my mate told him to piss off and pushed him away. Well, that started it all.

This boyfriend must have been mates with one of the bouncers, because within minutes they turned up and dragged my mate outside through a side door. I wasn't sure what was going on, so I followed them out, asking, 'What the hell is going on here?'

When I got outside they were laying into him, kicking him and punching him on the ground, and that's when I jumped in. I got a few good shots off before about four bouncers pinned me on the ground. One of them was holding my foot while another jumped on my knee, trying to break my leg. 'You're not playing footy next week, you prick,' he was shouting. He jumped on my ribs, then went back to my leg.

Someone at the nightclub called the police, but these hero bouncers kept me pinned on the ground, jumping on my guts from time to time. I had an eyebrow ring, and one of them decided it would be cool to rip that out. When the cops turned up, I was vomiting from all the work they had put into my guts. I'd only had one drink but it looked like I was blind drunk, spewing everywhere.

The cops realised pretty quickly that I wasn't drunk. 'You're not pissed at all,' one of them said. I told them what had happened, but the bouncers had made up some other story.

The cops chucked me into the back of the divvy van, saying that I'd have company in there. Some bloke they'd already picked up was in the van – I think he'd been in a domestic with his wife, and he was blind drunk. Anyway, he started screaming at me to get out, and we got into a scuffle. When the cops opened the door at the police station they were killing themselves laughing at this idiot.

By this time it was about three in the morning. They put me and the drunk bloke into separate cells, and I had to wait for someone from the football club to come and get me.

Brian Waldron was St Kilda's football manager at the time, and he turned up to collect me. Like the police, the first thing he said to me was, 'You're not drunk.'

'No shit,' I said, and I told him what had happened.

The next morning the media got onto the story and it became a bit of a circus. Malcolm Blight was okay. 'I know you weren't drunk,' he told me, 'but you shouldn't have been there because you put yourself in a vulnerable position.' That was fair enough, but I told him that, right or wrong, I would do the same thing if it happened again.

Malcolm had a 'three strikes and you're out' policy. Players could get strikes for all sorts of reasons such as missing a training session, and I got one after the Metro incident. There were plenty of 'experts' in the media who voiced their opinions that I should be suspended by the club, but I wasn't. They gave me a case of counselling and that was the end of it.

I was right to play the next week and, despite some far from great personal results, I continued at fullback. We played against Port Power in Adelaide in Round 4, and again it wasn't great for me at fullback. We headed back to Melbourne, and at the airport Malcolm came up to me and said, 'Where do you live? I'll give you a lift.'

On the way home he asked me if I actually wanted to play at fullback or not. I said, 'No, not really,' and his response was, 'I can tell you don't.'

I don't think he was too happy about it, but that was the end of Malcolm's experiment with me at fullback. I went forward the next week and kicked five against Carlton, but our team's fortunes didn't improve. After fifteen rounds, having won just three games, Malcolm was gone and Grant Thomas took over as coach.

I made a good first-up impression with the new coach, kicking eight goals, the most I had ever kicked in a game, but it meant little as we lost the game to the Western Bulldogs. From memory, we were up and going early, but they ran over the top of us and I think I got a few of those goals late in the game when it was over.

But that good impression for the new coach didn't last too long. In the next game, against Geelong, I got reported three times – for striking Joel Corey, for charging Matty Scarlett and for wrestling. I was a little bit grumpy that day. I ended up copping three weeks for the Corey hit.

I came back in time to go to Sydney to play the Swans, who touched us up in Round 21, then we played our last game of the season against Hawthorn at the MCG on a Saturday night. As it turned out, it would be my last game for St Kilda, and I finally got to do what I had been fantasising about all those years ago in the back paddock at home.

Hawthorn was expected to win – they were heading to the finals, while we were headed for the off-season. We trailed all night after a slow start, but we got back into the game and, with time running out, we had the momentum. Leading by four points, the Hawks kicked out from fullback but the ball was turned over. It quickly came back into our forward line and I marked it.

I was about thirty to thirty-five metres out, on a little bit of an angle. As I was lining up my kick, the siren sounded. I had to kick the goal for us to win.

Being in that situation is a weird feeling. The only thing going through your head is: 'I've got to kick this – I can't miss.' I was trying to tell myself, 'Just relax and kick it naturally,' but you can tell yourself that as much as you want – you still tense up.

While it wasn't for a flag, or even for our season's survival, there was still massive pressure. I definitely had a funny feeling in my guts as I was dropping the ball onto my boot. I kicked an absolute mongrel, but thankfully it went straight. It sailed through and we had won.

Having not kicked a goal in the first four rounds while I was playing at fullback, I went on to kick forty-four for the season, although I played just thirteen more games due to suspension. So, for the second time, I became St Kilda's leading goalkicker for the season, but that kick against the Hawks would be the last time I kicked a ball wearing the red, black and white of the Saints.

CHAPTER EIGHT

That I lasted at St Kilda until 2001 was probably due to good luck more than anything else. These days, I probably would have been sacked two or three times for some of the things I did.

Especially early on, when I was still living in Broadford, I was involved in a lot of incidents that didn't become public. But even the things that did get told to the club – like what happened at Seymour – you would get sacked for that these days, and rightly so. My biggest problem was that I kept surviving, and so I didn't do much to change the way I approached life. The reality was that I was a ticking time bomb.

I've already mentioned how I had a bad attitude and a chip on my shoulder, and like any young bloke I thought I was never wrong. I would always find a way to justify what I had done. When an attitude like that was mixed with alcohol, it sometimes became lethal.

My drinking was definitely a problem in those days. It got to the stage that, apart from drinking on the weekends, I was sometimes hitting it two or three times during the week as well. I didn't feel I had a problem – it wasn't as though I had to have a drink every day – but when I started drinking I just wouldn't stop, which obviously affected me in the head.

I was generally a happy drunk – until, just like on the footy field, something or someone sparked me. With my bad attitude being amplified by the alcohol, I used to explode. I couldn't control it, and when I was rubbed the wrong way I would get really aggressive.

But I didn't believe there was anything really wrong with me. I just thought that this was how I was. And, of course, if there was trouble I always convinced myself that I was a victim of circumstances.

Not all the off-field problems I had – and there were quite a few of them – were related to my alcohol consumption. Sometimes dickheads just wanted to have a crack at me. As I got better known – and hated by the fans of other teams – it seemed that every time I was out, someone would try to light my fuse. Of course, my fuse wasn't a long one back then, and I just couldn't bring myself to back down and walk away.

Even when I wasn't looking for trouble, it always seemed to find me. I'd go out for a night with my mates, and would be copping shit from imbeciles in the car park before we'd even gone inside. I'd try to stay cool but my mates wanted to stick up for me, and I couldn't let them fight my wars, so then I'd be into it too.

Truth be told, I still find it difficult to walk away even now, but I'm a hell of a lot better than I was. If someone had a crack at me, I just had to shoot him down. I always had to have the last word. Back then, it was always more about fighting physically than verbally, whereas now it's the other way. Nowadays, if some drunk footy fan has a go at me, I'll give him a few words back. Most of the guys who try this aren't very smart, so I can usually put them in their place fairly easily and then walk away feeling okay about it.

When I was a young hot-head, I didn't think about the consequences of what I did, and I didn't care too much about them either. I wasn't bothered if I got sacked, which probably explains a lot about my behaviour. Things did change for me, though, I think because I started to mature a bit, and because I started to care about my football career and my reputation. I realised I didn't want to carry on like I did when I was younger; I'd worked so hard to get ahead and I risked losing it all.

At that time I was on a better contract and getting good money. I thought, 'If I can keep improving, the potential is there for me to get a bigger contract.' Money drove me more than a love of the game.

I'm so lucky to have had the career I've had, and I believe that one of the main reasons I was able to have it was that I got out of Melbourne when I did. At the end of the 2001 season, I knew I just couldn't handle all the attention. Both out in public and in the media, footy was everywhere. The more high-profile you became as a player, the more recognisable you were in the street. When that happened, your private life disappeared completely, and you weren't able to do much at all resembling normal.

I was also lucky, too, that there wasn't the same sort of scrutiny on AFL players as there is now. I got into plenty of fights out on the town with my mates, but there were many which the general public never found out about. If there had been camera phones back then, I would have been stuffed.

The incident at the Metro in 2001 was one that went public, and if things hadn't worked out as they did, St Kilda would have had the perfect excuse to get rid of me there and then. But the reality, particularly early in my career, was that I never really got punished by the club for my off-field dramas. While I knew what I was doing was wrong, I didn't really think it was that unacceptable, so there was no real change in my behaviour.

I was involved in lots of incidents back then, and the club was contacted for probably half of them. Mind you, there were also times the club would get calls from people just making up stories. But there were plenty of true stories too.

My mates and I used to go to Wild Bill's at Southland, and one time a couple of blokes were giving us some lip in the car park. Then one of them picked up one of those yellow posts they put in the parking spots. I saw red and started running for him. I grabbed it, but instead of hitting him with it I just used my fists and bopped him. The next day he was on the phone to St Kilda, saying I'd hit him over the head with a pole.

One time, my girlfriend and I were out at Crown Casino with a mate and his missus, and we got into a blue. I ended up with blood pouring from my arm where a bloke had bitten me, no shirt on and wearing one shoe. I got a few strange looks when I walked through the joint to the other side to get a cab.

Like I said, not all the blues involved alcohol, but many did. It got to the point where I couldn't live anything like a normal life in Melbourne. I was getting even more public attention and was starting to struggle with it. I knew it would eventually bring about the end of my footy career, and possibly something worse. I needed to move away.

That was the main reason I decided to agree to being traded at the end of the 2001 season. I also felt that, despite having worked really hard over the previous few years, I wasn't getting anywhere at the footy club. Because of my past sins, I could see that I would never have the chance to take on a leadership role at St Kilda.

Leaving your club is not the sort of decision you take lightly. As it happened, the management at St Kilda told me there had been interest in me from a few clubs and asked me whether I would consider leaving. The money they mentioned was better than St Kilda's offer, too, and the more I thought about it, the more sense getting out of Melbourne seemed to make.

Grant Thomas had wanted me to stay. I remember him saying, 'We fought to keep you here when Malcolm Blight wanted to trade you,' but by that time I had decided it was time to move on.

Three clubs were interested – Fremantle, Carlton and Sydney. While Carlton's offer was a good one, I knew it would be best for me to leave Melbourne. Going to Carlton wouldn't fix my off-field problems – in fact, they would probably worsen – so the Blues quickly dropped off my list. My management and I still spoke with them, though, just in case things went pear-shaped with the other clubs.

John Andrews from Elite Sports Properties was the guy who was helping me out at that time. I had been with ESP as my managers since my second year at St Kilda. In the first season I'd had no need for a manager, as what I was getting was all set, so my uncle had just helped me out with anything I needed.

Then I saw an article in the paper about Craig Kelly – an ex-Collingwood player – setting up ESP. The fact that he was a former player and knew how the system worked impressed me, plus he seemed a genuine and honest type of bloke. My uncle and I contacted him, and I think I became one of his first clients.

Although money was important to me, it wasn't the main focus when we were talking to the clubs. It was more about how I was going to fit in, what the coach was like, and just the general gut feel I got from the place. We felt that if we got the first part right, the money would look after itself.

The one big advantage Sydney had, even compared to Perth, was that it wasn't an AFL city. Nobody would know me and I could get on with a normal, everyday life away from football, which was very attractive to me.

Sydney was far better organised than the other two clubs. They knew exactly where they were going. Rodney 'Rocket' Eade was the coach, and he had a real plan for me. As he described his game-plan to me, he said, 'This is what we want to do with you, and you'll have good support around you. We're potentially a top-four side, the location is great and we think we'll be good for each other.'

The way Sydney presented was so much better than the other two clubs. The whole time, I worked closely with their player-welfare manager, Phil Mullen – who would become not only a lifelong friend but also my manager – on things like how I would go about moving interstate, and selling my house and getting one up there, all those little things aside from contracts.

I went to Sydney twice before making the decision to move. I drove around and checked out the city – I didn't really know what I was supposed to be looking for – but it all felt good, and I felt like I fitted in up there.

Phil took me to Bowral to spend some time with Tony Lockett. I had played against him before but I'd never met him. I spent a couple of nights with him, sitting around the campfire, having a drink and a chat. We had plenty in common, quite apart from the footy side of it. He was a cruisy, laid-back country boy like me, and we had many similar interests.

We spoke about his move from St Kilda to the Sydney Swans some years earlier, and how getting out of the spotlight in Melbourne had worked so well for him. While he was living out of town at this time, when he'd first got up there he had lived closer to the city. He said he loved the place and told me how it had helped extend his career.

If moving to Sydney had worked for Plugger, whose profile in Melbourne had been so much bigger than mine, I knew it could work for me too. I told him about the issues I was having in Melbourne, and he reckoned I wouldn't have those problems in Sydney.

Plugger told me he would never go back to Melbourne. That he hadn't simply done his time at the Swans, collected his money and headed back to live in Melbourne spoke volumes for both the club and the city. When I left Bowral and went back to Melbourne, I was pretty happy about the idea of playing for Sydney.

Fremantle was the other club in the market for me. Kelly O'Donnell, my former coach at the Murray Bushrangers, was working there at the time, which was obviously a plus for them, but word filtered back to me that the Dockers' new boss, Cameron Schwab, didn't want a bar of me.

That made me wary. Kelly O'Donnell rang soon after to see where I was at, but I had to tell him that I had crossed Freo off the list because Schwab didn't want me. Kelly said it wasn't the case, but we didn't take it any further.

Carlton was still keen, although they did have a young forward at their club who had some big raps on him: Brendan Fevola. Their representatives must have thought I had gone up home to Broadford after the season, because they drove up to Mum and Dad's hoping to get the deal done. But Sydney had got wind of Carlton's plans, so they flew me up to Noosa for a week – which I spent with Phil Mullen – just to get me out of town so Carlton couldn't tempt me.

Sydney offered St Kilda three picks in the national draft – numbers thirteen, seventeen and forty-five – and it wasn't too much later that I signed the deal to become a Swan.

CHAPTER NINE

I moved to Sydney in late 2001. Although I had visited the city a couple of times when the Swans did their meet-and-greet with me, I didn't know too much about the place. Sure, I had been up there a few times to play, but on those trips you don't get to go sightseeing and you really don't see much more than the airport, the hotel and the footy ground. I have always done a lot of things in my life on gut feel, and this felt right.

One of the first things I noticed, though, was how invisible the AFL was there. You had to turn page after page to find any AFL stories in the newspaper, if there were any at all, and there might be a brief mention of the Swans on the nightly television news.

Not long after Kylie and I got to Sydney and moved in to a unit, we went out shopping. That was when it first hit me. There we were, in a busy shopping centre, with hundreds of people walking past us and bumping into us, and there was nothing. Not a thing. No one was coming up to me wanting to talk about footy or the Swans, no one was pointing fingers, no one was whispering 'Isn't that Barry Hall' behind my back. There was nothing at all. 'Serenity,' I thought.

Tony Lockett had told me that was how it was for him in Sydney when he first got there, and I figured that if they didn't know Plugger, they sure as hell wouldn't know me. But after a couple of years of that sort of attention in Melbourne, to actually experience such peace was a little weird.

We were only an hour away from Melbourne by plane, but this felt like a totally different world. One hour! It used to take me longer than that to drive back to Broadford each weekend. 'Geez,' I thought, 'if I'd known this back then, I probably would have gone to Sydney rather than Broadford after St Kilda games.'

These realisations came to me within the first few days of us moving up there. At least from an off-field perspective, I knew I had made the right decision in getting away from Melbourne and coming to a place where I had the chance of a normal life again.

My first challenge in Sydney was meeting all my new teammates, seeing how I would fit in, and then getting myself ready to have a real crack in 2002. I wanted to show the Swans that despite what some people might have thought – and there were plenty of people saying the Swans had taken too big a risk by signing me – they had made the right decision in bringing me to the club.

While most guys who came from interstate shared a house with other players, because I'd come up with a partner, we rented our own apartment in Paddington, right across the road from the SCG. It was a good place to live, and it was brand-new.

Our apartment was two floors up but it was situated right over the spa. One night Kylie and I were woken up late by a lot of yahooing and carrying on downstairs. I decided to go out and tell them to shut up, but when I walked onto our balcony and looked down at the spa, I saw five girls, all totally naked, either in the spa or running around having drinks.

As we were all new neighbours, they did the friendly thing of inviting me down for a welcoming drink, and I felt it was my neighbourly duty to go down and have that drink. Kylie didn't see it my way, though, and I was ordered back inside!

When I eventually met my new teammates, I realised that most of them were from interstate. I think the guys from the Riverina were considered locals! Because we were all together in a new city, away from our families and friends, there was a real sense that the club was a strong family environment. The playing group was a tight-knit bunch, and I soon discovered that they trained hard. The Swans had made the finals the year before and all the players desperately wanted to take the next step in 2002.

It wouldn't be long before these guys would become my good mates, not just my teammates. When we faced hard situations in games, I believe that the close bond we had helped get us over the line a few times. We just didn't want to let each other down.

But just because we were around each other the whole time, it didn't mean it was nonstop about footy. We loved getting out for a drink together. I know footy clubs frown on players having a drink and worry about what will happen, but because we were such a tight bunch, we always looked after each other.

At footy clubs you get on with most blokes, and that was the case at the Swans. There wasn't anyone I didn't get along with, but just like at any other job, there were a few blokes who weren't really my sort of people, and as a result I didn't spend too much time with them.

The ones in Sydney who I got along well with from the start were Tadhg Kennelly, Mick O'Loughlin, Leo Barry and Amon Buchanan, and then later on I got on well with a young bloke who lived with me for a while, Matty O'Dwyer.

Amon was a great guy, just a pure country boy and a funny little bugger, and we hit it off. Tadhg was like me – he just loved to train hard and play hard, but as soon as the weekend comes and the game is over, he loved to have a good time and we connected in that way. It was like that with a lot of the guys – Mick and Leo were exactly the same.

There was always a perception that the Swans players were the 'goody two shoes' of football in Sydney, and that it was only the rugby league players who went out drinking and carried on. I can confirm that we didn't always go straight home to bed after training.

We used to go out a lot. Sometimes we'd get hammered and not a soul seemed to notice. Having said that, though, the club did get a few phone calls from members of the public complaining about drunk Swans players. Just goes to show that not everyone in Sydney was a Swans fan, I guess.

The club would ask what happened, and I was always fairly honest with them. There was no point hiding things, I figured, because the truth would always get out somehow and make things a lot worse. Generally the club didn't make a big deal of things. What did surprise me was that not much ever reached the papers. It was Sydney, I know, but if I had done half that stuff in Melbourne, I would have found myself in the papers every second week.

We used to enjoy ourselves. We used to train hard, but we had fun too, there's no doubt about that. At Sydney during my time there, we had our share of 5 a.m. finishes, but the big thing was that I was never late for training or a recovery session because of a late night. I always made sure I got a lift in the morning, and that I put everything into training. I don't think there would be anyone who would dispute that.

I probably would have been in strife a few times if the club had breathalysers at training or recovery, but I think if any footballer – apart from those who don't drink altogether – says they haven't been to a recovery or training session under the influence at some stage, they're not being honest. The club certainly didn't condone it, but as long as we got there on time and did everything asked of us, there were no questions asked.

One difficult aspect of my first season in Sydney, especially when I was first signed, was that I was being held up as the Swans' new Plugger. That's like comparing any other boxer to Muhammad Ali – you just don't do it.

I was happy to have expectations put on me – and the team – to perform, that was fine, but saying I was as good as Plugger was just embarrassing. You can't replace a guy like him. And anyway, even as players the comparison was so off the mark it wasn't funny. But it was a good headline, I suppose, so the papers ran with it.

Those stories were silenced, though, when, just a couple of months after I joined the Swans, Tony Lockett announced that he was making a comeback, having retired at the end of the 1999 season. I don't know whether our discussions had revitalised his thirst to play, but he certainly hadn't mentioned anything to me at the time.

The news did come as a shock to me. I got to training one day and saw all these cameras there, which didn't happen too often in Sydney back then. When I heard what was going on, I was rapt. And why wouldn't I be? I had a chance to play in the same forward line as one of the greatest players our game had ever produced.

It was inspiring to see how hard Plugger worked to get fit and lose weight. He wasn't just coming back for the sake of it – he wanted to make an impact again. He's a pretty dedicated bloke. However, Plugger didn't get his famous number four jumper back for that season, and it was also time for me to make a change.

I had worn number twenty-five at St Kilda, but there had been no particular reason. Andrew Schauble had that at Sydney, so I would have to have a change. Someone at the club said to me, 'Hey, number one is available – do you want it?' I said sure, no worries. I had never been one of these players who wanted to play in low numbers, or who preferred certain numbers because they had special significance.

Expectation in Sydney was building as we approached the opening round of the season. The team had made the finals the previous season, Tony Lockett was back, and the club had signed some hot-head from Melbourne named Hall. All of a sudden, we were among the top three favourites to win the premiership.

We played the defending premiers, Brisbane, in our first game. After leading at halftime, we were overrun in the second half and comfortably beaten. We won our next game but struggled for consistency as the weeks went on. I was having trouble getting used to the Swans' style of game, and to playing regularly on the smallish SCG. There were a whole lot of reasons why it wasn't working for us, but the bottom line was that we just didn't perform. We lost six in a row, which made it eight losses from the first twelve rounds, and were near the bottom of the ladder.

And then it all happened. After playing just three matches, Plugger announced that his comeback was over – he'd suffered a bad corkie and just couldn't get over it. I was sorry to see him go – I had felt we were working well together. I would have loved to play alongside him at his best.

A couple of hours later, news broke that Rocket was quitting as coach. This was really devastating to me – Rocket had been a huge part of why I had come to Sydney in the first place. I'd been so impressed by the way he'd sold it to me, and I wanted to be at a club that was settled, had some stability and had a clear idea of where they were headed. Now, with only half the season over, everything had been thrown up in the air.

I hadn't seen it coming. When a coach quits, everyone says it was no surprise and that he got out before the club sacked him, but that has never been my way of looking at things. Although, like everyone else, I had heard all the rumours that go around a footy club, I hadn't read between the lines and looked at the politics. I always tried to keep my head down – I just wanted to win games, and I assumed my coach would be there for as long as me.

I had seen it happen a couple of times at St Kilda, but despite that, as a player, I never really thought the coach was going to be moved on. Most of my coaches have had a pretty good idea of the game, but if the players aren't doing what the coach is instructing ... well, it's pretty tough on the coach. But, having said that, part of a coach's job is to get the best out of his players. And, of course, it's easier for a club to get rid of one coach than a dozen players.

It's funny but I actually got to know Rocket better after he finished up as my coach. He was living two doors down from me, and he stayed in Sydney a while after that, so I still saw him all the time.

I remember going out on a Sunday drinking session once with Daryn Cresswell and Adam Schneider. We were plastered, having been drinking all day, and as we walked back to my place the boys said, 'Let's go and get Rocket.'

So Rocket joins us at my place, but within minutes of us getting there, the others had disappeared, leaving poor Rocket stuck with me. I was in no fit state for anything, and I started vomiting everywhere out in the backyard. What a good host! I can only imagine what he was thinking. It's a wonder he took a chance on me at the Bulldogs all those years later.

The club installed Paul Roos as caretaker coach, which everyone was happy about. He had been an assistant coach that year and knew the system. But almost instantly the chatter around the club was that Terry Wallace would be our coach next season. We weren't told anything officially, but it was everywhere in the papers.

As players, we didn't have any say in who the club would appoint as coach in 2003. All we could do was play out the year and see what happened. I hadn't had much to do with Roosy before he took over as caretaker coach, as he'd been the team's defence coach.

For a while I was worried about my own future in Sydney. Sure, I had a four-year contract with the Swans, but I didn't know what would happen at the end of the season. Our new coach, whether it was Terry Wallace, Paul Roos or whoever, might come in and say, 'Sorry, Hally, we're going a different direction, so we'll be putting you up for trade.'

But I quickly decided I couldn't let those concerns hold me back. All I could do was make the most of the rest of the season, which would make it hard for them if they were thinking of getting rid of me.

Rocket had been a very structured coach, who made use of lots of swaps and changes during a game. It was fairly complicated because he's a smart man and a smart coach, but not every player was as smart as he was. Roosy was different and wanted to keep it simple. He gave the players the licence to play how they wanted. Naturally, he had certain team rules we had to abide by, but he used to say, 'You blokes have got talent, so let's use it. Let's play some exciting footy and see what happens.' And it worked.

Roosy never ranted or raved at us. The one thing he always repeated was: 'If you make a mistake, that's fine, just don't dwell on it. I'm not going to drag you just because you stuffed up. Let it go, and move onto the next one.' It was good for all the guys.

We played Fremantle in Roosy's first game in charge, and we gave it to them, kicking twenty goals; I managed to get six. Then we lost a couple of matches, and in the second one, against Port Adelaide, I was reported for the first time since I had got to Sydney. It was a similar situation to when Grant Thomas took over at St Kilda. I did well for the new coach at first but then got myself into trouble.

As I remember it, Matthew Primus was running around intimidating some of our players, and I decided to take it upon myself to hit back. But I did it the wrong way, as usual. I grabbed him and got carried away, and I ended up getting outed for five weeks for eye-gouging. That's something you certainly don't want to have on your CV when your career is over, but sadly it's on mine.

I was probably lucky to get five weeks in the end. As with all my indiscretions, it was a spur-of-the-moment thing and I can't really explain why I did it. I'd never done anything like it before and I haven't since, and I have always felt pretty bad about it. I have spoken with Matthew since and he's been fine about it, but I still wonder – what if I had actually gouged his eye out?

I was also pretty pissed off that I'd let myself down, particularly as it proved all those sceptics right. Now I had given the cynics more ammunition, but – more importantly – I had also let the Swans down, and there was no excuse for it.

The club fined me, and rightly so, but that was the end of it. They said to me, 'Okay, let's get back on the horse and put that all behind us,' which we did.

When I got back there were two games left, and I made the most of them, kicking seven goals and then five. Personally, it was a good way to finish the season. In that last game – against Richmond at the Olympic Stadium – we belted the Tigers to give Paul Kelly and Andrew Dunkley a really good send-off. At the end, we all gathered around Roosy and hugged him, which was our way of saying we supported him for the coaching job in 2003.

We hadn't had any meetings or anything like that. While things would change over the next few years, at that time the players had no control over anything off the field, and we certainly didn't think we could pick the coach. But I think our show of support – along with that of the fans, too – may have caused those in the boardroom to take some notice. Whatever happened, Terry Wallace never arrived and Roosy got the job.

Despite our good finish to 2002 – we won six of those last ten matches under Roosy – missing the finals was really disappointing. Personally, I had managed fifty-five goals in my first season, playing a different style of game, on a smaller ground, and despite missing five matches through suspension.

Every year Broadford would host a big bikie festival. Even at a very early stage, you can see I got into the spirit of things on my favourite bike.

'That's right, Bert and Ernie, butter really wouldn't melt in that mouth.'

I've either cracked a really good joke, or my older sister Amanda just can't stop laughing at my two-dollar Kmart football.

You always had to do your chores before you could play footy.

The Halls of Broadford. My mum Helen, dad Raymond, sister Amanda, and the one with the skinny legs is me. My younger brother David was still a few years away.

I could say this is me at a young age about to take a screamer over my Uncle Teddy, or, I could just say, this was me on Uncle Teddy's shoulders in the backyard pool.

When it came to weekend footy with my cousin Billy (right) and my brother David (front), I did have a bit of a height advantage.

All siblings fight, I know, and my brother David and I were no different. I think he put the gloves on this time because he hated my mullet.

'Ball, umpire!' Some spirited backyard footy in Broadford. Reminds me a little of an incident against North Melbourne in 2010.

Under-10s footy for Broadford. Yes, that's me in the middle. Mum used to make me wear a helmet ... I hated that!

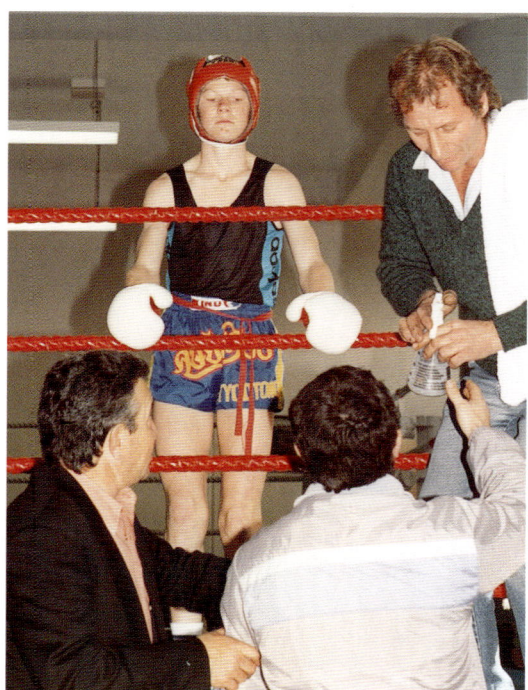

Barry Hall the boxer has his first bout, in Brunswick. That's my dad in my corner.

No, we weren't auditioning for *Dancing with the Stars*, it was just my cousin Billy and me, fighting in the front yard.

At dinner with my grandfather, Freddy, a Bulldog supporter through and through.

Standing with my nephew Jake on the stage at my twenty-first birthday party. It's really lucky that we have photos like this because, for some reason – maybe it had something to do with the drink or two I had – I don't really remember too much about this night.

And while I managed only three games with Plugger, that season was the start of a great partnership I would have with Mick O'Loughlin. I knew Mick was talented, but I didn't know just how talented until I played alongside him. With everything he did for the Swans and the code in Sydney, and simply as one of the best indigenous players ever, I reckon he was really underrated. He was right up there with the best, as far as I'm concerned.

CHAPTER TEN

There was a lot of enthusiasm among the players as we headed into the 2003 season. We had played well to finish off 2002, got some good results and our confidence was high. Roosy was confirmed as our coach, he had the full support of the players, we enjoyed playing for him and his style of play seemed to suit us.

It didn't impress some 'good judges', though, who still thought we'd again miss the top eight. Some even picked us to win the wooden spoon.

It was a new era for the club. Roosy had come in as coach, and both Paul Kelly and Andrew Dunkley had retired after long careers at the club. Things had also changed dramatically off the field, with the players instituting a system that would ultimately shape the club and help us win the premiership a couple of seasons later.

Stuart Maxfield replaced Paul Kelly as our captain. Just as significantly, it was at this time that we started a leadership group, and the code of 'the Bloods' was born.

At the end of the 2002 season, the club had hired a leadership consultant called Ray McLean. All the players and coaches had a meeting with him at the club. His ideas about the leadership within our club were based on how we wanted to be perceived. The Brisbane Lions were the AFL's best team at that time, having won the past two premierships. Ray asked us how we perceived Brisbane, and we agreed that they were hard, tough and played without compromise. Then he asked us how we thought we were perceived by others in the competition, and our conclusion was totally different.

The consensus among the majority of our team was that we were perceived as soft. We were good at times, we felt, but other teams thought that if they kept us under pressure, we would crack pretty quickly. As a club, this was exactly what you don't want to be, and you certainly don't want to be known for it. We were being honest with ourselves, though, and from that moment on the direction we felt we had to go was clear.

It was quite a reality check. At first, I'm sure many of our players thought, 'Geez, we're not going that bad, are we?' But upon closer consideration, we knew it was something we had to deal with. I remember thinking, 'Hey, this is good – everyone is being honest and realistic, and they are on the money.'

As a team, we made a pact to change the perception that we were soft, regardless of what it took. We wanted to gain some respect in the AFL. I know it sounds like a cliché, but we wanted teams to really feel like they'd played a game after meeting us. That's the way it was when you played against Brisbane.

We came up with some ways we could change our behaviour, which in turn would change our opponents' perceptions of us. In fact, they would change us as a footy club. There were a lot of words thrown up at the meeting about how we wanted to be portrayed as a team. The overriding theme was that we had to be uncompromising and hard as a group, both in games and at training. Just as importantly, if we wanted to be successful we had to live by that code. Of course, we had other things like a game-plan and team rules and so on, but these described our overall approach. We agreed to live by these ideals, no matter what. This was not negotiable.

We decided to revive the name 'the Bloods', as a dedication to the club's players before us, and to our club history. A group of players had come up with the idea that we could incorporate the 'blood-stained angels' of the South Melbourne Football Club into the modern-day Swans.

Most of the actions decided upon at these meetings were driven by the players. That was something Ray thought was important. It wouldn't have been the same if the coaches had just told us what to do – that wasn't what was needed. This was about the players being brutally honest with each other and themselves. In saying that, however, the coaches were right behind us and supported our decisions.

Many people who knew me thought I would have treated that sort of stuff as a joke, but I didn't. I backed it fully.

It all made good sense to me. Anyone who was even a little bit sceptical soon got on board when they started seeing the approach working for us.

Things were pretty different around the club after that. I was one of those old-fashioned blokes who was all about playing footy – I liked to train hard, play footy and then have a drink to celebrate or commiserate. But I enjoyed the new changes – well, at least at first.

The new system certainly promoted leadership. If a player wasn't doing what was expected of him, his teammates were supposed to pull him into line. Likewise, another objective was to encourage our teammates when they did things right. There was a leadership program tacked onto that as well, but it was important for everyone to step up and behave as a leader.

At training, we all could see that things had changed immediately. We were harder on each other, and we were more open and honest, and if blokes weren't doing the right thing or could have done things better, they were told in no uncertain terms.

Our formal leadership group was voted for by all players, which was a fairly new idea in football at that time. There wasn't any certain number of leaders we had to have, but if you thought there was someone who would be a good addition to the group, you could put his name forward. The players voted, and then we decided how many blokes we would have as leaders for that year.

I wasn't voted into the leadership group at that time, but the next season Stuey Maxfield told me that he thought I could be a leader. He wanted me to speak up more, both on the field and around the club. 'You've got a big, loud voice – people will listen to you,' he said.

Until then, I never used to say much on the field. I just went about my business. Stuey reckoned I could be pretty influential if I opened up and used my voice constructively. So I started to work on that and over the season I improved, and in 2004 I was voted to join the leadership group.

While I hadn't been much of a talker, I had always enjoyed playing practical jokes on blokes, and that never really changed throughout my career. One thing I used to do was hide my teammates' cars. I'd get their keys out of their lockers and hide their cars around the corner. The looks on their faces when they came out and couldn't find their cars were priceless!

Another trick blokes would play was to get a banana, peel it and hide it inside another guy's locker. All of a sudden there would be fruit flies everywhere and the poor bloke couldn't work out why they were pestering him.

Daryn Cresswell once decided to put a dead rat in my locker to get back at me. I found it quickly, thankfully, and I decided to put it in the pocket of his suit pants, which were in his locker. After our match, he put his pants on, put his hand in his pocket, pulled the dead rat out and went off his head. Ah, good times!

Anyway, just because we had a new philosophy at the club, it didn't mean we became robots. We still went out for a beer – in fact, that fitted in well with the overall theme. We had some guidelines. If a teammate had had enough, for instance, you'd make sure he got home safely. We played hard, but we loved to enjoy each other's company away from the game. As always, of course, you had to make sure you got to recovery or rehab the next day, on time and not reeking of alcohol.

I think having a reasonably young playing group was the key to our new approach. I don't know how older guys, such as Paul Kelly or Andrew Dunkley or Tony Lockett, would have gone with all this stuff, but with the young and enthusiastic group we had, the timing was perfect.

In fact, Ray McLean's approach had been tried when I was at St Kilda. But there we had a lot of senior players, and that made the whole thing more problematic. Having a young bloke tell Stewie Loewe or someone else who had played 250 games that he had to train a bit harder didn't go down too well.

At the Swans, though, there weren't really any standout superstars with huge numbers of games to their credit. Everyone was pretty much on a level footing. Sure, some players were probably more talented than others, but the important thing was that our egos were all on the same level, and that helped a heap.

Early on, we felt that the process was working for us, but we knew that if we achieved something big with it, there would be a whole lot of fuss, so we did try to keep it quiet. But somehow it got known in the media, and every headline from then on seemed to make reference to 'the Bloods'. That was okay, because while the media knew the name, they didn't really know what we were doing. People sometimes asked me, 'What is it – a secret society or a cult or something?' It definitely wasn't that. There were no secret handshakes or passwords, and we didn't swap blood with one another, but a few of the boys did get tattoos representing the Bloods culture.

Instead of putting any of those motivational 'Bloods' words on the whiteboard in the change rooms, we used stars as a substitute. This meant we could have those stars on the board before a game, or at training, and every player would know exactly what they stood for. If anyone else saw them, they wouldn't have a clue what they meant.

It wasn't as though we ever gave much away to the media anyway. That wasn't something that was drummed into us, but I think we all learned along the way that it was best to say very little, rather than risk saying something that might be construed as controversial. It had occasionally happened that a player would make an innocent comment – something not at all controversial – and it would be twisted around and become an issue. So we basically decided that we should always play a straight bat with the media. Let them write whatever they wanted, and we'd respond on the field.

As for our key words we wanted to abide by, I'm sure other clubs had the same sorts of ideas, so that wasn't a massive development. The important thing was that we actually lived by those ideals. At St Kilda, we had words and signs and things on the wall, and it just didn't work. For the Sydney Swans players, they were more than simply words. It was the actions they inspired that mattered, and the honesty players had with themselves and each other.

The new system did come as a shock to a few blokes, though. We had a few players who were really talented but who weren't pulling their weight, yet they were still doing enough to stay in the team. They were told they had to learn to play the way we wanted to play – which was hard and unforgiving – or find another club. The key thing about our system was that you really couldn't hide anywhere.

From then on at the Swans, if players were missing little things or their training wasn't up to scratch, it was known straightaway. There were forty blokes with their eyes on you, watching to make sure you were doing everything you were supposed to. That could naturally create a bit of tension, so strong leadership was vital. Stuey Maxfield was always quick to deal with things if conflicts ever occurred.

Our new philosophy at the club brought about some different training methods, including pre-dawn sessions at Sydney's eastern suburbs beaches. The players would be told the night before, and we would have to turn up the next morning at around 5.30 or 6 am. These weren't intended as a punishment for a loss, though. There were reasons for them, but they were usually things that happened during the week, such as someone breaking a team rule or players not training at the level we expected of everyone – things we felt might affect our performance on the weekend. But it wasn't always about those sorts of things.

Occasionally, we would do it just to realise how lucky we were to be playing footy. It sounds stupid, but there are so many people in the world much worse off than we were. Some people have to spend their whole lives in wheelchairs.

If we have a bad game one week, some blokes think it's the end of the world. Footy is a hard sport, but really we're pretty lucky. At the end of our beach sessions it would always be made clear to the boys why we were doing them. 'We are lucky to be doing what we're doing, and we should appreciate it.' That was the message. They were tough sessions at the beach but it's a lot tougher not being able to walk.

Stuey initiated that sort of stuff, and I was all for it too. If some blokes weren't pulling their weight, they should know that their actions affect their teammates too. That, in turn, would make us get on the backs of the blokes who need to pull their fingers out.

With around forty blokes required to turn up that early, though, there was almost always someone who slept in and arrived late. When that happened, the punishment was that the team had to back up again the next day at 5.30 am.

It happened to me once, but it had nothing to do with a big night out. Leo Barry and I lived around the corner from each other, and one night the power cut out during the night and our alarm clocks didn't go off. No excuses mattered, though.

The sessions weren't just running in the sand or standing in the icy water. They lasted thirty to forty-five minutes and were pretty intense. We would have wrestling matches on the beach, do laps of the beach carrying bricks, or do push-ups on our knuckles on the concrete pathway – and you can imagine how tough that is on a freezing winter's morning. After one of these sessions, a lot of blokes were left with their knuckles bleeding. Adam Goodes' hand actually got infected, and he was in serious doubt to play the next weekend. After that week, it was decided that we shouldn't do as much of that.

By the end of the 2003 pre-season I could see the change in everyone. The entire group had adopted the changes and wholeheartedly jumped on board with what we were trying to do. Despite everyone outside the club giving us very little hope of making the finals that season, we had a real sense of belief.

CHAPTER ELEVEN

By the time we reached Round 1 of the 2003 season, there was a confident feel around the club. The most important thing was that we were all on the same page. The Bloods culture was in place and appeared to be working well. Now it was a matter of taking those improvements onto the field.

We got off to a perfect start in front of our fans at Homebush, beating Carlton by twelve goals. It was a nice way to start off, but they had won the wooden spoon in 2002 so nobody in the footy world took too much notice of our performance. Still, we were reasonably happy at the club.

But then we went to Perth and lost to Fremantle, Adelaide came to Sydney and beat us, and Hawthorn gave us a touch-up at the MCG. We were four rounds into the season and only percentage was keeping us off the bottom of the ladder.

When you start off like that, or when you lose a number of matches in a row, you start to doubt some of the things you are doing. It's just human nature. And there were some things we knew we should be doing better. Yet the team never lost focus on what we felt it was that made us a good team. We had a game-plan, we knew the way we had to play, and we stuck with it.

Things did turn around soon after. We beat Melbourne and Collingwood, and then had a great win over Brisbane at the SCG. The next week, we made it four in a row when we beat Geelong. Suddenly people were starting to mention us.

The reality was that our skill level wasn't the best, but we felt we compensated for that in other ways. Most times, our will got us over the line. Our low skill level was amplified by our game-plan, which would at times make us look terrible. There's no question it was a boring style of footy, but when our skill level improved our footy started to look marginally better too.

There wasn't anything really special about our game-plan. We'd looked at the talent and the personnel we had, and we'd come up with a style of play that we thought would still allow us to win some matches.

We could have done what other teams did and played a style beyond our skill level. Then we would probably have bottomed out and been able to draft some talented kids. In three or four years we might have been able to climb back up to the finals. But we decided to make the best of the talent we had. We felt that if we stuck to our game-plan, played as a team and didn't worry about individual stats or glory, we could do alright.

Our coaches emphasised to us that this would be our best chance of success. We just had to be disciplined, they said, and they were right. This approach would lead to five pretty successful years at the Swans.

While Roosy was our coach, it was a real team effort in terms of coaching. His three assistants – John Longmire, Steve Malaxos and Peter Jonas – worked with different areas of the team. John 'Horse' Longmire was the forwards' coach.

Horse was great. We got along really well and he was a good coach. He certainly put a lot of work into the forward line as a whole and into individual players as well. Especially early on, he helped me enormously to tweak some small things in my game.

The crux of the Swans game plan was one-on-one footy. This style went well with our new philosophy at the club; if a player wasn't pulling his weight, there was nowhere for him to hide. If you had a bad game or your opponent got away from you and got thirty touches, it was there for all to see. That was a good thing, because it meant problems were dealt with quickly. Also, our game-plan was good for the guys who weren't overly talented. If their defensive mindset was right and they applied themselves well, the game-plan would work.

Even when we won, we rarely blew teams away. There were games where we should have really destroyed our opposition, but we didn't. Playing close, tight games was what we were good at.

I found it a bit hard to get used to playing that lock-down style of game. But, as I said, everything was about the team, and the game-plan wasn't to get the ball in quickly to me. It was all about getting results, and as the season wore on, we did.

The club was getting bagged about the way we were playing – even the AFL bosses didn't like it. Like many others, I'm sure, they wanted to see exciting, free-flowing footy, especially up in Sydney, where they were still trying to win over fans.

But, quite frankly, if we hadn't played that lock-down, one-on-one type of footy, we wouldn't have been anywhere near as successful as we were over the next five or six years. We didn't have the midfield to be a quick-running side, but we had a game plan that suited our midfield. The bottom line was that game-plan was tailored to the group of players we had.

As the wins kept coming in that 2003 season, the players' belief in our game-plan, and in our new culture, grew. At the halfway point of the season, we were in the top four. We got as high as second late in the season, then we dropped back before winning our last home-and-away match, against Melbourne, to grab fourth spot. That earned us a Qualifying Final in Adelaide against Port Adelaide, who had finished on top.

Very few people gave us any chance of beating them. We were missing Mick O'Loughlin, Jason Ball and Jason Saddington. Port had lost just four matches during the home-and-away season; they had won all but one of their home games. Coming into the Qualifying Final, they had won fourteen of their past fifteen.

Only the true believers would have expected us to win that day, but we played out of our skins. By half time we had raced away to a big lead. Then we did the typical Swans' thing of grinding out a tough win in the second half. It was a great way to open my finals' account with the Swans.

Under all the circumstances, this win – against the best team in the competition on their home turf – vindicated what we had put in place before the season and what we had lived by all year. It was working for us. You never want to get ahead of yourself and start thinking about how far you might go, but the win certainly didn't hurt our confidence.

We had won the week off before we hosted the Brisbane Lions in the Preliminary Final at Stadium Australia in front of a crowd of around 70,000. That was the second time in a month we'd attracted that many to watch us play in Sydney, having packed in a record crowd of more than 72,000 to watch us play Collingwood in Round 21. I couldn't believe that so many Sydneysiders would ever go to watch the Swans play. Brisbane had done it a harder way: they'd lost their first final, then beat Adelaide, before coming to Sydney.

It was a strange game. We stuck with them early, then they got away. We came back to trail – just – at three-quarter time. Because we'd had the week off and had the fresher legs, I reckon everyone expected us to go on with it from there and book a Grand Final spot, but Brisbane, being the champion side they were, met the challenge and just blew us off the park in the final quarter. Considering we'd used our will to overcome teams during the season, we were disappointed that, this time, they'd out-willed us.

The result showed that we weren't yet ready for the big stage. Sure, we had made big strides and improved through the season, but that loss gave us a kick in the pants. It demonstrated to us all that we still had a lot of work to do if we wanted to be as a good as a team like Brisbane.

At the same time, though, losing to a champion side in a Preliminary Final showed us how close we actually were. It vindicated what we were doing and how we were playing, and demonstrated that our game-plan was working and we should stick to it.

Towards the end of 2003, a fair bit was made of how a lot of people had tipped us to finish last, and it was claimed that that had driven us to prove people wrong. But it wasn't like that at all. The fact was that we'd had a very poor 2002, going from being one of the three favourites to win the flag to missing the finals. In 2003, proving people wrong wasn't motivation for me, and I'm sure it wasn't for my teammates either.

At the end of the 2003 season, I was selected in the squad to play for Australia in the International Rules series, and I managed to keep my spot when they cut the squad down to form a team. It was a great honour to be picked – the only disappointment was that it was Ireland's turn to tour that year as the series was being played in Australia. It would have been great to have had an end-of-season getaway to Ireland.

But it was still a really good experience. The public got right behind the series and we had a sellout of over 40,000 for our match in Perth, and then 60,000 in Melbourne. While we lost the Second Test in Melbourne by three points, we ended up winning the series as we had won by ten points in Perth.

The game itself wasn't difficult at all to adjust to. While there were some subtle changes in rules, and of course a different ball, I thoroughly enjoyed it. It is a game for the runners, though, and there are not too many big blokes who get a game.

I had three fellow Swans – Leo Barry, Brett Kirk and Jared Crouch – in the team with me, as well as future Bulldogs' teammates Brad Johnson and Bob Murphy. Apart from them, getting to know blokes from other teams was terrific. I found myself getting along with guys I had never expected to.

At the start of 2004, when the critics came out against us again, it did hurt a bit. We'd played well in 2003 – we'd finished fourth and made a Preliminary Final. To be written off again the next season was a kick in the pants. The players had spoken at the start of 2003 about winning the respect of the footy world, and we all thought we had made great strides in that regard, so for everyone to tip us not to make the finals again was a slap in the face. We wanted to be consistent from one year to the next, and now we had a little more incentive to do that.

By 2004, other teams had worked us out a bit and knew how we were going about our footy. While those on the outside may not have given us too much respect, our opponents generally did. That they were trying to find ways to counteract the way we played showed that. We hadn't changed our game-plan much from 2003 to 2004, and in my view we became a little bit too predictable in the way we played. As a consequence, we knew that our challenge that year was simply to execute our game-plan better.

We lost a close one at the Gabba against the Brisbane Lions, who were again the reigning premiers, to start the season, but after three straight wins we were moving in the right direction. But a run of losses followed and then some wins; finding consistency was proving to be a real problem for us. We did make it to the finals again, though, finishing sixth on the ladder, and in our Elimination Final we beat West Coast at Telstra Stadium. But the following week St Kilda belted us in the Qualifying Final and our season was over.

It was pretty evident towards the end of 2004 that the Swans players were worn out. The way we played was pretty taxing, and I think it really took a toll. We peaked well before the finals and couldn't keep up our intensity through the long season. Maybe in hindsight we could have rested a few players throughout the year, but that's easy to say now.

While it again didn't end the way every player wants, the 2004 season was a pretty good one for me personally. I didn't miss a game, didn't do anything stupid on the field and kicked seventy-four goals for the season – the most I had kicked at that time in my career. But the stat that pleased me most was that I was number one in the AFL for goal assists.

Late that year, I got a phone call from Andrew Ireland, Sydney's football manager. He told me I had been selected in the All-Australian team. I'm not really one for awards, but that was pretty special. There had been a bit of talk in 2003 that I was in the running but I missed out. When I was selected in 2004, I found it hard to comprehend that I was alongside so many great footballers.

I capped off my good season by winning the Bob Skilton Medal for the Swans' best and fairest, and the Paul Kelly Trophy, which is effectively the players' player award. Those meant a lot to me. I had never seen myself as the sort of player who would win those kinds of awards. Aussie Rules is a team game, and that's the way I've always looked at it.

With no disrespect to Bobby Skilton, who's a legend of the Swans and the game, I probably valued the Paul Kelly Trophy more highly. The coaches vote for the best and fairest, and in reality it was more prestigious, but the opinions of my teammates were what I cared about above all others.

CHAPTER TWELVE

After making the finals for two seasons running, there was a serious feel around the club that we were close to becoming one of the really good teams. We knew that our so-called 'premiership window' was open, and we wanted to make sure we didn't let any chance slip by. The intensity of our training and our discipline, and our scrutiny of each other, really ramped up as we headed into 2005.

We got off to a good start with a ten-goal win against Hawthorn, but things soon turned ugly for us. When West Coast flogged us in Perth in Round 6, they had yet to drop a match all season. We were struggling with just two wins.

We tried extra early-morning sessions, we tried players' meetings at the pub – anything we could think of to try to turn it around. We'd suffered an extra blow in Round 6, when we lost our captain, Stuey Maxfield, to a bad knee injury. It looked like it might be the end of his career, but he was really good about it. Inside, he must have been gutted but he didn't show it around the club.

Stuey had been captain at the Swans since 2003, after Paul Kelly retired, and he'd led us into a completely new era. Kell had been a real on-field leader. He never used to say a lot, so when he did say something, we listened. Kell's on-field leadership had made him a great captain. Stuey was a bit different, and off the field he was probably as good a captain as I've ever been under. He was terrific at rallying the troops and hardening us up, and that was how he drove us.

Honesty was a big thing under Stuey – he was brutally honest at times. He really pushed us to be honest with each other, and everyone got on board. I reckon Stuey's legacy would still be having an effect at the Sydney Swans today.

Stuey relinquished the captaincy, but not really due to the knee injury. The club had granted him permission to spend a few days in Melbourne with his kids each week, and there had been some criticism in the media about how he could still be captain. Stuey being Stuey, he put the team first and decided it was best to stand down.

Most people thought it would be Brett Kirk who would take over. He did get the job first-up. But our leadership group had a meeting – there were nine of us in it at the time – and we decided to see if the club would allow us to rotate the captaincy. Kirky would do a couple of weeks, then the next guy in line would, and so on until the end of the year. Kirky went first, then Leo Barry, and then in Rounds 11 and 12 it was my turn.

Captaining a footy club was not something I had ever dreamed of doing. None of my childhood footy dreams involved holding up the Premiership Cup as the captain of the winning team. Because of Stuey Maxfield's situation, though, I had fallen into it.

I wouldn't say there was a lot of extra pressure on me when my turn to be captain came around. At that stage, all of us in the leadership group were learning and we didn't really know what to expect. Thankfully, Stuey was there to guide us, and we were continuing what he had put into place. We were all hard on the group, like Stuey had been, but we recognised that every captain would naturally be different.

As the season progressed, it wasn't only our slow start and Stuey's injury that unsettled us. When we were getting belted around and struggling, Andrew Demetriou, the chief executive of the AFL, came out and said that the way we played the game was ugly. If we didn't change the way we played, he said, we wouldn't win many games. Gee, thanks for your support, boss!

Roosy was pretty pissed off by that, but he didn't show it publicly. That was part of our strategy of giving the media absolutely nothing that might end up haunting us. I can tell you, though, behind closed doors there was some anger there. I have no doubt that Demetriou's comments really got us going at a time when we needed a kick along.

Whether rightly or wrongly, we started to develop a mentality that it was everyone against us. We had a meeting about it at the time, and Roosy was pretty animated; by the end of the meeting, there wasn't a single player who didn't think the world would do anything to stop us being successful.

We weren't going well at the time, but we all knew we could improve significantly. We knew that what we were doing wrong and why we were losing games was totally in our hands. If we could stick to our processes and get better at certain things, we would win more games. Eventually, we did start turning things around.

Was our game style 'ugly'? Well, it was a slow brand of football, there's no doubt about that; if I was just your average footy spectator I probably wouldn't have gone and watched the Swans play. We didn't have a midfield that could break the lines and run with the footy, which is why we had to stack our defence and play defensively. It was as simple as that. Otherwise, our members and fans might have seen us play some pretty football, but they would also have seen us lose pretty consistently. I don't think most of our fans cared if we were called ugly as long as we were winning games. There have been plenty of teams that played really attractive football and never won a flag.

However, we did sometimes feel we were getting some poor treatment from the umpires, and it was even suggested that the AFL might have directed them to stop us slowing games down with our tight, contested footy. A lot of free kicks were being awarded against us around stoppages, for things that other teams weren't getting in trouble for.

That was just all speculation, of course, and I'm not suggesting it was correct, but even the impression of it gave more fuel to our us-against-them mentality. As a team, we became even more intent on achieving something special that season. It's funny, looking back on it now, and it was pretty smart motivation because we all swallowed it.

I did think to myself at the time, 'Are we just crying over nothing, or are these things really happening?' But analysts at the club searched for, and found, footage of all these free kicks that shouldn't have been there, and there were heaps of them. In the end, though, nothing was done and we were told to stop sooking and get on with it.

So we did, and after starting with just two wins from six matches, we went on and won thirteen of our next sixteen. By the end of the home-and-away season, we had finished in third place on the ladder, winning the double chance for the finals.

CHAPTER THIRTEEN

Our Qualifying Final opponents were the West Coast Eagles, who had finished second on the ladder. They had given us a touch-up earlier in the year but we had improved a lot since then. In fact, we'd been one of the few teams to beat them during the home-and-away season.

That had been at the SCG, though, which was a small ground and suited us well. Now, for the first final in 2005, we were heading back to their ground, Subiaco, the biggest field in the competition. Still, we were in good form, and we headed west reasonably confident that we could match it with them.

In the end, we were beaten by less than a kick. From memory, there was at least one decision that caused a bit of grief among our fans, who thought we were dudded, but the reality was that we'd had our chances to win.

Who knows how things might have fallen if we had won that game. We would have got the week off and gone straight into the Preliminary Final, as we had in 2003, and then we would have faced Adelaide, who had the wood on us around that time.

As it turned out, we came through that West Coast game without any major injuries, and even though we had a long trip back to Sydney and immediately had to prepare for the Semi Final against Geelong, we took a fair bit of confidence away from Subiaco.

That Geelong game was on the next Friday night, which was pretty rare in Sydney at the time. Although it hadn't rained that day, it became a wet-weather match for us.

I never found out exactly what had happened, but the sprinklers had definitely been on before the game and the field was really wet. I didn't personally see them on, but I was told that someone from the club had rocked up earlier and seen them on. A few players had checked the ground earlier in the day, and they couldn't believe that it was now wet.

There were all sorts of rumours flying around about what happened. Some thought the sprinkler system had sprung a leak, while others even suggested that it was an AFL plot to get us out of the finals because we weren't as well suited to a wet surface. Talk about paranoia! All I know was that the ground was wet and there hadn't been any rain.

That match has become almost as famous as a Grand Final. At three-quarter time we were in big trouble, down by seventeen points. The field was wet and slippery and we weren't even looking like we were a chance. We had only kicked three goals all game.

There was no memorable three-quarter time blast from our coach or from me as our captain. But this was a Semi

Final, a couple of steps away from the big one, and while it might have seemed unlikely that we could get back into it, everyone came out of our huddle feeling like we could get it done.

I have to admit that confidence took a shot when, a couple of minutes into the final quarter, Geelong kicked another goal to extend their lead. Nick Davis had fallen away from his direct opponent and copped a serve from Kirky, who told him he owed us that one back.

Davo repaid it – and then some.

It was one of the most amazing games I've been a part of. Davo's locker was next to mine, and for some time after that he kept reminding me – and anyone else who would listen – about 'his' final quarter. It really was an unbelievable individual performance, no doubt, and he got us out of a hole.

He just kept finding the ball and kicking goals. We kicked four in that last quarter and Davo got the lot, the memorable last one coming with just seconds to go from a Jason Ball tap.

There was every reason we shouldn't have won. We had come back from a hard game on the road in Perth, it had been a long, taxing season – especially with the style of game we played – we were four goals down with less than a quarter to play, and the ground was wet. Somehow, though, we found a way to win. For the team in general, the most significant thing was that we had shown the never-give-in attitude we had been striving for.

It was a real turning point for the club. Just two seasons earlier, we had been in a similar situation against Brisbane in a Preliminary Final – no, we'd been in a better situation – and we hadn't been able to do it. This time we had. We'd been forced to dig deep and we had. In reality, the win had just got us into the next final, but the way we had done it was hugely significant for the players.

There were guys who hadn't played that well against Geelong, and I was one of them, but the next Monday our team focus was on all the little things everyone had done. A tap here, a block there, a chase, a spoil, the desperation to keep the ball in play – our coaches stressed that all these little acts had created goals for us. For those of us who hadn't played well, seeing and hearing this was a real boost.

The win meant we booked a Preliminary Final against my old club, St Kilda, the following Friday at the MCG. They had had the week off after beating Adelaide in the first week of the finals, but they still had some injury concerns. Among others, Aaron Hamill and Justin Koschitzke were struggling to be fit to play. It surprised us when St Kilda made an early call on both of them and announced that neither would play. Someone from their coaching staff said that the club was confident they would both be right for the next week, if they got through the Swans game.

To me, it seemed like they were resting these guys for the Grand Final. St Kilda had flogged us earlier in the year and were coming off a good win against Adelaide, but we'd had a massive boost of confidence in our comeback win over Geelong.

All we were hearing was how they were short-priced favourites, and how their fans were getting ready to line up for Grand Final tickets. I was really pissed off about that.

By the afternoon of the match, before we left the hotel to head to the ground, I was so fired up that I got everyone downstairs and had my say.

I told the boys that we had done all this work to get some respect, to get some sort of reputation as a tough, hard team, and now these arseholes were so confident and cocky that they were going to rest their players. That wasn't the respect we had been striving for over the past three years.

I started pounding my fist on the wall as I told the boys how we were going to hook into these bastards, how they would limp off the MCG tonight knowing they'd played against the Swans. 'I don't care if we win, lose or draw – they are going to feel it,' I shouted, 'and by the end of the game they will have some respect for us as a club.'

I was pretty fired up. As a leader, I had from time to time grabbed the boys if something pissed me off, and I used to be on the backs of blokes who didn't train hard, but this was bigger than that – this really got my goat. 'Those arrogant bastards,' I thought.

I made sure our whole team knew how I felt, and that while we thought our hard work to gain respect had paid off, we weren't getting any from St Kilda. 'Let's go out there and get it tonight!' I shouted. Even on the bus going to the ground, I was so wound up that I couldn't sit still: I was bouncing around, firing everyone up again.

Once we got out onto the ground, I could sense that we were going to give St Kilda a big shake. Having given that speech, and being as pissed off as I was, I was trying to be as physical as I could be when we got out there, and I got a bit carried away. I even managed to hurt my shoulder as I tried to tackle someone in the first quarter.

As most teams did, St Kilda was trying to get under my skin. Every time I went to lead for the ball, my opponent, Matt Maguire, would grab me by the arm or try to hassle me. I quickly got sick of that, and then every time he did it I'd give him a bit of a jab in the ribs. But on one occasion I got him in the sweet spot and he wasn't ready for it. He wasn't bracing for it, as you do when you know contact is coming, and he went down.

I didn't think too much of it at the time. In fact, I just thought he'd taken a dive trying to get a free kick, because it hadn't been a hard punch. I realised when I saw a replay of it, though, that I did get him in the midriff when he wasn't expecting it. Having been hit there once or twice myself, I can vouch for it that if you're not ready for it, the wind is really taken out of you. When I saw that, I had no doubt that he wasn't taking a dive.

Like the week before against Geelong, we were down at three-quarter time, but only by a kick or two. We were all confident – confidence gained from the week before – that we could go on and win it. We kicked seven goals in the last quarter, and suddenly we were into the Grand Final. Well, the team was – whether I would be was another matter.

The next day and the day after, there was media everywhere at the Swans. I think everyone expected I would get charged when the Match Review Panel met on the Monday, but the story was saturating the news, even in Sydney, a city getting ready to celebrate being in the AFL Grand Final for the first time in nine years.

Among all the frenzy, there was one person who certainly thought I should play – my mum! I had to laugh when I saw the headline in the paper: 'Let My Barry Play'. Someone from the paper had rung my mum and got her opinion on the matter, and even though she hadn't actually said those words – she hardly said anything, in fact – I suppose they thought it looked good as a headline.

Mum hadn't said anything other than that, naturally, she would love me to play, and that we'd have to let the tribunal take its course. Apparently that became 'Let My Barry Play.

It might sound strange, but my biggest concern at the time wasn't whether I would play or not, but more that the whole business might distract the rest of the Swans team. So I made sure I didn't walk around the place looking worried – I just tried to be exactly the same way I was every week.

Away from the group, though, I was a little worried. 'Shit, this is the Grand Final,' I thought to myself one night. 'This is what we've been playing for, what we have worked so hard over the past three years for, and I might miss out.' I thought back to the 1997 Grand Final. I knew how big it was to play in one, and how good a week it was, and I didn't want to miss a minute of it. The West Coast Eagles had beaten Adelaide in their Preliminary Final, but the result had been small news outside Perth among all the hysteria about me.

Even more significantly, I was our captain at the time, due to our rotation system. While the trend throughout the season had been for each member of the leadership group to captain the side for two games at a time, when we made the finals we decided that it would be best to take one captain all the way through. As it had turned out, I'd been the lucky one. So I had the honour of leading this great group of guys – of mates – onto the MCG on Grand Final day, and now I might miss out on that.

When the Match Review Panel made its announcement on the Monday, I faced a charge that would have ruled me out for two matches. If I pleaded guilty, I would get just one match, but since that match was the Grand Final there was no doubt that we would fight the charge.

All I could do was let the club's legal team deal with everything. I was lucky it wasn't like the old days when players defended themselves, or I might have said something like, 'Well, he deserved it – he wouldn't stop holding me.' I guess I could have called Mum as a character witness, though.

Our legal team decided to fight to have the charge downgraded. The Panel had charged that I'd hit Maguire behind play, but we could argue that it had been in play. If the charge was downgraded, I would cop a week, but if I then pleaded guilty to the lesser charge, it would be reduced by enough that I could still play in the Grand Final.

We also had a backup plan. If I was found guilty and suspended, we could go to the Supreme Court; according to our legal team, I would eventually be allowed to play. This was the same loophole that the Swans had used in 1996, when they fought to allow Andrew Dunkley to play in that Grand Final.

It was a relief for me that the legal team thought I would be fine to play in the Grand Final, regardless of what happened at the tribunal, but I still wanted to beat the charge so that the matter was dealt with on the Tuesday night. It would be far better for us to move on immediately, rather than having the Supreme Court stuff going on all week.

The media attention was pretty chaotic, and while I didn't want it to disrupt the team, it did get to me. I was expecting to fly down on the Tuesday for the tribunal hearing, get mobbed by media at the airport in Sydney, and then again in Melbourne. I was relieved when I was told we wouldn't have to worry about that. One of the club's board members, Peter Weinert, flew us down to Melbourne on a private jet about lunchtime. It was handled so well, and it must have been expensive for him to arrange it. I truly appreciate what Peter did – it made the whole episode run so much more smoothly than it might have.

We flew into Essendon Airport and, with not a camera or microphone in sight, got straight into a limousine and drove to the offices of our legal guy. There, we discussed how we would approach the hearing. As we still had some time before the tribunal, Phil Mullen and I decided to go for a coffee. The media was everywhere out the front, so we snuck out the rear and into the back door of a cafe.

Phil and I were sitting there, having a coffee and trying to relax, when a journo was suddenly standing at our table, saying, 'Barry, can you just come out and make a comment? Then everyone will leave you alone and go away.' I just laughed, but Phil reared up. He stood up and really gave the bloke a serve. I thought he was about to whack him, and then we'd have another striking charge to worry about! The journo, who was obviously scared, turned around and walked straight out the door.

The tribunal hearing went smoothly enough. It took about an hour of argument and evidence. At one point I remember the chairman telling the jury that they shouldn't have any sympathy for me just because my Grand Final was at stake. In the end, it took around five minutes for them to decide the charge should be downgraded. I put in my guilty plea and walked out free to play.

I had tried to play it as cool as I could all along, but of course I had been worried. It was the most amazing feeling of relief when they said I was free to play. It was pretty emotional in the room. I went out and faced the media – keeping Phil and that journo from the coffee shop apart – and thanked all the supporters who had stood by me over the previous days. I told the media pack that I was now looking forward to Saturday.

Then it was back to the airport, onto our plane and back to Sydney. After a good night's sleep, on Wednesday morning I could finally start to think about preparing for the biggest game of my life.

CHAPTER FOURTEEN

It actually started to feel like the build-up to a Grand Final the next day. With the tribunal hearing behind me, now I could focus on footy and prepare for what would most likely be another tight battle with the West Coast Eagles.

For me, the situation was similar to the Grand Final week I had played in with St Kilda in 1997. The Swans hadn't won a flag for a long time – seventy-two years. All the old South Melbourne fans came out of the woodwork as well. While that wasn't really a surprise, it did shock me a bit how much the whole city of Sydney got behind us.

The support we had was massive. Who would have thought we would ever get anyone to come to training to watch us? It wasn't the 20,000 Collingwood might get for a Grand Final training session, but that didn't matter to us. We saw that Sydney people really were interested in us. Someone said at the time that there were more at that week's training sessions than the club used to get to home games during the early 1990s.

The week was more enjoyable for me than 1997 had been. I was older and a bit more mature, so I could handle it a bit better. It wasn't as though I couldn't handle it back at St Kilda, but in 2005 I felt I could enjoy it more.

The Grand Final Parade was different too, because I was captain. I couldn't blend into the background like I had done as a young player back in 1997. I had press conferences to do on Grand Final eve, and when the parade reached its end, I had to stand up in front of the crowd and pose for photos with Ben Cousins, the captain of West Coast, as we held up the Premiership Cup.

I'd never even touched a Premiership Cup before. Holding it was a strange feeling. 'Geez, this is real,' I thought to myself. It was a bit unbelievable. The boys had told me beforehand that it would be bad luck if I let it go first. I don't know whether Ben Cousins had heard the same thing, but there was no way I was going to release it first.

My shoulder, which I'd hurt in the match against St Kilda, was still pretty sore. In the week leading up to the Grand Final I hadn't been able to get my arm above shoulder height. Now, here I was with Ben Cousins, having to hold the cup up above our heads. I was straining pretty hard just to manage it. I had to keep doing it, though, because the boys were watching and we didn't want the bad luck. Plus, I couldn't let the West Coast guys see that I had a crook shoulder.

One thing that pleased me in the days leading up to the Grand Final was that Dad was coming to watch it live. I had played in the AFL for ten seasons by this time, and the only game he had been to watch was my first, way back in 1996 against Carlton. He hadn't even made it to the 1997 Grand Final. I wasn't sure whether Mum was making him come to this one, but I was pleased that he would be there.

I woke up nice and early on the Saturday morning, excited as a kid on Christmas Day. That was exactly how it felt. I turned on the telly and watched a few replays of great Grand Finals, and saw a bit of the North Melbourne Grand Final Breakfast too. I remembered back to how I did that every Grand Final day when I was kid.

I went downstairs in the hotel for breakfast. The room was really quiet, and it was fairly obvious that everyone was nervous. But I wasn't – I was just excited, and I just wanted to get out there and play. It was a feeling I'd never had before.

I went back to my room – on this trip we'd been given our own rooms instead of sharing – and I lay down again, thinking I'd love to have a crystal ball right then to see what I'd be doing at 5 o'clock that afternoon. I said to Leo Barry later that what would make this day more enjoyable would be if we could see the future and know how things were going to turn out, so that if we were going to win we could really enjoy the experience all day. A bit weird, yeah, but that's what was rushing through my head.

The bus ride from the hotel to the MCG was pretty special. There were people everywhere on the streets, and everyone was waving at the bus; well, most of them were waving – some others were giving different hand gestures. But the support we had was amazing. There was red and white everywhere.

The atmosphere on the bus, too, was a bit different from usual. It was pretty quiet – blokes had their iPods on, others were reading the paper – but there was a special feeling in the air. I can't describe it precisely. You hear people talk about this sort of thing all the time, and until that day I had thought it was crap, but we had a real sense that this was our time. Our moment was here.

It was business as usual – well, as usual as it could be – when we got into the rooms at the MCG. I had to have a painkilling injection in my shoulder as it was still pretty painful, but there was never any doubt about whether I would play. We had to push our warm-up back because of all the pre-match hoo-haa going on, but other than that everything was exactly the same as it was every other week of the year. It was important to keep it that way.

In the rooms, as we were getting ready to go out, Roosy gave his pre-match speech. What did he say? Was it inspirational? Did it fire everyone up for the game? Well, I'm not sure. It probably would have been, but to be totally honest I wasn't listening.

I was so focused, and I just wanted to get out there and do my thing. I didn't really even notice whether he was giving us a rev-up. I hope the other blokes were listening, but I wasn't. It was nothing personal, but I was just in this zone. I could hear him and I was looking straight at him, but what he was saying was just going straight over my head. I was lucky he didn't ask me a question. But I knew what I had to do and how I would aim to play.

When we got out onto the field and lined up for the national anthem, the adrenaline was really pumping. I just wanted the match to start. I hadn't just been waiting all day for this, I'd been waiting since 1997 for another shot at a Grand Final, and I just wanted to get into it. I went into the centre for the coin toss – making the right call – and finally it was time to play.

Nobody was surprised how tough and tight the game was, and while West Coast might have had the better of the first quarter, we got a goal right on quarter time that meant we actually had the lead at the break.

The second quarter was all ours, and we led by twenty points at half time. However, we knew that we'd missed some shots and should probably have been five or six goals up by then. When you have the momentum but miss opportunities, it often happens that the other team manages to kick a goal or two to get back into it and halt your momentum. I remember thinking at half time that we'd expended all this energy but hadn't really achieved much.

We knew we had to put it on the scoreboard early in the third quarter, but then the momentum did turn. West Coast came charging back at us, we couldn't kick a goal, and the game was set up for an arm-wrestle in the final quarter.

We were up for it. This was our type of match. We had shown we could win the tight ones, and we drew confidence from that at the final break. Soon after the last quarter started, however, they kicked a couple of quick ones and led by ten points or so.

This was it for us. We had to step up. The Eagles now had the momentum, and unless we swung it around we knew that they would run away with 'our' Grand Final.

It was only a few minutes later that I led out towards the

fifty-metre line and marked the ball. This is where I should tell you that, as I walked back to line up the kick, which was on a bit of an angle, I was thinking to myself, 'I'm the captain and have to lead from the front. I have to kick this goal to get us back into the game – not only on the scoreboard, but to regain the momentum ...'

I should tell you that, but it would all be crap. As I said, I was pretty focused all day and I wasn't thinking about anything but kicking the goal, which I did. People later said to me, 'Gee, that was an important goal you kicked – that really turned the game,' but at that moment of the game I wasn't thinking about any of that stuff. It was the same as always: kick the goal and get on with the game.

That last quarter was tough and we only got one more goal, but it was the goal that gave us the lead. Amon 'Monty' Buchanan kicked it from a stoppage – it was similar to the one Nick Davis had kicked against Geelong two weeks earlier. Stoppages were our thing, but it was still an amazing goal.

There were thirty-odd players inside our fifty-metre zone but somehow Monty had managed to get free and kick the goal. Everyone had done their little bit, which was what we were all about. Tadhg Kennelly was standing thirty metres off the stoppage but it was his job to keep his man out of the play. It was on little stuff like that which we put a big emphasis. We practised it, not knowing when the opportunity might come up to use it, but in two important games that season our preparation had come through.

Our runner told us there was hardly any time left. I was on West Coast's side of the centre wing watching the play. We were all doing what we were supposed to, playing the ball towards the boundary and trying to soak up the time. The Eagles managed to work the ball forward but Tadhg Kennelly rushed it through for a point. From the kick-in, Tadhg found Leo Barry short, he kicked long towards the wing. Dean Cox used his muscle and marked it, then pumped it back into the fifty.

As a footy player, you have to stay switched on for every second of the game, but at this point I kind of stopped thinking about what I was supposed to be doing. I knew there were just seconds left on the clock and thought, 'No, they can't take it away from us now.' Then I experienced this weird feeling. It was almost like I was jogging on the spot, but not actually in the game. It's hard to explain, but I felt like I was no more than a spectator. Like I wasn't out there on the ground. I've never felt anything like that in a game before. I guess I just felt helpless, like I was a spectator.

The ball was in the air. This was their last chance to snatch it from us, and we had to hold them off for one last time. There was nothing I could do and I felt helpless, anxious and nervous, but that's footy. You have to rely on your teammates to do their best, and mine did.

Two seconds later, Leo – who was my best mate – became a legend.

It was an amazing moment, and it still is when you watch it. He came from nowhere, from the side of the pack, and while most defenders would have gone for the punch, Leo went for the mark – and it stuck.

I instantly felt a great sense of relief, then just as quickly I wondered when the siren would sound. I only had to wait a few seconds. Fittingly, Leo's mark was the final piece of action in that Grand Final. We had won it. The match hadn't been handed to us – we weren't ten goals up and able to cruise home and soak up the atmosphere in the last quarter – and that made it even more special.

As in our finals against Geelong and St Kilda, the whole match felt like we could have won it or lost it. We had been made to really, really fight for every minute of the game. That, plus the journey we'd had – the fact that we'd worked so hard for this since 2003 – made it an incredible moment.

I remembered watching the Grand Final presentation as a kid and thinking how good it would be to be standing there, waiting to get called up to get a premiership medallion. Now it was actually happening. I thought about what I should do up on stage. 'There's literally millions of people watching,' I thought. 'Should I carry on like a dickhead and show how excited I feel, or should I just play it cool?'

As the captain on the day, I would be the last player called up. It was so good to see all my mates get up there and get their medals. Then it was my turn and I decided against carrying on like a dickhead. I walked up to the podium, got my medal, and then Paul Kelly came over with the Premiership Cup and presented it to me and Roosy.

By that time, the injection I had in my shoulder had worn off. I stood there with Roosy, holding the cup up, and I thought to myself, 'How good is this! But, geez, it hurts.' I wouldn't be feeling any pain in the few days that followed, though.

Someone asked me later whether I felt lucky or guilty that I was the one who got to be the captain and hold the cup up that day. I sure felt lucky, and I guess I did feel a little bit guilty, too, that it was me and not Leo or Kirky or Jude Bolton or any of the other leaders. I made a point of mentioning to the guys that although it was me standing up there with the cup, I was representing the leadership group as a whole. In the end, the boys didn't really care who was standing up there – we just wanted to win it!

The presentation ceremony was pretty special, but the lap of honour was just amazing. I was surprised by the number of people I knew in the crowd. Every fifty metres there seemed to be someone I spotted: 'Hang on, he's from Broadford! ... I know that bloke from back home!' Then we saw Shannon Noll on the fence dancing away. It was so funny.

The lap was awesome. It was the first chance we had as a team to soak up all the atmosphere and realise what we had done. We were interacting with the fans but we could also interact with each other while we were walking. There were that many celebrations going on, and the Swans staff had all come out onto the ground. That walk around the MCG was something I'll never forget.

When we got back into the rooms, the players and the coaches were taken into a separate room, and there were Crown Lagers there for each of us. Surprisingly, it was really quiet – the idea was just to have a beer for ten minutes, just to chill out and relax. After that, Roosy – who had been pretty excited – spoke to us as a group and told us how proud he was of us, and particularly of the way we'd won the match. We had shown our critics that it could be done our way, despite what they all said.

After that, we all wanted to see our families. They're the people you want to be around at a time like that. And during that week my parents had been forced to deal with all the controversy and stress of me at the tribunal, so it was important to me that I could share the victory with them.

Pretty much all my family was there, and they came into the rooms. It was a pretty good moment, because we all hugged. In fact, that was the first time I had ever hugged my old man. I'd just captained a premiership side; you wouldn't think things could get much better for me that day, but at that moment they did.

We then mingled with all the well-wishers, officials and media in the main room, and by the time it all cleared out, it was dark. One of our assistant coaches, Peter Jonas, suggested that we do what the Adelaide Crows had done when he was there and they won the flag. All the players and coaches went out into the middle of the MCG, formed a big circle with the cup in the middle, sang the team song and took some great photos. I was especially happy that Stuey was there with us too.

We had a club function that night and the celebrations just continued and continued and continued. I don't know if anyone got to bed. We went to the Lindsay Hassett Oval on the Sunday morning to be presented to the South Melbourne fans, and then we got on the plane back to Sydney, where we went straight to the SCG to see our home fans.

I remember borrowing a pair of sunglasses from one of the boys when we were about to go out. I couldn't let the kids see me like I was. I was pretty drunk for a few days, I think. Wins like that are rare, so we had to make sure we celebrated it properly. Who knows when the next one might come?

It was announced that we would be given a ticker tape parade down George Street at the end of the week. To be honest, when I heard that I was a little worried. Sure, we'd won and Sydney as a whole had got on board, but this was still a rugby league town. Added to that, the rugby league grand final was on that coming weekend, and a Sydney team was involved. What if we had a parade and only a couple of hundred people turned up?

We had to meet at the loading docks for the cruise ships down near the Rocks. On the way there I didn't see too many people gathering for a parade. 'We're going to have 5000 people here and it's going to be embarrassing,' I said.

'You might be surprised,' one of the officials replied.

Anyway, we jumped in the cars and got going. It was pretty quiet through the Rocks, then all of a sudden – shit! There were people everywhere, there were planes in the sky writing messages, there was ticker tape falling. I was stunned and humbled. It was awesome and I couldn't believe it was happening. Some reports later said there were 50,000 people there, while others said 150,000. I don't know the actual number but my tip was way off!

That night we had our club champion dinner. Brett Kirk won the Bob Skilton Medal, and I was pretty pleased to finish second to him. I also won the Paul Kelly Trophy again – being in a premiership year made that accolade even more special.

It was yet another big night out in a long list of them for us, and it just seemed to go on and on and on.

CHAPTER FIFTEEN

It's not every year you win a premiership. When you do, you have to make the most of it, and I think the Sydney Swans' boys did a fair job of celebrating our success in 2005.

We continued our celebrations offshore when we headed away on our footy trip to Hawaii. Most of the guys went on the trip – partners stayed at home – and the bonus was that the club was nice enough to pitch in. It felt like they were rewarding us for all the hard work we'd put in and for winning the premiership. I suppose the club did get the prize money, so maybe they felt they should share the cash around.

When we got back, and before we got back into training, the club came up with a great initiative. They decided they would send the Premiership Cup, accompanied by a few players, to various country venues around New South Wales. It was a great idea and the cup was well received everywhere it went. It was the club's way of rewarding the fans, the people who had supported us through thick and thin.

One of the places I got to go was Coffs Harbour. To be honest, just like that ticker tape parade in Sydney, I was truly surprised at the number of people who came out when we hit town.

I've had my moments with some fans over the years. I usually cop gobfuls from opposition fans, which is fair enough. They pay their money to come along and give it to the players they don't like. Some sporting fans are lunatics, living and breathing their chosen sporting team with a passion. Good on them, I say – there's a lot to be said for loyalty in this day and age. Footy fans certainly stay loyal through the good times, and the best of them through the bad times too.

Fans continue each year to put their hands in their pockets to pay to go out and watch their teams play, and while I admire that passion and devotion, I have to admit I just don't get it! I don't want to bag anyone, but I don't understand how some people get so wrapped up in it – that how good their week will be depends on whether their team has won or lost. That's just me personally, though, and while I don't get it, it's a great thing they do, and footy clubs need it to survive.

While opposition fans have always enjoyed sending a few choice words my way, the fans at the clubs I have played have always been fantastic towards me. The support they have given me, through thick and thin, has been overwhelming, really. When I've come back from my indiscretions, they have cheered me back onto the field. That was always the case, which was a bit odd, I guess.

The Sydney supporters, in particular, were really good. But I also remember how the St Kilda cheer squad greeted me the first year after I'd gone up to Sydney. It was game day, and I happened to park my car right in front of them. They were fantastic. They all jumped out of the bus and shook my hand, saying it was great to see me and that they hoped I did well with the Swans. There was no negativity at all.

A lot was written and said about our Grand Final win in the press, but one of the common themes was that we'd been lucky to win it. People said that everything had fallen perfectly into place for us, that we'd avoided the teams we struggled against – like Adelaide. They even said we'd been lucky to sail through the season with hardly any injuries.

It was pretty clear that, still, no respect was being given to us. We had won the whole thing, and still people wanted to bag us and say it was a fluke. The reality was that we were lucky – there's no doubt about it. You've got to have luck to win a premiership. You need things to go your way, and things did during that season. It was a very close, tight season, and any number of teams could have won if they had the luck going their way.

By that time, though, the players really didn't care what was being said. We knew full well what to expect from the media and parts of the public – it was the usual Swan-bashing – so it was just business as usual for us. It didn't bother us, and we never spoke about it in depth.

We all had a fairly good break over the 2005–06 off-season, but like any job, if you get away from your normal routine and what you are used to doing, you miss it a little bit. After eight weeks away from footy and training, I couldn't wait to get back into it. I was always like that, whether we had won the premiership or not.

One of the things to be decided soon after we got back was the captaincy. It was unlikely that we'd go with six rotating captains again, and there was a lot of media speculation that if we went back to one captain I would be it.

The players voted, Roosy discussed it with the match committee and the leadership group, then the board signed off on it. The result was that we would have three captains: Brett Kirk, Leo Barry and me.

To be perfectly honest, I wasn't too worried about the whole captaincy thing. The other two guys – particularly Kirky – probably held it in a higher regard than me. I was happy being a leader on the field, but all the other stuff that went with the captaincy wasn't really for me.

When the 2006 season got underway, the Swans had the same old slow start. We were blown away by Essendon in Melbourne in Round 1, then we had a huge day at the SCG where we unfurled the premiership flag. We had past players there and a big crowd, but Port Adelaide gave us a beating.

As in 2005, we tried hard to find a solution to our slow start. We did it pretty much every year, and every year we'd say, 'We can't keep dropping games so early – we need to get them in the bank for later in the season,' but it kept happening. We were making silly little mistakes – uncharacteristic things for us – that were costing us.

After four rounds we had just one win, and again only percentage was keeping us out of last place. As usual, the critics were saying this proved that the year before was a fluke. But six wins in a row had us back in the top four, and our season was back on track as we neared the halfway point.

Unfortunately four losses from our next five games meant we were about to tumble out of the eight. It was that last loss, though – against West Coast in Perth; a two-point loss this time – which seemed to spark us, and we went on to win six of our last seven. With that, we managed to grab fourth spot on the ladder on percentage from Collingwood and St Kilda. The prize for fourth place was a trip to Perth to play the first-placed Eagles in a Qualifying Final.

We thought back to our Qualifying Final against Port Adelaide in 2003. Back then, we had snuck into the top four, Port – who were almost unbeatable at home – had finished on top, and nobody gave us a chance. Yet we'd gone there and won.

Now three years on, we had to go to Subiaco, where we hadn't won since 2001, and play in front of a hostile Eagles home crowd. West Coast were flying, and their midfield was at its best. In the media, the game was being written up as the Eagles' chance to get some revenge for the previous year's Grand Final loss.

We got off to a good start, which was crucial. We had a good lead at half time, but then, as expected, the Eagles came back at us. We knew we had to hold on. The turning point came with Mick O'Loughlin's famous goal – and his equally famous celebration in the faces of those West Coast fans on the fence.

I had led up the ground as we brought the ball out of defence, then Nick Malceski booted it long into the forward line. It went over the top of everyone, and Mick just turned up out of nowhere, as he often would, and the ball bounced up into his hands. Just in time, he dropped it onto his boot as he ran in, kicking the goal.

It was pretty exciting stuff, but the thing that got me was the silence that descended on the ground. It's a hard thing to explain. People try to describe how it feels to have loud crowds, and big crowds, but it's just as difficult to explain how this silence felt. It was silent, but at the same time it wasn't. The entire crowd went quiet but we could hear our teammates shouting and yelling. It was a great feeling.

The siren went as I was contesting the ball with Darren Glass, and then again, the silence was amazing. All I could hear was our boys cheering. I could hear my teammates in the backline, and Subiaco's a pretty big ground. The crowd was just stunned into silence that we'd been able to win, and by a point.

A few of the boys came to me and we hugged. Someone said it looked like we'd won a Grand Final again. We all knew how important this win was for us. To be honest, it was one of the better wins I have ever been involved with.

I actually liked playing at Subiaco. It's a big ground and there's plenty of space, and I always had good battles with my old foe, Darren Glass. Of all the fullbacks who played on me, he was one of the better ones. He's just an all-round good player. He doesn't worry about getting the footy himself – he's very much a stopper. He will run to get you out of position, but generally not to get the footy. He's strong and he's quick – everything you need in a fullback. Simon Prestigiacomo is another who's quick in a straight line and strong. Those guys just tick all the boxes for a good defender.

Winning in Perth meant we enjoyed a week off, which really helped us because we had a few players carrying injuries. Next, we faced Fremantle at Homebush, and while they were playing some good footy, we went into the game fairly confident we could get through to another Grand Final.

But Freo really surprised me. We had a big crowd of more than 60,000, and it was in the game straightaway as we got on top of the Dockers early. While the old Freo would have crumbled, this version wouldn't go away. The match was a very physical one, and they just hung in there for most of the night. It wasn't until the last ten or fifteen minutes that we were able to get on top, although the margin at the end made it look like it had been a lot easier.

After the game, the feeling among our group was very different from the year before. Perhaps it was because we had been there twelve months earlier, but there wasn't as much celebration this time. Although there hadn't been a hell of a lot in 2005, we'd been hugely excited that we had actually made it, after working so hard to get there. In 2006, it was almost like we expected to make the Grand Final.

For me especially, the 2006 Grand Final week was very different to the year before. There were no private jet flights to Melbourne for a tribunal appearance, so I could just think about the match we were about to play.

I think the whole of Sydney was approaching it differently too. There wasn't anywhere near the level of hype of the year before, which was understandable. The year before, the

Swans hadn't won a Grand Final for seventy-two years. Now, the Swans hadn't won a Grand Final for twelve months.

I don't know whether our fans thought we weren't going as well as in 2005, or that West Coast were going better, or just that they had seen it last year and would watch this one on TV. Whatever the reason, the Eagles had all the fan support at the MCG this time around. Still, that didn't worry us. We just had to make it silent again, like we'd done at Subiaco.

It was a different lead-up for us as a team. For a start, there were no surprises. Whether that was good or bad, I don't know, but we knew what to expect because most of us had been there a year earlier.

Some said West Coast had more to play for than we did, because we had the win from 2005 in the bank; that they didn't want that same terrible feeling they'd had a year before, and so would go into the game more fired up than us.

Maybe that was true, but once you're out there on the ground I reckon all that stuff disappears. I knew every one of our blokes would have a red-hot crack, and none of those thoughts about them wanting it more would enter our minds.

While we had three captains in 2006, it wasn't like we all did everything together. Leo did the captain's press conference and held the cup at the end of the parade with Chris Judd, the new West Coast captain, while Kirky was the one who would toss the coin on game day. But there was one thing we hoped to do together.

As I said, I had felt a bit guilty about being the lucky one to receive the Premiership Cup as captain in 2005, so I came out in the media ahead of the game and declared that if we were to win it this time, I wanted all three of us – plus Roosy – to accept the cup together. It wasn't something we had spoken about in-depth – I just came out with it. The only problem would be that the cup didn't have four handles.

CHAPTER SIXTEEN

I've never watched a replay of the 2006 Grand Final, and I never will. Why would I? What good would watching it again do? I know the result, and I know I had one of those bad days that every footballer dreads.

For me, the story of the Grand Final was that all the Eagles' good players played outstandingly, particularly in the first half. They blew us away at first. We fought back and could have pinched it, but we didn't.

In the end, they outplayed us, but our boys could still hold their heads up high. We hadn't played all that well and had gone down by a point – not that that made us feel any better.

At the Swans, we never felt we were out of a game. We might be getting flogged early on, our midfield might be getting smashed, but we always stayed in a match. In the Grand Final we did exactly that. We weren't playing well, but we hung in, prevented some goals that should have been kicked, kicked a couple ourselves and earned a chance as we headed into the final quarter.

The fourth quarter started perfectly: we got the clearance, it came to me, Goodesy ran past and I gave him the handball, and he kicked the goal. That got us within a kick. From there, it was back to the usual tight Sydney–West Coast style of play, and you just knew it would come down to a kick.

There was a feeling, with that first goal from Goodesy, that things had swung our way. We could feel that the momentum and belief were there. That belief was a great trait of the Swans then. We'd been down and out, with everything going the Eagles' way. Their good players were dominating, we weren't playing well, and the crowd – which was probably sixty–forty in their favour – was going stupid. But we just kept plugging away and eventually turned things our way through pure persistence.

We were on top everywhere but the scoreboard, yet we never felt that we wouldn't catch them. Every time it looked like they would get a break on us, we would kick a goal and get back to within a point.

When the siren had gone at Subiaco a few weeks earlier and we had won by a point, as I said, it was the most incredible feeling. When it had sounded the year before and we had won the premiership, it was an unbelievable feeling. When it went on Grand Final day in 2006, it was an amazing feeling, but one of massive disappointment and despair. We hadn't done it this time. Despite sticking at it all day and never giving up, it hadn't been enough. We had fallen one point short.

It was the worst feeling I'd ever had in my life. It was horrible, then after the pure disappointment, my mind started to tick over: 'What could I have done to bridge the gap of just a point?' That was when the guilt started to come in. I'm sure all players get that, but when you have played badly – and especially when you can't stop hearing about it afterwards – it's twice as bad. I ended up getting pretty down on myself.

For me, it was just purely and utterly a bad day. My effort was there – I was busting my arse all day – but the facts were that I was playing on a good player, our team was struggling generally, and I had a bad day. It was pretty tough to handle when all that combined, particularly on the main stage of our game.

It was so frustrating because I was trying so hard. Everywhere I ran, it seemed the ball wasn't there. Some games the ball just seems to follow you around, but not this day. Even when I did get a crack at it, I stuffed up, dropped the ball or didn't kick straight. It was just one of those days. I've had plenty of them, like any player, but this was the Grand Final and everyone was watching. It seemed that, regardless of what I'd done in previous games – and my final series had been good in 2006 – the only thing that mattered to the critics, in the end, was how I played that day. That's fair enough. But to be branded as 'going missing' ... to me, that was saying that I wasn't even trying. That just wasn't right.

After the game, we were all gutted. Like the year before, we were given time with our families. I was pretty upset. I stayed with them for an hour or so, and there were a few tears. I found the whole day pretty upsetting, and then having people saying 'Hey, it's not your fault' almost made it worse. I was thinking, 'Are they saying that to make me feel better because they actually do feel it was my fault?' All that sort of stuff was running through my head.

I didn't go storming out of the rooms or anything like that, which was suggested later. I went to the club function that night but I didn't stay long. People were dissecting the game and wanting to talk to me about it, and I just didn't want to hear about it. The last thing you want to do is go to a Grand Final function and talk about footy when you've just lost.

We headed home the next day. There were some media people at the airport, and then I got home and they were out the front of my house. It was a joke. I was walking up my driveway and this dickhead with a microphone was saying, 'Do you think you could have done anything different, Barry?' I just stared at him, bit my tongue and said nothing, and went inside the house.

I knew that if I spoke to them it wouldn't really have been the end of it. And anyway, what could I say? I decided to say nothing and that was the end of it. It wasn't as if I had dogged it – I knew I'd put in the effort.

I guess the media wanted to be able to blame someone for the loss, and I copped the brunt of it. I was certainly disappointed after the game – I was shattered – and if I could have wound back the clock or played another quarter, then of course I would have. But I couldn't. It was done.

Not that I read too many papers – it's just not worth it – but at that time I couldn't get away from it. My family was ringing you up, saying, 'What about what so-and-so has written about you ...' I just didn't want to know!

There were a few people in particular in the media who aimed up at me. The thing that disappointed me most is that I let it affect me. I was pretty angry about it, and I thought, 'Stuff the media – that's it, I'm not doing anything for them again. When everything is sweet again and they want an interview, stuff 'em. I'm not going to take time out of my day for them to write an article – it's not going happen anymore if this is how they want to play it.'

People kept saying to me, 'Don't worry about it – you can't win, so let it go,' but I just couldn't. I had people at the club, and even the coach himself, saying to me, 'Just smile and do the interviews.' But I just wasn't going to give them the satisfaction. The way I saw it, things didn't work that way.

I've got no doubt that my reaction to it then had an impact when I stuffed up later on. The media probably went harder on me then, as a result of my refusal to play their game. Oh well – I just have to cop that.

I'm me. I can't change who I am, and my beliefs are my beliefs. I couldn't just smile and give someone an interview and not tell them what I really thought about them. And I don't believe I should have had to.

My stand-off with the media did create a problem the next season, though, because I was still one of our captains. The club felt I needed to speak to the media more. I had a weekly column in the *Sydney Morning Herald*, though, and I told the club that that was where people could read what I thought about things. I probably said more each week than most players.

What really annoyed me, in the months after the Grand Final loss, was that the media went to my family for comments. Mum said something about it being disgraceful that the media had sung my praises a week before the Grand Final and that now they were kicking me in the guts.

Everyone in my family now knows better than to give comments when the journos come calling. The frustrating thing, though, was that I had told them before it happened exactly what to do. A journalist will ring you up and be really nice to you, I had told them. They'll say they're on my side and want to write something about all the unfair treatment I've been copping ... Exactly this had happened, and I think Mum had been sucked in.

Mum is mad. She's kept every single article written about me at that time. I told her once that I'd read them and find out exactly who said what, but I never have and I don't think I ever will.

I'm really not into looking back and reflecting on stuff that happened in the past. A few years ago I threw all my trophies out. Mum loves all that stuff and went off her head at me for chucking them away. But to me they don't mean anything. I don't want them sitting on my mantelpiece for everyone who walks into my house to see them. It's like saying, 'Look what I've done!' Who cares?

It's the way I am. People who know me know what I've done and respect me for it, and that's enough for me. I don't need memorabilia or my premiership stuff hanging on the wall. Maybe when I get older I'll eat my words and I'll love it all, but at this stage it doesn't interest me. I would actually feel embarrassed if someone walked into my house and I had all that stuff hanging up.

I have got some memorabilia from our 2005 premiership – some limited-edition stuff which only the players got. So there's only twenty-two of those, some signed pictures and my premiership jumper, but it's all put away and I won't ever bring it out. The only reason I'm keeping those things and haven't sold them on eBay is to have something for my kids down the track. The premiership itself means more to me than any memorabilia could.

The other thing after the Grand Final loss that annoyed me was a report claiming that someone at the club had said I was shitty and had left town. I didn't leave town. I was still at home in Sydney. I wasn't doing much at all, but we were on holidays. I might have gone up to Noosa for a few days later on, but that was it. Yet it was made out that I had gone into hiding, which – surprise, surprise – was total crap.

I reckon I probably had two weeks off and then was back training again. I was so filthy about the way things had turned out that I just wanted to get back into it. I was pretty hard on myself and certainly felt guilty about my bad Grand Final. My state of mind was pretty low, to be honest. I was fed up with footy and the way the media treated players. I even thought briefly about chucking it in. But after two weeks off I decided to do everything possible to prove all my critics wrong.

So, although we weren't officially training again, I would do weights and go running by myself. I planned to get super-fit. I wanted an outlet and I needed to find a way to resolve what had happened. Training was the best way I could think of doing that.

Soon after that, I was off to Ireland with the International Rules team. For me, the timing of the trip was perfect. It meant I could get back on the field that month, instead of waiting four or five months for the pre-season games to begin. I knew I had to keep my mind active and play some footy again, because the criticism had made me doubt myself.

CHAPTER SEVENTEEN

Going to Ireland in October 2006 was a great experience. I was made co-captain of the side in that series, which was a real honour. It helped to put the disappointment of the Grand Final behind me – for a couple of weeks, at least.

The best part about the trip was getting to know and play with some of the great players in our competition. I saw a different side of blokes I'd played against in the AFL, some of whom I probably had some preconceived ideas about.

Back in 2003, one of the guys I was on the International Rules team with was Matty Scarlett. I'd played against him plenty of times, and until then I had absolutely hated him. But once we were on the same team, we got along like a house on fire. In 2006, there were guys on that trip who I hadn't liked one bit when we left Australia, but by the end of the trip we ended up good mates. There were probably a few blokes who felt the same way about me too.

This was the first time I'd ever played a game of footy outside Australia. Our biggest challenge was to gel as a team, since we only had about a week and a half of training before we played the First Test. And we were playing a game where nobody really knew all the rules or how to kick the ball properly.

There had been a few brawls in the previous series, and we were all put on notice that if there were any incidents like that – or any blues at all – we would be red-carded, which would wipe us out for the whole series.

So we wanted to make sure there was none of that. We stayed disciplined, but Ireland came out and used some dirty tactics – little things like hitting blokes in the guts behind play. It worked for them and they won the First Test by eight points.

'Bugger this,' I thought. So for the Second Test I said to the boys, 'We've got nothing to lose here. They came out and gave it to us in the first game and we had to just cop it. Bugger it, if you get a red card, bad luck.' I told everyone to make sure the Irish knew they were in a game – bump into them, give them some niggle and give them some lip.

The team certainly listened. Before the ball was even bounced there were fights breaking out everywhere. There were more than 80,000 people at Croke Park in Dublin for that game, and they got to see a fired-up Australian team smash their boys.

But while it worked for that game, the Irish authorities didn't like our tactics. Nor did the fans or media, and the upshot of the outcry after the game was that the series was dumped for the following year. But it's back now and it's good that it is.

The biggest drama of the tour happened in Galway, but it wasn't on the field. It was in a pub, and – for a change – I wasn't in the centre of it. Well, not quite.

Brendan Fevola got into an altercation with a barman, who, to be honest, was being a bit of a tool and bagging most of the Australian players. Anyway, Fev put him in a headlock. I was actually the one who stepped in and broke it up.

We left the pub and all the other blokes went to another bar. I didn't fancy it and decided to walk home. As I was making my way, the police came along and stopped me. 'We've got you on the footage,' they said. 'You obviously know the bloke who did it. We know you play for the Australian team, we know you guys were in the bar and we know where you are staying. If you don't help us out you'll be locked up.'

'Hang on a minute,' I thought. 'This isn't right.' I wasn't concerned for myself because – for a change – I knew I hadn't done anything wrong. 'What do you want me to do?' I asked.

They asked where Fev was, and I said I didn't know, which was true. They said to tell Fev to come to the police station to sort it out. They were pretty sure that if he went and apologised to the bloke, that would be the end of it.

When Fev got back to our hotel, I said to him, 'Look, we should go to the cop shop and get this thing sorted out. It was a headlock, it's no big deal. If you apologise to the bloke, that will be it.'

I thought I was doing the right thing and that it would all

blow over quickly, but instead it blew up. As it turned out, this guy wanted to press charges, and that's what he did.

I often wonder what might have been if I hadn't helped the coppers that night. They knew where we were staying anyway, and I'm sure they would have eventually done something, but I did feel a bit responsible for how it played out.

I had to go to the police station and make a statement. In Fev's defence, I told them that he was well within his rights to give the barman a piece of his mind. I had felt like doing it too. Thankfully, I hadn't done that. When I was younger I probably would have done something worse than putting the bloke in a headlock.

Fev received a caution from police and was sent home from the tour. I later heard that the barman was chasing him for some sort of compensation. It was a disappointing part of the tour, but overall it had been a terrific experience for me and the team.

As soon as I got home from Ireland I got straight back into training, and I worked my arse off. Throughout my career I always trained hard during the off-season, and usually during the time off the club gave us as well. I love doing weights and cardio stuff, so while I worked hard in late 2006, it wasn't anything drastically out of the ordinary.

The pre-season went well for me, and I felt great heading into the 2007 season. It was probably the fittest I had ever been, and I felt strong. All through that pre-season I ticked every box we had as players, and I was raring to go when Round 1 arrived. First-up, we faced none other than the West Coast Eagles. We always knew what to expect going into a game with the Eagles. It would end up being a tough, tight, close game that could have gone either way.

We had an incredible stretch of close games with West Coast over that period. People always said it was because we were so evenly matched as teams, but I don't think that's right, to be honest. They had a far better side than us, but we were able to clamp down on them in a way that only we seemed to be able to do. As a result, we always ended up with close, tight games. I don't mean any disrespect to any of my teammates, but the Eagles were ultra-talented; we had to drag them down to our level and make them play our style of game.

Darren Glass and I had a bit of an ongoing joke for a little while. If the Swans were a couple of goals down and fought our way back, he would look at me and say, 'Here we go again,' and I did the same a few times to him. As soon as one of our sides kicked a goal to be within a point, we would both look at each other and think, 'Here we go again – how's your heart?' It was a running joke for us.

I was pretty fired up for our Round 1 encounter. It wasn't a chance for redemption or revenge. The Eagles had won the Grand Final, while this game was worth just four competition points. A win in Round 1 would hardly avenge a Grand Final loss.

Despite my keenness, they jumped us and kicked ten goals in the first half. That alone was very rare in matches between Sydney and West Coast. They led by six or seven goals at half time. We clicked into gear in the second half and charged home, but for the third time in three games the margin would be a point. For the second time on the trot, we would be the losers.

As a team, we made the finals again in 2007, but personally I was plagued by injuries all season. It was my groins again. I think I had over-trained in the off-season, and probably for the wrong reasons. I was too fired up because of all that had been written about me, and because I wanted to show everyone I was better than my bad performance in the 2006 Grand Final.

Halfway through the 2007 season, I missed a game with the injury, which was the first match I had missed since being suspended back in 2002. I had a week off to rest the injury, then I played a couple more, had another one off, played a few more and went okay, then needed another week off. I missed the last week before the finals, then I battled through our Elimination Final against Collingwood, which was to end our 2007 season.

My groin injury was a problem that just needed rest. It was the same thing I'd had earlier in my career. It generally happened every pre-season when I had to get used to the training workload again. It was a chronic injury, and I realised then that I'd always have it and would just have to manage it.

Sitting games out that season was tough, but what was even tougher for me personally was to play games and find that my body refused to obey my mind. That was just so frustrating. I would see a ball bounce in front of me, which generally I'd be able to get. But with the injury I couldn't get there in time – it was like my body had a defensive mechanism to prevent me from moving quickly. I'd see a bloke come in and grab the ball and run away, leaving me standing there cursing like an idiot.

I was pretty glad to see the back of the 2007 season, which had been the most frustrating I'd had in a while. It wasn't the type of year that would put the disappointment of 2006 behind me.

My relationship with the media hadn't improved over the course of the season, and I still didn't want to have anything to do with journalists. Our media manager at the Swans, Stephen Brassel, got pretty annoyed with me, although I was still doing my weekly column in the *Sydney Morning Herald*. He said that, as one of the club captains, it was my responsibility. We had words about it several times, but I wasn't going to budge.

We had a meeting with Roosy and Andrew Ireland to discuss the matter, and I told them how I felt about the media's treatment of me at the end of 2006. They wanted me to forget everything that had happened, but I said it wasn't going to happen, simple as that.

When we returned after the 2007 off-season, I had an inkling that they didn't want me to be one of the captains anymore. The reality was – and I'm being 100 per cent honest now, even though it's easy to say after the event – that I didn't really want to be a captain.

I reckon I was a pretty good clubman and did my bit to keep the club happy and vibrant, but there was more to being a captain than that. You have to be responsible and grown-up and smile if you're a captain. That doesn't sound too much like me, does it?

My character doesn't really suit being a captain, I reckon. As an on-field leader I was good, and I always did the hard stuff and all those things, but I'm a light-hearted bloke and

I play practical jokes and I didn't want to stop doing that. Footy is an awfully serious sport and it can really weigh down on you if you don't keep it fun, just like anything.

And there are so many meetings you have to attend as a captain, not to mention match committee, media stuff and speaking at functions. It's a big responsibility, and once I had made the decision to let all that go I didn't feel at all devastated or shattered.

Before I officially resigned from the captaincy, though, I had a general chat with Roosy about the coming 2008 season. He said to me, 'You go and get your body right,' and then – almost in passing – 'Oh, and the captaincy thing ... If you don't want to continue that, to take a bit of pressure off ...' He didn't actually ask me to quit, but he said it in a roundabout way.

That confirmed my decision for me, and I announced my decision to step down as captain soon after. Roosy was probably the happiest bloke in the world that he didn't have to make the hard call of dumping me.

Roosy and I had always got along okay, but that had been when things were going well for the club in general. From about 2007 onwards, I sensed that our relationship was starting to get a little strained. He never told me that, but I reckon I'm a pretty good judge. A few things happened that made me think that way.

I had a few concerns about our game-plan and how it was working for the forwards. I went to Roosy and the other coaches and told them my ideas, suggesting some new ways of doing things. They put it back onto me, saying I was blaming the game-plan because I wasn't getting a kick.

Mick O'Loughlin and I went into a meeting about it – Mick agreed with me about the game-plan – but it all got turned back onto me again. 'You let the media affect you,' I was told.

'Hang on, let's stop the meeting here,' I said. 'This is ridiculous – what are you talking about? I'm here to help us try to win more games, that's all. I'm not suggesting this so I can kick ten goals next week – I'm here because I want to win.'

I was told that my body was not letting me do what I wanted it to do, but I said it wasn't about that. They just didn't get it.

Another time I asked the coaches if they still valued me as a player at the Swans, because I didn't feel like that was the case. They denied it, of course, but I could see what was happening. My relationships with the coaches at the club were starting to fracture. In hindsight, it's clear to me that the end of my time at the Swans had begun.

CHAPTER EIGHTEEN

So much happened in my footy career both before and after that April night at ANZ Stadium in 2008. I managed to achieve quite a few significant things during my time in the game, most notably holding aloft the Premiership Cup as the Swans' captain in 2005. But there's one moment, one incident, that will forever be associated with my playing days: 'that punch'.

Moments after it happened, I heard the crowd give off an almost deafening groan. My punch of Brent Staker was instantly being replayed on the big screen. Amid all the commotion, I managed to sneak a quick look.

I was actually really surprised when I saw the replay. I hadn't realised until then how bad it was. I knew I'd connected, and of course I saw him lying there on the ground, but when I saw the replay – and particularly saw how graphically his jaw wobbled – I immediately thought, 'That is not good. I'm in a bit of trouble here.'

I was really disappointed in myself, but I didn't let it get to me for the rest of the game. It was a strange feeling. I kept playing and actually went okay, until I crashed into the fence late in the game and broke my wrist. Talk about karma, hey?

There were so many rumours flying around straight after the game – including that Roosy had torn strips off me at half time because I had thrown the punch at Staker. Apparently, during the second half of the TV coverage, they had shown vision of Roosy standing toe-to-toe with me at half time, having a chat with me in the rooms; the suggestion was that he was giving it to me for letting myself and the team down. The fact is he didn't even mention the incident then. Nobody spoke about it at half time.

I had tweaked my hamstring in the first half and Roosy was asking if I wanted to come off. I told him I was fine and that I could get through the match, and that was it. End of story. He knew that right then wasn't the time to be trying to get inside my head about the punch.

As I've said earlier, I was used to being niggled on the field. I got it in every game I ever played. Because of that, people often ask me why I cracked this time. Let me take you back to that night.

There was a lot of niggling stuff going on – much more than usual. Staker wasn't even my man; I forget who he was on, but perhaps it was Mick O'Loughlin. Anyway, it seemed that West Coast had decided they would give it to me that night. Staker would run past me and – with the ball nowhere near us – he would go out of his way to blindside me or drop a shoulder into me. He did it two or three times and we exchanged a few heated words.

That sort of play is one thing that always really annoyed me. Players can do that and there are no consequences. The umpire might come in and shoo them away or break it up, but there's never any penalty. And of course, the umpire usually happens not to see the first contact, only when I retaliated. But it was like that my whole career.

In the aftermath of the incident I remember some people – so-called experts – coming out and saying, 'If that happened off the football field he would be charged ...' Well, imagine someone in everyday life coming up to you – say, in a pub – and jabbing his elbow into your ribs or dropping a shoulder into you from behind. He'd get whacked. But the rules of the game seem to allow it, and if you retaliate then you're penalised.

As a young bloke, I was brought up not to let anyone have anything over you. That was drummed into me from day one, although of course it would get me into trouble off the field as well. But what was happening to me on the field that night really pissed me off.

I was being held quite a bit that night, not only right before I threw the punch but every time I led for the ball. I was screaming to the umpire every time to keep an eye on it. He was standing twenty metres away, just watching what was going on and doing absolutely nothing. My jumper was being pulled, Staker was holding my arms, pushing me in the back, and the umpire could see how animated I was about it.

A lot of crap was written afterwards about my relationships and the mental state I was in before the game, but that was just bullshit. The truth was I was continually wound up by Staker, and by the umpire who didn't intervene. I got frustrated, and the result was ... well, we all know what it was.

I had a reputation as a very animated player out on the field, but a lot of the time that was just a tactic I used to try to intimidate players. Generally, it wasn't because I was angry. If things didn't go my way, then of course I'd get annoyed – that's just human nature. I'm the same as anyone else, and I showed my frustration openly, particularly later during my time in Sydney.

Contrary to what those 'experts' think, I don't believe I had a tiny fuse. I put up with a lot on the football field, and I gave a bit back too. But if you wound me up enough, of course I could explode, just like many people.

The aftermath was equally frustrating. You can't talk about umpires, so I couldn't say openly that this bloke hadn't intervened before the situation escalated. And I didn't want to put any blame on Staker, because the truth was I really felt bad enough for him as it was. Anyway, it wouldn't have looked great if I started playing the blame game.

I'm sure my 'mates' in the media would have had a ball if I'd said I belted him because he deserved it. To be honest, though, it was really hard to stay silent, when I knew the reasons it had happened. But I just had to sit there and cop everything that was thrown at me. And it was amazing how much of that there was.

Having said all that, though, the bottom line is I shouldn't have done it. I regret punching Staker and I always will. If I had my time again, it certainly wouldn't have happened, but all the excuses in the world aren't going to change it now. That moment left the darkest of marks on my career.

I'm not trying to justify my actions then in the slightest –
I never can and I never would try to do that – but I am able
to tell my side of the story, which I haven't before now.

I held a press conference the next day, in which I
acknowledged that I'd stuffed up and said I would cop
whatever came my way. I had no idea what that might be.
It could have been seven weeks, but there was talk of fifteen
weeks or even the whole season. Some people wanted me
rubbed out for life, and some wanted me charged by the
police. I didn't need to start speculating before the media –
I knew my penalty wouldn't be good.

The club was hoping that holding a press conference
might help take the spotlight off me until the tribunal
hearing. Fronting the media was a little awkward,
considering the frosty relationship I'd had with many of
them over the past year or two, but the club was convinced
it was the way to go.

Like me, the club wanted to get the whole thing over and
done with as soon as possible. The intention was never to
get some brownie points ahead of the tribunal hearing; we
couldn't talk about specifics before the hearing anyway. It
was an opportunity for me to acknowledge what I'd done
and to apologise. I guess it was also about saving the public
image of the Swans, who probably wanted to be seen to be
doing something about it too.

I rang Brent Staker to apologise but couldn't get on to
him, so I left a message. There was a story going around in
the papers soon after that I hadn't called him, that I was just
saying I had in order to make things sound better for me
at the tribunal. But I had rung him, and I showed Andrew

Ireland my phone record to prove it. In fact, I called him again as we were waiting to go into the hearing.

He was fine. We didn't get into details about why it had happened. We both knew what had gone on before I threw the punch. I told Brent I hoped it didn't mean he had to miss a week. I apologised and said I regretted what I'd done, and said that if I had my time again it wouldn't have happened.

He said, 'That's part of footy. If it happened to me, I would take it like you have.'

'The next time I see you I'll buy you a beer – I think I owe you one,' I said.

'I think you owe me two or three,' he replied.

In the days between the game on the Saturday night and the tribunal on the Tuesday, the media and photographers and TV cameras were camped outside my house. What made things worse was that I didn't sleep for those four days. As I said, I had dislocated and broken my wrist late in the game, and I had to wait four days to have an operation. I couldn't sleep a wink and was doing laps around the house going stir-crazy.

As I would obviously be pleading guilty, there was no real point going to Melbourne for the tribunal. I was taking responsibility for what I'd done, and I would cop whatever came my way – there wasn't much else I could do, really. We did a live video-link cross from Sydney. There was media everywhere there too, but it would have been massive chaos had we gone to Melbourne.

The hearing lasted a bit over an hour, and it really wasn't that difficult. I'd been there a number of times before and was ready to accept my punishment. I wasn't denying the charge at all. I wasn't putting blame on anyone else and it hadn't been an accident. I had already owned up to it at the press conference. It was really just up to the panel to decide how many weeks I got.

Because of this, it was probably the least nervous I'd been at a tribunal hearing. It sounds silly, but I just knew I'd done the wrong thing and was prepared to cop my punishment. In the end I got seven weeks, which I thought was fair. It was rare that I agreed with the tribunal's penalties, but I did this time.

With the hearing out of the way, I had the operation on my wrist, and from that moment on I wanted to focus on getting back onto the field. But it wouldn't be that easy, I soon discovered.

The football club was trying to come to terms with why I had punched Staker. In the end, to be honest, I just agreed with whatever explanation they wanted to make. I knew why it had happened – there had been a build-up of things, and my frustration at being ignored by the umpires had peaked. I did tell the club that, but at the same time I was trying to be careful. All I wanted to do was get my punishment done, get the situation and my wrist fixed, and get back to playing.

But I had to be careful about what I said. I didn't want to appear to be whingeing and making excuses. It was very important within the whole Bloods culture to accept responsibility for your behaviour. If I'd whinged about the umpires, for instance, the response would have been: 'You still shouldn't have done it, and now you're not taking responsibility for it.'

I decided that the best way for me to get back to doing what I wanted – playing football – was to take responsibility and move on, and that's what I tried to do. I was responsible for throwing the punch, and it was stupid. I'll never deny that, and I was honest and up-front about it at the time.

But the club wanted to dig deeper. They asked me if there was anything that had happened off the field, in the lead-up to the game, that had been unusual. I had to meet with Grant Brecht, the club's psychologist, and I told him the only thing that had been slightly different to any other game was that my ex-girlfriend Kylie had rung me up; we'd had a blow-up on the phone for ten minutes. It had been pretty heated, but when I'd hung up, that had been that. It was done and I was fine.

Kylie and I had split up, and I was seeing another girl, Talia. On the day of the game I had gone shopping with Talia to get some food for my game preparation, and as we were driving out of the car park of the shopping centre, Kylie drove up the ramp and saw us. That had triggered something, and I got a phone call that afternoon from her, saying, 'How can you do this to me?'

That was basically all there was to it. A heated phone call, sure, but that was it. It's absurd to say that was the reason I hit Brent Staker. If you look at the game, I had been playing really well until it happened – I finished the game with ten marks. If you're wound up mentally, that's going to have an impact on your game. I'm not good enough to play well if I'm off my game because I'm thinking about my ex-girlfriend. And anyway, how could they think that I run around the footy field thinking about girls?

But I was willing to do whatever it took to get myself back on the field. If I had to say there were matters in my private life that affected me, and if I had to lie on a psychologist's couch a few times a week, I would do it. I knew I was going to miss playing footy, and I wanted to serve my seven weeks, get my arm right and get back out there again.

While it was always going to be a huge story, I wondered whether not talking to the media after the 2006 Grand Final, and during 2007, had an influence on the way some journalists covered the story. I knew they'd been waiting to take a shot at me, and I'd given them the perfect opportunity.

The club announced to the media that there were 'private matters' I had to deal with, and that these had affected my mental state going into the Eagles game. The media, as they often do, put one and one together and came up with three – a triangle. A love triangle, actually. There were headlines every second day and photos of both Talia and Kylie. The whole thing made me look like a bit of player – someone called me the Hugh Hefner of the AFL. Now that was a laugh.

In those situations, if you say nothing the story ends, but unfortunately – maybe because both Talia and Kylie didn't know how to handle it, or perhaps just because they wanted to have their say – the story kept on bubbling. I'm not saying I'm a guru, but I've got a fair idea of how things work in the media, and you really are better off saying nothing. But both women had their three minutes of fame, and that kept the story alive.

I didn't read the papers, but someone always called me, saying, 'Hey, did you see what was in the paper about you today?' The funniest media story was that Kylie was by my bedside in hospital after I had my wrist operation. That was just not true. I don't know where Kylie was, but she certainly wasn't at my bedside.

As a result of all this extra drama, the story didn't die down as quickly as it should have. It got pretty ridiculous. I'm not Tom Cruise and we weren't in Hollywood, but I was being stalked by the media and I just had to live with it.

CHAPTER NINETEEN

I couldn't believe how much publicity the Staker punch got. Talk about the shot heard – or seen – around the world. Someone even said at one point that the AFL should be paying me for promotion. It was even shown on American TV. I was surprised, but it was very graphic and they love that sort of stuff.

Even today it's still often shown on TV – I wish I had the copyright to it. Every time there is some story about violence in sport, they tend to show that Staker punch. It's hardly surprising. It was a clean hit, and the shock factor is always there with that sort of vision.

Whether it was good or bad for me to play it the way I did with the Swans, I don't know. The way I saw it, they thought they had found the problem, so I'd grin and bear it for seven weeks, sit on the couch and have a chat with Grant Brecht, say all the right things and get back on the field as soon as possible.

The problem with that, though, was that whenever something happened involving me on the footy field from then on, it was decided that 'he must again have all these women problems going on in his private life, taking his focus off footy'.

In those first few weeks after the Staker incident, there mustn't have been much important news around at the time. There always seemed to be something about me on TV or in the paper, and everyone wanted to have their say about it.

I was a pretty easy target. There were girls who could be tied into the situation, and a big angry bloke ... it made for a good story that ran for a few weeks. And I knew that when it eventually died down, it would be back when it came time for me to return after my suspension.

It was difficult for the club, because the Swans' public image was so clean-cut. There hadn't been any negative publicity about the club for years and years.

It was also a pretty difficult time for my family, and that was one of the hardest things for me to deal with. I could handle myself and everything that was thrown at me, but they didn't deserve to be copping any crap. They were harassed by the media, and, being family, they wanted to defend their son and brother.

My old man speaks from the heart. He's your typical down-to-earth country bloke who calls it like it is and doesn't deal in crap. He got hassled by reporters and he said some things he shouldn't have. He was just sticking up for me, but actually it just inflamed things. He thought that because I couldn't say anything, he was doing the right thing for me.

Then my sister came out and defended me too, saying I was a better role model for kids than Ben Cousins because I wasn't a druggie. Shit! They all thought they knew what they were doing, but they just didn't.

I had a run-in about it with my parents and my sister. I told them to tell the media absolutely nothing. If they rang, I said to say, 'Sorry, I can't comment on that – you'll have to talk to Barry.' If they said nothing, I told them, the story has nowhere to go and will soon stop.

I was pretty angry with them because I had told them all this before, when the drama after the 2006 Grand Final came up. I didn't think they'd make the same mistake again, but I was wrong. In fact, after we had this run-in, I didn't speak with my family for several months. I didn't call any of them, and if they called me, I didn't answer.

A similar thing was happening on the other side, too. Brent Staker wasn't speaking about the incident and so the media headed for his parents, from whom they got exactly what they were after – lots of raw emotion and great headlines.

I wasn't surprised his parents called me a 'weak mongrel' and were demanding that I be rubbed out for a season, and saying their son should take legal action against me. I wasn't surprised one bit, but that didn't mean it had no impact on me, especially when I wasn't able to respond. Not that I would have, in that forum.

There were a lot of things running through my head, and it would have been quite easy to say something in the media to respond to everything being thrown my way. I could have used my weekly columns in the *Sydney Morning Herald* and the *Age*, but the reality was that I didn't believe in playing things out in public through the media. That just gives the media exactly what it wants – a slanging match, back and forth, which sells more papers.

And I don't believe the way to do it is over the phone, either. If you have something to say to someone, particularly if it's something difficult, you say it to their face. Everyone's got a bit more courage on the phone. I might give someone a call if I don't agree with something they've said, but I'll arrange to meet with them face-to-face to talk about it.

I totally understood Brent Staker's parents coming out and saying what they did; if it were my son I'd be fired up as well. When the media start to go for the parents, it gets really emotional, and I know that's exactly what they are looking for. Parents will stick up for their son and say plenty against anyone who caused him any harm. It would have been exactly the same with my parents, and as we all know, things come out of our mouths which we may later regret. But that's all part of the whole saga.

One of the biggest criticisms at the time was that the incident looked dreadful for the code and was an awful example for all the children watching. Of course I don't want kids running around pretending to be me and throwing punches at their opponents. I'd prefer that they were lining up for a goal like me, just like I pretended to be Simon Beasley when I was a kid. But the reaction I got from kids was strange – my popularity with them soared.

Don't get me wrong, it was a bad look. Violence doesn't belong in sport, but bizarrely, in the aftermath of it all, it made me more popular than ever. People wanted to know all about it. I was asked to speak at more and more functions, so people could hear me speak about 'the Staker incident'. Even people who hadn't watched AFL told me they started watching Swans games after that incident. Rugby league fans especially started coming up to me when I was out, saying, 'That punch was great – we watch now to see if you do it again.'

That attention is never going to go away, I know, and people are genuinely interested in what happened and why, and everything that followed. People probably don't want to hear that, but that's what happened.

I learned a lot of things throughout that period. Most significantly, I learned who would stand by me, and who I'd want in the trenches with me. But I also learned a lot about marketing and popularity. As the old saying goes, any publicity is good publicity, and that's how it proved to be for me.

At no stage was there any talk at the club that I might have been sacked. I had to keep seeing Grant Brecht, but that was it. And there was no way I was going to walk away either.

I was still contracted. I loved playing footy. I didn't necessarily like many of the things that came with it, but I loved training, the camaraderie and the team environment. And I was on fair money. You hear footy players saying they don't care about the money and it doesn't drive them – that may be so for some, but for most of them it's crap. It may not be the sole motivating force, but you've got to eat. I was building for the future, for my family.

So it never crossed my mind to do something else. I still had a lot to offer footy. My plan was just to cop everything that came my way and then to get back out there and try to get people to forget what happened. That last part didn't work out too well.

One thing that hit me harder than everything else was the way some of my teammates reacted in public. There was stuff said by the club's management, and by some of the players, which I was pretty pissed off about. I thought some of what had been said – about respect and trust, in particular – was terrible, and I wasn't the only one.

I felt it was pretty ordinary for my teammates to be saying that stuff in public. I made a mistake and I had said I'd take my punishment, but I'd played in a premiership with these blokes and they knew me pretty well. If they couldn't trust me enough to play footy with me, then that was a massive statement.

I felt very alone and it made me think about my future in Sydney. How much did the club value me, not only as a footy player but as a person? How did they see me? Did I still belong here? The words 'trust', 'respect' and 'selfish' kept coming up in their public interviews, and I wasn't too happy.

First and foremost, in any sporting arena, one thing I've always been taught is that in a team environment you always support your mate. Right, wrong or otherwise. At no stage condone what he's done, if it's wrong, but let him know you are there to help him through it. That was all I was asking for. The public and media was on my back, and now it felt like some of my teammates were as well. It was pretty difficult to handle. But I just had to sit there and cop it all, walk around and act insane for the psychologist, and try to get back to playing footy again.

When I returned to training it was a bit awkward, but I had decided that the best thing to do was walk back in there and try to move forward. I suppose I tried to pretend that certain things hadn't been said or hadn't happened. I went back to training earlier than I was due to come back, and when I turned up I still couldn't train. I had my wrist in plaster, but I decided to walk back in there and show a bit of character.

I didn't want to hide away from things, though. I confronted our leadership group about what some of them had been saying publicly. I figured it was better for us to talk about it, rather than butt heads for the rest of the season.

I told them that I felt abandoned by my mates, that I felt alone and empty, and that some of the things they were saying were pretty hurtful. I said I had expected better from my mates. 'None of you contacted me to give me any support,' I said. 'All I heard was shit on the radio and TV, and it was all negative.' I told them that the next time someone did something like this, they should be mindful of what they say.

When they had heard this from me, and how I was feeling about things, I think they walked away agreeing with what I had said a little bit. We basically called it a truce. I told them that I wanted to move forward and put all that stuff behind me.

CHAPTER TWENTY

The counselling sessions I had with Grant Brecht continued for some time. While I was really only doing them so I could get back onto the field as soon as possible, I didn't make a mockery of them.

I get along pretty well with Grant. I think he's a nice fella, but in saying that I just felt he was looking for stuff that wasn't there. Having said that, though, I do feel I got something out of our chats.

I guess they gave me a chance to lift a bit of weight off myself. I told Grant things I hadn't told a lot of people, and while that was useful for me, those things had nothing to do with the problems I had been having on the field.

Rather than the things that had happened in my past, or things to do with my relationships, I think my frustration with the footy club was more to blame for my outburst. I can assure you I wasn't thinking about my past or my girlfriend when I hit Staker. I understood what Grant was trying to do, but I struggled to get my head around how all of that could possibly affect what happens out on the footy field.

Naturally, my relationship with my father was brought up in my sessions with Grant. He tried to set up a way for us to resolve the differences we had, but trying to do that from afar – without my old man being there – was probably too difficult.

We spoke about a hell of a lot of other things, too, including my relationship with the football club in general, and my relationship with Roosy in particular. At that stage I felt like I was running on the spot with the club, not going anywhere. I don't know whether Grant told Roosy about our discussions, but nothing really seemed to change in that area.

It was good to get that stuff off my chest by talking to someone, but it clearly didn't work, given that the goal was to resolve things and to help me on-field. Off the field our discussions might have done me the world of good. I'm not sure, but they didn't hurt.

I think one of my problems was that I put pretty high expectations on myself. Since 2006, I felt that I had underachieved at the Swans. Not just because of all the misdemeanours and those things, but in a purely playing sense. I knew I had a lot more to offer.

The expectations I put on myself were unhealthy and did put extra pressure on me. If things weren't going my way – even if the whole team was going badly – I would think that I had to do something about it, that it was up to me to lift. If things weren't going well for me, then that pressure just built up. I don't think it had anything to do with my disappointment about my performance in the 2006 Grand Final – I had just begun to ask more of myself.

I told Grant about the frustrations I'd had during the previous season about our game-plan, and the feeling I'd had that Roosy was trying to give me a gentle shove out of the captaincy. 'I think the footy club has lost faith in me on the field and off the field,' I said.

Eventually, I did tell Roosy what Grant and I had been talking about in there, but he told me not to be stupid. It was all rosy and hunky dory, according to him, and we pulled up just short of having a hug.

I found that frustrating and a bit insulting to my intelligence. Roosy is a master manipulator, I reckon. I'd gone in to talk to him, I'd been brutally honest about the things that concerned me, I'd told him exactly what I thought – and then suddenly I'd come out and we were best friends and I was told that everything I thought was happening was totally wrong.

'No, Hally, we don't think that at all. You're way off track,' he'd say.

'But that's exactly how I feel,' I'd reply.

'No, that's just not the case.'

Nothing ever got resolved. At the end of the day, though, I have proved to myself that I was right at that time.

My seven weeks' suspension ended in Round 11. The club was on a bit of a streak with four wins in a row, and there was talk that Roosy should consider sticking with the set-up we had, instead of rushing me back in. But the match committee decided that, provided my wrist was ready, I would come straight back into the senior team.

I hadn't expected to be brought straight back in. I thought they might wait a few more weeks and ease me back into playing, but I was ready. My fitness levels were really good. I had trained pretty hard and I was ready to go.

My first game back was at the SCG against St Kilda, and the Swans fans were brilliant. I felt like I had robbed them of something by not being there for the previous seven weeks, but they cheered me warmly upon my return. It was pleasing to get that game out of the way. I went okay, but I had a better game the following week against Melbourne, kicking five goals.

Then we had our so-called 'blockbuster game' against Collingwood at ANZ Stadium. There were plenty of rumblings about me going back to the scene of the Staker crime, but I just treated it like any other game. There was pressure, but no more pressure than usual, and I knew that when I came back from suspension I would be targeted by defenders hoping to get me to snap like I had with Staker. Grant, to his credit, had tried to put together some strategies to pre-empt frustration on the field, but when you're in a game it's hard to do those things.

After that Collingwood game, I wouldn't know where my career stood. There was an incident in the second quarter with Shane Wakelin which again landed me in trouble. Suddenly, I was back in the papers, on TV and radio. I was labelled a thug and the cries telling the Swans I was beyond redemption grew louder.

First things first, I didn't hit him. I've watched the replay and it looks like I was trying to, but I certainly wasn't trying to whop him, that's for sure. Wakelin was a good defender in his day, but he was a scragger – he held onto you because he had to. He did it well and it was damn annoying at times. I won't lie. Frustration got the better of me again, and all the psychological theories obviously just didn't work at the end of the day.

I certainly didn't try to hit him in the head, even though it looked like I was going high. I was trying to push-punch him in the chest – that was what I was going for. There was really nothing in it and no force at all. I wonder what would have happened if it had been John Smith or Joe Nobody instead of me. And if I was trying to punch him in the head … well, seriously! Did he dive? Of course he did! He should have been a soccer player.

I was charged with 'attempting to strike'. I attempted to kick ten goals that night too. It was a one-match suspension, but before I had time to think about fighting it or not, the Swans told me I would be stood down indefinitely until I was cleared by Grant Brecht to play.

I couldn't believe it. Everything had been blown out of proportion. After the club's reaction to the Staker punch, I suspected that things weren't great for me there, and this confirmed it. I was pulled into a meeting where the coaches told me they were going to stand me down until I got my issues sorted out.

'You might as well sit me out for the rest of the season,' I said, 'because nothing is going to change. The issue I've got is right here in this room.' I stormed out and that was it. All I had to do then was turn up for training and wait to get the nod from Grant that I could play again.

Once again, the media circus started up, as did the

problem of blokes not sticking up for their teammate. It was pretty clear in my mind then what sort of people I was dealing with – people I'd thought were my mates.

My recent relationship with Paul Roos hadn't been fantastic up until then, but after this latest episode it wasn't good at all. Once again, the worst thing was that our disagreements were never openly discussed between me and him. Whenever there was a meeting, there were always other people – on his side – around. All the coaches would be in there and I'd be there by myself. I felt like telling him to grow some balls and tell me what he thought face-to-face, but that never happened.

There's probably not a person who will have a bad word to say about Paul Roos – what he's done in the game, what he's done for Sydney and the footy club and so on. That's all great, but I couldn't respect the way he went about things. I thought Paul was a good coach, but one thing he lacked was the ability to confront people directly. He would do it to some people but to some others he just wouldn't. That was my experience.

Other people might have seen him as God's gift to coaches and the saviour of Sydney, and that's fine. I'll nod my head and half-agree with them. He's got a great record. I have to say, though, that I lost a lot of respect for the bloke over the latter stages of my time at the Swans.

When the club suspended me for the Wakelin incident, I know some of my teammates were pretty surprised. I don't know about the leadership group – I had stood down from it during the Staker saga. It took just two weeks before I was given the 'all clear' by Grant to play again. What an amazing recovery, hey? There must have been some really big issues! In truth, nothing had changed from when I had these apparent 'issues' two weeks earlier, but suddenly I was officially okay again.

I came back for our last six games of the home-and-away season, and I also played in our two finals. I managed to stay out of trouble on the field, but I had begun planning for the future.

I didn't try to get out of the Swans immediately. The reason was that I wanted to buy a new house. I know that sounds weird. But I was selling my house, and I was all set to buy a place which was basically my dream home. I had only one year left on my contract, and so Phil Mullen – who was helping me out unofficially at that stage – and I tried to get an extra year's extension. Even though it wasn't ideal for me, I was prepared to spend another year at the Swans in order to have the security of the house.

Andrew Ireland told me the club was not in a position to give me the extension, which I fully understood. In hindsight, I'm glad they didn't.

Not long after that, Rodney Eade – the man who'd brought me to Sydney in the first place, and who now was coaching the Western Bulldogs – contacted Phil. I met with the Bulldogs and they were definitely keen to get a trade done and get me there.

I went to speak to Roosy. 'Look, if I'm able to get a two-year contract elsewhere, you've got to expect that I'll be keen,' I said. 'I want some security. If I have a bad year here in 2009, it could be all over for me and I'll have nowhere to go.'

Forget about focusing on all the hair I had back in 2000 – look at that speed and balance and determination. I should've been a dashing midfielder.

It's not what you might think. Actually, what I was really asking Collingwood's Anthony Rocca, who spent a couple of years in Sydney, was, 'What's it really like at the Swans? You never know, I might end up there one day.'

Stan Alves was the first of six coaches I've had during my AFL career, and – not just because he gave me my first chance by drafting me to St Kilda – he was a great coach, one of the better ones I played under.

Brett Kirk would often come to me after I kicked a goal and tell me how much he loved playing with me. It went both ways. This photo was taken during one of our better wins, when we went to Perth and beat the red-hot West Coast by a point in the 2006 qualifying final.

The moment I knew I was going to be in a fair bit of trouble. With West Coast's Brent Staker being attended to on ANZ Stadium, and after hearing a collective groan from the crowd, I looked at the replay of 'that punch' up on the big screen, and saw how graphic the incident looked.

One of those few occasions I got to leave the AFL tribunal with a smile on my face, and the most important time too. Here I am telling the media how relieved I am to have escaped suspension for striking St Kilda's Matt Maguire, clearing me to play in the 2005 grand final.

Don't ask me why I thought the Premiership Cup would look good as a hat, it just seemed to fit well. And who says I never smiled on the footy field? This moment, this day, and sharing it all with my teammates, will forever be some of the best memories I will take away from playing AFL football.

To this day I still can't believe how many people turned out for the 2005 ticker tape parade in Sydney. I thought it might be embarrassing with nobody showing up, but there were people everywhere. In my wildest dreams I wouldn't have imagined holding the premiership cup aloft with Paul Roos, in front of thousands, outside the Sydney Town Hall.

The grand final ... it can deliver the greatest joy, as we experienced in 2005, and the harshest of pain as we felt here in 2006 when we lost by a point. You just feel so empty. Shattered. Gutted. The worst feeling I have ever had on a football field.

Okay I have to admit that I was pretty happy I'd had a reasonable game for the Bulldogs this day, in Canberra in 2010 when I came up against the Swans for the first time since my departure. Coach Rodney Eade looks fairly pleased too.

You do tend to get a few groupies hanging around in football as this picture shows. No, seriously, it was good to have a few chats from time to time with the Bulldogs' number one supporter, Prime Minister Julia Gillard. Especially after she made it clear she wasn't after my job as full forward.

I might look happy here having kicked a goal against the Swans in the 2010 semi-final, and we did go on and win the game, and end their season, but there were no smiles the next week when we fell short in the preliminary final. While close might seem okay to some, in football, getting close was never good enough for me.

Roosy said to me he understood what I was getting at, but they still wanted me at the club. Despite him saying that, I had an inkling that if a deal could be done they would do it.

I certainly would have thought that, with the year I had and all the issues we were having, the club would have been happy to get rid of me. I didn't see what value I held for them anymore, considering the obvious problems we were having.

But I still believed I had a lot more footy left in me, and so I was keen to move on. Because I was still under contract for 2009, and because the Bulldogs had already committed their top draft pick to get Ayce Cordy, there was nothing they could offer the Swans to get the deal done. I would have to wait twelve months before I would end up going to the Bulldogs, but under circumstances that were totally different to what I expected.

CHAPTER TWENTY-ONE

I might still have found my way out of the Swans – maybe to the Bulldogs, maybe somewhere else – a year earlier than I did, had Sydney been able to strike a deal with Carlton and Brendan Fevola.

It was in early July 2008, around the time of the Wakelin incident, that I first heard Paul Roos was meeting Brendan Fevola for a coffee in Sydney. One of Fev's good mates had contacted me. 'Just a heads-up,' he said. 'Fev is on the way to have a chat with Roosy.'

I can't categorically say that Roos and Fevola met up, but the mail was that Fev's management had received a call from the Swans in 2008 saying they were interested. Hearing that confirmed for me what I had suspected for a while – that if the Swans could get rid of me, they would.

When the story broke in the press a week later, Roosy was emphatic that it hadn't happened. He said the club wasn't remotely interested in trying to entice Fevola to Sydney.

I never asked Roosy about it myself, mainly because I knew what sort of response I would get. He'd treat me like a fool, just like every other time I had tried to talk to him about things. The rumour about Fev wasn't discussed much among the players, either. We didn't really speak about that sort of stuff. What could we say about it?

If there was ever speculation about players' futures, we'd just put it out of our minds. 'If it happens,' I used to think, 'well, there's nothing I can do about it.' That's just the way professional sport is. And in this case, because I already had an inkling that the club was looking to move me on, it wasn't anything new. I'd had my suspicions for a good twelve months beforehand.

After I parted ways with the Swans midway through 2009, Roos was asked for an article in the *Age* about rebuilding his club's forward line, and specifically about whether he might chase Fevola. He said he wouldn't now because Fev had signed a new contract with Carlton. But he also added: 'If Brendan Fevola was available for trade last year, would we have been interested? Yeah, we would have been.'

The thing that annoyed me was that when the Fevola/ Roos coffee story broke in the media, so too did a story that I'd hit Wakelin – sorry, 'attempted to strike', as the Match Review Panel put it – because I had heard about the meeting and was filthy that the club was trying to get rid of me and bring Fevola in.

That's just not true – it certainly wasn't on my mind. As I said at the time, it was the club's decision if they wanted to speak with Fevola – it was nothing to do with me. It was out of my hands. I was quoted at that time as saying that Fev was a great player, and that if I was the coach, I would be sourcing out the good players and chasing them if they were available. Even when I left the club I said that the Swans should go after Fev. Maybe it would have worked out better for him than Brisbane did – who knows?

By the time 2009 came around, all that was forgotten. I was professional enough to put everything that had happened in 2008 behind me and focus on footy for the last year of my contract. But there was also another option for me, and I came reasonably close to taking it. It was a case of back to the future – boxing was back on my radar.

I'd got back into boxing a little bit at the Swans when Johnny Lewis worked there as a trainer. When I wanted to do some extra training outside the Swans' training hours, Johnny told me I had an open invitation to come to his gym and work out. One day there I did some sparring with Danny Rowsell, who I think was the Australian cruiserweight champion at the time. It was good. I enjoyed it.

I met Angelo Hyder around the boxing traps – he's one of Australia's best boxing trainers – and we became pretty good mates. Through Angelo, I got to meet up with Danny Green, who, during the 2008–09 off-season, invited me to come over to Perth and spend a week training with him, to see if boxing might be something I would be interested in getting into professionally.

Since the Swans had been unable to get a trade done with the Bulldogs, and with all the stuff that had gone on in 2008, I agreed to make the trip. I told Danny that if he could match what I was getting paid to play footy, I would seriously consider switching.

The only downside was that I was still contracted to the Swans for 2009. If I was to go and box, I'd have to rip up the contract. Regardless of how things were going now, the Swans had been good to me and I didn't want to leave them in the lurch. It was then two weeks before the cut-off date for the club to submit its playing list to the AFL. If that date passed and I then decided not to play on, the club would be left one player short for the whole season.

I really enjoyed the week with Danny. From the first day I was there to the last day, I felt that I improved out of sight. I sparred with Pieter Cronje, a tough and experienced South African heavyweight. It was a real challenge and he certainly pushed me, but I did okay. The experience clarified for me that if I wanted to give boxing a real shot, I could do it.

But it was also a reality check, since it took me back a few years. I remember as a teenager sitting there at night having to eat dinner with a massive headache because I had copped a few punches to the head. I hadn't missed that.

And I also realised that while I was fit for footy, I wasn't fit for boxing at all. It's a sport that requires a totally different type of fitness. That side of it was really challenging during my week in Perth, but I enjoyed it.

I also enjoyed sparring with Danny Green. He was a lot smaller than me, obviously, but I reckon he could have taken me out at any stage, if he'd wanted to. But he looked after me and I learned a lot from the experience. When I made a mistake he would stop sparring and show me what I was doing wrong. He was really good.

Danny was reasonably impressed with what I could do and told me he certainly thought I had the tools to give boxing a crack. I hadn't done much proper boxing for a while but Danny said I looked like I hadn't stopped fighting. He put that down to having been trained well as a young bloke. 'The potential is there,' he said, 'but you still need a lot of work – there's no two ways about that. But if you want to do it, we can give it a go.'

I also talked to my old man about the idea. I realised he might have been getting a little bit dirty because he was reading all this stuff in the paper about me getting back into it, with Angelo Hyder and Johnny Lewis saying I could be this or do that. My old man was probably sitting there thinking, 'Well, I trained him – I put in all the hard work when he was a kid.'

If I ever do get back into boxing, I wouldn't have my old man train me. I'd certainly have him there – I would want to reward him for everything he did – but I know that at a high level you need the best coaching. I reckon Angelo is probably the best trainer in Australia.

When I talked to my old man, he said, 'If you really want to do it, do it – but if your heart's not 100 per cent into it, don't.' I started to realise then that, at that stage, my heart wasn't 100 per cent in it. There was still a little bit of footy left in my heart.

Time was running out, too. Danny and his management team put a contract in front of me just four or five days before the AFL lists were due in. The window was just open but it was closing quickly, and they knew I wasn't going to leave the Swans in a hole.

As with any contract, the first one is never the real one, but there wasn't much time for negotiation. The money Danny offered me was close to what I was getting paid at the Swans, but the contract was of a different type; the management group would receive a big percentage of endorsements and things like that. There were a lot of things in the contract that went against me as an athlete, and that didn't feel right. It would have taken far longer than a few days to work through all those details, so in many ways my decision was probably a foregone conclusion.

I was still earning really good money at the Swans, and although it was never all about money, it was important. If I was going to take a risk in a new sport and still make similar money out of it, that wasn't too bad. But I knew I could play another year of footy and not have any worries about whether I would succeed or not.

As the money in boxing didn't quite match the money I stood to make in footy, I would have been taking a huge risk. The potential earnings beyond that year were unknown as well. With footy, if I had a good year, I knew I'd be able to play on and maybe get another contract. While I was confident I could make it in boxing, its unknown factors meant that the future would be much more uncertain if I switched.

If I'd been asked nine months later, when I got sacked from the Swans, whether I'd made the right decision about turning down the boxing contract, I would have said no. But now I can see that, in the long run, playing on in footy was the right choice to make.

CHAPTER TWENTY-TWO

Spending a week in Perth with Danny Green certainly generated plenty of interest in my boxing 'career'. The year before, I'd had some brief talks about organising a fight with Willie Mason, and now I was apparently getting offers to fight all sorts of rugby league players.

When I heard about these 'offers' I'd supposedly had, I laughed about it. I reckon the newspapers just threw figures out there. It was always something like 'Barry Hall offered $1 million to fight so and so'. As I've always said, give me a million bucks and I'll fight anyone you want!

I never saw any proof of these so-called offers. Never any contracts, never any proposals at all. The only exception was Danny Green, who called me after he was quoted in the paper talking about setting up a fight between me and Mason, an idea that never went anywhere.

When I got back from Perth for the Swans pre-season, they had no problems that I'd spent a week in Perth boxing with Danny Green. It had taken place in the off-season, so they hadn't known about it beforehand, but there were no problems when I returned.

The fact that I had decided to continue playing footy rather than accept Danny Green's boxing offer meant that it wasn't an issue for the Swans. If I had chosen to box, then it would have impacted on them, but I hadn't. There were never any warnings that I shouldn't be boxing while I was on my break.

A few of the guys around the club asked how it had gone, whether I'd actually sparred with Danny Green – just the usual banter. But my future was clear by that stage – it would remain in footy.

What with all the dramas of 2008, including the fact that I had looked into getting a trade to the Western Bulldogs and the tension which was obviously there between me and our coach, it wasn't surprising that some at the club were concerned about how I would front up for pre-season. But I was a professional, and regardless of whether I had issues with the coach or the club or the players, I didn't let those things get in the way of what I had to do. I was able to put everything else aside and give myself every chance to be fit and ready to go for Round 1.

And anyway, it wasn't like Roosy and I were at each other. There was no animosity at all. We were both professionals, and I certainly felt I could work around whatever issues we had. At that stage, that's exactly what I did. We never had long conversations, but our professional relationship was fine.

While my life on the field had been better, off the field things improved in a big way during that off-season – in

February 2009, to be exact. I lived around the corner from the Eastgardens Shopping Centre in Sydney's eastern suburbs, and I used to go there a lot. In fact, I actually turned into a bit of a stalker that summer.

I walked past a shop called Diva one day and saw this gorgeous girl working there. From that moment on, I went there regularly just to perv on her. I didn't know anything else about her – I didn't know her name or anything. I just used to call her Divalicious. I'd say to whoever I was with, 'I'm off to have a look at Divalicious – I'll be back in a few minutes.'

I would then head to Eastgardens and do a walk-by. I used to go there three or four times a week just to look at her. I don't know what it was, but something about her just attracted me to her. Obviously, her looks were a big attraction, but she also just looked like a really nice, sweet person. But I never had the balls to do anything about it.

It's a wonder she didn't call the cops to get an AVO taken out against this bloke who was stalking her ... now wouldn't the newspapers have loved that story!

Anyway, one day I finally worked up the courage to go and speak to her. A mate and I were sitting in a cafe four or five shops down from where she worked, and I had a plan. I wrote my number on a piece of paper, so I had it ready to give it to her, but when I walked over to the shop, it was busy. It was a girls' shop, a jewellery shop, and I knew I would have looked pretty odd standing there with my piece of paper, waiting to be served by Divalicious.

So I went back and sat down with my mate again. He said, 'I'm sick of hearing about this girl – just go in there and give her your number. If it doesn't work out, just move on – who cares?'

I said, 'No way – I'm not going in there.'

'Give it here,' he said. 'I'm sick of this.' And he snatched the piece of paper out of my hand, went into the shop and gave my number to her.

She had obviously seen me around – it would have been hard not to since I walked past the shop seven or eight times a week – but of course she thought it was a bit weird to get my number like that. I still hadn't even spoken to her, I didn't know her name and she didn't know me at all.

She still gave me a chance, though. She sent me a text message saying, 'Your mate gave me the number – it's a bit bizarre. Are you a bit shy or something?' I wrote back and we met for a coffee, and we just hit it off from that first time we went out.

I know it sounds a bit like a high-school introduction, but that's how I met Sophie Raadschelders. Twelve months later, we were engaged. Sophie admits that before we met she had no idea who I was. She said she thought my face was familiar, but she had no idea that I played footy.

As I'll explain, 2009 proved to be a really tough year for me – the toughest of my footy career. But the one thing that made it so much easier for me than it might have been was having Sophie there. She's a really positive person, while I'm probably pretty negative. Sophie knows when I'm down on myself, and when she sees that she gets into me about it, telling me there are tougher things in life than football or playing a bad game. She tells me to snap out of it and we go out for a walk or a bite to eat. It's as easy as that, but it's exactly what I need.

She had a massive influence on me from that time on. I know she helped my temperament on the field, too, because I became a calmer person. I still got frustrated and angry at times, but I seemed to be able to calm down more quickly.

Sophie is always fully supportive of what I do, but she has never been one of those girlfriends who are so into footy that they're almost like groupies. She was a total footy novice when we started going out, and I really enjoyed that. The last thing you want is to come home to a girlfriend who knows everything about football and rattles off your stats for the game you've just played.

In all ways, what I had with Sophie was perfect. It was no wonder I asked her to marry me, but I was still pretty surprised when she agreed!

CHAPTER TWENTY-THREE

Despite a 'different' type of off-season, I worked hard through the pre-season and was reasonably happy with my preparation heading into the 2009 season. I wanted to put 2008 behind me and have some more success with the club.

Things began well enough. In Round 2, we belted the defending premiers Hawthorn. I kicked four goals but strained a muscle in my groin. It wasn't the recurring injury I'd had so much of but just a pulled muscle. But it was still very difficult to run. I played against Brisbane in Round 3 and really struggled. I just couldn't run around at all. I was lucky the guy I was playing on didn't run off me too much, because I wouldn't have been able to chase him.

I was forced to sit out the next match. One game was enough, to my mind, but the next week we were travelling to Perth and it was decided I should miss that one as well. The aim was that I should be ready to go with no problems the following week.

We had a rough start to the season – we struggled to find consistency and really found it tough going on the road. We would win one, lose one, win one and so on. After ten rounds, we had five wins – all at home – and five losses on the road. Despite that, we sat just inside the eight. I had kicked six in Round 10 in Canberra against the Western Bulldogs, but they were worth nothing, really, because we lost the game.

Our next match was a big one – against Hawthorn at the MCG. The Hawks were sitting just behind us on the ladder. Midway through the final quarter, Hawthorn was leading by less than a kick. The ball came into our fifty-metre area and I tried to get to the contest and spoil, but Robert Campbell was holding my arm. I cracked the shits and yelled at the umpire, asking how he could have missed the free kick and saying I just wanted a fair go.

True to form, the whistle went straight to the umpire's mouth and a fifty-metre penalty was awarded against me.

Jarryd Roughead had taken the mark as I was being held, and as I stood there with my arms out, pleading with the umpire, Roughead ran into me. I threw an arm out and grabbed him, and naturally he hit the deck. Wham, another fifty-metre penalty.

Then, as I jogged up the ground to where the mark would be, Sam Mitchell was giving it to me. I put my forearm into him – nothing savage, just a bit of push and shove – and guess what? Another fifty-metre penalty.

It was the biggest overreaction by the umpire. Were there three fifty-metre penalties there? No, definitely not. Maybe one, because I had yelled at the umpire, but the rest was bullshit. It was wrong, for sure. It seemed like every time I looked at the umpire he called a fifty. I know I should have shut my mouth, but three in a row was ridiculous.

And then came my pet hate. I knew I'd stuffed up, but what did the coach do? Drag me off the ground. I knew full well that he would be pissed off, but taking me off the ground just made it worse. Of course, I copped a hiding from the whole crowd, which had erupted.

Roosy didn't say anything to me when I came off, nor later on. He said something in our team meeting after the match but he didn't direct it at me, which was typical.

I knew I was going to cop it in the media. It was going to be another 'brain snap for Hall', but what I didn't see coming was our coach publicly blaming me for the loss. He said it had been the turning point of the game, and that we'd had momentum at the time it happened. In fact, less than a minute before the fifty-metre penalties, Hawthorn had kicked a goal which gave them the lead. The goal had come from one of our defenders giving away a free kick about twenty metres out. Was that a turning point too?

Anyway, after Roughead kicked his goal from the 150-metre penalty, Hawthorn was ten points in front with about ten minutes to play. There was plenty of time for us to get back into the match, but we couldn't quite do it.

Don't get me wrong – I stuffed up badly and I shouldn't have let it happen, but really, would it have been three fifty-metre penalties if it hadn't been me? Maybe, but probably not.

What really pissed me off, though, was that Roosy again came out in the media and vented his thoughts there. He said nothing to my face, but he didn't have a problem telling the journos, who were happy to have a headline.

Of course, the players were all disappointed. We'd lost a game we could have won. I was happy to cop my whack for my role in the loss, but it shouldn't have been turned into the circus it was.

I think Roosy really wanted to rip into me after the Hawthorn game, but instead the leadership group were the ones who got me out in front of them and grilled me that week. That was the way it went. The only people who spoke were Kirky and Craig Bolton. They said they were disappointed but that we'd move on and try not to let it happen again.

I'm a big boy and I can take my medicine. Certainly, if you admit your mistakes, which I had no problem doing, the whole leadership group process is a lot easier than if you argue with them. So I sat there, copped my whack and moved on. What else could I say? Sorry? Okay, I'm sorry – I'll try not to let it happen again. But it might.

I knew where the guys in the leadership group were coming from. I knew whose idea it was, and I knew why it was happening, but what disappointed me was that Roosy never confronted me about it one-on-one. He had someone else pass the message on.

By that stage of his coaching career, Roosy was very results-driven. He had totally changed from the coach he'd been when he first came in – the coach who had taken us to two Grand Finals. That cool, calm, relaxed guy might still have appeared to the public to be there, but away from the television cameras he would regularly lose it.

To be honest, when Roosy had announced at the 2008 club champion night that he had signed a new two-year contract extension, I was pretty shocked. John Longmire, one of our assistant coaches, had been told he was next in line when Roosy finished. At that time, it had seemed to me that Roosy had had enough.

He often seemed uptight, and a number of things he did seemed totally different from what he had been all about in the earlier days. There were a few blow-ups, but he would certainly pick his mark, no doubt about that. That alone showed us that things had changed, because he'd never used to do that. From what I heard, in 2010 – his last season at the club – he blew up on a regular basis.

Everyone changes, I know, but I wasn't alone in thinking that it was time for him to step down. The whole playing group was surprised when he signed on again – although I wouldn't expect the other players to say it. But there was genuine shock when he announced he would stay on.

The following week we played Collingwood. I think I surprised a few people with my 'new attitude' towards the umpires. At one stage I was given a free kick and I gave the umpire a thumbs-up. I just thought I'd try something different, and I think it shocked him. Umpires weren't used to seeing a smile or a nod of approval from me.

Over my career, I had tried a number of things to see if I could have a better relationship with the umpires and get an even break with calls. I tried talking to them, I tried being nice to them, but nothing seemed to work. No matter what I did, I just had to put up with whatever I copped.

But the one thing I never did was whinge about the umpires publicly. The way I looked at it, I just had to cop whatever came my way. All I ever really wanted, though, was a fifty-fifty chance. Sometimes I got it and sometimes I didn't.

I don't really know what had sparked my bad relationship with umpires, but it seemed that every time I went near the ball one would put his whistle to his mouth. I wasn't the only guy who copped that sort of treatment – I know that other big, imposing figures would sometimes get it too. It's just the way it was.

The Swans once sent some video tapes to the AFL that highlighted some really bad calls against me, but that was basically all they could do. Jeff Gieschen – the umpire's boss – actually agreed with us. He conceded that the club was right but there was no change – it was back to the same old thing the following week. I think the club lost interest in it after awhile, and quite frankly so did I.

Of course, one of the media outlets got hold of the tape we'd sent to the AFL and did a story on it. Suddenly, it was made out that I was whingeing about my poor treatment from the umpires. In fact, it hadn't even been my idea to send the tapes – it was the club's.

The week after that Collingwood game – which we lost, sliding to a record of five and seven – we were to play the Adelaide Crows in Adelaide. It would be my 250th senior game. I had never thought I would play anywhere near that number of matches. Certainly, when I thought back to the early days of my career, playing fifty games would have been a major achievement. Not many people at all get to play

250. Considering the journey I'd had, it was a pretty good milestone to reach.

Strangely, though, the occasion had crept up on me. In fact, I only realised it when I was asked to do some media that week. Being in Adelaide, it was harder for me to have my family and friends there. Soph flew over but my parents couldn't make the trip. As a result, they missed out on seeing my last game in the red and white.

CHAPTER TWENTY-FOUR

As soon as it happened, you could see a look of shock on my face. I was genuinely surprised. The umpire came up and I was reported. From that moment on, everything was a bit of a blur.

I had tried to punch Ben Rutten in the chest. I certainly hadn't meant it to be high – that was the thing that surprised me the most. I really hadn't intended to hit him there. But the fact was, I had, and so I would have to deal with the avalanche of consequences.

It all happened so quickly. At the time, I didn't know if I had hit him or not. A free kick was given against me but I didn't really know what to think at that stage. Soon after, Rutten said to me, 'You got me a beauty.' Right at that moment, I thought, 'Shit, this is not good.'

I was already struggling in the game, having pulled a hip muscle early on, but I was able to put the punch and being reported behind me. Unfortunately, I'd had a bit of practice at that. There wasn't anything I could do about it. I was more worried about my hip than anything else.

I sat off for a stretch in the last quarter, and I remember Roosy actually gave me a pat on the back. That made me think he wasn't aware of what had happened. He later told the media he hadn't seen the incident. It wouldn't be long before he did.

We flew back to Sydney that night, and when I got home there they were: TV cameras waiting in my street. 'Here we go again,' I thought. That's when it started to hit home for me that I was in a bit of trouble.

That night and the next day I was pretty shattered. Naturally, things started going through my head. What would happen? Had I used up all my chances? Would the club sack me? Had I just played my last game? What hit me hardest was that I was really disappointed in myself. I had not only let myself down, but I'd let down a lot of people who had put their faith in me.

I felt I had been playing good footy up until then. I had put 2008 and the Staker and Wakelin incidents behind me and had turned a new page. I had started the long journey of winning back some credibility so that I could be remembered as a footballer, not a thug.

But now I was feeling sick in the guts. It felt like my missus had cheated on me or something. I was afraid of what was ahead, although I think that, deep down, I already knew what was going to happen.

The best-case scenario would have been if the Swans let me play for the rest of the season and then told me I was done. And I probably would have accepted that at the time.

The other option, as I saw it, was that the club made me play the rest of the season in the twos and hope – like footy clubs do – that I got so pissed off that I retired at the end of the season.

On that Saturday night, and especially on the Sunday, I was doing it pretty tough. I knew I'd made yet another real stuff-up, and I realised what the consequences might be. It could be the end for me, and if it was, I had nobody to blame but myself. It's hard to explain the empty, lonely feeling I had. I was lucky I had Soph there, and Phil Mullen to talk to. If I'd been single and if Phil hadn't been around, who knows what I would have done. None of my teammates rang, and I couldn't get onto the one man I wanted to speak to.

Sleep wasn't great that night, but as soon as I got up I rang Roosy to see if we could have a chat. Obviously, something had to happen, and I decided I should get on the front foot and be a man about it. I was under no illusions that some serious shit was about to go down, and I was prepared to cop my punishment.

But his phone rang out. I left a message saying that I understood it was Sunday, but if he could call me, I really wanted to have a chat. If not, we could catch up on Monday. I didn't hear back from him that day. When we eventually did meet up a couple of days later, Roosy said he'd been too angry to take my call.

But on the Sunday, I wanted – and needed – to make contact with someone at the club, just to talk about things. I hadn't had a manager for a number of years, but Phil Mullen had been a friend and confidant to me for quite some time and I called him. He was the only person at the club who actually helped me then. I didn't know why I'd done it – did I need help? I really needed to talk to someone because I felt pretty alone. Thankfully, I was able to catch up with Phil and we talked about the whole situation.

I was really surprised that Roosy hadn't taken my call or rung me back. Maybe I shouldn't have been, but I just wanted to spill my guts to him. I would have felt a lot better about the situation and we could have talked about what we had to do. I think that by then Roosy had already made up his mind that this was the end for me. Now, it was just a matter of how I would leave the club.

There was plenty of speculation in the papers and on TV that weekend, but neither Roosy nor I nor the club had said anything at that point. The matter was going before the tribunal, so we couldn't really discuss it anyway.

We had the day off on the Monday, but I knew something had to be done. Having not heard back from Roosy, I went in to the club to see him. The coaches had their match-review session on, though, so I left a message with Gina, the girl who sat out the front of his office, to ask him to call me.

That afternoon, Roosy popped into Phil Mullen's office and said, 'Can you let Hally know I'm going to speak to the media now and tell them this and this?' Phil rang me and asked whether I'd heard from Roosy. I had tried to call him again but he still hadn't rung me back.

This was ridiculous. The only contact Roosy had tried to make was with Phil Mullen. My phone had been on all day and I was waiting for his call. I wasn't interstate, I had reception, my phone was working. But still I hadn't heard from him directly.

I don't know whether I intimated Roosy or not, but all I wanted was to hear the news from his mouth first. I understand he had to talk to the media sooner or later, but if he had told me his thoughts first then I'd have been able to cop them a bit better. I knew he disliked confrontation, but to hear Roosy's response on the news was disappointing.

Look, I stuffed up – no arguments, no complaints – but I did lose a bit of respect for him for not having the decency to call me personally.

I watched the news that night while I was cooking dinner, and I saw Roosy saying that there needed to be some discussion with me to find out what I wanted to do. He said my actions showed I didn't want to play footy, and that perhaps I wanted to move in a different direction, whether it be to boxing or something else. All he was seeing was a guy who didn't want to play football.

I could read between the lines. The club had decided that I should be moved on, and in their view this was the moment for me to quit and leave with some dignity. I could understand that – I'm not a total idiot. It's just how the whole thing was handled that I felt was ordinary.

If they had come to me and said, 'Hally, you've had one too many chances – you've left us with no option but to sack you,' I would have been disappointed, but I would have known it was my fault and I wouldn't have blamed anyone but myself for that outcome.

And look, I don't blame anyone for the outcome which did occur, either – I think it was inevitable after the Rutten incident – but the way it was done did leave a sour taste in my mouth.

To say that I didn't want to be playing footy was just crap. It certainly upset me to hear that; the people who knew me well and who played footy with me knew that wasn't the case. Roosy knew me well too. He knew I was pretty passionate about footy and how I went about it – I always had been. I had always been a pretty animated player, too, and that was due to my passion. He knew that. And I think he had actually said after the Adelaide game that I'd played well.

My head was still very much in the game and I did want to keep playing. This was the last season of my contract. I had made it clear to the club when I asked Andrew Ireland for an extension at the end of the previous season that I wanted to play on beyond 2009, which meant I had a pretty big carrot dangling in front of me that season. I believed I was pulling my weight on the field; I certainly felt I was in better form than I had been over the previous couple of years.

I realised that if my season just petered out, that would have probably been it at the Swans for me when the end of the season came. Perhaps I'd be able to get another one-year contract and then pull the plug at the end of 2010, but that didn't look likely.

I did one interview that night, with the *Sydney Morning Herald*, just to get my side of the story out there. I said I wasn't going to retire, and that I hadn't lost the desire to play. I pointed out that I'd played well for three quarters against Adelaide with a torn muscle in my hip.

Later that night, after I'd seen Roosy on the news, my phone rang. It was John Longmire. He had a go at me about why I hadn't contacted Roosy and why I hadn't talked to Roosy about the whole thing that day.

I just sat there dumbfounded. 'Horse, are you serious?' I asked.

'Well, you should have at least come in and interrupted the match-review meeting to talk to him,' he said.

'Hang on, mate, you were behind closed doors in there. I told Gina that I had come in to see Roosy. I'd already tried ringing him on Sunday but he never called me back.'

'Well, you've got to make a better effort, Hally,' Horse said.

I was just stunned. 'Look, Horse,' I said, 'no disrespect to you, but I don't know why the hell you're ringing me. Why isn't he ringing?'

'I don't know, Hally,' he said.

'Well, why don't you get off the phone and tell him to call me?' I said, and we ended up shouting at each other. I felt really bad about that, as I had the utmost respect for Horse – he'd done such a lot for me as a coach. I didn't want to be fighting with people I really respected, like him.

A little while later, my phone rang again. This time it was Roosy. He told me that I'd said in my message on Sunday that there was no need for him to ring me back, that we'd catch up on Monday. Of course, I'd never said that. In any case, he later claimed he'd been too angry to talk to me. I told him how I'd come in to the club earlier that day and left a message with Gina for him to ring me as soon as he got out of the match-review meeting.

The argument went back and forward and we both thought we were right. I knew I wasn't in the wrong because

I'd made the calls. All of this was just over why we hadn't been in contact – we hadn't even mentioned the actual incident. The call ended with Roosy telling me to come in and see him the next day.

CHAPTER TWENTY-FIVE

When Tuesday morning arrived, I wasn't anxious about going in to the club and seeing what consequences I was facing. I'd had enough waiting and wondering. I just wanted to meet with Roosy and find out what he was thinking and what we were going to do.

I walked into the Swans' offices, thinking we would be having a chat in Roosy's office, but I was told that we'd meet in the meeting room downstairs in half an hour. I thought that was a bit weird, but I had a coffee and headed down there to face the music.

When I got there I was confronted not by just Roosy, but also by Andrew Ireland, John Longmire and another assistant coach, Johnny Blakey. I was stunned – it was like a show of power. As I've said, Roosy never wanted a one-on-one chat with me, so while I was surprised, I really shouldn't have been.

The meeting started, and straightaway Andrew Ireland

brought up that I had said a couple of years earlier that if anything like this happened, I would retire – they wouldn't have to sack me. And it was true, I had said exactly that. So it was instantly clear – that's what they wanted. They wanted me to quit right there and then.

Thankfully, before I had gone in for the meeting that day, I had got some advice from a friend of mine in case they put this on me. His advice was categorical: do not retire. If they wanted me out, they would have to sack me – if I went of my own accord, I wouldn't be entitled to any payout of my contract.

As I sat there in front of the club's football manager and coaches, I realised that if I did what they were asking and made the call on my future, their job would be so much easier. They wouldn't have to make the tough call of sacking me.

So I played a straight bat about retiring. 'No, I don't want to do that,' I said. 'I want to keep playing footy. I'll take my two weeks' – which was the suspension I'd been given by the AFL – 'and be ready to play again when it's done. I'm still passionate about playing, so that's what I want to do.'

At this, they brought out newspaper clippings about me, including ones which had Bobby Skilton and others making comments about my future. 'Look at what the club legends are saying about you,' they said. 'How can you keep doing this to the club?'

I pushed the articles off the table. 'I don't give two shits about what they are saying,' I replied. 'They can say what they like. I don't even know why you brought them in –

they've got nothing to do with this. It's about me and you guys – it's got nothing to do with media articles. This is ridiculous.'

The meeting was becoming pretty tense. Roosy and I then had a fair blow-up, another shouting match over how the whole thing had gone down. That was the ridiculous thing, though – we weren't screaming about the Rutten punch or what I should do, but about how the matter had been handled and why there'd been no contact between us for two days, and who was right and who was wrong.

In the end, I said, 'We're getting nowhere here. Let's agree to disagree – this is friggin' childish. At the end of the day, if you don't think I made enough attempts to contact you, fine.'

John Longmire then asked me what I thought they should do. I knew exactly what he wanted me to say, and being totally honest, I think that I deserved to be sacked. They had given me enough chances and I had slipped up again. As a result, I had to deal with the consequences. But I wasn't ready to walk away, and so I said, 'I don't know, Horse. I'm going to do my two weeks, train hard and then play if I'm picked. If you want to play me in the reserves, that's fine – I'll do that.'

I'd had enough of the argument, so from then on I just shut down everything they tried to argue. Believe me, they tried everything. So I walked out of the meeting with nothing resolved. They wanted me to quit and I wasn't going to. If they wanted it that way, they would have to make the call and sack me.

Afterwards, John Longmire pulled me aside and we went and had a coffee. I decided to put it on him. 'John, I'm getting a vibe here,' I said, 'but I want to hear it straight from your mouth. What do you think I should do? Don't beat around the bush.'

There was an awful, awkward silence for about thirty seconds, and then he said, 'I think you should retire.'

During the rest of that week I stayed away from the club as I thought about what to do. Our club co-captain, Kirky, fronted the media on the Wednesday and was asked about me. He came out with the now famous quote that he would trust me with his kids, but he didn't know if he could trust me on the field. Great – I can start Big Bazza's crèche.

A lot of people thought that his comment would have been devastating to me, but Kirky actually told me what he was going to say before I heard it from anywhere else. I truly appreciated that. Whether I agreed with him was irrelevant, but I really respected that he told me about his comments before I heard them on the news, which made them easier to cop.

Kirky and I had met for a coffee. Of course, the club had already made it clear to me that I couldn't play on, and I'm sure the leadership group would have known that. Kirky and I talked about it, and I told him I wasn't going to resign. Kirky said, 'Well, that's your decision. Let's wait and see what happens.' That was when he told me what he would be saying to the media that day. I was grateful for his honesty – if some other people had manned up in the same way, the whole situation wouldn't have been as messy as it was.

I always got on really well with Kirky. People used to think that was unusual, considering we were from very different walks of life. But I respected him for what he had achieved, and because if he ever had any issues with you, he'd come straight out and tell you, and he would make sure you heard it from him, not from someone else or in the media.

I also talked to my old man. He didn't want me to resign, but not because of the payout I'd lose. He reckoned that if I walked away, that would be it for me in the game. He just didn't want to see me go out that way. I told him I had to have some time away from football, and I was starting to think it was the right thing to do. I'd just about had enough. I'd been advised by my mate not to resign, but I couldn't take it anymore.

Not long after, I went back to the club and told them I'd had enough and I wanted it to be over. It was as though I'd already been delisted anyway. I told Phil Mullen that if the club paid me out, I'd resign. That way they could look like the good guys, as I knew they wanted to, and they wouldn't have to worry about any fallout from sacking me.

In the end, that was exactly how it all panned out. The club agreed to the payout if I resigned, and the deal was done. I think it was the best result for everyone, really. If I'd been sacked, the drama in the media would have carried on for another few weeks and I would have been harassed outside my house again. The club got the result it wanted too, but I just wish they could have handled it better. Maybe it was badly managed because nothing like this had happened before. All I wanted, though, was some honesty.

I don't think it would have made any difference if we'd been in finals contention or up near the top of the ladder. I think Roosy had made up his mind about what should happen on the Sunday, and that wasn't going to change regardless of where we were on the ladder.

After the deal was done, everyone smiled, shook hands in public and moved on. That's how it was at the press conference the day we announced my resignation. I was asked if I was worried about my actions, and about how they might impact on me in society – at a nightclub or driving on the road. I said I was worried, which was true. I said my reactions were always instinctive, and as soon as I did something wrong, I'd always think, 'Why did I do that?' But I also said I was going to do my best to fix the problem.

People walked away not knowing the full story, but it was an outcome where there were no real bad guys. I was judged to have done the right thing, and those at the club were seen as the good guys for not sacking me.

I had spoken to the Swans' players before I made the announcement. That was difficult and I got a bit emotional. I told them I'd decided that it wasn't fair on them or the club for me to continue, and that the best thing was for me to resign. Of course, I wanted to tell them I had wanted to keep playing but that the club had shown me that there was no chance of that happening, but I didn't. I just said, 'Look, it's not fair to have you blokes being forced to answer for me in the media. It's not fair on my family either' – which was also true – 'so I've resigned.'

I think most of the players knew what was coming before I addressed them that day. With all the media stuff that had been going on, and then with a players' meeting called at the club, they would have had a fair idea. But the fact that they probably knew what I was about to tell them didn't make it any easier. I tried to keep it fairly light-hearted, but eventually my emotions did come out. I had spent nearly ten years at the club, after all, and I'd spent most of my days with the blokes in that room. It hurt me to lose that and to go out the way I did.

I can't actually remember what their reaction was – I was trying my best to keep it together. Roosy stood up and said a few words about how much I'd done for the club and for the game in Sydney. That was good to hear, but it was a shame the club hadn't treated me with that respect when we were dealing with the situation.

Afterwards, Roosy asked me into his office. He said he thought he had let me down as a coach. I don't know whether he was feeling guilty or just trying to butter me up, but at that stage I was past caring. I said, 'No, look, I accept all responsibility – my actions have put me in this spot.' That's where I left it.

In the weeks afterward, I received a lot of letters from old and young people saying really nice things. I was sorry that they couldn't know the full story. I hope they will now.

People who have known the real story sometimes tell me it's a shame that Roosy and I ended up the way we did, considering we were the two blokes up there on the stage accepting the 2005 Premiership Cup in what is the greatest moment in Sydney Swans' history. It is, but as I have said, the problems that got me to where I was were my own actions. I had no one to blame but myself for where I ended up. If the club had handled it a bit better, I would have no bad feelings about the place at all.

If I saw Roosy tomorrow, I would stop and shake his hand. We've spoken a couple of times since I left, and it's been fine. We just aren't best mates.

CHAPTER TWENTY-SIX

When I walked out the door of the Swans, that was it. I didn't know for sure, but I didn't expect to ever be back there.

I didn't even bother to clean out my locker. I didn't know what was in there, but I told Dougie, who was in charge of our gear, to just throw it all out. At the time, I didn't think I'd be needing any of it ever again.

I had no immediate plans after I quit the Swans. I certainly wasn't thinking about playing footy for another club. Contrary to speculation, I didn't have any boxing contracts lined up and waiting for me. Some interest did come, and I did entertain the possibility, but I knew that, first, I had to step away from the game and get it out of my system.

I didn't watch much footy during the rest of the 2009 season. I needed to see whether I missed it, whether I still had a passion to play it again. When the time came for me to make a decision about my future, I was feeling itchy to get back into football. I still thought I had something to offer.

But long before then, I had a farewell to make. The club wanted to give me a farewell lap of the Sydney Cricket Ground at half time during its Round 15 match against Essendon. At first I said, 'Okay, sure,' but by the day of the game I had decided I would pull out. I just thought it was corny, and I honestly didn't want to do it.

Phil Mullen called me when he heard, and said, 'Look, they have it all organised. This is a chance for the Swans' fans to say goodbye to you. Just think of them.' That convinced me to go ahead with it.

I was genuinely surprised by the reaction I got from the fans that afternoon. Going there in the car, I was fine – really, I just wanted to get it over and done with. I was feeling a bit over footy at that time and wanted to get away from it. But when I saw the reaction of the fans, who gave me a standing ovation as I was driven around the field in the back of a ute, I became pretty emotional.

It hit me that this might be the last time this would happen to me, the last time I would be in this sort of atmosphere. This was my farewell to the Swans, the Swans' fans and the SCG. It was really tough to keep it together. When the lap was over, I didn't stay for the rest of the game. It was over.

While that was my official farewell, I did return to the SCG seven weeks later after being asked by the club to present Leo Barry with his jumper before his last match for the Swans. Whether I had been officially involved or not, I would have gone along anyway that day just to watch two of my good mates, Leo and Mick O'Loughlin, play their final games.

Giving Leo his final Swans' jumper was a huge honour. We had been such good mates for a long time, and we'd done so much together. It was a special moment for me, but at the same time it felt strange.

Part of the reason I'd chosen to leave the club on good terms was so that I would always be able to walk back in the front door and not feel awkward. But coming back for that game that day, I actually felt like I didn't belong there one bit. I suppose by then the bond had been broken. I was no longer a Swans' player, and that became really clear to me then.

I don't think it had anything to do with the fact that I had just decided to try and find another club and play footy again in 2010. I had announced this in my newspaper column the day before the Swans' final match.

A couple of other past players were at the match too – Paul Kelly and Paul Williams – and we went out for a drink after the game. We walked into the Kings Cross bar where the players all went after the game. When we saw all the players sitting there in a group, it hit me again that I wasn't part of their team anymore.

I felt excluded from the group – and of course, technically I was – but that day it also felt like I'd never been a part of it. I only stayed about an hour and then left.

Someone asked me a while ago whether I'd feel awkward at a Swans' reunion, or whether I'd even attend one. To be honest, if one was on next week I probably wouldn't be there. It's got nothing to do with the players or the club, really, but I just wouldn't feel comfortable. That is a bit sad, and I hope that, over time, my feelings might change.

Making the decision to play footy again was difficult. I thought long and hard about it and spoke to a lot of people, including Phil and Sophie, of course. I knew that playing again would mean moving interstate, so we put some serious thought into it. But I felt like I had unfinished business in the game, and I really didn't want my football career to end the way it had.

The last Swans' function I went to was the best-and-fairest dinner, which took place a week after the club's last game. I didn't want to go. I had never really enjoyed going to nights like those – they just weren't my thing. But I had agreed and we had our tickets before I'd really thought it through. As the night approached, I was feeling unsure. I had already closed the book on my career at the Swans after my lap of honour.

But Sophie and I went along, and as it turned out it was not a bad night. I was taken aback a little when I was called up to the stage to receive an award honouring the players who were retiring. I didn't know what sort of reception I would get, but the audience gave me a massive ovation. That was a nice feeling, but still I knew that this was no longer my club. There would be no late night for us – we left as soon as all the presentations were done.

Once I had made the decision to play again in 2010, the big question was whether I would be able to find a club willing to take me. One club where I knew I would never be was Collingwood.

Soon after I'd left the Swans, Collingwood coach Mick Malthouse had made it very clear he would not consider me if I did choose to come back to the AFL. He came out and said, 'If Paul Roos and Brett Kirk can't get the best out of a bloke, and he's prepared to move [away from] those blokes – who I have the highest admiration for – then I am not about to take that on.'

Mick Malthouse was an experienced guy and had been around for a long while, but he wasn't at the Swans and didn't know me. I was surprised by his words, but anyone can have an opinion. I did think it was strange for him to buy into the whole affair. If he wasn't interested in me – and that was the question asked of him – then he could have simply said, 'No, he's not on our radar.' I didn't think his little pot shot at me was necessary.

CHAPTER TWENTY-SEVEN

Mick Malthouse might not have been interested in signing me, but Alastair Clarkson, the coach of the 2008 defending premiers, Hawthorn, was keen. I was surprised to get a phone call from him, but Hawthorn had problems with their ruckmen, who were all injured. I think Alastair's plan was to use Jarryd Roughead in the ruck and slot me in as a forward, and perhaps rotate us. When I thought about it, it actually seemed like a decent idea.

I flew down to Melbourne with Phil Mullen and we met with the Hawks at Clarko's house. I hadn't had a manager since I left ESP several years earlier, but I needed one now, and Phil, who had resigned from his role at the Swans, agreed to look after my affairs. While we were careful not to appear to be asking for too much – after all, we didn't have a lot of bargaining power – we still had to be realistic. For starters, I wasn't going to go just anywhere. There was no point in me going to a bottom club just to play out a year or two more of footy – I might as well just stay retired. Sure, I wanted to work to change my image by finishing my career well, but realistically I was only interested in going to a club that needed a key forward and had a chance of winning the flag.

Once I had met with Clarko, I started to entertain the idea of playing alongside Lance 'Buddy' Franklin in the Hawks' forward line. It wouldn't be too bad at all, I reckoned, but in the end it still had to be worth it for me to play. We told the Hawthorn blokes exactly what we wanted – we weren't trying to be demanding, just realistic, to make things easier. We told them what we thought I was valued at, although we recognised that naturally my value would have dropped a bit. We also stipulated that it had to be a two-year deal.

Sophie's needs were another big consideration. We would have to move interstate, and I was adamant that she should be comfortable wherever we went. Sophie was going to have to leave all her friends in Sydney to come to a place where she would know nobody. There would be a lot of pressure on me but I would have the footy club to fall back on. Sophie wouldn't have that, which was a real concern for me.

The deal had to be worthwhile. Phil and I thought the number we'd stated was fair for both parties. I wasn't going to play for $100,000 and have a truckload of pressure and the spotlight on me, especially when I could go and push a wheelbarrow around and get paid, or even hop back into the ring.

We told the Hawks that we couldn't negotiate on our stated figure; if they couldn't match it, then we'd look elsewhere. It was a risky strategy and we could have left ourselves with nothing, but the reality was that if playing wasn't going to be financially worth it, then it was pointless me doing it.

Hawthorn's offer came up short. I think it was all they could afford, because their number-one target at that stage was Josh Gibson. So we pretty quickly realised that it wouldn't work out with them. I was firm that I would be staying retired if I couldn't get the deal I needed.

The Western Bulldogs were also an option. They'd tried a year earlier to get me to their club with a trade, but that hadn't worked out. Obviously, a lot had happened in those twelve months, though, and I wasn't sure they would still be keen.

I had a phone call from Paul Williams, who was an assistant coach at the Bulldogs. We'd stayed in touch after he retired from the Swans, and it was just a normal mate-to-mate phone call – nothing out of the ordinary. But the fact that I was considering playing again was mentioned, and that sparked talks between Phil and the Bulldogs.

By no means were they dead keen on me at that stage. The talks just covered where I was at and what my thoughts about playing on were. The fact that Willo and Rodney 'Rocket' Eade – who had got me to move to Sydney in the first place all those years before – knew me made a difference. They showed a fair bit of faith in me, which was comforting.

There was a lot of work that had to be done, and plenty of talking. Obviously, taking me on as a player was a big risk for the Bulldogs, and when it emerged that they were interested they copped a bit of heat. But they were genuinely interested and we worked out a deal. Then we just had to organise a trade with the Swans.

When trade week arrived, the Swans tried to get as much as they could for me. That was what they had to do, and that was fair enough. I was never worried that a deal wasn't going to be done. I was thirty-three years old and an unwanted player at Sydney, so the Swans knew they couldn't demand too much for me. And if a deal hadn't been done, I would simply have gone into the draft and been selected by the Bulldogs – if that happened, the Swans wouldn't get anything in return for me. In the end, the Dogs gave the Swans pick forty-seven in the national draft, which was a reasonable result for both clubs.

Contrary to some media reports, there weren't any specific clauses in my contract about on-field behaviour. It was simply a standard footy player's contract, and all of them have clauses about your responsibilities as a player.

As soon as the trade was done and I was officially a Bulldog, I started to get a flood of text messages from all the Bulldogs' players, welcoming me aboard and saying they were looking forward to playing alongside me. Most of the guys in the team sent messages, which meant a lot to me.

Rocket had let me know that before they'd made a decision on me, the players' leadership group was asked about it, so it had been a combined decision. It was good to hear that the leaders were keen to have me there, and the messages I was receiving confirmed it.

Leaving Sydney was a bit emotional for me. It was the city where I thought I would settle after my footy career ended. I really had no intention of going back to Melbourne. If anything, leaving Sydney and going back to Melbourne showed how much I wanted to play in the AFL again – that

I was willing to pack up everything and head back into that sort of environment, with all the scrutiny that would go along with it.

I was willing to give the Melbourne lifestyle one more shot. But in saying that, I had matured a lot since leaving Melbourne back at the end of 2001, and I felt I would be able to handle it ten times better now than when I was at St Kilda.

But it wasn't just about me – there was Sophie's well-being to consider as well. She was from Queensland but loved her life in Sydney, and so I was probably more concerned about how she would like Melbourne and how she would settle in. I had a footy club to fall back on if the going got tough, but she didn't.

Once we made the move, though, Sophie settled in really well. She got a job soon after we got there and she hit it off straightaway with many of the other players' partners.

I think it was a bit of shock to her when we went out on the town one night to see just how fanatical and passionate the locals are about their footy. She was taken aback by how much it's in your face. She became quickly aware of the huge difference between Sydney and Melbourne in that area, and so far it hasn't been a problem for us.

Everything was positive from day one at the Bulldogs. Once we got into our serious pre-season training, all the players saw I was fully committed and that I was there for the right reasons. There was still a negative hanging over me, waiting to raise its head at some stage, but thankfully it never did.

No team goes out to lose games in the NAB Cup, but obviously some teams take it more seriously than others.

For some clubs, their preparation for Round 1 might mean they play under-strength in the pre-season competition.

We went into our first match – against Brisbane in Canberra – but I didn't play. A lot of the other senior guys didn't either, but the young kids played well. After being well down at half time, we came back and won the game. The coaches' plan for the pre-season was that we would filter in the more experienced players from week to week, and so be able to play with our full squad in the final practice matches.

I'd known Rocket since he'd coached me for half a season at the Swans, but now he seemed a totally different person. Naturally, he was still very smart and a great tactician, but the way he carried himself was so much better. I hadn't known him so well back then, but I could see that leaving the Swans had been a good move for him. I hoped it would be equally good for me.

I made my debut for my new club the following week. Funnily, the match was against Hawthorn and Josh Gibson came to play on me. Things couldn't have gone much better for me. I kicked four goals in the first quarter and ended up with six for the game, but more importantly, I seemed to fit into the team well and we won quite easily. It couldn't have been scripted much better.

I went okay the next week against Port Adelaide, and we just got home with a late goal. Suddenly, despite it still being the pre-season, the hype around the club started to build.

It had been forty years since the Bulldogs had won a trophy, and while we were only competing for the NAB Cup, it was still great for the club when we beat St Kilda to win it. My dream beginning with my new club had continued through the competition – I kicked seven in the final and won the Michael Tuck Medal for best on ground. Talk about fairytales!

But as we all knew, it was only the pre-season. Our goal was to win premiership games. The pre-season victory did heighten the expectation of our fans heading into Round 1, when we met Collingwood. The club was abuzz and membership sales were going through the roof. It was terrific for the club.

Also, it showed me that if the fans were this rapt about us winning the NAB Cup, then if we finally could win the flag, the place would go crazy. Melbourne wouldn't know what hit it! The Bulldogs fans have been starved of success for that long they were just craving it. There were a lot of older supporters and people who had stuck by the club, and it hadn't been an easy ride.

I thought back to one young fan they had many years before who used to kick the footy around his back paddock pretending he was Simon Beasley, getting handballs from Dougie Hawkins. It had taken me two clubs and fourteen years, but I was finally at the club I supported.

We were beaten in Round 1 by Collingwood, and for me it seemed like déjà vu when we won and then lost, then won and then lost. After seven rounds we had four wins and three losses. Our next opponent had got off to a flying start and won five of their seven games. It was the Sydney Swans.

When I'd left the Swans, I remember saying that I'd find it very difficult to play against my former teammates. But when I finally decided I wanted to play again, realising that

I still had a lot to offer footy, playing the Swans was the furthest thing from my mind. I wasn't going to be at the Swans, and I just figured that if I wasn't playing for them, I'd eventually come up against them.

And now the time had come – in Canberra, of all places.

The lead-up was a little bit different. There was obviously a lot of media interest in me facing my former teammates again, but I just tried to put it aside and not let it get to me. And I'm pleased to say it didn't. During that week, Rocket asked me about how I was handling it all, and I said I was fine. I wasn't nervous and I was feeling confident. For some reason, I always seemed to play well in Canberra. Maybe the Swans should have played me in the reserves after all, since they played in the Canberra league.

Naturally, our team's focus was simply on winning the game, not on me kicking goals or getting the better of my old team. It was a bit weird playing against them, though, more so than it had been when I'd arrived at Sydney and played against St Kilda.

At the Swans I used to mentor Lewis Roberts-Thomson, and now, at the start of the game, he was playing on me. That was strange, but in the end it couldn't have gone much better for me. I kicked five goals, and more importantly, we won the game.

We met Sydney again later in the season. By that stage we were in the top four and they were in the eight. I'd enjoyed playing at the SCG and so it was good to go back. It was my first time on the ground since the farewell lap I'd made in the back of the ute. I didn't need to say goodbye to the fans this time, but I was keen to say hello again.

The match was a special one for the Swans, though – it was the last home game for both Brett Kirk and Paul Roos – and their team was pumped. We started well but lost Adam Cooney really early in the game. Sydney overran us in the second quarter and didn't give up their lead – they were just way too good for us that day. It wasn't the return I'd hoped for, but it was still good to get back there.

I did cop some stuff from the fans that night. When I'd walked onto the ground, for example, there were little kids running up to me and calling me a traitor. It was clear that had come from their parents, who were too scared to say it themselves. When a reporter asked me about the abuse I'd copped, I fired a shot at those fans. I said I'd thought they were better than their behaviour showed. I even added that I'd nearly put them in the category of Collingwood supporters.

I was pretty pissed off, but I hadn't meant to tar all Swans' fans with the same brush. There were probably twenty-five per cent who'd had no idea of the circumstances when I'd left the club, and they were the ones carrying on. I got a lot of letters after that from other Swans' fans who said they supported me – they urged me not to let those other dickheads get to me. That was good, and I almost felt like doing another article to apologise to the other seventy-five per cent. I didn't, but I am doing it here and now.

Anyway, the AFL scriptwriter must have been working overtime, as I was to face the Swans one more time in 2010 – in a Semi Final at the MCG. We were battered and bruised and coming off a ten-goal loss to Collingwood, while Sydney was full of confidence, having beaten Carlton the week before.

It was a remarkable game. The Swans led by five goals in the second quarter, and everything was going their way. Nothing was working for us. But we came out after half time and pulled ourselves out of the hole, and in the end we somehow got home for a terrific win. It showed that we had what it took mentally to go all the way. It was a truly memorable win.

Some thought it must have been all the more satisfying for me to know that I'd helped win the match that was Paul Roos' last as a coach, but that wasn't the case at all. We were playing finals football and the win was all that mattered. I did enjoy seeing Kirky chaired off after the game and getting a great reception from the crowd.

The following week we played St Kilda in the Preliminary Final for a shot at a Grand Final berth. While we came out hard and led at half time, the Saints got over the top of us in the second half and we were beaten up a bit.

Sometimes you need a bit of luck to go your way to win a flag, and at the business end of the 2010 season we didn't get a lot of it, especially with injuries. But we fought it out right to the end. Naturally, it was gut-wrenching, but there was no shame in that loss. It would have been great to go further but it wasn't to be.

The rooms were pretty emotional after the game, as that was the end of the careers of Brad Johnson and Nathan Eagleton. It became crystal-clear to me then that you can be a legend of the game, as Johnno is, but that doesn't guarantee you that you'll have the highest success and win a premiership.

It's always tough when you don't achieve what you set out to, and for us that was winning the flag. On a personal level, though, I was pretty happy with my first season at my new club. I'd worked hard, done all the little things that a team needs from every player. I finished with eighty goals for the year, the same number I had managed at the Swans in 2005, and the equal best tally I've had in my career.

There had been a bit of talk towards the end of the season that I had a chance to win the Coleman Medal. I mean no disrespect at all, but winning that award really has never been something I've worried about. I think that my actions show that I don't go out there chasing personal glory.

In 2005 I had gone into the last game of the home-and-away season five goals behind Fraser Gehrig, but winning the Coleman was the furthest thing from my mind. In fact, I almost used it to make a bit of a statement to my teammates that day. I was looking to give off goals if a teammate was in a better position, and I tried to be as team-oriented as I possibly could. I wanted to show them that I wasn't interested in individual honours – it was all about the team. No single player is ever bigger than the team, and I think that my message that day bonded us as a team more tightly than ever.

There was one incident that caused plenty of headlines for me during the 2010 season. It was in Round 9 against North Melbourne. I was tying up my bootlaces when North defender Scott Thompson came over and pushed me to the ground. I grabbed him, flung him to the ground and put a headlock on him.

I ended up getting a fine from the Match Review Panel, but some people wanted me rubbed out. It was ridiculous. Thompson had been at me all game, but when he shoved me to the ground for no reason I thought he had crossed the line and I reacted.

I was in complete control. It was said at the time that I could have choked him and that I had lost it. For starters, I didn't have his windpipe – I had him by the head. It was just a little wrestle and there wasn't going to be any harm done. But some parts of the media thought more of it.

When I was taken off the field to get me away from the drama and let things settle, a few of the North players came at me and got into my face. I tried to put my arms in the air and run past them, but Rodney Eade actually thought I had lost the plot and was going off my head.

When I got to the bench he phoned down and said to one of the guys, 'Get him down to the rooms and let him cool off!'

'I'm not going down there,' I said. 'I'm fine! Don't make things look that much worse.'

The guy relayed back to Rocket that 'Hally is fine – he's got his wits about him and he doesn't need to go down there'.

I spoke to Rocket about the whole thing the following week. 'Mate,' I said, 'you've got to trust me that I'm not going to lose it. I was completely in control. The bloke did something that I thought was unacceptable and I wasn't going to let him get away with it. If I'd lost it, I would have whacked him, I wouldn't have put him in a headlock.' Rocket was fine with that and we moved on.

I took a lot of positives out of my first season with the Bulldogs. One thing I noticed about myself was that every day I just felt so much more relaxed. I wasn't stressed or worried about footy – or anything – at all. The move back to Melbourne, as well as being in a great relationship, had done me the world of good. A stable and relaxed life off the field can only help your performance on it.

I had also gone from struggling with my relationship with Paul Roos to having a coach who I had a very good relationship with. At the Bulldogs, I felt Rocket was willing to give me another shot, and it was only fair that I repaid him that faith. With Rocket, you always know where you stand, which is all you can ask from anyone in any walk of life. It's been refreshing to have that. He knows me and what I'm about, and he's willing to back me.

If I do something wrong, I couldn't imagine Rocket going out defending everyone else but me. He wouldn't condone the stuff I did but he would certainly support me, I know that much.

I also discovered – to my surprise, really – that all footy clubs are not really the same. Life at the Bulldogs was totally different to at the Swans. The Dogs players are a really relaxed group who are really hard-working and yet so humble. There is just no bullshit about them. It reminds me of a country footy club: you come in, you train hard and then you go home. It's as simple as that. It's a really close bunch of guys and they use an easy system. That has been a breath of fresh air for me.

The club trusts that everyone is going to do the right thing off the field, and so they don't have to be militant about it. And thankfully there aren't as many meetings as there were at the Swans.

The style of play we go for at the Dogs is more free-wheeling. At Sydney there were so many rules: 'We can't kick there …

We can't do that … You can't do this …' Of course, we still have a few guidelines, like any team does, but we want to play unpredictably and take the game on. The Swans' style was very, very structured and so we had to have meetings to get everyone doing the same thing. The Swans still do that well, there's no doubt about it, but the Bulldogs take a different approach, which I think is a good thing.

Another benefit of being at the Bulldogs was that I got to catch up a few times with one of our biggest fans, the Prime Minister, Julia Gillard. Before she became Prime Minister, she had famously said that she had a better chance of playing full-forward for the Bulldogs than taking over from Kevin Rudd. I would have been happy to swap jobs with her if she wanted!

We got on really well. She seems really nice – pretty down-to-earth, very cool, calm and collected – a bit like me! At the start of 2011, the club made a presentation of a Bulldogs jumper to Julia to recognise her support. I was lucky enough to make the presentation and I got a kiss on a cheek. One photographer snapped us from an angle that made it look like I was going in for the kill! It wasn't the case, of course, but I did cop plenty over it from my teammates.

CHAPTER TWENTY-EIGHT

Whenever footy players are asked about milestones, they always say they don't mean too much now, but they'll mean more after their careers are over. It's true – it's not really possible to think of your career as whole until there is no more present-day footy to worry about. Until then, your focus has to stay on the current season and your upcoming games.

My career is close to the end now, so what do I see as I look back over it? Well, if nothing else, it's been turbulent.

When I came back to footy after leaving the Swans, I wanted to change the way people thought of me as a footballer. For some people that might be impossible now, but I hope that during my time with the Dogs I have made some others think twice about me.

I think I'm a better footballer than I was a fighter. I want to be remembered for what I did as a footballer, rather than all the incidents that made me 'Big, Bad Barry'. I'm not proud of all that stuff, and I'm trying to do my best to make people forget it. I want them to see me as a footballer who played for fifteen years in the AFL because he was good enough and desperate enough, not because he was getting chances or getting lucky breaks all the time. People don't see much of the hard work that happens behind the scenes at a football club, but there is a lot of it. That's why success is so rewarding.

After I've finished playing footy, I have a few ideas of what I'll do. I think I would be able to coach – I know enough about footy and I've got enough ideas – but I don't think I would want to. I'm just not a massive footy fan, and to be a good coach you have to sit there and watch footy vision all day, every day. But I could perhaps coach part-time, coming in and helping out on the track once or twice a week. That's something I would be more interested in.

Other than that, I'd be interested in doing some media work. I've made a few appearances on *The Footy Show*, which I enjoyed, but anything longer-term would have to be a light-hearted role. I just don't want to sit there and talk serious footy. Maybe even player management is an area I might be interested in as well.

What I would love to do is build cars for clients who want something unique, something specific and special – a bit like the stuff West Coast Customs do on TV. I do want to get into that. I've got a fair bit of knowledge about cars and some pretty good ideas. I've been working with cars as long as I can remember. You need paying customers, though, to get a business like that off the ground and I'm not sure whether there's enough of a market here for that. If one develops, though, I'm there.

The career I've had has enabled me to buy the cars I've wanted. I reckon I've owned about thirty different cars over the years – GTS Monaros, HQ Monaros, HRs, a real mixed bag. The best one I've owned, though, was a black ZR6 Corvette. I'd wanted one ever since I was a kid. I fantasised about owning and driving a Corvette, and when the opportunity came up to buy one in 2009, I thought, 'Bugger it! I've always wanted this car and I've got some money – I might as well do it.' So I did!

Of course, Dad was totally into cars too. A little like with boxing, he put everything into passing his knowledge on to me. Even now when I'm building a car, a little bit of me wants to get it done to prove to him that I can do it. Sounds like a classic case for the psychiatrist's couch, doesn't it? In fact, the issue did come up when I found myself on the couch at the Swans.

But I do love cars, both working on them and driving them. I know a lot of people do, but I have a real thing for them. I guess it comes down to being a bit of a show-off as well. I don't do burnouts or carry on like an idiot; I just love driving around in really nice cars. It makes me feel good about myself, I guess.

You get a real sense of achievement if you've done something to a car or created it from nothing. It makes you feel proud to drive around in it, and you feel pretty good when you can tell people, 'Yeah, I've built this.' As I said, perhaps it's because I'm a bit of a show-off.

I've got a real problem, too, in that I can't leave them alone. I'll get a car and say, 'I'm not going to touch this one – I'll leave it alone.' But sure enough, two months later I'll have done something to it to make it go just a bit quicker. Every car I've owned has been modified.

But it's not just about driving the cars around the street or working on them – I race them too, at Heathcote Park. I know the guy who runs the place, and it's pretty close to home, just half an hour away. My old man, my brother and I go there to race each other. It started out as a bit of fun but it developed as we learned more, and now it's a pretty high standard of racing. Putting so much work into your car and then getting it moving the way it does ... I get a pretty good buzz out of it. And going fast is a real thrill too.

My dad and I now get along much better than we did when I was younger. The good thing is that I can have a different opinion to him now, whereas before I always did what he wanted me to do. Even though we still have the occasional blue, we always get over them quickly. We can at least talk things out now, and I'm not scared shitless of voicing my opinion. If I think something is wrong I'll say something, which I was never able to do before.

Naturally, there's always a bit of rivalry, particularly with me and my old man. He's as competitive as they come – that's where I get it from – and he doesn't like losing. If I beat him, the next time we go racing I know he'll have done something special to his car to beat mine.

I've never had any dramas with my footy clubs banning me from racing. I didn't do it that much while I was in Sydney because I didn't have room to store my cars so they were all down in Broadford. When I joined the Bulldogs, they didn't have a problem with me racing at all. It's safer than driving on the road. The cars have roll cages and you wear a helmet and fire suit, so the risks are well controlled.

As I look back over my career I can see that it's been one hell of a ride. But is there anything I would change? A lot of it, probably! No, that's not true. I believe everything happens for a reason and it's all part of the journey.

These days, my temper and my anger-management issues are certainly nowhere near as bad as they used to be. I'm much better at letting things go now. Sometimes the bad side of me rears its ugly head, but I do feel that my stubbornness has improved significantly over the years. I'm not kidding myself, though – I know it's still there. But I guess it's just a part of my make-up.

I'm really happy where I am now. There's been a lot of heartache and pain on the way through, and all of it has been my own doing, make no mistake about that. But the journey has brought me to where I am now, and I'm really, really happy. My footy and my life in general – especially my wife-to-be – are going just so well.

The road has been a very bumpy one, and while it might have been easier for me to take a different route, I can't complain about how it's all worked out.

MY THOUGHTS

It's been enjoyable – and sometimes therapeutic – to tell my story. I hope the journey has been interesting for you, the reader, too.

I know that not everyone is a cover-to-cover reader – some of us like a quick fix from time to time! I'm often asked by fans and the media, and even by my friends and family, all the standard footy player questions: who is the best player I've played against, what's the best goal I ever kicked, and so on.

So, for those looking for some short, sharp insights into my career, here goes!

Best player who played on me: Matty Scarlett of Geelong.

Best player I played with: Robert Harvey at St Kilda.

Player I most enjoyed playing footy with: Amon Buchanan at the Swans. He was just a good old country boy, hard as nails, but he's the funniest bloke.

Player I would most like to have played with: Technically,

I did play with him, but it was during his brief comeback. At his best, though, and over a longer period, I would love to have played alongside Tony Lockett.

Toughest player in the game during my time: Glenn Archer of North Melbourne. There was no one tougher.

Stan Alves: A very good coach – in fact, he was definitely one of the better ones I played under. He had a bit of a temper and could really be a bit of a lunatic at times, but he's a lovely fella, Stan, and I get along with him well. When I talk to him now, he's a totally different person to when he was coaching.

Tim Watson: Very, very knowledgeable about football. In my view, Tim would probably have been more successful as a coach if he'd done an assistant's role first, just to guide him into what he was in for as a coach. He really threw himself into the deep end.

Malcolm Blight: Very different. He certainly had different ideas, and he just put a different spin on everything, which is sometimes what you need. He got a lot of success out of that approach – his record of leading his team to five Grand Finals and two premierships speaks for itself.

Rodney Eade: A very smart man. He can be sarcastic, though, but he's very funny. He'll have a go at you and then ten seconds later he'll be laughing about it, saying, 'How funny was that?' These days, while he still gets animated, he handles the tension of footy a lot better. Tactically, I reckon he's one of the best coaches I've played under.

Paul Roos: Although we didn't always get along, especially towards the end of my time in Sydney, I have a lot of respect for Roosy as a coach. He's a good coach, there's no doubt about that. I can't say a bad word about his coaching or what he's done in Sydney – his record speaks for itself. He led the team to more wins than losses, and the Swans made the finals year after year.

Umpires: I have always been confused about umpires, and I probably always will be. I've tried to work them out but I never have. My relationship with umpires was always a strange one. I don't know why, but they just never seemed to like me, and as a result I rarely got a call my way. I tried everything to rectify what I thought the problems were. At one stage I thought that perhaps they got a negative vibe from me so I changed my behaviour towards them, but nothing's changed at all so I thought, 'Oh well, I might as well just yell at them.' There's not much more to say about them, except that nothing really changed in the fifteen years I've been playing AFL footy.

Broadford: I used to absolutely love Broadford, and I always raced home every opportunity I had. But now I can't wait to get out of there. What was I thinking? Seriously, though, I have a lot of great memories of Broadford. It will always be my home, but there's nothing much there for me now except my family and some mates. While some might say that's quite a bit, I now prefer to encourage my family and mates to come down to Melbourne to visit.

Sydney: I really liked the city of Sydney. Just before I left the Swans, I was about to buy a house and stay for good, which shows just how much I enjoyed life there. I'm liking being back in Melbourne now, though, so we'll have to wait and see what happens when my footy days are over.

Melbourne: I find Melbourne totally different now from how it was when I first arrived in 1995. That's mainly because I'm a lot more settled as a person these days. Going out in public can still be difficult at times, but that's part of the job I signed up for.

Drugs: I absolutely hate them. I'm very anti-drugs. I just can't for the life of me understand why people take them. It disgusts me. I even hate smoking. My vice is that I'll have a drink at times, which is a bad habit, I know, but I still have no time for drugs at all.

Drugs in football: I just shake my head. I don't see why blokes would dabble in it, knowing that we get tested all the time, and knowing that the testing is only going to get more and more stringent. They'll be caught eventually. But blokes want to roll the dice, and that's up to them, but they're playing with their careers and their livelihood. Let's face it, AFL players have it pretty good, getting paid to run around and kick a footy. Why jeopardise that?

My most memorable goal: The one I kicked in the last quarter of the 2005 Grand Final. We needed one at the time, and thankfully I kicked it straight.

My most memorable game: Without doubt, the 2005 Grand Final. Winning a Grand Final is the reason we all play footy, and when you do you realise that all the hard work, all the battles and struggles through injuries, have been totally worth it.

My most forgettable game: The 2006 Grand Final. Let's not mention that again, hey?

If I hadn't been a footballer ... I would have had a flatter nose. I would have been a boxer.

Other sports I enjoy playing: Boxing and basketball, both of which I loved as a kid. More recently, I've got into tennis a little bit – they used to call me 'The Hammer' because of my forehand.

Sports I enjoy watching: I really like watching tennis. I don't mind boxing and the Ultimate Fighting Championship. Footy – not so much.

If I could have been anything ... I could say Prime Minister, but with mates like Julia, I haven't given up on that dream yet! Seriously, though, I'd just wish to be a millionaire and not have to work, so I could have all the access I need to all my toys and everything I want. Some say I have that now ... well, I do have a few toys.

Any regrets? Yeah, all the notorious incidents I've been involved in. In fact, I regretted them as soon as I did them. But I guess they're all still part of my journey, and they've played a part in getting me to where I am now. For that reason, I wouldn't change anything.

Worst thing I did in football: There have been a lot of things I've done in footy that I'm not proud of, but the one which really wasn't any good at all – the very worst – was when I tried to eye-gouge Matthew Primus.

Best thing you did in football: Woke up to myself.

ACKNOWLEDGEMENTS

Whenever you have to step up and accept some kind of award, and make the accompanying speech, there's always that slight worry you are going to leave out someone you shouldn't in your thank-yous.

Perhaps I should simply start these acknowledgements by saying that I'd like to thank everyone who has helped me – no matter how big or small – throughout my football career, from the juniors at Broadford, to Avenel, to the Murray Bushrangers, to St Kilda, to Sydney and finally to the Western Bulldogs ... you know who you are. I truly appreciate your help.

I must particularly thank all of my teammates along the way. You have all had an effect on me and my career in one way or another. As the cliché goes, footy is a team game: no matter how good you might think you are, you can't do it on your own, and I've been fortunate to have played alongside some very, very good players during my football journey.

Generous thanks go to each of my coaches who have given me a chance – some more than one chance – in particular the first man in the AFL to do so, Stan Alves, and the second, Rodney Eade, who gave me two chances, one in bringing me to Sydney, the other giving me one more shot when plenty wouldn't have bothered.

It would also be remiss of me not to thank all the fans who have supported me during my time in the game – regardless of some of my hiccups – at all three AFL clubs I have represented.

A special mention must also go to Paul Cleary. Everyone has a moment in their life they can look back on and say 'that was pivotal'. For me, one of those moments was when Paul talked me into playing footy again in my late teens. I didn't realise it at the time, but if he hadn't, my life would have been totally different to the one I have enjoyed.

I want to thank my parents, my sister and brother, and all my extended family for everything they have done for me along the way, both in the good and the bad times, and all my close mates – and they really do know who they are – who have always been there for me through plenty of thick and thin, both on and off the field.

To the team at ESP, my first management group, and especially John Andrews who I worked with a fair bit, sincere thanks for setting me straight about a lot of things early on, and giving me the kick up the bum I needed at the time.

To Phil Mullen, my current manager, not only are you

the the person who helped me the most during my time in Sydney, but you've been a true friend and confidant, the one person I could always turn to, no matter how difficult the situation I found myself in. Phil and his wife Astrid are my Sydney family.

One special person I owe a lot to is my partner, Sophie Raadschelders. She was a rock for me during a pretty turbulent time, my last season in Sydney. She then stood by me, offering her full support, and never questioning the decision to make the major move of packing up and heading to Melbourne. She has been such a positive in my life, is such a well-grounded person, and always has the knack of showing me that it really is only football, and things are never as bad as I may think they are.

After being convinced my story was worth telling, when it came to putting my life on paper for this book, the only person I would have trusted to help me with it was Michael Cowley. Having worked together on newspaper columns for a number of years, he was someone who knew the real me, and knew exactly how I would want my story told. My sincere thanks for all your work, Michael.

I must give my thanks to Fitzroy Boulting of Equinox Literary Management, the man who believed in this project for day one, was responsible for getting it off the ground, and steered us in all the right direction throughout the entire process.

To the team at Murdoch Books, particularly Colette Vella, Elizabeth Cowell and Sarah Hazelton, thank you too for believing in this book, and giving me the opportunity to squeeze my life into 200-odd pages.

And finally, thanks to all those hotel, nightclub and pub owners, and particularly their bouncers. I was a bit of a handful at times over the years, and I'm sure it could have ended a lot uglier than it usually did. Thanks for putting up with me.

Dedicated to Bruce and Judy

PART

1

As the twig is bent

1

THE BLACKNESS OF THE NIGHT DESCENDED ON ME as I made my way down the back steps of the old house. And the perfume of the frangipanni flowers filled the warm evening air.

We lived in the country in a house that seemed quite ancient, with an old thunder-box shithouse at the far end of the backyard. It was to this monstrosity that I was heading when, out of the gloom, this eerie apparition came towards me emitting blood-chilling noises that made the hair on the back of my neck stand up. The fear I felt made me piss my pants and, unable to scream—frozen into immobility where I stood—I waited for the horrifying end I thought was imminent.

The nightmarish creature moved towards me, pale and ominous, still making hissing and gurgling noises. Then the top half of the monster expanded before swooping down to devour me. But instead of being consumed I was lifted up, given words of comfort and kisses to calm me.

The creature wasn't a fiend from hell, it was an ordinary person with a sheet over her head. And it is the first memory I have of my mother. I never did find out what her motives were for putting me through this terrifying time and it wasn't till years later, when I met people who knew her, that I was told 'She was a lovely girl, but always a practical joker.'

My father was away with the Army. How long he'd been away I didn't know, but towards the end of the Second World War my mother developed a fatal illness, God rest her soul. My natural aunt was also alone, with her husband off at the war, and being pretty hard up, what with three children of her own to look after, she couldn't afford to take on three more kids even if she'd wanted to. So, unable to cope, and being ill and depressed, my mother placed my brother and myself in an orphanage while my sister went to my grandmother's.

I don't remember anything about the orphanage, so it couldn't have been that bad. But I do remember being taken out of it at the age of three and fostered out to people, if you could call them that, who had no children of their own. Probably God didn't want them to have any. But why in the name of Hell did he allow me to be put into the clutches of these two sadistic bastards? It's a question I must ask him one day. There are two types of Hell as I see it. First, there's the one the Bible-bashers tell you about—punishment for having led a bad life. The other is the one that fate, for reasons known only to itself, lets the innocent stumble into through no fault of their own.

I was four years old when my mother came to see me at my foster parents' home. That visit came shortly before her death and, apart from scaring the living shit out of me, and a dim memory of going for a walk with her to the old milk factory, it was all life let me have of her. Now, apart from a faded photograph and these dim memories, there is little I can say except that I believe life could not have been worse for me.

It was in Hell on Earth that I spent eleven years of my life. They were terrible people, my foster parents, human monsters who were ugly in looks but uglier in character. My foster father was called Eric. A stoop-shouldered, bald-headed little Rumplestiltskin of a man, he didn't just have a chip on his shoulder, but a bloody great log. And my foster mother . . . well Ruth was the witch out of 'Hansel and Gretel', with her hair tied back in a strict bun, a wart on her nose and a screechy, cackling voice. What other people called Hell in those days, I used to call home. I truly believe that when God created the scorpion, the spider and the toad there was a substance left over which he had no idea what to do with, so he created my foster parents to see the result.

They believed that children were to be seen but never heard. To speak without first being spoken to resulted in 'Get to your room . . . I'm going to flog you.' And when they said flog they meant just that. It wasn't just a parental whack on the arse you received, it was the razor-strop. And the thrashing stopped, not when they realised that they had inflicted physical injury on me, but when their arms got tired. I never learnt my table manners courtesy of an explanation or through illustration . . . I learnt them by way of a heavy backhander, as if I was expected to know all from the beginning . . . that the knowledge was implanted from birth. So I learnt early on to keep quiet as much as possible, to speak only when spoken to. I learnt fear. But I also learned to hate.

My foster parents not only wanted me to tell them I

loved them, they demanded constantly that I tell them that they had my love. But they sure went about it in a funny way. I used to have to attend Sunday school while they went to church. Oh yes . . . speak like angels on Sundays, they did, though with vacuous smiles. But they played spiteful cards with the Devil for the rest of the week. I was screamed and yelled at constantly . . .

'The Bible says you have to love and honour your father and mother.'

Honour and love them? . . . I wouldn't have pissed on the pair of them if they'd been on fire.

'I do love my mother and father,' I used to tell them. 'But you're not my mother and father. You don't treat me like other parents treat their kids.'

The fury that this would bring on was something you'd have to have been there to believe . . . They would smash my head against the nearest wall, spit in my face and scream at me.

'You're nothing but a spawn of the Devil,' they'd say. 'Your father and mother were Satan and his Mistress.'

They were a miserable pair of bastards. They'd buy any cheap item of food, irrespective of its condition. Meat would be bought when it was on the verge of decay, under the pretence that it was 'just for the dogs, you know'.

I never wore clothes like the other kids did. I had cut-downs that had the other children at school laughing at me. Dripping was the main topping for sandwiches. Pocket money was something I never saw. Toys that had been sent as Christmas presents were placed in a high cupboard . . .

'You'll be allowed to have them when you show us some love.'

6

I was never allowed to leave the property, to go visit and play with other kids.

'You have your work to do.'

Chopping wood, digging the gardens, hoeing tussocks out of the front paddock, polishing floors, washing up and drying the dishes, feeding the dogs. There were always a million and one things that I had to do and there was never time for play. If we ever went to visit anyone it would be one of their Bible-bashing friends from church. And the lectures before we went! Don't say this, and don't say that. But in reality I was too bloody scared to say or do anything, with the threat of a flogging always at the back of my mind. They would sit there, sipping cups of tea and trumpeting what joy they found in the Lord. Hypocrites! Sitting there, in a simulation of virtue and goodness, camouflaging their insincerity. There may have been some sort of an excuse for their stinginess if they had been poor, but my foster father had a good job. He was a bank manager. Still, they always depended on charity. We never owned a car. If it was too far to walk when we went anywhere, they would bludge a ride. Other kids at school had bikes. I had to run four miles to and from school. And there was a set time I had to reach home.

'If you're late you'll be flogged . . . '

I was like a junior John Landy, always trying to beat my own record for the distance. I tried to please with my silence and cooperation just to have some peace for myself, but no matter how I tried it was never sufficient . . . 'It's just not good enough.'

Shit! Did I hate those bastards. My hate was like a living thing. It ran through my body like quicksilver and

7

grew into a fire that ate and burnt through me. Their death was the only fuel that would be able to quench it. I'd lie in bed at night trying to work out how I could kill them and have some peace. I didn't care what the penalty was . . . Let them hang me, at least I'd be free. In the early mornings, just after daybreak, I had to run to the dairy farm and get the daily milk, about two miles away. I didn't have any shoes to wear. 'They're only for Sunday and church,' I was told.

In the winter I learnt to run because it seemed to make the burn of the frost easier to accept. So, in my childish mind, I dreamt up plans to kill them. There was an old shed in the backyard and I would lure them in there and bar the door from the outside. Then I'd douse the walls with kerosene and light it. Oh! And my thoughts of pleasure as I imagined their screams for mercy and clemency, calling on God to save them. These two hypocritical, cruel, inhuman bastards. Jumping up and down with pleasure and glee at their pain and their screams became my dream of pleasure. And of freedom.

Things came to a head more quickly than I imagined. As I grew older I remember thinking I'd simply run away. And that's just what I did.

I got out of bed one morning as if I was going to get the milk, and when I went through the front gate I started running. I remember throwing the billy-can to the shit-house and thinking I wouldn't have to see the bloody thing ever again. All morning I trudged on. We lived in the small country town of Coraki and the city of Lismore was 15 miles away. I headed for there. Later on, as I walked, I managed to hitch a ride on a farm truck.

My natural uncle and aunty lived in Lismore and at last I found their place. My aunty was my true mother's sister. But on arrival there, and telling them I had run away, they did the only thing I suppose that was open to them. They listened to my story, and I could sense that my Aunty Freda was concerned. Then, after assurances that 'Everything will be all right now', they called the police. The coppers treated me as a general bloody nuisance, put me in the police car and took me back to Hell again. I was dismissed from the room as the police spoke with Eric and Ruth. I ran out the back of the house and into the old shed, to hide from the flogging I knew had to come.

I waited in that dark shed, clinging onto the wooden workbench in front of me to stop the trembling that was running through my body. My foster mother had three mongrel dogs she kept chained up there. And, apart from the odd occasion when she'd take them out and chain them to a tree, they spent the whole of their miserable lives in that shed. The building had an earth floor and it was infested with fleas. It was one of my chores to carry the wood I had chopped from the shed to the kitchen to fuel the stove. I used to dread having to go over and get the wood. The moment you entered the shed, fleas would jump onto your legs and go to work immediately.

But on this day the shed seemed to be my only haven. As I stood there, hanging onto the bench, I could feel the fleas jumping and crawling over and up my legs ... feel their itchy stings as they started to suck my blood. But for some reason I just stood there, knowing I had to do something ... that there had to

9

be another life for me. I had no one or nowhere I could go to call for help. I just clung to that bench like a friend that I was afraid to let go.

I heard the police car drive away and, not long after, the door to the shed swung back and there it stood, this gnome from Hell. He had the razor-strop in his hands and he snarled as he came towards me.

'I'm going to flog you and flog you till you can't stand. You won't run away from us again.'

I stood stock still, feeling hate and revulsion. Memories of his cruelty flooded through my mind. As I turned towards that voice, my hand brushed against the handle of a hammer. I picked it up.

'You touch me again you bastard and I'll kill you.'

I'll never forget the look on his face. It started as one of fear, then slowly turned into a malevolent grin. He had never heard me speak to him in this fashion and a rage spread across his ugly face. He made a further move towards me.

'Put that hammer down,' he shouted.

'Fuck you!' I said, and hurled the hammer. It struck him above the left eye, high on his forehead, making a fleshy thud as it landed. A spurt of blood fountained out and he bent over at the hips, like someone bowing, then grabbed at his head with both hands.

'Oh! you mongrel!' he shouted.

Panic grabbed me for an instant but washed away just as suddenly, replaced with a feeling of utter pleasure. I had finally struck back and hurt the beast who had caused me so much pain and grief. I felt like David, who had just slain his own Goliath. He crumpled to the dirt floor of the shed, moaning and yelling out.

'Ruth ... Ruth ...'

I took a pace towards him, doubled-up on the ground, and spat on him. And I remember thinking this childish thought ... Hope the fleas eat you alive.

I rushed out into the yard just as my foster mother came running down the back steps of the house. She must have sensed something from the look on my face and from the groans and the barking that were coming from the shed.

'What have you done,' she yelled at me. 'What have you done, you little beast?'

I didn't answer her. I just spat in her direction, ran down the side of the house, out the front gate and up the street.

I ran for what seemed like hours, and all the while I only had one thought in my mind ... I just had to get away from them.

NIGHT CAME QUICKLY. IT WAS AS IF SOME GUARDIAN angel knew I needed cover and gave me the darkness in which I could hide from my tormentors.

When I finally stopped running I found myself at a quarry, about five miles from town. It had a supply shed made out of corrugated iron and with no lock on the door. I went inside, waited till my eyes became accustomed to the gloom and sat on a box. Pent-up thoughts started to rush through my mind. Hope the bastard's dead ... Hope the fleas eat him ... He won't flog me any more ... I should have whacked old Ruth with the hammer, too ... They'll have to do all the bloody work themselves now ... Hope I killed the bastard.

I had no feelings of remorse that night, and no fear of punishment. In fact I just felt happy and, for the first time in my life, free and at peace.

Eventually I got up and started to fossick around. I found an old flashlight, got it to work after a bit of fiddling around and started to examine the shed more thoroughly. At the far end was a cupboard with no door on it. It was full of all sorts of stuff that you usually find in a kitchen ... a tin of tea, an old teapot, a biscuit tin with a big parrot on the side. I flipped up the lid and, inside, there were a few biscuits and a million bloody ants. I took out a biscuit, knocked the ants off it and started to chew. But it had that anty, acid taste so I threw it away. I found two tins of condensed milk and, after hunting around, a rusty old can-opener. I punched a couple of holes in one of the cans and sucked down the milk. It was the most beautiful food I had ever tasted and I kept at that tin until I'd sucked every last drop from it. But the sweetness of the milk left me thirstier than I had been earlier. Outside, there was an old water tank that was fed by an overflow pipe from the roof. I went out to it, put my mouth to the tap, turned it on and drank . . . Oh, Jesus! What a shitty taste.

There couldn't have been any strainer on the tank and rats, or frogs more likely, must have drowned there and rotted in the water. I spewed my guts up all over the ground and all that delicious milk was gone. I was tempted to open the other tin to get the taste of vomit and dead animals out of my mouth, but I fished out another anty biscuit instead and nibbled a piece of it.

The battery wasn't much good and the torch was giving off only a dull orange glow, but behind the door of the shed I came across a pushbike covered over with a couple of corn bags. I'd never owned a bike but had learnt to ride one at school. That is, I could keep my balance and pedal one in an upright position. I uncovered the bike and had a bit of a gander at it. All the bits seemed to be in the right places, the tyres weren't flat and, apart from the chrome flaking off it in numerous places, it seemed to be okay. There was a little generator attached to the front forks with a wire leading up to a lamp on the handlebars. I fiddled around with

13

it, using the last of the power in the torch, and found a lever that let the small wheel on the generator come in contact with the front tyre. And presto! As you pedalled the bike the lamp came on. To me, this was all magic, something to be marvelled at. After I had taken the bike for a couple of turns around the loading area I decided to use it in my bid for freedom.

Armed with the clothes on my back, the spare can of condensed milk and the stolen bike, I pedalled towards Lismore. The seat on the bike was too high but I managed to pedal my way along despite this inconvenience and a chafed arse. I had the occasional buster but it sure beat the hell out of walking. Even so, I didn't reach Lismore till around daybreak. I thought my uncle and aunty would help me, even though it was only yesterday that my appeals for help had come to nothing. I only half-realised it at that age, but they had no alternative other than to call the police, whether they wished to or not. There was no phone at my foster parents' place, so no discussions could be entered into. Not that my foster parents would even have allowed them anyway.

Years later, I found out that my uncle and aunt knew that something was terribly wrong, but in those days ... well, one didn't interfere.

So, tired, hungry and thirsty, I made my way up the front stairs and knocked on their door once more. It took two or three knocks to rouse somebody, and in the end it was my Uncle Ted who answered the door. His look of annoyance turned to one of surprise when he saw me.

'Jimmy! What the bloody hell are you doing back here?'

14

'Uncle Ted,' I said, 'will you help me? I'm not going back there to Eric and Ruth. I've hit the bastard with a hammer.'

'Shit! You'd better come inside, mate.'

We went into the house, down the hall and into the kitchen.

'Sit down, Jimmy, I'll go and wake your aunty.'

When he left the room I just sat there, waiting. I heard mumbling coming from their bedroom which I couldn't understand and after what seemed like an eternity they both came out to the kitchen. My aunty was in the lead, belting up a pink dressing gown.

'Hello Jimmy,' she said. 'What have you done, love?'

I broke down in tears and poured my heart out to them. I tried to explain all and everything that had happened to me. The floggings, the cruelty, what they called me, my mother, father, everything. They listened to me sympathetically, with the occasional look at each other.

'Now look here, mate,' Uncle Ted said to me when my torrent of hurt had been poured out. 'How bad is this Eric? How hard did you hit him with the bloody hammer?' .

'Stuff him!' I said. Then I explained how Eric was moaning on the floor with blood coming out of his head. 'I hope I killed the bastard,' I added.

Aunty Freda got to her feet.

'I'm going to make a cup of tea and get some breakfast for you. Then Ted and I will have a talk. We've got to work something out because the police will be looking for you.'

'I don't care! I hope they lock me up. At least I won't

have to go back to that rotten Eric and Ruth.'

While my aunty was preparing breakfast, Uncle Ted made one or two trips in and out of the kitchen, having mumbled conversations with my aunty. I simply sat there feeling peaceful and safe. I didn't think very much about the consequences of my actions, and I didn't really care. I was away from *them* and that house in Coraki. That was enough.

My uncle returned to the kitchen, sat down and rolled a cigarette.

'How did you get here this time? Did you hitchhike again?'

'No, I found a bike in a shed at the quarry.'

'Christ almighty! You mean you pinched a bloody bike as well? Boy oh boy, they're really gonna love you. What do you think the coppers are going to say about that?'

I shrugged my shoulders.

'Well . . . where's the bike now?'

'Down at the side of the front stairs.'

'Shit! We could be had up for possession of stolen property. What did you bring the bloody thing here for?'

I shrugged my shoulders again once more.

'You know we're going to have to notify the coppers again, don't you?'

'I suppose so.'

'Well you'd better get a bit of breakfast into you before you face the music. Shit!' He shook his head.

Nothing more was said about the matter during breakfast. Just some small talk and a lot of silence. Two of my cousins came into the kitchen dressed in

16

their pyjamas. We looked at each other sheepishly, the way relations do when you don't see each other too often.

'Say hello to Jimmy,' my aunty told them. Then, 'You kids go up to the lounge for a while. We've got a little problem here we have to sort out.'

'Why? What's going on?' my eldest cousin Pamela asked.

'Just go and do as you're told. I'll bring some breakfast in to you in a minute.'

My cousins left the room mumbling their hurt feelings out loud. I was amazed that nothing happened to them when they answered back like that. If that had been me back with my foster parents I'd have been flat on my back by now.

When breakfast was over and done with, I sat there with my aunty, who had come to my side and was holding my hand.

'You're so much like your mother,' she said. 'But you walk and move just like your father. I still miss your mother very much.'

Well if you miss her still, I thought, how the Hell do you think I feel? But I kept it to myself.

I heard the handle of the phone in the hall being cranked and Uncle Ted talking quietly for a minute or so. Then I heard the phone being hung up and he came back into the kitchen.

'Well, that's that,' he said to my aunty as he sat down at the table with us and rolled another smoke. 'I've just been talking to the coppers and they're not real happy with you, Jimmy. Eric's all right, though. He had to have his head stitched up, and he's reported that you've run

17

away again. They didn't say anything about the bike.'

After a while my cousin Terry came running in excitedly.

'Hey Dad, the coppers have just pulled up in the yard.'

'Righto, Terry, go on back to the lounge and I'll go and talk to 'em.'

With that he stood up and went down the hall to the front door. 'Gidday,' he called out, loud enough for us to hear, and then I heard his footsteps going down the front stairs.

I still held no fears for what I'd done. The only worry was that they'd take me back to Coraki again. Nothing they could do to me would be as bad a punishment as that. After what seemed an eternity, Uncle Ted returned.

'You'd better go down and talk to the coppers, Jimmy. Just tell them the truth and things will probably work out all right.'

As I stood up my aunty got up too and gave me a hug and a kiss on the forehead.

'It'll be all right, love. Just do what Uncle Ted has told you. Tell them the truth.'

I looked at my uncle for reassurance and he nodded to me.

'See you later then,' I said. 'Wish me luck . . . and thanks.'

I walked through the hall and down the front stairs, where two coppers were waiting for me.

'Gidday!' said the one who must have been in charge. 'I think you'd better come with us.'

The other one took my arm, led me over to the police car and opened the back door.

'Hop in,' he said to me.

My uncle and aunty were watching from the front verandah so I waved to them and got into the car.

'See you later,' the coppers said to them. Then they climbed into the front and drove away.

Once we were inside the police station they took me into a room that was furnished with a couple of desks and filing cabinets.

'Sit down there for a while,' one of the coppers said.

They left the room, closing the door as they went out. There was a window across the room and I noticed the bars. Outside the sun was shining brightly and the shadows of the bars made funny patterns on the floor. I remember counting the bars and noticed how the paint had chipped off in places, leaving rusty red marks. Muffled voices sounded throughout the building. Someone started laughing, about what I didn't know, but I remember that the sound of it brought a smile to my face. Footsteps sounded in the hall and a police-woman came in.

'Hello, Jimmy. Would you like a cup of tea or something?'

'Yeah,' I said. 'I wouldn't mind something. How'd you know my name?'

'We'll talk about that later when Mr Ward gets here. I'll go and get you a cuppa.'

She left the room, closing the door behind her, and returned a while later with an enamelled mug of tea.

'There you are,' she said. 'Try that. I'll be back in a tick.'

She returned a minute later with a cup and saucer

which she placed on the other side of the desk. Then she sat down and looked at me.

'What's been going on down there at Coraki with your foster parents? You can't go round hitting people with hammers, you know.'

'They're just a pair of bastards. You wouldn't understand.'

'Why don't you try and explain it to me. Then I might.'

So I went through the whole sordid story again. From time to time she would interrupt me to ask questions, but by the look on her face and the questions she asked I got the impression that she didn't believe a word of what I said.

After some time the door opened and another copper came in and beckoned with his head to the police-woman. She got up and went out the door. A few minutes later she returned with a guy in a suit.

'Jimmy,' she said. 'This is Mr Ward. He's from the Child Welfare Department and he'd like to ask you a few questions.'

As I looked at what in those days was an extension of the constabulary, I felt no alarm or unease. But the memories of the floggings, face spitting, head smashing, spite and cruelty all raced through my mind. Well whatever they do to me, at least the people who do it won't be those mongrels at Coraki. They won't be trumpeting biblical passages at me. At Coraki I got two hours of Heaven on Sundays and six and a half days of Hell for the rest of the week. Fuck 'em all, I thought. Let 'em do their worst. They can't hurt me any more.

'You've got yourself into a heap of trouble, young

20

fellow,' were the first words this Welfare guy said to me.

Shit! I thought. I've been in trouble from the day I was born and never planned or asked for any of it.

'You're not going to send me back to Eric and Ruth are you?'

'Well ... that's not up to me. You're going to have to go before the Children's Court. The magistrate will decide.'

'Righto!' I replied to him.

The Welfare bloke and the policewoman turned their backs on me, walked out into the hall and started talking in mumbo-jumbo that I didn't understand. I guess it was all technical stuff about my seeing the magistrate, so I went back to studying the room and thinking. Wonder what's happening at school? They probably think I've wagged it. So what? When they find out the truth some of the kids will understand. In fact I really liked school. It was a release from *them*. The morning school bell was hope, while the afternoon bell tolled a message of gloom and heralded a return to all that I hated and feared. Not only that, but I did well at school. Even the austerity of some of the teachers was a relief from what I got at home.

A copper came and took me down a long corridor, out through the back and up to a steel door with a big bolt and a shiny brass lock. It was the biggest padlock and bolt I had ever seen. He put a key in the padlock, undid it and pulled the bolt back. Gee! I remember thinking. Look at all the grease on that bolt.

The copper pushed the door open, stepped back and nodded to me to go inside. I found myself in an exercise yard with a high brick wall on three sides. Across the top there were bars, with steel mesh on top of them.

'We'll be back later,' the copper said. 'In the meantime, you'll have to stay in here.'

He closed the door and I can still hear the sound of the bolt when it was shot home and the rattle of the padlock being locked back in place. There was a sink and a tap against one wall and I felt thirsty, so I turned on the tap and had a drink. On the fourth side of the yard was another door like I'd just come through, but it was open. So I walked in and found myself in a cell. There was a small barred window high on the back wall, and wire mesh over the bars. In one corner there was a toilet. Jesus, I thought, look at that. A flush toilet in the gaol. Better than those maggot-infested things I was used to at home.

I walked up to it and looked into the bowl. There was a green ring at water level. Further up the wall there was a metal plate with a flat ring and a button in the centre. I gave it a push and water gushed into the bowl. I felt strangely guilty at the intrusion of noise because everything was so still and quiet.

High up in the ceiling there was a round dome light fitting which was covered with more metal mesh, but it was dark inside the cell and I looked around for a light-switch. There wasn't one. Against one wall there was a bench, attached to the wall by brackets. And there were four thick wide wooden planks bolted onto the brackets. At one end was a thin hard mattress that had been rolled up, and a couple of folded blankets. I rolled the mattress out and lay down, using the blankets as a pillow. I guess the events of the night before had caught

22

up with me because the next thing I remember was someone yelling at me from the door.

'Hey! Wake up. Come on, hurry. You're wanted over at the court.'

There was a copper standing in the doorway. 'The little bastard's asleep,' he said to someone I couldn't see.

I don't know how long I had slept, but when I sat up on the bunk I felt drugged and really fatigued.

'Come on. Come on,' the copper kept saying to me. 'They're waiting for you in court.'

I'd never seen a court before so I didn't know what to expect. There were four big ceiling fans turning slowly. Sitting at a table up the front with Mr Ward from Welfare was the *toad*, Eric. He had a bandage on his head.

Hope it hurts, I thought.

The cop led me to a table on the other side of the court. Eric didn't look around as the copper motioned me to sit down. He just kept staring at the high bench, where the magistrate was sitting. The magistrate looked down at me. I noticed how red his face was. Shit he looked cranky! I wondered if he was feeling the heat. He sure looked hot. He mumbled to a cop who had some stripes on his arm and the copper mumbled something back. The magistrate wrote in a big book in front of him, looked at me and mumbled again. I couldn't understand a word he said and I glanced across at the copper with the stripes. The magistrate must have thought I was ignoring him and I found out that he could get pissed off pretty quickly.

'Do you understand?' he boomed at me. His face was even redder.

23

I shook my head and looked at him. He said something else in a mumbling tone, wrote in his book, looked up again at the copper with the stripes and nodded his head.

The copper bowed at the hips. 'Very good, Your Worship', he said and scribbled something on a piece of paper. Then he walked over to Mr Ward and Eric. They spoke in soft tones and nodded a lot. I remember wondering why they were all whispering. Must be something like being in a church.

The copper who'd brought me to the court then came and tapped me on the shoulder, motioning with his head that I was to follow him. Out we went, out of the court, down the hill at the back and into my cell.

'What are they going to do with me?' I asked.

'They'll explain all that to you later, mate,' he said as he locked the big steel door in the yard.

I hadn't been there long when the door clanged open again and another big copper came in with a tray which he placed on top of the sink in the yard.

'Get that into ya,' he said, and left as quickly as he'd arrived.

Two big fat sausages, a heap of mashed potato and two slices of buttered bread sat on an enamel plate. And a big mug full of tea. I had never had these red sausages before . . . saveloys. I picked one up and took a bite. Shit that tastes good, I thought. I wolfed the food down, drank about half the tea, and the yard door opened again.

'Someone wants to see you, mate,' a copper said to me. 'Come with me.'

I went back into the police station, and was told to sit down outside an office that had the door half-closed. There was more than one person in the room and their words came out in bursts.

'Christ! He's only a minor. Can't keep him out there' ... 'Uncle and aunty says it'll be all right' ... 'How long?' ... 'Today. Well, as soon as you talk to him' ... 'Shit! Hope he doesn't take off again.'

Two coppers walked out of the room. One of them had silver pips and some braid on his shoulders. He looked down at me.

'Everything okay, son?' he asked.

I nodded. He smiled at me, nodded to the other copper and they walked off. Mr Ward then came to the door. He gave me a kind of grin and patted me on the head like a dog.

'Come on in, Jimmy,' he said. 'Let's have a talk.'

Seated in front of a table, Mr Ward then started to give me a lecture. Can't go around assaulting your foster parents with hammers ... blah, blah, blah ... Good, God-fearing people ... Lucky to have foster parents like that.

Lucky my arse, I thought. You go and live with the bastards. You'll soon find out. But I said nothing, just taking it all in one ear and letting it out the other. I was pretty used to saying nothing. I had been taught to shut up from nearly the time I could first talk.

'You're very lucky, you know. You've been given a chance.'

Alarm set in. 'Are you gonna send me back to Coraki?' I blurted out. 'I'll run away again.'

'No no no. You can forget that. You're going to live

with your aunty and uncle and go to school up here in Lismore.'

Boy, oh boy. A joyous feeling swept through me like an electrical current. The big dark cloud that was my constant companion vanished and I found myself trembling with emotion. I wanted to jump up and scream out to the world . . . *I'm free. Someone cares. I'm going to my own family. Even if it's not my real mum and dad, at least it's my real mum's sister.* I wanted to get up off that chair, hug that man, dance, yell, scream out.

Instead, I simply let my head fall forward and cried with relief. Then I looked up at Mr Ward.

'When can I go?' I said quickly.

He got up and left the room without answering. A policewoman came in and sat down beside me and smiled.

'Will you be happy with your uncle and aunty?' she asked me.

Happy, I thought. Christ! This lady doesn't know what she's on about. I didn't have the words to explain it to her properly, so I nodded my head and said 'Yeah.'

Mr Ward came back into the room and he had that rotten Eric with him. Eric looked at me with those malevolent close-set eyes of his. I could feel his hate. He knew I'd beaten him . . . checkmated him in the game of violence. He was afraid now, not me. I could see it in his eyes. But in front of these other people he had to put on an act. Just like Sundays at the church.

'We're very disappointed in you, Jimmy,' he said. 'I hope you treat your aunt and uncle better than you did us.' He said all this in a tone of voice that was quite alien to me, and that wasn't for my benefit.

You bastard, I thought. Why don't you show these people the real *you*? I looked at Eric, stared at him, and the revulsion and hate I felt for him wouldn't be quiet. I gazed right into those cruel, beady, close-set eyes of his and spoke with all the loathing that I could muster.

'I *hate* you and Ruth. Do you hear me? I hate you.'

He reeled back as if I had struck him, this stinking little coward of a man.

'See, see what I mean?' he bleated in a voice that bordered on the falsetto.

I glanced at the others and thought I saw a look of understanding for me. They knew from my outburst that something just had to be wrong. The looks on their faces said it all as they watched and listened to Eric gibbering on about me.

The policewoman ushered Eric out of the room. Mr Ward wheeled around to me. He was about to say something but, instead, he just stopped and looked at me.

'It'll be all right now,' he said, patting me on the shoulder. 'Don't worry. We'll get going in a moment.'

3

WHEN I WENT TO LIVE WITH MY UNCLE, AUNTY AND four cousins, life began to take on a different meaning for me. It was strange at first. The lessons I learnt from those bastards at Coraki were deeply ingrained. But gradually, with the love and understanding that my relations showed me, I adapted to their way of life. I met relatives I didn't even know I had. I learnt all about my mother and father, not that anyone knew where he was. There was laughter, fun, games with the other kids in the street. I was at a new school. I ate different food, dressed in different clothes, went fishing with my uncle in his boat. I had never been to the beach before, let alone gone fishing. My uncle and aunty taught me things, explained things, my worries and concerns became their worries and concerns. I got on well with my cousins. We shared and romped, did the household chores that were allotted to us, went shopping, ran messages. It was easy to please them, because I wanted to. And so, gradually at first, the fear slipped away and was replaced with confidence. Instead of being withdrawn, I became outgoing and adventurous. I was starting to live. I became a member of the under-12 Rugby League Club, Eastern Colts. I loved the game and threw myself into it with enthusiasm. Life was good.

It was during this period that I fell in love for the first time. Puppy love, they called it in those days. Two houses away from my uncle's place lived a family by the name of Chesterman. They had two daughters, twins, and it was Anne that I fell in love with. My cousins and I and the Chesterman girls often played together. We went to the same school, caught the same bus, had the same interests, joked and chided one another. And, somehow, Annie and I always seemed to end up together. There was a big chook house down the back of their place and their father had built a fair-sized cubby on the end of it for them, with an old army camp stretcher in it, made of wood and canvas.

One afternoon we were sitting on the stretcher, talking away, and a wrestle started over an old clock we were examining. I ended up on top of her and for no apparent reason I let my face drop towards hers and kissed her on the mouth. She threw her arms around my neck, pulled me down even tighter and kissed me back. Then we just looked at each other and there was this bond between us.

It was our secret, no one else knew. We used to meet there after school and kiss and touch, take our clothes off, feel, fondle and examine each other's private parts. We used to get sexually excited, but no matter how many times we tried to fuck, it never worked out. We didn't have the know-how or experience. I would try to stick my cock in her, but she'd say 'It hurts!' and I'd stop. Still, we were in love. We rode the bus together. Sat in school together. Wrote each other love notes. Whispered things to each other when no one else was paying attention. My cousins used to jibe me about the time and attention I showed her, but I didn't care. And neither did Annie.

'I hope you two aren't up to anything!' Aunty Freda would say to me, but it was usually said more in the way of guidance than with a nasty bite.

The day after my thirteenth birthday is the one I remember most about Annie and myself. It was a very hot March and we all used to swim a lot. Annie and her sister Margaret came to the house and gave me a box of sweets for my birthday. Pamela and Margaret slipped off to talk about things and Annie and I were left on the front verandah, talking and clowning around.

'Why don't we go for a swim, Jimmy?'

'The bloody place'll be packed,' I said to her.

'Well why don't we just go down to the river, to the sand spit? There'll be no one there.'

'Jesus! Aunty Freda won't like that. She's always asking what we get up to?'

We were leaning over the front rail of the verandah, close to each other. She moved till we were touching and put her arm around my back.

'Why don't you tell her you're going to check your fish traps?' she whispered.

I had about half a dozen traps along the river. They were all the rage back then. They weren't hard to build, you didn't need a boat, and the river was deep enough along the banks to just throw them in and tie them to a tree so they wouldn't wash away. It kept us in a steady supply of fresh fish. Perch, bream, the occasional flathead, not to mention turtles and eels which we didn't eat and were a source of annoyance more than anything.

'She'll know we're gonna go swimming when we take our cossies.'

Annie gave a giggle and tickled my side. 'We won't need swimmers down there. There'll be no one to see us.'

I turned and looked into Annie's eyes. A silent message passed between us. I gave her a quick peck on the lips, disengaged her arm and walked to the kitchen where Aunty Freda was knocking something up. She lived in that kitchen.

'We're just going to check the fish traps! Be back later.'

My aunty turned around from the sink top where she was working and gave me a look that said . . . Oh yeah!

'You be careful down there, you hear. There's a clean bag down in the laundry, you can take that with you.'

'We'll be right, don't worry. See you later.'

I raced down to the laundry, grabbed a bag, tore through under the house, which was built up high so the floods wouldn't reach inside, and waved the bag up at Annie.

'What are ya waitin' around up there for?' I yelled.

Annie gave a laugh, flew down the steps and ran up to me.

'What did she say?' she asked in a conspiratorial whisper.

'Nothing. Just said to be careful.'

We looked at each other and smiled. There was no need to hurry. It was the weekend and we had all the time in the world.

It was beautiful down by the river. I can close my eyes, even today, and still see and remember how it was. The

31

willows draped their lazy arms down into the water and the tide played music as it rippled over the pebbles and around the stones that littered the banks. The occasional plop as a water goanna dived in from the low branches and roots of the willows and gums that lined the banks. Shoals of long-beaked garfish swam lazily among the reeds and weed at the edges, searching for shrimps. The song of the birds, all singing their different tunes as if proclaiming peace and happiness. Butterflies, in a myriad of colours, floating in the air, then landing on the wild-flowers to taste the nectar. Dragonflies hovering above the water like miniature helicopters, forever adjusting their flight control to compensate for the warm breeze that washed over everything.

Annie and I had never been down there alone before. We simply stood there for a while, hand in hand, taking it all in.

'Let's go for a swim,' Annie said. 'The water looks beautiful.'

'Last in's lousy!' I yelled at her.

We started shedding our clothes at a furious pace. I couldn't help looking at Annie as she removed her top . . . she had gorgeous boobs.

Our clothes off, we sprinted down the bank and dived into the river. We both came up, laughing and yelling out, filling our mouths with water and spurting it in each other's direction. Splashing, diving under each other, grabbing a leg and pulling down to share a hurried kiss underwater.

After a while we found ourselves standing in waist-deep water on the sand of the spit. We held on to each other, kissing for what seemed like an eternity. Then, hand in hand, we walked in under a big weeping willow. We lay down on the cushion of soft leaves and the branches of the willow folded down all around us, concealing us from the rest of the world. We were kissing, slowly exploring each other's mouths with our tongues. I kissed and licked and sucked her beautiful boobs. The pink nipples had gone hard and stood up. Annie reached down and took my cock in her hand. It was hard and throbbing and she caressed it as if to soothe it. When I slid my hand down over the wispy soft pubic hair she gave a little moan and spread her legs wider. I pushed down further. She was slippery and wet, and my finger entered her further. Annie was moving around, pushing against my hand, and she kissed me furiously.

'Let's try again?' she said in a hoarse whisper.

I got on top of her, like I'd done many times in the past. She had always left her legs straight out before, but this time she lifted her knees and, reaching down, she guided me to the right spot. I gave a little push and she caught her breath, then she pushed up hard and I felt myself sink deeply into her. Oh God! What a feeling. It was warm and smooth and wet and held me in a velvety embrace. I pushed in and out, in and out. Annie was making little mewing sounds and kissing me wetly. I felt this strange feeling starting to rise up from deep in my balls. It sort of rose and rose in waves, making me more eager and frenzied. I placed my mouth over Annie's and kissed her.

'I love you Annie,' I said into her mouth. 'I love you.'

She moaned and pushed faster and harder and then a dam burst inside me and the feeling, the flood spurting out of me, deep inside, into Annie.

The world seemed to stop for a moment and we lay there, side by side, holding onto each other. Annie started to cry softly against my shoulder.

'What's up? Is something wrong?' I asked her.

She was silent for a moment.

'Nothing's wrong,' she said quietly, rubbing her hand over the side of my face.

'Then why were you crying?'

'I don't know. Just being silly I suppose.'

She kissed me and sat up. She looked down at me for a moment, then turned her head away.

'You won't say anything to anyone, will you?'

' 'Course I won't. What makes you say that?'

'I just thought you might tell the other boys.'

'Don't be bloody silly. What'd I want to tell them for?'

Our secret was safe and belonged just to her and me.

'You promise . . . Promise me you won't tell anyone.'

I sat up and took Annie in my arms. 'I promise I won't tell anyone.'

Annie got back to her old self after that.

'I'm going back into the water,' she said. 'Come on.'

We spent the rest of the afternoon going along the river, collecting a good feed of fish from my traps, then made our way home. We were happy and felt closer than I imagined possible.

When Annie and I arrived home we went straight under the house to the old cement tubs outside the laundry where I started to clean and scale the fish. Aunty Freda came down the back stairs and walked over to us but we didn't look up. I just kept scaling away while Annie stood there silently, watching.

'I was starting to worry about you, Jimmy. What took you so long?'

'We went looking for birds' eggs.' I had a small collection of different eggs and hoped that this excuse would get us by.

'Did you find any? You must have gone a long way. You haven't even had any lunch.'

I looked at my Aunty Freda and smiled. I could see by the look on her face she wasn't exactly happy with the explanation I'd given her. Then she looked at both of us and smiled. She knew we'd been up to something, but it just wasn't her nature to accuse unjustly.

'I'm sorry, I guess the time just slipped away. What do ya think about the fish?'

I leaned over and gave Aunty Freda a kiss on the cheek, which seemed to end the matter and quell any fears she had. Annie took this as her cue to leave.

'See you later, Jimmy. Bye everyone.'

We looked at each other for a second and that silent promise flashed between us, again unspoken.

Not long after this Annie went away. Her father worked for the government in some capacity and he was transferred to Sydney. I was devastated, heartbroken and I hardly ate anything for a week. I had lost Annie. I pined and pained. We wrote to each other for a while, but in time the world turned again. The hurt was gone.

At this stage of my life a lot of things changed for me. I had a good friend at school, Lenny Gee, and we got on like a house on fire. He used to travel from Coraki to school in Lismore because the nuns in the convent down there had expelled him and the Marist

Brothers wouldn't take him. They said he'd put one of their God-fearing pupils in the family way and the shit really hit the fan. The girl had to go up to Brisbane to have the baby, and then it was adopted out. Lenny swore black and blue that any one of a dozen could have been the father, including the Father, the parish priest, who he said was a randy old bastard.

But, good mates we became. After some requests from me, and some phone calls between my aunt and uncle and Lenny's folks, he became our weekend guest. We put another bed in my room and he'd come home with me on Friday after school, spend the weekend, then return to Coraki on the school bus on Monday afternoon. At other times I'd go down to Coraki on the bus on Friday and return Monday. This went on for a couple of years.

They were great times. And the things we did on these weekends gave us enough during the week to talk about and laugh and make plans for the next one. We rode horses, went rabbit trapping, duck shooting, fishing, teased the local sheilas and teased and tormented the Abos. Lenny's dad taught me to drive in his old fishing ute. Christ, we had some fun!

Round about this time my Uncle Ted got very sick. He was always a heavy drinker, ever since he'd returned from the war. But with all the drinking that he did he never said a word out of place to my aunty or us kids. And even when we kicked over the traces, he was fair but firm. I was nearing the end of my school days, had passed my Intermediate Certificate and wanted to become a mechanical fitter and welder. There was an opportunity for me to take on an apprenticeship at the

Broadwater Sugar Mill, but it was twenty-five miles south of Lismore and transport was going to be a problem. It was decided that I could go and live at Lenny's place and pay board. Lenny was taking on an apprenticeship at the mill too, as a fitter and turner, and we could go to work in the bus together.

So I moved camp back to Coraki, where the mongrels who had been my foster parents lived. But Lenny's mum and dad thought the sun shone out of me. They both knew Eric and Ruth and, like all the others who didn't belong to their church group, they thought they were a pair of pricks. After six months I was asked to call Lenny's parents Mum and Dad. They showered me with all the love and affection and understanding that parents would show to their own child. In fact their eldest daughter Zelma, always said they loved me more than them . . . 'and we're their real kids.'

But this never caused any problems. The kids didn't mind me being loved like that because I returned it. And this is how things stayed for 18 months or so.

Lenny's dad was a professional fisherman with a big prawn trawler, a couple of mullet boats and all the paraphernalia that was associated with the job. When I wasn't at the mill I was working on the trawler or the smaller boats, repairing, painting, mending the trawl nets or the mullet nets, corking and leading lines or fixing lobster pots. There was always something to do. Lenny hated the sea, but I loved it all. Lenny and I became more like brothers than just mates, but he was transferred to the Condong Mill up near Brisbane and the only times we saw each other after that were on long weekends and such. I became Dad Gee's compan-

ion every moment when I wasn't at the mill. The work
he did was hard, but he always seemed to be laughing,
which made it much easier. I saved my pay, gave Mum
some board and bought a motorbike with the money
Dad gave me from the fishing.

Shit! I was proud of that bike. A Norton Dominator,
it was my pride and joy. I kept it polished and sparkling, bought some leather boots and jacket, just like
Marlon Brando. I'd taken up smoking and used to think
it was shit hot sitting astride the bike with a durrie
hanging out of the corner of my mouth, squinting with
one eye so the smoke wouldn't sting it. And did the
local sheilas love that bike!

The way it worked back then was on a ride for a ride
basis and I used to encourage things a bit with a trick
I'd been shown. You'd undo the studs that kept the
seat's weather cover in place and peel it back to expose
the passenger section. Then you'd cut a tennis ball in
two and tape one half onto the seat, replace the cover
and clip it back down. When the sheila's got on there's
this nice little mound that fitted right in the slot where
it did the most good. It must have been all right because
none of them complained about it. In fact they'd shift
around a little when they got on, till it hit the spot.
You'd no sooner be down the road when you'd feel
their arms around you tighten and a hand would start
working down till it found your cock, and once it got
that far you only had to travel a little further and find
a parking spot. We had a favourite special spot at Evans
Head, called Lovers' Lane. It was a big patch of scrub,
between the beach and the river, and there were tracks
running all through it like a bloody rabbit warren.

Many of today's citizens of sterling character in the area had their first taste of the forbidden fruits in old Lovers' Lane at Evans Head.

The local police sergeant was Jack Clifton. 'Slobbery Gob' we called him, 'cause when the bastard spoke to you he'd spray you as well. He had an old Indian motorbike with a sidecar, it was the police vehicle, and we used to bait him. When it got dark we'd ride by the police station and retard the spark on the bikes. They'd backfire with a report like a 12-gauge shotgun and out he'd come, throw a leg over the Indian, kick it over and get after us in hot pursuit. That's what he intended anyway, but the Indian didn't have the pace to catch us. We even used to slow down so he could catch up a bit, then accelerate away again.

We were all in a bunch outside the movie house one Sunday night and he walked up to us and sprayed away.

'There's a couple of real smart bastards making a racket with their bikes outside my place and scarin' the shit out of my missus. If I ever catch the bastards they're gonna get the greatest boot up the arse that they'll never forget.'

He could spray all he liked but there was nothing he could do. The Keystone Cops were a model of efficiency compared to him.

There was less fun for me at the mill. One of the shift engineers really had it in for us. I don't know why, but I didn't like him much either. Harry Blake was his name. We all called him Joe Blake, and he *was* a bloody snake. He'd sneak up and watch what you were doing and then whinge and whine away at how it should be done. And if it was his shift things would have to be done his way. He made you feel like telling him to piss off, but we just had to put up with him. It wouldn't matter that we were doing the job exactly the way that some other engineer had instructed us, Joe Blake would still have to have a whinge, the silly prick.

When the mill was in full production during the cane harvest we used to work long hours and if you pulled the two-till-ten shift in the evening it was the usual practice to slip across the road to the Broadwater pub and get a couple of quick beers into us at tea time. One evening a few of us were sneaking a couple of cold ones at the break and it was decided we'd have one more for the road. Jack Swampy Marsh was the shift engineer and he was a good bloke. He didn't mind if you were a bit late getting back, as long as the job got done. But, unbeknown to us, Swampy had gone home sick and Joe Blake had been called in. Jesus! Did he go off his brain when we got back late.

'Ya sacked! The whole fuckin' lotta ya, sacked. Do ya hear me? There's a boiler down and where are you bastards? . . . Across the road on the piss. Well ya sacked. And as for you two . . . ' pointing to Bobby Claven and myself . . . 'I've got a good mind to call the bloody coppers and bung that bastard in across the road for servin' minors. Bloody look at ya. Ya both pissed and ya both sacked, along with these other drunken bastards. Go on, get . . . the bloody lotta ya.'

At that moment, we couldn't have given a hoot in hell. We were half-tanked, so off we went back to the pub and got properly pissed. And laughed about old Joe Blake till the tears ran down our faces. He was a miserable cunt of a man if ever there was one.

Somehow, I managed to ride home that night and fall into bed. In the morning I had a hangover like I'd never had before and I swore black and blue that I'd never touch another drop. I couldn't bring myself to tell Mum and Dad that I'd been sacked, so around lunchtime I rode down to the mill as usual. Mum had made me some sandwiches for my tea and I hadn't told her a thing. I felt a real bastard.

I went to the mill manager's office and asked to see him. He called me in.

'You've made a real mess of things, haven't you, Jimmy? What got into you blokes?'

'I'm sorry. Can't you give me another chance?' I all but pleaded with him.

'It's a bit late for that now, Jimmy. Harry's already rung the Apprenticeship Board and they agree with his decision. You blokes know what drinking on the job means if you're caught. Christ almighty! What came over you? You all know what Harry's like. I'm sorry, Jimmy, but it's out of my hands.'

That was that. My job was gone. I went to the pay office and collected my wages. I finished up with about a hundred and thirty quid with holiday pay, etcetera.

4

TO THIS DAY I CAN'T GIVE AN EXPLANATION FOR WHAT happened next. I went over to the Broadwater and got a few more beers into me. I still couldn't bring myself to tell Mum and Dad ... couldn't even pick up the phone and ring them. So I just hopped on my bike, headed south and rode to Sydney. I got a room at the People's Palace, which was a cheap dive run by the Salvos, and ended up working in a factory making lollies with a bunch of wogs.

I met up with a bloke called Merv Allen. He was a few years older than I was, but was someone to talk to and we seemed to get on okay. We met in the Civic Hotel, on the corner of Pitt and Goulburn Streets. I didn't know it at first, but he'd just finished a stretch in Long Bay. In fact I don't think it would have mattered all that much if I had known. That was the frame of mind I was in.

These were the days of the Bodgies and Widgies. I remember when I first met Merv, how his clothes looked so much better than mine. Black trousers with 12-inch cuffs, pink shirt and a white sports coat were the order of the day. And suede shoes with thick rubber soles. I felt like a country bumpkin and wanted to learn. All thoughts of who I was or where I had come from had to be erased. I wanted to be like a Sydney Bodgie.

They were sharp. But to dress like that took money.

It was money I didn't have, but I soon learned from Merv how to obtain it. We bashed and robbed the poofters. There seemed to be an unlimited supply of them around Sydney, and being young and handsome, with a baby face, I was the perfect bait. I would simply lure them to a place where Merv would ambush them. Some of the buggers could fight like hell, but with two of us pounding the living shit out of one it was a no-win situation for the poof. Not to mention that the first whack that Merv usually gave them was with a foot-long leather sock packed with lead shot. It would have put Iron Mike Tyson down for the count, though there was always the odd one that took a little extra.

We usually did the job on pay nights, when they were loaded. One of the poofters' favourite haunts was the Rex Hotel at the Cross . . . nobody ever referred to it in those days as Kings Cross. It was the Disneyland for adults. Merv and I would enter the pub separately. I'd go to the bar to get a drink, and it usually didn't take long before I'd have some cocksucker whispering sweet nothings in my ear. I'd play him along and suggest we go down to a nearby park. Merv would be watching proceedings from a distance. We had signs that would look quite natural and innocent to the casual onlooker, or victim, but Merv knew all right. He'd make his way to the park where he'd act like a drunk.

One night this guy followed me at a discreet distance. Still, I got him to the park, led him to a bench near where Merv was sprawled over, acting pissed.

Whack! . . . I heard the sound of the sap and I spun around, expecting to see this guy laid out. But was this poof going! He'd taken hold of Merv's throat and had him pushed back over the bench, right off balance. I ran back, got behind the poof and hit him with the hardest punch that I could, right into the kidney. His hands came from around Merv's throat at once and he straightened up, trying to suck in some air.

'You dirty bastard,' Merv croaked. 'Come on, Jimmy, let's do this cunt over properly.'

Merv smashed a wicked punch right into the poof's face and I whacked him in the kidney again as he staggered back. Merv grabbed one of his arms and swung him around hard. As the poof was going down the back of his head crunched down onto the metal armrest of the bench. He slipped over the end and went down like a rag doll.

'Shit! I think we've killed the bastard.'

'Fuck him,' Merv said. 'Grab his fuckin' wallet and let's get outta here.'

I bent over the still form of the poofter and patted around his clothing till I located his wallet. Blood was pouring out of his head and collecting in a dark pool. As I straightened up my eyes came in contact with the top of the armrest and I felt sick to my stomach as I found myself looking at a big piece of the poofter's scalp. Skin, flesh, with a tuft of hair sticking up out of it.

'Christ almighty! Look at that,' I said. Then I started running.

I was out in the street by the time Merv caught up with me.

'For Christ's sake ... slow down will ya,' he said between breaths. 'The fuckin' coppers'll be right onto us.'

'Where the fuck are we going?' I asked as I slowed down to a fast walk.

'Hampton Court, mate. We'll take it from there.'

The Hampton Court was a pretty flash sort of a pub back then. We walked into the bar and went straight to the shithouse. Over to the wall basins for a quick wash to get the sweat off our faces.

'Where's that wallet Jimmy?' Merv asked.

I took it out of my pocket, and for the first time noticed how bulky it was.

'Shit! Look at that,' I said.

The wallet was crammed with money, most of it in big bills. We went into one of the cubicles and I pulled the bank notes out. I handed them to Merv, grabbed a heap of paper from the roll, wiped the wallet all over, wrapped the dunny paper around it and dropped it into the toilet. Merv was still counting and I kept peeking out the door to make sure the coast was clear.

'Jesus! There's over two grand here, Jimmy.'

'You're kidding aren't ya?'

'Bullshit I am. No wonder the bastard put up a fight. Christ! This is our lucky night. Two fuckin' grand.'

There was twenty-three hundred quid all told, so we split it down the middle and decided to meet up down the Civic in a couple of days. With over a grand in my pocket I was on a high. I'd never had that much money at one time and I got a cab to Chequers nightclub. I felt like I owned the whole town but that the further I got away from the bloody Cross the better.

I got a table and ordered the best feed I'd ever had. Then I made my way to the bar, where there was a show on stage. I was so high on being loaded and the event that preceded it that the beer didn't seem to be having much of an effect on me. And any thought of keeping a wallet stuffed with money in low profile never occurred to me. All of a sudden these two guys sort of appeared, one each side of me, and started talking about anything and everything. They shouted me a drink and I returned the shout. This must have gone on for about an hour, till I felt this tap on my shoulder. I turned around and looked into the face of the most amazing looking woman I had ever seen in my life.

She was a dazzling blonde. Her face could only be described as beautiful . . . more than that . . . stunning. Not tall, but with a gorgeous figure, great boobs and a smile that made me melt.

'Hi sweetie,' she cooed. Then turned to the two guys with me. 'Why don't you pair of creeps fuck off and leave him alone. Can't you see he's only a kid?'

'We're only having a beer and a yarn, Margo,' the one on my left said.

'Bullshit. Piss off right now or I'll go and have a word with Tony.'

I didn't believe it. The two guys took off like a couple of scalded cats. They didn't even bother to finish their beers.

'You come over and sit with us, love,' this woman said, taking my arm. 'All those pricks wanted to do was roll you. Half the bloody joint knows you've got a quid in your pocket . . . You've been flashing it around enough. You come over with us. No bastard will worry you while we're around.'

I picked up my drink and she led me over to a table with two other sheilas and a guy sitting there. She pulled out a chair next to her own.

'You sit there, love, you'll be right. By the way my name's Margo. Margo Colenzo. What's yours?'

'Jimmy Diamond,' I replied in a voice I hardly recognised.

'That's Abe Stafford,' she said, indicating the guy. 'And that's Sue and Mandy.'

'Gidday!' I said to one and all and extended my hand to Abe.

'How ya doin'?' he said. 'Didn't ya know those two were linin' ya up?'

'Never considered it. Just thought they wanted to have a beer and a chinwag.'

'A beer and a yarn my arse. Those two mongrels'd rob their own bloody mothers.'

'How do you know that?'

'How do I know . . . Christ! Did you just come down in the last bloody shower or something? Jesus, Margo, explain it to him will ya.'

'Where are you from, love?' Margo asked me.

'Lismore.'

'Lismore! Where the fuckin' hell's Lismore?' Abe broke in.

'Right up north.'

'Never heard of the fuckin' joint. Have you?' he asked, turning to the other sheilas.

'Yeah, I have,' one of them replied.

A guy walked over, bent down and said something quietly in Abe's ear. He nodded a couple of times and turned to Margo.

'We've got to go,' he said. 'See you later.'

'Yeah, righto love,' she replied. 'Take it easy.'

I broke the silence after they'd left. 'Would you like a drink?'

'Yeah, that would be nice.' She lifted her arm and signalled. A waiter seemed to appear from nowhere with a tray in his hand and a cloth over his arm.

'What'll it be, Margo?' he asked.

'I'll have a gin sling. What do you want, love?' she asked me. 'Why don't you get off that bloody beer? It'll rot your guts.'

'What do you recommend?'

'Why don't you have a brandy, lime and soda, that's nice.'

'Try anything once,' I replied, nodding to the waiter. The waiter took off to collect the drinks. I was looking around the club.

'How long have you been in Sydney, Jimmy?'

'About three months.'

'What brought you down here?'

'I got the sack.'

'Well, where do you work here?'

'I had a job in Redfern making lollies, but I left.'

'So you're not working at all now?'

'No, not at the moment.'

The waiter arrived with the drinks. I reached into my pocket, but Margo put her hand on my arm.

'It's okay, love, I'll get these.'

It was the first time a woman had ever bought me a drink. All I could do was say 'Thanks'.

We yakked away for a while, Margo asking the occasional question as we went drink for drink in shouts.

48

The grog loosened us both up and we were laughing and having a great time. Then she asked me where I was living.

'People's Palace.'

'The People's . . . What the bloody hell are you doing in a dump like that?'

'Stuffed if I know. It's cheap.'

'It's bloody cheap all right. Jesus, you can do better than that.'

'Yeah, s'pose you're right. I might start looking around.'

'Look,' she said. 'Let's get out of here. This place is starting to give me the shits.'

'Yeah, righto. I've just about had a gutful of it too.'

When we walked out into the foyer I fully expected that we would go our separate ways. Out in the street Margo turned to the doorman.

'Get us a cab, Lou.'

'Yeah sure, Margo.'

He walked out to the kerb, whistled at a passing taxi and opened the back door.

Margo walked over and got in while I stood there, but she ducked her head down and looked over at me.

'Well, come on,' she said. 'Aren't you coming?'

I just about jumped in from where I was standing. Margo gave the driver a number in Roslyn Street, wherever that was, and the cab weaved its way uptown and headed towards the Cross. We never spoke in the cab until it pulled up outside her house.

We went through a fancy iron gate and up a couple of stairs onto a small concrete and tiled landing. Margo unlocked a grille door and then a big wooden front door. There were windows on each side of the landing and I noticed that these had bars on them. The place is a bloody fortress, I thought, as Margo walked inside and turned on some lights.

'Come on in,' she called out.

I walked past her into the hall while she relocked the grille and pushed the front door closed. I just stood there looking up and down the hall.

'Come on through.' She breezed past me. 'I'll get us a drink.'

I followed her down the hall and into a beautiful room with wall-to-wall carpet and soft rugs strewn around. There was a bar against one wall with a huge mirror behind it that made the room look larger than it actually was. A low oval table decorated the centre of the room, surrounded by soft comfortable lounge chairs, and to one side there was a big settee with cushions piled on it. Velvet drapes covered the windows and the walls were decorated with paintings and prints in gilded frames.

'Sit down and take the weight off,' she said. 'Would you like a Scotch and soda?'

'Yeah, sure,' I said, though I'd never had one before.

I sat down on the big sofa while Margo left the room and came back with a tray of ice-cubes and a mesh-covered soda siphon. She popped a couple of cubes into two tumblers, poured some Scotch over them and squirted in the soda water with a hiss. Kicked off her shoes, twiddled her toes, picked up the drinks and came over and sat down beside me.

'Here,' she said, passing me the drinks. 'Hold these.'

I took the glasses out of her hands. She got up and pulled on the oval table, which glided over to us on its castors. Then she sat down beside me again and took one of the drinks out of my hand.

'Cheers,' she said.

I clinked her glass with my own and returned the salute.

After a few drinks and general talk I started to yawn.

'You're not going to go to sleep on me are you?'

'I'm pretty stuffed. It's been a long day.'

Margo got up from beside me, left the room and came back a moment later with something cupped in her hand. She offered the hand to me. Lying in her palm were two tiny purple tablets, shaped like little hearts.

'Here. Get these into you. They'll fix you up.'

I didn't even question her as to what they were. She made me feel so comfortable and at ease I simply washed them down with some of my drink.

'Thanks a lot,' I said.

'Don't worry, love. You'll come good in a moment when *they* hit the spot.'

It could have been potassium cyanide that I had taken for all I knew. But one moment I was half-pissed and ready to put my head down, the next I could have run a bloody marathon. I was yakking away and laughing, full of life. The pills gave me a confidence I'd never had before. They made me unafraid, bold. I reached over and put my arm around Margo and drew her closer to me. I put my other hand under her chin, lifted up her beautiful face and looked into her eyes for a moment. They were dark blue, and as they looked back into mine they seemed to have the power to look right into my

51

soul. I lowered my face to hers and kissed her softly on the mouth. Her lips parted. They were delicate, soft and warm.

It was as if someone had turned on a switch, I felt such a strong current charging through me. As I slowly lifted my face from hers, our lips stayed together for just a fraction of a second, as if they were trying not to be parted. I sat back, then reached forward and took my drink off the table and took a gulp. Margo straightened up beside me. I felt her fingers lazily caressing the back of my neck.

'Has anyone ever told you, Jimmy, that you're a real beautiful boy?'

'Nah,' I said. 'Don't be silly.'

'You are you know. You're a very pretty boy.'

Any other time this sort of talk would have had me red in the face. But for some reason—maybe the pills, or the charisma from Margo I felt washing over me—I didn't mind it when she said it.

'You're pretty nice yourself,' I said to her. 'You really are.'

That night was my introduction into the Sydney underworld. My baptism. I never left Margo's place that night and I stayed there with her for two more years. In that all-too-short time Margo taught me something new about everything. I was a kid of eighteen, she was thirty, but something was there that drew us together.

Margo Colenzo had been an orphan, just like me, and had grown up taking all the knocks that life could dish out. It hadn't left a blemish on her beautiful face or body but, deep inside, it had left some terrible wounds. Like me, she hid them from the world. When she was going to school she'd been a thief. Been shunted from home to home. Spent time in Parramatta Girls' Reformatory. Become a prostitute, walking the pavements of the Cross and Darlinghurst. Gone through the trauma of backyard abortion, performed with a crochet needle, that left her unable ever to conceive children. She'd been arrested on numerous occasions for procuring, and had spent time in Long Bay Women's Prison. She was also reputed to have shot dead the person who had stabbed and killed her only real lover. She was a beautiful velvet glove that concealed an iron fist, but when she opened to me she became soft and comforting. Now she owned a string of brothels and sly grog joints around the Cross and in the outer suburbs.

Margo became my lover and companion, my friend, mate, confidante and confessor, my everything. She taught me how to make love in slow easy lessons that were full of feeling, emotion, care and consideration. I never knew how to make a woman climax. Margo taught me how. I always knew when she wanted me to make love to her in a special way. She would take hold of me, and gently whisper . . . 'Be nice to me.'

Margo was also a mother figure. Teaching me what clothes to wear, how to wear them, what colours suited me best. She showered me with gifts of clothing, never saying a word. I would come home and hanging on the front of the big wardrobe I would find a couple of shirts, or trousers, a nice jacket. I'd try them on, and they always fitted and suited me. She gave me a gold ring with a diamond in it, a solid gold bracelet and watch. The bracelet had our names engraved on it, together with the word '*Forever*'.

We went everywhere together. She was proud of me, and I was proud to be seen and be with her. I gave her all my love, all my devotion and loyalty. She was like an intoxicating drink that I couldn't get enough of. She was my guardian angel and the most unselfish person I ever met. She would do anything for me, without question. At times it was as if she were clairvoyant, knowing exactly what I was thinking, and would please me with the very thing that was in my thoughts. Nothing Margo asked me to do was too much. I lived to please her and love her. We had each other. It was as if we were looking at a street lamp on a summer's evening, and the rest of the world was a myriad of bugs, busily bashing their brains out, getting nowhere.

In the world we inhabited, Margo was respected, and the very fact that I belonged to her made everything right. I met cops, bent, and on the take, who took her money to look the other way so she could stay in business. Cops on the Vice and Consorting Squads, 21 Division, from sergeants to inspectors, and all on a first-name basis. Even they respected Margo. She was the true Queen of the Underworld. There were a couple of pretenders for the position, but it really belonged to her. With her love and protection I was safe even from the Devil himself.

A couple of days after I moved in with Margo the story of the poofter in the park broke. The guy was in hospital, in a critical condition, and not expected to live. I was reading the paper and the story was on the front page.

'Christ!' I said. 'I hope he doesn't die.'

'Why?' she asked me. 'What do you know about it?'

Slowly at first, and then with a gush, I told her what had happened and how I had been living. I couldn't tell her any lies, she was like a truth drug. One look at me with those deep blue eyes and I would melt. I couldn't hide anything from Margo, not even in the early days.

'What arrangements have you got with this bloke . . . what's his name . . . Merv?'

'I told him I'd meet him in a couple of days down at the Civic. Shit! That's today.'

'Jimmy, if you've got any brains at all you won't meet him. And by the way, we've got to get your stuff out of that bloody rathole you were living in.'

'What about my bike?'

'What bloody bike?'

I explained to her that I had my Norton in the basement garage.

'Well we'll have to get that too. How long have you known this Merv?'

I told her how we'd met, and answered every question that I could about him.

'Has he got any form?'

'What do you mean?'

'Is he known to the police?'

'He came out of the Bay not long before I met him.'

'What did he go inside for?'

'Assault and robbery. He got eighteen months.'

'Jesus Christ! He'll be one of the first buggers the cops'll want to talk to. Let me tell you something, Jimmy. This guy you bashed was Silver Phil Parker. He's an SP bookie and he'd have been paying off someone on the Gaming Squad. They'll have a score to settle, not to mention Phil's mates. He might be a poofter, but he's got some nasty friends.'

'Do you know the bloke?' I asked her.

'No, not well. I've seen him around, and I know a few of his connections.'

I watched her. She had stopped talking and was looking into the distance, thinking.

'Right!' she said at last, 'I'm going to call a cab. Go down to the Palace and get your stuff and your bike. Then come straight back here. Please, Jimmy, I know what I'm doing. Listen to me, love.'

'I give you my word,' I said.

To be honest, I really didn't want to go at all. I'd only known Margo for a few days but it was like I'd known her all my life. The ride down in the cab wasn't too bad, but when I walked into the foyer of the Palace I imagined every set of eyes was glued to me and a thousand coppers were about to pounce. But I got my gear, turned in the key, made my way down to the basement and rode away with one eye glued to the rear-vision mirrors all the way back to Margo's.

'See,' I said. 'I'm back. I told you I would.'

She gave me that smile of hers that was worth a king's ransom.

'I knew you would, Jimmy. You wouldn't be staying here if I'd thought you'd let me down. Take the bike down to the garage.'

She opened the high gate at the side of the house and I rode the Norton into the garage, where she kept a Humber Hawk. I left the stuff I had in the saddle-bags and the duffel bag tied to the back. I walked up to Margo and she put her arms out and held me to her. We went inside and I kissed her softly once more, tasting her mouth, taking in the scent that only came from her. I kissed her eyes, her nose, her chin. I put my face in her beautiful blonde hair and breathed in her perfume. She put her hand at the back of my neck and pulled my face down to hers and kissed me a long time.

'Be nice to me Jimmy.'

We lay naked in bed, exploring each other's bodies. Margo's skin had the texture of soft rose petals. I wanted to eat her, and still have her. Tasting, nibbling, fondling, caressing and feeling. She sat up and, facing away from me, she took my penis in her hand, caressing and teasing it. She bent down and licked the top of it, round and round, then she took me into her mouth, working away with a slow wet rhythm, stopping now and then to lick and play with me. I pulled her over until her knees were on each side of my chest and pulled her back until I could look right into her. I pushed my tongue against the lips of her vagina. I loved the taste of her. The more I used my tongue to lick and probe, the wetter she became. I put my mouth over her and kissed her as if I were kissing her on the mouth, my tongue exploring. I reached forward and took a breast in each hand and squeezed the nipples softly. She stopped sucking me and turned around, lowering herself down onto me until I sank into her all the way. Leaning forward she kissed me and moaned.

'Oh my baby boy don't ever leave me. Say you'll never leave me.'

She worked herself up and down, moaning and kissing me. I could feel myself near that point of no return and she moved faster and faster until I exploded into her with a gush.

'I love you, I love you,' I yelled. ' Oh God! I love you Margo.'

Her back arched and she clenched her teeth together, then opened her mouth in a silent scream. I pushed hard and fast up into her to assist the climax I knew was coming and, placing the palms of my hands over her lovely breasts, I kneaded them gently. Something inside her let go and the scream broke ... like the pound of a wave that has hit the shore, then runs up the sand till its momentum has abated.

'Aaaaaaaaa aaaah ah. Oh! you're beautiful,' she said. 'I love you. You're beautiful.'

She lay down beside me, holding me in her arms, stroking my damp hair and placing little light kisses on my face. She looked right into my eyes.

'Nobody has ever made me come like you do, Jimmy. What is it?'

I didn't answer. I couldn't answer. There were no words to describe it. Maybe we filled that lonely hurtful gap that only those who have experienced it could recognise. I was the child she could never have. I was the lover she had lost. She was the mother I'd been denied and she was the lover, the girl that I'd lost. She had known cruelty and hurt, just as I had known cruelty and hurt. Men who had payed to 'love' her, the short time, had meant nothing to her. They were a means to an end, a source of income. We were two wounded animals whom fate had brought together, to lick and soothe each other's wounds. Our spirits were locked together, we were immortal.

Jimmy and Margo Forever. The bracelet said it all.

5

SIX MONTHS WENT BY, AND DURING THIS TIME PHIL Parker recovered from the coma and was placed in a convalescent home. He was a walking vegetable. Life for Margo and me had become one big game. We went out a lot. Spent hours at Tamarama beach, Bondi and Manly. We were invited to parties, and we threw parties. Jesus! They never seemed to end. You'd just get over one hangover and you'd have another. Sleep was never a problem. If we were tired we'd just drop a couple of the old purple hearts and—whammo!—we'd be right as rain.

I had her name tattooed on my wrist for one and all to see. Margo was thrilled. I had branded myself with her name. Whenever we sat close, her fingers would rub back and forth across the tattoo on my wrist in an effort, as she explained, 'to rub it in deeper . . . so it never comes off.'

We would sit in the Cashmere restaurant till the early hours. Passing time with friends and acquaintances who were the people of the night. We both loved the place. It had an intimacy about it that kept drawing us back. Since the moment of my involvement with this beautiful person my life had undergone a complete metamorphosis. From the brash country boy, riddled with doubt and uncertainty, I had become a man who was sure and confident. Instead of taking the knocks that life dished out and withdrawing into my shell, I said fuck the world and spat in the face of adversity. The world was mine. We lived only for the day and lived each one as if there were no tomorrow.

There was a power about the Cashmere that enveloped Margo and me whenever we entered. It was like a pair of welcome arms that hug and embrace and give assurance after a long and hazardous journey. The lighting was subdued and the pungent odour of coffee hung in the air. The place had the ability to put us in a thoughtful frame of mind and we often philosophised for hours on end on life's misfortunes and achievements, its successes and sorrows.

One of the walls inside the Cashmere was covered with a gigantic painting of women, all of them with the same face. The women were depicted in a satanic ritual, in lurid, lustful and exotic contortions. The face of the women was demonic and had a hypnotic effect. The body was emaciated, and scarred like an anorexic who had been flogged and beaten with the lash. This evil angel danced and cavorted on cloven feet as she meandered her way across the mural of life, on her way home to Hades.

The painter was known as Rosalie the Witch and she became a close friend of ours. We spent hours together, discussing her beliefs and habits. She believed that if God created man—stressed with the biblical text '*Let us make man in Our image, according to Our likeness*'—then evil was also part of God's doing and planning, that dropped like a storm from heaven. She riveted our attention to the words '*us*,' and '*Our*,' and '*likeness*,' emphasising that God, with these very words, existed in the plural and thus there must be two. If we were made in their likeness, then the Gods must also be good and evil. It was a fascinating idea and one, I think, that must hold some credibility.

Rosalie would come around home armed with a concoction she made and always drank. It had a gin base and some herbs and spices, boiled in an old coven recipe to which she had added her own ingredients. Margo and I often had a glass with her. It had a strange taste. It seemed to scald and chill the mouth both at once and then take you to another time and dimension in a pleasant, euphoric journey. She called us her children and though others would shudder and cringe from her, we felt completely at ease in her presence.

The three of us were sitting in the lounge room late one evening, drinking and listening to a record that Rosalie had brought around. Wagner's 'Ride of the Valkyries.' Rosalie would get up from the lounge when it came to an end and start it again and again. We were drinking our own grog at the time, while Rosalie was sipping away at her special brew. On impulse, we decided that we'd have some too. Rosalie's Elixir of Life we christened it. After a few glasses the music took on a new meaning. It seemed to pulsate and burst within us. Margo and I became oblivious to the outside world as the music thundered and raced through the corridors of a different time, a different place. We reached for each other as if our minds and thoughts were one. We kissed deeply and passionately, tore the clothes from each other's bodies. Depravity became a sweetness, an exotic essence of love as we probed and sucked the very

61

juices from each other's bodies. Savouring the taste of each other, exploring areas that we had never travelled into before. Our love was out of control, raging and beautiful. Like two suns that had reached a critical mass, that finally imploded and exploded at the same instant. We were totally naked and unashamed. Rosalie was there, but not as a person or a voyeur. She was one of Odin's handmaidens, hovering over us like an angel over a battlefield. And as the memories of our hurts and wounds lifted away from us like the souls from slain warriors, she gathered them up and carried them off to Valhalla.

After the love, we didn't even bother to dress again. We just sat there, holding each other, with tears of joy and happiness, sorrow and sadness, running down our faces. We kissed each other's faces to pick up the droplets, not wanting them to fall away and evaporate. It was a saline communion, welding us together into a perfect coexistence.

Finally, we showered and dressed. Then, linked arm in arm with Rosalie in the middle, we skipped and danced our way to the Cashmere.

6

BUT THE OUTSIDE WORLD WAS STILL THERE, AND WE couldn't keep it at bay.

One night Margo's collector, Bernie Walker, was found shot dead outside Thommo's two-up school. Margo had known Bernie since she was a kid and he not only managed her business empire but was also like a big brother to her. I had only known Bernie for a year but had come to like him pretty well, so it was as if we had lost one of the family. After his death, the doorbell never stopped pealing, the phone ringing, coppers arriving at all hours of the day and night, asking questions. Some were coppers we knew we could rely on, others were not. But the law of *omerta* applied. In front of the coppers, nobody knew anything or said anything. Of course *we* knew who did the job on Bernie, and a time would come when the score would be settled, out of court. But that time would have to wait.

As far as the police were concerned I had been in the background up to this point. I was just Margo's bloke and they knew I had no part in her business. But with Bernie's demise, I got more than my fair share of attention. When the coppers we couldn't rely or depend on came around and started firing questions at me, especially the bulls from the Homicide Squad, Margo was always there. She never left the room and refused point-blank to do so, even under the threat of arrest.

'Why don't you leave him alone,' she'd say. 'He knows nothing about any of this.'

Of course the coppers always relied on their favourite line at this point. 'We're only doing our job, Margo.'

'Well why don't you just piss off and do it somewhere else,' she'd snap back. 'You know where Jimmy was at the time, you know where I was, so stop wasting our fucking time and yours and bugger off and leave us alone.'

This line of attack worked until Detective Sergeant Jack Kelly came around with his offsider. Kelly was a real cunt. He might have looked more like a headmaster than a copper, but he was worse than the crims he arrested and had more notches on his gun than Trigger Davis—and that's putting it mildly. The crims hated Kelly and most of the cops did too. But he had rank in the CIB, and that meant when Kelly said jump all anyone could do was ask how high.

To Kelly, Margo's outbursts were like water off a duck's back. He drilled me with those cold eyes of his that were always magnified a little through the rimless spectacles he wore.

'You're coming downtown with us,' he said. 'Right now.'

An enraged tigress was calm in comparison with Margo. She screamed, spat, cursed and abused Kelly till I thought she was about to have some sort of a seizure. Kelly just stood there with a sardonic smile on his face. He knew he was hurting Margo by taking me away, and causing grief in the greatest possible way.

As sudden as Margo's outburst of fury might have

been, so too was the silence that followed. She became pensive for a few moments, then slowly turned to face Kelly and addressed him in a voice that dripped with vitriol.

'If you harm one hair on his head ... I swear that you will rue the day you ever walked into this house.'

Kelly's offsider was visibly shaken by her remark. He took a pace back from me, as if his proximity placed him in some jeopardy. And the smile vanished from Kelly's face, too, but he reached out nonetheless and tapped me on the shoulder.

'Righto,' he said. 'Let's go.'

Not another word was spoken till we were in the car and a fair distance from the house. We were heading down William Street. The offsider was driving, I was sitting in the back, and Kelly was in the front passenger seat. He slowly turned round, pushed his hat back a little and looked at me, seething.

'You think you're a real fucking smartarse don't ya? Well let me tell you something you cunt. You think you're all safe and sound because you've got that pretty blonde moll of yours fuckin' looking after ya. Well she might have some people in this town scared shitless but she doesn't fuckin' scare me. I could push you out of this car right here and now and blow your fuckin' head off—attempting to escape, that's what we'd call it. What have you got to say about that, smartarse'.

A demon rose inside me. I had learnt more about Kelly with his little speech than if I had read his whole case history. He was a coward, just like that rotten Eric from my childhood, and I wanted to see him bleed. This cunt Kelly. A hate spread through me like blood on blotting paper, getting wider and darker all the time.

'Well, what have you got to say, smartarse?' he yelled.

'Fuck you!' I screamed at him. And spat in his face.

He recoiled and wiped his arm across his face. Then he looked at his sleeve in the gloom of the car and felt his face with his fingers, as if my saliva had scarred him.

'I'm gonna kill you . . . you dirty bastard,' he roared. 'Come on,' he said to his offsider. 'I want this cunt downtown quick. I'm gonna give him something to remember.' He turned back to me. 'Yoooou fuckin' smartarse.'

His partner glanced back over his shoulder for an instant and spoke for the first time during the trip.

'You want to take it bloody easy, mate. What the hell are you trying to prove?'

'He'll take it fuckin' easy when I'm finished with the bastard.' Kelly ground the words out between clenched teeth.

With my hands manacled behind my back I was pushed and half-dragged into the Police Headquarters building. Up the lift to the CIB Homicide Squad section. A few faces turned as Kelly dragged me in by the shirt-front.

'We've got a real smartarse here,' he said to one and all. 'Get in here you bastard.' He dragged me into an office, then slammed me down into a chair. 'Keep an eye on this cunt,' he said to his offsider, who had been tailing behind. Then stormed out of the room.

'Fuck me, mate,' Kelly's partner said. 'What did you have to carry on like that for?'

'He can go and get fucked,' I replied as venomously as I could.

'Jesus, you're really asking for it aren't you?'

I didn't reply. I just sat there seething with anger and hatred for Kelly.

He came back into the room at a fast pace. It was obvious from his damp hair that he'd been washing his face, and I could smell Lifebuoy soap.

'Come with me, bastard. I've got something for you.'

Kelly dragged me up and off the chair, out the door and down the hall. Pulling me into a small bathroom, he got behind me and pushed me over the front of the washbasin. It was full to the brim with the water he must've just washed in. It had a milky colour and a few suds still floated on top. He placed a hand on the back of my neck and grabbed the handcuffs on my wrists with his other hand.

'So you like to spit do you, ya cunt. Well spit a bit of this out.'

Pushing down on my neck and lifting up on the handcuffs at the same time, he forced my head into the basin. Soapy water cascaded over the sides, pouring onto the lino-covered floor. I held my breath and tried to straighten up. I couldn't. He had a vice-like grip on the back of my neck, and with my arms up behind me acting like two levers I couldn't get my head out of the water. I held onto my breath until my lungs were on fire. My eyes and nose were stinging from the carbolic in the soap. When my breath finally exploded in a cloud of bubbles I lifted a foot and kicked backwards with my shoe. It connected heavily with one of Kelly's shins and, as he went backwards, he dragged me out of the sink.

'You fuckin' bastard,' he yelled.

Gulping for air, I heard him only faintly. My ears and nose and throat were full of soapy water and I started gagging. Kelly tried pushing me forward again, but he lost his footing on the wet floor and went down backwards, pulling me with him. We slammed into the half-opened bathroom door, closing it with a crash. Then we toppled down onto the slippery floor together. I fell back on top of Kelly and the air whooshed out of him. Running feet came pounding down the hall. Someone was trying to open the door but we were jammed against it. Kelly had released his hold on me and I rolled off him. He got to his hands and knees and, as he did so, the door half-opened and a copper jammed himself in the space and looked down at us.

'Jesus, Jack! What the fuck's going on?'

Kelly got to his feet, panting and puffing. The other copper came over and helped me up. Both Kelly and I were soaking wet and dripping water.

'Hang onto this bastard . . . I'll be back in a minute. I've got a bit more to say to him yet.'

Kelly left the bathroom. The copper who had helped me up led me back down the hall to a closed door with 'Interview' written on it and led me inside. The room was empty, except for a table and two chairs.

'Wait here,' was all he said.

In less than a minute, he was back.

'You'd better dry yourself off a bit,' he said, tossing a couple of towels onto the table. 'You're dripping bloody water everywhere.'

'How the hell do I do that with my hands locked up behind my back?' I asked.

'Shit! Hang on a minute.'

He left again and returned in a short while. Turning me around, he undid the cuffs.

'Righto,' he said. 'See how you go now. Are you okay?'

I didn't reply, but picked up a towel and started to dry myself off. My left wrist was bleeding where the handcuff had cut into it during the struggle. I dried myself as best I could.

'Yeah,' the copper said. 'That'll have to do you for a while.'

He came forward with the handcuffs, to put them back on, and when I lifted my hands he saw the blood.

'Oh Christ! Look at that. Listen, wrap a bloody towel around that and follow me. Don't try anything silly.'

I did as he said and he led me back to Kelly's office before going off in search of a first-aid kit. Kelly's off-sider walked into the room, looked at me, and sat down.

It was an hour before Kelly came back, still looking the worse for the scuffle we'd had. No one had said a word to me in all this time. They all seemed to be avoiding me like the plague. A uniformed cop had replaced Kelly's partner and, apart from me requesting something to drink and a cigarette, which he gave me, we both sat in stony silence.

'Righto now,' Kelly said. 'What do you know about this Bernie Walker thing? And I don't want any fuckin' bullshit.'

'I don't know what you're on about. And I don't have

to give you any bullshit, or any of anything. I don't know a thing.'

Kelly turned to the uniformed cop. 'I think this bastard would like another trip to the bathroom.' He turned around to me. 'Now you . . . you fuckin' smart-arse, you're going to sign a record of interview, one way or another.'

'I told you,' I said. 'I won't be saying or signing any bloody thing.'

'*Where are they?*'

It was a stern voice that interrupted Kelly. A voice of authority. There was the sound of chairs scraping hurriedly back. Someone said 'Sir?'

'Where's Detective Sergeant Kelly and the prisoner? Is everyone deaf here?'

'In his office, Sir.'

Footsteps approached and a grey-haired uniformed officer came through the door, followed by a tall neatly dressed guy carrying a briefcase. Kelly jumped to his feet.

'Evening, sir,' he said.

Kelly's greeting was met with a stony look. The uniformed cop looked at me for a moment, then spoke.

'My name is Superintendent Windsor. This gentleman with me is a solicitor. He would like to have a few words with you. Do you want to talk with him?'

I nodded my head.

'Okay,' he said, and turned to the solicitor with a nod. Then, pointing a finger at Kelly: 'You . . . Come with me.'

'Right, Sir,' said Kelly.

He made towards the door in the wake of the superintendent, but looked back over his shoulder at the last moment and gave me a look that said . . . You'll keep, you bastard.

The solicitor sat down at the table and offered his hand, which I shook.

'Mr Diamond, my name, for the record, is Lawrence Galbally. I've been retained by Miss Colenzo to represent you. That is, of course, if you are agreeable. It looks as though they've been giving you a rather hectic time.'

'What have I been charged with?'

'That's the point. You haven't been charged with anything. They have no right to keep you here like this, and they certainly can't question you in this manner. Now would you like me to represent you?'

'Well if Margo sent you I suppose you'd better.'

'Miss Colenzo is really quite concerned about you. I'm going to have a word with the superintendent. You wait here. In the meantime, is there anything else I can do?'

'I wouldn't mind something to drink and a smoke.'

'I'm afraid I don't smoke myself, but I'll see what can be arranged.'

With that he left the room.

Some minutes later a plain-clothes cop came into the room with a mug of coffee, a packet of cigarettes and a box of matches.

'I believe you can use these,' he said with a smile. 'Don't set fire to Kelly's office, for Christ's sake, will you?'

'What's going on?' I asked him.

'Look mate, I don't know anything other than I was

ordered to bring these to you. I don't even work on the same squad as Kelly.'

He left the room and I drank some of the coffee, smoked a couple of cigarettes and waited. Half an hour later, Lawrence Galbally was back. He sat down beside me again and talked in quiet tones.

'There will not be any charges laid if we don't press the matter of this assault on you. Apparently Detective Sergeant Kelly is not too impressed with you spitting on him. But the police are prepared to waive their right if we play ball. Do you understand what I'm saying? You do know don't you that, technically, spitting is an assault? My recommendation to you is that we grab what we've got. In other words, we agree to their proposal.'

'I'll go along with whatever you say. You know best. Thanks for the smokes and the coffee.'

'Don't mention it,' he said and left the room again.

Five minutes later he was back with the superintendent.

'You're free to go,' said the super. 'And keep your nose clean.' He nodded to Galbally and left the room.

'All right then. We can make tracks. I'll give you a lift to Miss Colenzo's.'

When we got back to Roslyn Street Margo gave a little squeal when she saw me and tried to reach me through the grille before she had even unlocked it.

'Here he is, safe and sound,' said Galbally. 'I'll be popping along then.'

'Thanks Lawrence,' Margo called.

Galbally just gave a wave and walked back to his car.

The grille opened and Margo grabbed me. I held onto her, rubbing my face in her hair. Her face lifted up to mine and I kissed her, slowly and tenderly.

'Thanks sweetheart. I love you,' I said to her.

'What did the bastard do to you?'

'Please Margo, let it go. I'm back home. That's all that matters.'

'Whatever you want, Jimmy,' she said, still holding me. 'Whatever you want.'

She made a bath for me and we both soaked in it for at least an hour, washing each other and doing great things. She put a dressing on my wrist, muttering 'That bastard. That dirty rotten bastard.'

We went to bed and fell asleep in each other's arms.

7

WE THREW A PARTY TO CELEBRATE MY VICTORY OVER Kelly. Rosalie came along, accompanied with her special brew, and I asked her for the recipe.

'We mustn't play at making the potions unless we are the chosen,' was her knowing reply.

One and all came to the party, including a couple of coppers who were on the take and promised to cocka-too for us, so a raid from the Consorting Squad was out of the question. We drank and danced and sang, told dirty yarns, teased and poked shit at each other, downed purple hearts and sent out for food. It was more like a Roman orgy than a party. Some of Margo's girls were there, on the job to keep the unescorted gentry amused.

Christ! The money that was spent on enjoyment and having fun around us could have paid off the national debt. But Margo's philosophy was that we can't take it with us. 'We may as well live well, play hard, die young,' she said grandly, 'and have a good-looking corpse.'

I received pats on the back and 'Good on ya son' from one and all. Not because I was home, but because I hadn't said a word. Being staunch was the name it was given. Once you had established that, you were accepted, you were in. No amount of money could buy acceptance like that. You had to earn it the hard way . . . be arrested by the worst cop . . . then cop the worst he and his mates could dish out and come away saying 'Fuck you' without uttering a word of assistance. The word travels down the grapevine awful fast. The coppers on the take soon let it be known if someone had squealed. After all, if the enterprise that was feeding them their dirty money came unstuck they didn't receive their pay-offs. So it was in their interests to eradicate the gutless, and their reports were given with ruthless efficiency. Even down to carbon copies, at times, of signed confessions and such.

The vacuum left by the death of Bernie Walker had still not been filled. Margo was running around trying to keep it all together. The bloody phone never stopped. What about this? Who's going to take care of that? Will it be all right if this or that is done? Can we take this bloke's promissory note or cheque? Who's going to pick up the grog and deliver it? All of the million and one things that Bernie used to take care of. Abe was used to handle a bit of it, but that was not his role. He helped out to oblige, but not really willingly. His main role was one of retained enforcer, and running the gaming rooms for Margo and Joe. Oh, Margo coped all right. However, it was not in her best interests to be in the front line, so to speak. The further she could distance herself from the organisation without losing control of it the better. She had accumulated quite a string of brothels, the 'shops' we called them, and sly grog outlets where you could get beer and spirits after pub hours, seven days a week. We did more business after hours than the bloody pubs did all week long. She also had an interest, more of a partnership with Abe and Joseph Flood, in a gambling den. But running these things was really men's work. She was known as a no-nonsense lady and well respected. No one dared cross her. But it was the guys she kept on the payroll who took care of the dirty work.

One night we were lying in bed. 'You can't keep this up,' I said to her.

'I've got to. With Bernie gone ...'

'Well you've got me.'

'Oh Jimmy, what do you know about the business?'

'Bugger all, but you could teach me. At least I could do the collections for you. Take some of the pressure off.'

'Would you really like to?'

''Course I'd like to. I wouldn't have volunteered otherwise. Look, let's face it, love. Spending time with you and loving you is everything to me, but I just can't go on sitting here day after day like a stale bottle of piss. I've got to do something. Just let me have a go. If I can do it with you, so much the better.'

She sat up and looked down at me. 'I don't like it, Jimmy. I don't want what happened to Bernie to happen to you.'

'Oh bullshit, Margo. For Christ's sake, I haven't been around as long as Bernie was and I may still be a little wet behind the bloody ears but let's be honest here ... How can I put this? ... I don't want to hurt you but ... you know and I know why Bernie got the chop. He went outside the circle and asked the *Famiglia* to do him a favour. But when they called it in he didn't play ball. Christ almighty, I heard you and Abe talking about it for two bloody hours at my party. What harm can come to me doing the collections and delivering piss? Come on, sweetie, let me help. I feel like a bludger.'

She bent down and kissed me, then lay back and propped her head in her hand, just looking at me. Then she smiled. God, she had a glorious smile. I would have crawled over a mile of broken glass just for one of Margo's smiles.

'You'll be careful?'

' 'Course I'll be careful . . . I'll carry a gun if you like.'

She dropped back down on the bed, her eyes shut tightly.

'God, Jimmy,' she said, 'don't start talking like that.'

I gathered her into my arms and kissed her lovely face.

'I'm sorry, I'm sorry . . . But you know what I mean. I'll be careful, real careful.'

She didn't say a word, as if she was afraid to speak. Just nodded her head in approval.

We lay for another hour or two, going over the pros and cons and how things were usually done. She'd call Lawrie Galbally to take me around the shops and introduce me to the boss girls and she would personally call all of them first. It wasn't wise, not in a legal sense anyway, to be seen around the shops. She owned the houses and paid the rates, but as far as the law was concerned that was all they'd be able to prove. If ever there was trouble, and the shit hit the fan, I was to keep out of it and call Abe. I didn't have to worry about the girls' commission as the boss girls had all that in hand, and I wasn't to carry any receipts. Margo would give me some unlisted numbers to call if there were any raids. The instructions went on like this for quite some time. I was the new kid on the block and it was important that I learn fast. Real fast. After a while she said . . .

'I'm still bloody worried, Jimmy.'

'It'll be okay, love. Don't worry.'

But deep down I was as concerned as she was. Margo was so important to me I didn't want to let her down. The pride I felt whenever she and I went somewhere was beyond words. Heads would turn to look at her and there was the occasional wolf whistle from some unseen admirer. The looks I received when walking arm in arm with her were looks of downright envy. But above all this she made me feel strong. I felt I could beat everything and everyone.

When I was living with my uncle and aunty, two nights a week I used to train at the Police Boys' Club, boxing. Our instructor, Alf Smith, had been a light-heavyweight champ, and he took a lot of time with me.

'You've got a lot of natural ability there, Jimmy,' he kept telling me. 'You should use it and take up fighting.'

I always felt confident. I never ran away from a fight at school and after a while the other guys didn't want to tangle.

'You've got a real killer instinct there,' Alf kept saying. 'It makes you hit hard. That's the difference in the ring. Some blokes can box, but when it comes to delivering a killer punch something inside them puts the brakes on. They're afraid they might hurt him or somethin'. But you're goin' for the jugular all the time, like you want to hurt 'em. And you hit real hard, Jimmy.'

Some people, I feel sure, were born better fighters

than others. But in my case, even if I was a little better equipped than the next bloke, every time I hit someone I was bashing that bastard Eric and his razor-strop. So when anything started I was dynamite, with a very short fuse.

It was this type of intense emotion, coupled with the protectiveness I felt for Margo, that had me in the eyes of the constabulary again. It wasn't as if I went looking for trouble. It just happened. We were in the right place but at the wrong time.

EARLY ONE EVENING WE HAD DECIDED TO SEE A MOVIE and had caught a cab downtown so we could eat at Chequers beforehand. After the meal, we were ambling up George Street, where we received the usual looks and wolf whistles and such. As we dashed across the road to the movie theatre we were forced to go between some parked cars. Margo was in front and there was a guy leaning against the boot of the car on our left. When he saw Margo he called out, with a strong foreign accent.

'Oooh la la! Hello darleeng.'

Margo ignored him, but as she was just about to pass this mongrel he reached down quickly and pinched her on the left cheek of her arse. Margo jumped and gave a little squeal of fright.

She spun around to say something, but in that instant I saw red and erupted. I virtually leapt at the guy. He saw me coming but I didn't give him enough time to lift his hands up as I smashed him square in the face with the hardest right I could throw. I felt the bone and cartilage in his nose give way, and the shock of the punch travelled up my arm. The force of the blow, plus this bastard's backward defensive movement, hurled him onto the pavement. There were a dozen or so people standing around out front and all their eyes were focused on us. I jumped onto the footpath, and from somewhere in the background I heard Margo scream out . . .

'Jiiimy no.'

'Get up you bastard,' I roared and kicked him in the side as hard as I could.

As the wog slowly got to his feet, there was blood pouring out of his nose, running down over his mouth and chin, dripping onto the footpath. His eyes were already starting to puff and close up. The damage I had done held me back for that fraction of a second and from nowhere the bastard pulled a knife and lunged at me. I reached forward to deflect the thrust, but at the last moment he hooked the knife and stuck it into my right forearm, all the way through. I looked at my arm quickly, taking in the knife embedded in it, then up at this bastard.

'You cunt,' I said.

Someone was pulling at my other arm. I glanced around to see Margo tugging at me.

'Please Jimmy, don't.'

She had no idea I had a knife through my arm and I shrugged her off, stepped forward quickly and kicked the wog as hard as I could right in the balls. He screamed and sprayed blood everywhere. I grabbed him by the hair, dragged him over to one of the parked cars and smashed his face down onto the roof. He collapsed down between the car and the gutter. I couldn't kick him because he'd sunk down below the level of the footpath, so I lifted my leg and stamped down on him. Suddenly my arms were grabbed from both sides and I was dragged away by two big burly uniformed coppers on foot-patrol.

'Righto, that's enough,' one of them said. 'Settle down. What are you trying to do, kill him?'

'Too right I am,' I said, 'if you buggers'll let me go. The rotten bastard assaulted my girl, then stabbed me.'

'What? Where?' they asked. And let go of me.

I extended my right arm and displayed the knife.

'What do you think that is? A bloody wart or something?'

'Jesus Christ! It's gone right through!' The copper on my right had turned ashen.

I reached over with my left hand and slowly took hold of the short black handle of the knife. Now that fury was ebbing away, it didn't look the best. The coppers saw my movement and one of them took my left arm in a firm grip.

'Jesus, mate! Leave it.' There was alarm in his voice. 'It might be through the artery. If you pull it out . . . '

He left the question unfinished and I let the reason for his concern sink in. Margo came rushing up to me. She was crying as she held me tight and pushed her face onto my chest.

'Jimmy, oh Jimmy.'

'Who's this?' one of the coppers asked.

'She's my girl,' I said.

This started Margo sobbing even more.

'We'd better get a car and an ambulance down here on the double,' said one of the coppers before running into the theatre. His partner and a couple of bystanders had meantime lifted the wog up out of the gutter and laid him on his side on the footpath. Bloody gigs, I thought. This will give them something to talk about for a couple of days.

A fair-sized crowd had gathered around us by this time, all ooohing and aaahing, and the remaining copper was waving his arms at them like a farmer trying to chase chooks back into their coop.

'Move back . . . Come on, move back,' he yelled at them in an authoritative tone. 'Give us a little room here.'

Even though I had a knife through my arm, there wasn't what you'd call any pain. It just felt funny when I clenched my fingers. What surprised me even more was the lack of blood. There was only a slight trickle running down my arm. Which was more than could be said for the moaning bloody wog on the footpath. He was a fuckin' nightmare to look at. I felt like going over and kicking the bastard again.

'Jimmy, oh Jimmy,' Margo sobbed.

'I'm all right, love. This won't kill me.'

She lifted her head, looked down at the hilt of the knife and started a fresh outburst of sobbing.

'Oh look at your arm,' she kept saying. 'Look what he's done to your arm.'

The second copper came running back to us from inside the theatre. He had a couple of handtowels with him and a blanket.

'Car and ambulance on the way,' he said to his partner. 'Here, you'd better wrap these around that arm.' Then he went over to the wog and said something I couldn't hear. Probably assuring the bastard that he'd be okay, I thought. The copper covered the wog with a blanket, then gently lifted his head and placed a towel beneath it.

Margo took the towel out of my left hand and, as

83

gently as she could, wrapped it around the knife, and my arm.

'Is it hurting, Jimmy? . . . God it looks terrible. I feel like I'm going to be sick.'

'No it's not too bad, love, I'll live.'

'Move back! . . . Will you all move back and give us some more room here,' yelled one of the coppers. They were both pissed off with the crowd, but one of them came back to me, a notebook in his hand.

'Now what's your name and what's this all about?'

I was just about to answer him when a police car and an ambulance pulled up, with flashing lights and sirens wailing. The medics ran onto the footpath and one stooped down over the wog while his offsider came up to me.

'Let's take a quick look, mate,' he said, raising my arm and slowly unwrapping the towel. 'Shit! How did this happen?'

'That bastard down there,' I said, pointing with my other arm. 'Fuckin' stabbed me.'

'We'll have to get you to the hospital. We can't remove it here.'

'When you're finished there, could you give us a hand,' the other medic called out. 'This bloke needs a stretcher.'

Two plain-clothes coppers, one quite tall, had climbed out of the car by this stage and they watched as the wog was loaded into the back of the ambulance. The CIB blokes were asking questions and the medics were nodding and saying things I couldn't hear, sometimes shrugging their shoulders. The wog was saying nothing. He probably didn't even know what planet he was on. My right hand was starting to go a bluey colour and was half tingling, and half numb.

'What's the story here?' a plain-clothes cop eventually asked me.

'I haven't been able to get all the facts yet,' one of the uniformed men answered, 'but it appears the bloke in the ambulance stabbed this bloke here.'

'Can we take a look?'

I extended my arm and the medic unwrapped the towel once again.

'It's going to have to be removed pretty quick,' he said. 'It looks to me like the knife is obstructing the circulation.'

'Bloody hell!' the plain-clothes guy said. 'It's gone right through.'

I turned to the medic. 'Is that bastard in the ambulance dead yet? Let me in with him and I'll finish the prick off on the way to the hospital.'

'You get going with the bloke you've got loaded,' one of the CIB men said. 'We'll follow behind with this one.'

'I'm coming too,' Margo told the cops.

Loaded up in the cop car, with Margo and me in the back, the coppers asked if I knew the bloke who knifed me.

'Never seen him before in my life.'

'I know you, don't I?' asked the tall copper, looking at Margo.

'I don't know. Do you?' Margo replied.

'You're Margo Colenzo aren't you?'

'So what if I am?' she said.

The copper faced the front again, and looking out

the windscreen said to his partner: 'This'll turn out to be a nice shitty job.' He turned around again and asked me my name.

'Jimmy Diamond.' He wrote something in his note-book, resting it on the back of the front seat.

'Jimmy Diamond eh! Have you got any form, Jimmy?'

'No.'

'Well it won't be long if you keep hanging round with these types.' He indicated Margo with a nod of his head.

When we arrived at the hospital, I walked in to the accident and emergency section with Margo hanging onto my left arm and flanked by the two coppers. A hospital sister led us into a room with an examination table. She unwrapped the towel with a long-handled pair of forceps, as if it were contaminated, then dropped it into a receptacle at the end of the table. Felt my hand, which had turned a darker blue and which by now had puffed up. Put a big piece of cottonwool and lint under my arm on the table, removed a clean white cloth from a stainless steel box and placed it over the knife and my arm with the forceps. 'The doctor won't be long,' she said. Just before she closed the door, I noticed the plain-clothes cops talking to Margo.

Not much later two doctors entered the room.

'How are you feeling?' they asked.

'Not too bad, but my right hand has gone numb.'

They lifted the cover off my arm and started dis-cussing what they saw. 'Mmmm nasty ... causing obstruction' ... 'Looks like we may have possible arterial obstruction' ... 'Partial severance?' ... 'Depends how sharp the blade' ... 'He'll need a general' ...

'We're going to have to put you to sleep to remove that,' one of them said. 'You'll have to sign a consent form.'

'Can I talk to my girl, doctor? She's just outside.'

He went to the door and beckoned to Margo.

'Are you related to each other?' the doctor asked.

'Sort of,' said Margo. 'What's going to happen to Jimmy?'

'Well we'll be taking him down to the emergency theatre in a moment or two. We can't make any further diagnosis until we've removed the knife.'

Just then the door opened and the sister came back in with a kidney tray in her hand. 'We're going to give you a couple of injections. One's a pre-op, and the other's a tetanus shot.' Just as she banged the two needles into the shoulder muscle, another nurse came in with a clipboard.

'Here's the consent,' she said.

'I can't write with this hand,' I said to the doctor. 'Can't Margo sign it?'

The doctor and the sister conferred before nodding in agreement. As soon as the form was signed two nurses came in and started to manoeuvre me towards the door and down to the operating theatre.

After I recovered from the operation a doctor informed me that I had been lucky. The artery hadn't been severed, just jammed against the bone, and they didn't anticipate any complications.

'What happened to the wog who stabbed me?' I asked the quack.

'Yes well, I'm really not at liberty to discuss that with you.'

Margo said she couldn't find out anything about him either. She wanted to remain with me but it was almost 4 a.m. and I begged her to go home and get some rest.

About 10 o'clock I received another visit from the doctor. My arm was stiff and sore but he said it would loosen up in a few days and return to normal soon enough. Then I received a visit from the cops. Two plain-clothes detectives. They pulled up a couple of chairs and started firing questions about the incident. They weren't hostile towards me, more curious in a way. I explained how the wog had made advances to Margo, grabbing her on the arse, and had pulled a knife when I went to her defence. Then I had clobbered the bastard.

'Am I being charged with anything?' I asked.

'No. Not at this time. We haven't been able to interview the other bloke yet.'

'What's wrong with him?' I fired back.

'Well you've really done a job on him all right. He's got a fractured nose and cheek bone, a fractured skull, along the forehead. There's a rib or two broken and he's not feeling the best. He doesn't speak much English, so we won't have his story till we can get hold of an official interpreter.'

They then asked me how I had defended myself. 'In light of the injuries to the other bloke, it's hard to believe that there was no weapon used in your part as you claim.'

'Well,' I said, 'there were two uniformed cops there too. They pulled me off him.'

'Yes, well we'll be having a talk with them today also. Look, we understand you have some sort of a relationship with Margo Colenzo. And that you were also taken in and questioned in relation to the homicide of Bernard Clarence Walker.'

'Questioned my arse! I was taken in all right and that Kelly tried to fuckin' drown me. He and everybody else knows I knew fuck-all about who shot Bernie. Kelly doesn't like Margo and he used me to get back at her. There's something wrong with that Kelly ... He's not the full quid.'

'Yeah, well we'll pass on your regards when we see him. But let's stop beating around the bush. We understand your name is James Francis Diamond, is that correct?'

'Yes.'

'Do people call you James?'

'No, I've always been called Jimmy.'

'Okay, Jimmy it is. Let's start from the top. Where are you from originally, and what's your date of birth?'

'Lismore, in northern New South Wales, and the ninth of March 1940.'

'Have you ever been in trouble with the police up there?'

I gave them a quick run-down on the troubles I had with Eric and so forth.

'You haven't been in gaol or a juvenile institution?'

'No, never.'

'Righto then, let's get back to your involvement with Margo Colenzo. How well do you know her?'

'Real well. I live with her.'

'Jesus Christ! He lives with her. Do you believe this?'

the cop said to his silent partner. 'How did you come to meet her?'

'We met in a club . . . Chequers.'

'How long ago was this?'

'About a year or so.'

'Are you aware that Colenzo has had trouble with the police and that she has a criminal record?'

'So what. I'm not bothered about that,' I said testily.

'Do you know what consorting is?'

'Yes, Lawrie Galbally and I have spoken about it. But I don't have a criminal record. I'd have to have done time or have a record to be consorting.'

The cop turned to his partner. 'Christ! It doesn't get any better does it?' He turned back to me. 'Where do you work? What sort of a job do you have?'

'I'm not working.'

'What do you do for Colenzo then? Are you working for her?'

'I told you I'm not working, or doing anything.'

'She's keeping you then . . . In other words, you're living off the earnings of prostitution, gambling and sly grog.'

I could see where this was heading. These two coppers weren't that interested in me, they were trying to get something on Margo.

'That's a load of bullshit,' I said. 'You can't prove that.'

'Look, you could be charged with assault occasioning grievous bodily harm, even attempted murder.'

'Come off it! I was the one who got stabbed. All I did was defend myself and Margo. I didn't know it was against the law to defend yourself.'

'Look. Why don't you come clean and tell us what you know about Colenzo and company ... We'll see you right.'

'Stuff this ... I told you. I don't know anything. I'm ringing for the sister and asking her to ring Lawrie Galbally.'

'What do you need Galbally for?' asked the other copper, speaking for the first time. 'You haven't been charged with anything yet. We're just asking a few questions.'

The door opened and the sister poked her head in. 'You've got another visitor.'

She stood back and Margo walked into the room, carrying a couple of loaded shopping bags. She completely ignored the coppers, walked to the opposite side of the bed and kissed me.

'I've brought you a few things,' she said quietly.

'Well well well, speak of the devil and in she walks,' the talkative copper said to his partner.

'What's that supposed to mean,' I fired at him.

He ignored me, looked at Margo and said: 'Talk about cradle-snatching ... You're nearly old enough to be his mother, Margo.'

'She's not that much older than me,' I chipped in.

'She could give you a good ten years, mate. Don't you worry about that.'

I turned to Margo. 'Do you know these buggers?'

'Yes I do unfortunately ... And we don't have to put up with this kinda shit. I'm going to ring Lawrie right now.'

The copper who had been asking all the questions stood up.

'Don't worry your pretty little head about it. We're leaving now. But we'll be talking again after we've checked on a few things . . . Have fun.'

He motioned to his partner and they left the room, having a quiet chuckle to themselves.

'Bloody pricks,' Margo said. 'How long have they been here?'

'Not that long. They were trying to get me to rat on you, but I got a bit pissed off and threatened to call Lawrie.'

Margo bent over me and kissed me once again. Those soft lips of hers were magic when they touched me. I remember one night, after some hectic lovemaking, that I had bruised the lower one, kissing her. I could feel myself getting hard under the covers. I explored the inside of her mouth with my tongue. Reaching up I gently squeezed one of those lovely boobs and moaned. She slid her hand under the covers, inside the front slot of my pyjamas, took my penis in her warm hand and stroked it.

'Don't worry, sweetheart,' she said. 'I'll take good care of that when you get out of here.'

We spoke about all and everything for a while. What had happened outside the movie theatre. The bloody wog and the extent of his injuries. How I was going to get out of this joint as quick as I could.

I told her all the questions that the coppers had asked me, what I had said to them and so forth. The best bit of news she gave me was that she had spoken to Lawrie Galbally and as long as we kept to our stories, there was no way possible that the coppers could charge me and win the case. In fact it was the wog who was in trouble, not me.

9

I WAS RELEASED FROM HOSPITAL THREE DAYS LATER AND, apart from a sore arm that was healing nicely, I was none the worse for wear. The police paid us three or four more visits and asked all the usual damn-fool questions that they must in the course of their investigations. They knew they couldn't get an assault charge against me to stick, in the light of the knife being produced. Lawrie Galbally had tutored me carefully and I was to stress at all times that I had been in fear of my life, negating the police case that I had used undue force while protecting myself.

Of course, the police hate coming out the losers, and when they fully realised the hopelessness of their situation they tried to influence me to give evidence against the wog, who turned out to be a Greek seaman. But there was no way that I was going to get up in court and do that. As far as I was concerned, justice had been meted out already and fuck the wog and fuck the coppers too.

So the whole thing just died a natural death. The wog missed his boat and was deported and we had a bit of a laugh about this amongst ourselves. In fact the incident helped Margo and me. Some of our opposition, who were a bit cocky, started treating me with a little more respect. I remember Abe taking me aside one day not long after my release and giving me a wink and some friendly advice.

'Way to go, mate. Horses for courses, oats for goats, and straight lefts for fuckin' mugs. Never waste your breath arguing with pricks, Jimmy. Talk won't earn you any respect in these circles. Just keep the bastards down and hurt 'em good. That puts the fear of Christ up the next joker who comes along and tries to get smart with his mouth.'

It was advice I never forgot.

Margo and I had also gone a step forward in our relationship. It grew even stronger and she became less the mother hen, more tender and submissive towards me. Of course her concern for me still persisted, but my protecting her in a physical way gave her confidence that I could look after myself, and her too, if I had to. She loved me more than ever, and she felt proud of me. I was her Paladin, and that's just how she treated me after that. As if I was her own White Knight.

In the Sydney underworld in those days Margo had another name, though it was never uttered in her presence, or within hearing of those who were close to her. Although sweet and innocent to look at, she was known as the Angel of Death. To cross her in the line of business or a personal insult usually resulted in a trip to intensive care, or an appointment with the Grim Reaper. No one fucked about with Margo. What was hers was hands-off to others. I often noted alarm in the eyes of others, who were physically capable of breaking her into little pieces, when she got pissed off with them over something.

Yet, from the first moment we met, I never felt fear

of any kind. She was always sweet and tender towards me and I treated her like she wanted to be treated—a sweet girl who needed someone's real love and understanding. She was a human being with feelings, just like anyone else, and I accepted her totally. She had done me no wrong and could do no wrong, but she lived in a dog-eat-dog world where only the rough and tough survived. Margo, to her credit, had come through without a scratch to her beautiful skin, and this said something for the mind that she possessed. It was as sharp as a razor, brilliant.

On the other hand, I had been an ordinary country boy, abused by those the state had promised would love and raise me as their own in an atmosphere of care and understanding. But I didn't have the burden, as Margo did, of being raised in an area where murder, muggings, bashings, rape and reprisal were the order of the day. Yet fate brought us together. It was as if our every action from birth till our first encounter had been planned by the gods, so that gradually they brought us within reach of each other. Each and every one of the things that Margo and I had done separately had manoeuvred us closer together till the distance was just right. Then that natural magnetic power had taken over and drawn us together, to cling and bathe in the power of this natural attraction.

Margo and I were opposite only in as much as she was a woman and I was a man. Negative and positive if you like. But that's where it ended. We never tired of each other's company and hated being separated from each other. Our minds seemed to be as one. We found out we even had the same blood group. We were Peter

Pan and Tinker Bell, and were called that in a friendly sense by the old hands around the Cross. We romped like a couple of kids and didn't seem to age. Both of us looked a lot younger than our actual years. When we were alone, at times we would just sit and gaze at each other, saying absolutely nothing, and messages seemed to flash between us. If a problem arose that I couldn't solve or fathom, Margo always had the solution. And if she was discussing something with me, I could usually provide the answer she was looking for. Both our lives were a giant jigsaw puzzle and we had each other's missing pieces to complete the picture.

Rosalie became our closest companion and confidante. What drew us even closer together was the death of her lover, Garry Green. There was a maniac getting around Sydney, a kind of serial killer. He murdered only men and, after stabbing them to death, he would cut off their genitals. But even in devastation and loss, humour has a way of bubbling to the surface to those not directly involved. 'Dick Hunter' they nicknamed him. And if you went to a shithouse in a pub to take a piss, it wasn't uncommon to find 'Use it before you lose it!' scratched into the paintwork above the urinal. The dirty bastard was eventually run to earth and arrested, but not before Garry had become one of his victims.

As far as I knew, Rosalie had never had any other lover. And after Garry's gruesome death I can't remember ever seeing her in a relationship with another man. The loss of Garry hit her hard. She muttered curses and incantations against his attacker that would have sent chills down the spine of Lucifer himself. We gave her what comfort we could and she came to stay more and more with us until Margo and I invited her to move in. She became a voluntary slave to us, showering us with a devotion that defied words. Her room was done out like a shrine, with all sorts of occult and satanic paraphernalia decorating the walls and ceilings. It was enough to have the uninitiated and uninformed scared shitless, but it never worried Margo or me. We both loved Rosalie, and never belittled or made fun of her beliefs.

However, Abe never got used to her. 'Jesus!' he used to whisper. 'That fuckin' room of hers gives me the bloody creeps.' Rosalie sensed Abe's dread and often ribbed him in a friendly fashion. Abe hated coming to the house unless it was a dire necessity, believing that Rosalie would turn him into a toad or something.

10

A FAIR BIT OF WATER HAD PASSED UNDER THE BRIDGE since that day at the Broadwater pub when I'd mounted my bike and headed for Sydney. Since that day, I hadn't written or phoned the two people who had taken me in like an adopted son and given me love and shelter. For all the contact we had, I may as well have been dead. I knew that they deserved better than that and my conscience often pricked me. I could never explain even to myself how I just rode away without even a goodbye that day back at Broadwater. But somehow I fought the urge to phone or write and assure them that I was okay. Maybe it was that I had happiness enough, and didn't want to leave Margo.

Looking back, it was a casual conversation that made me pick up the phone and ring them. One night we were talking at home and I mentioned their names.

'Why don't you call them and say hello?' Margo said.

'They probably think I'm dead by now. What good would it do? It's been eighteen months. They're probably still pissed off with me for not saying anything.'

'Well you'll never know until you ring, will you,' Rosalie piped in.

'Yeah, well I'll give it a try and see how it goes. The poor buggers deserve better than the shitty trick I pulled.'

98

I went down the hall to the phone and got their number from the operator. I'd forgotten it after all this time. I had to make a trunk call because they weren't on an automatic exchange. I heard the phone ringing at the other end and then a click.

'Hello!' It was old Mum Gee's voice. I was sort of speechless and didn't know what to say. I heard her again. 'Hello, is anybody there?'

'Hello Mum, it's me. Jimmy.'

'Where the bloody hell are you?' There was an angry tone in her voice. 'Dad and I have worried ourselves sick over you. Where are you now?'

'I'm in Sydney, Mum. Look, I know I did the wrong thing leaving like that without a word, but you've got to try and understand how I felt at the time. I just couldn't face you. I've often thought of getting in touch, but at the last minute I just haven't had the guts. You don't know how hard it is for me to be ringing now.'

Mum seemed to quieten a little.

'What are you doing down there? We really have worried, you know. Someone said they saw you in Brisbane and we had the police up there try to find you. Tell you to come home.'

'I'm sorry, Mum, I really am. You both deserved better from me than this . . . '

As I continued to apologise I heard some muffled talk and then Dad's voice came on the line.

'By Christ, Jimmy, you're a beauty. Not a bloody word out of you all this time. Now you've got Mum standing here crying her bloody eyes out. What the bloody hell came over you?'

'I don't know mate, I really don't.'

He mumbled something on the other end of the line to someone. It must have been poor old Mum.

'What are you doing in Sydney? You're not in any trouble are you?'

'No, Dad. I finally plucked up the courage to ring. To apologise, actually. I just hoped that you and Mum can forgive me. Try and understand.'

'Understand! . . . Christ, we might have if you'd only said something before you cleared off. We've had the bloody coppers lookin' for you all over Brisbane trying to find out if you're all right.'

'Well you needn't worry any more. I'm not in trouble, and I'm all right.'

'What are you doing down there? What sort of job have you got?'

I didn't know what to say to this. I certainly couldn't tell the truth. The job was done for me by the operator. 'Your three minutes are up sir,' she piped in. 'Do you wish to extend?'

'No thanks,' I replied, and then quickly to Dad: 'I've got to go, Dad. I'm on someone else's phone. I'll write. Say bye to Mum for me.'

'Righto. See you do then. Thanks for ringing.'

And we were cut off.

'Well, how did it go?' Margo asked.

'They're pretty pissed off. They've even had Missing Persons trying to locate me in Brisbane. I didn't tell them where I was living, just told Dad I'd write. That seemed to ease things a bit. Jesus, I'm glad I didn't just turn up out of the blue.'

'Well at least they know you're alive and well,' Margo said. 'Be thankful for that, Jimmy.'

A month or two later, after writing and a few more calls, Margo and I decided that we'd slip up for a visit.

Since I had started doing the collection work, Margo had got me a brand new Holden. I was pretty proud of it and, just like the old Norton, which was still sitting out in the shed, I kept it spick and span. In fact Margo and I often climbed on board the bike and, with the wind whipping us, would make our way to the beach to spend the day frolicking and swimming, sunbaking and anything else that took our fancy.

The visit back to Mum and Dad Gee's place was not a screaming success. They treated Margo well enough, but their questions were awkward and our evasive answers obviously worried them. Then one evening after an afternoon on the piss, Dad said: 'You're up to something dodgy down there, aren't you?'

I tried all sorts of ways to lay his mind at rest, but he was having none of it. I got a big lecture on how they always respected the law, and had never broken it. No member of the Gee family had ever brought disgrace on the household, he told me, and that was the way it was going to stay. If I thought that I was fooling him then I was making a mistake. How could I afford a new car, flash clothes and gold jewellery at my age? Mum and he had slaved all their lives to get where they were, and we should do likewise. Shit! It went on and on.

We left the next morning after he'd cooled down a bit, but it was a long time before I was to pay another visit. Down the road a bit from their place Margo started to sob quietly. I pulled the car over.

'What's the matter, sweetie?'

'I just feel awful, Jimmy. I can see those people love

101

you. They think the world of you, and they're worried about you. I feel responsible.'

'You can cut out that sort of thinking right now,' I said to her. 'I'm leaving with you because I want to leave with you. You're not responsible for anything. You weren't with me when I left in the first place. There's nothing here for me now and I'd go stark raving mad if I had to spend the rest of my life in this dump. So let's not get all silly about it.'

She turned her lovely face up to me and wiped away her tears. I kissed her and felt her relax. She hugged me to her, and with a voice full of love and emotion pleaded . . .

'Don't ever leave me, Jimmy. I've never begged anyone for anything in my whole life, but I'm begging you. I don't think I could live with it if I lost you now.'

The emotion in her voice and the way she was holding me made me feel proud. I was wanted, I was needed, and the fact that it was Margo who needed me made it all the better. Because I needed her too. Too afraid to speak, in case the emotion I felt would burst, I took my arm from around her, moving it over her head and down in front of her face, so she was looking at the bracelet she had given me.

Jimmy and Margo Forever.

She gave a sigh and kissed the bracelet, and then kissed me. I started the car and we drove back to Sydney.

11

A WEEK OR TWO LATER ABE CAME ROUND FOR A discussion about one of the girls who had been arrested. She said she'd had enough and wanted out. Unlike others in the industry who believed that once they were in they were in forever, Margo never did that to her girls.

'Let her go,' Margo said after we'd gone over pros and cons of the matter. 'She's no good to us if you force her to stay. You say she wants to go to Melbourne. Well, make that the condition. She can go with no strings attached, as long as she goes to Melbourne.'

'Right,' said Abe. 'I'll give her the message. That brings up another matter I think we should discuss. Isn't it about time we did something about that bastard who took Bernie out?'

'Can it be done without bringing too much heat on us?' Margo asked. 'We aren't what you'd call Driscoll's flavour of the month and he'll know for sure that we had a finger in the pie. What have you got in mind?'

Abe thought for a moment. 'There's two ways we can go about it. We can hit him straight up front, and fuck Driscoll and the bloody Italians. Or we can take Driscoll out at the same time and kill two birds with one stone.'

'Jesus, Abe,' Margo said. 'Isn't that a bit risky? When

you think of the Italian connection Driscoll has. What do you think Don Luigi's going to do? He's going to be really pissed off.'

'Not really ... Well anyway, not so's he'd be pissed off with us ... Look we know that Bernie reneged on the deal he had with the Eyeties and was hit by Driscoll's bloke ... He took the contract, well he didn't really have a choice. As far as old Luigi is concerned, what happened between him and Bernie was a matter of honour, and that's how they settled it. In their way. It's also a matter of honour for us to look after our own, Margo. But let me ask you this ... What if Driscoll fell out of favour with the Italians? Suppose I told you that the Don isn't going to be too happy when that joint of his at Paddington gets raided, and our sly grog joint gets a going over at the same time, just after Driscoll gets pinched. But with the help of our blokes on the Vice and Gaming Squads we'll tip Luigi off in time. That'll leave the Don owing us a favour.'

'What're Driscoll and Flood going to be arrested for?'

'Suspicion of murder.'

'Whose murder?' Margo yelled at him. 'What are you talking about, Abe?'

'The murder of Bernie. Can't you see this would put Luigi in the hot seat? The job was done on his order. But when Driscoll and Flood are pinched on suspicion and the Dago's joint gets raided while they're being questioned, he's going to be really pissed off. The raid on our joint has to be done. If not the Don'll smell a rat. This way we'll be in a position to ask him for a favour and take out Driscoll and Flood at the same time. It's got to work, Margo.'

Margo sat sipping her drink, deep in thought. I hadn't said a word. It wasn't my place to put my two bob's worth anyway. This was Abe's department.

Margo looked up. 'I've got to have time on this one, Abe. There's a lot at risk here, too much to give an answer straightaway. I'll get back to you in a couple of days.'

I saw a look of anger flash across Abe's eyes, and he straightened up in his chair.

'But Margo I . . . '

'I said a couple of days, Abe.' Her tone had the lash of a whip in it. 'Do you understand? A couple of days.'

Margo went back to her drink and lapsed into silence. Abe was absently doodling with the wet ring his glass had left on the table. He felt embarrassed and a look of anger passed across his face. Margo's lashing remark in front of me made him feel like a child and he didn't like it one bit, you could sense it. I still hadn't said a word. Abe suddenly got to his feet.

'Well that's that then,' he said. 'I'll be off. I'll wait for your call, Margo. See you later, Jimmy.'

Margo looked over at me and smiled. 'Would you mind doing the honours, darling, and let Abe out?'

'Sure, love.' I hopped up and walked down the hall, ahead of Abe. As I moved out onto the porch he must have noticed that I'd taken keys out of my pocket.

'How long have you had your own keys to the joint?' Abe asked. His tone was acid.

'Months I suppose.'

'I've never had that privilege. Must be nice to be trusted.'

I walked down the steps towards Abe, who was nearly at the gate.

'What's the matter, mate?'

Abe turned around and his manner had completely changed.

'Look, Jimmy, you talk to her. She'll listen to you. Can't you persuade her that I'm right?'

'I don't know, Abe. I'm just the new boy in this game.'

'Bullshit, Jimmy. You know what I'm on about. Look, just talk it over with her?'

'Righto, Abe, I'll do what I can.'

'Thanks mate, I'll see you later then.'

He walked to his car and drove off. When I went back inside Margo was still sitting in the same spot, as if she was frozen in that position.

'Abe gone?' she asked with a smile.

'Yeah, love. Don't you think you were a bit hard on him?'

'Maybe. Still, there's a lot to think about here. But don't you go getting involved. It'll work itself out.'

'Margo, Abe asked me to talk to you. Try to get you to see things his way.'

' 'Course he would. He can't stand losing. I've known Abe for a long time now. At times he can fly off the handle. Do things a bit too quickly. I appreciate you telling me he talked to you.'

'Jesus, Margo, I couldn't keep something like that from you.'

'I know, Jimmy, I know. I just meant thanks for letting me know.'

The subject was dropped, but there was more to come, and I'd play a bigger role in it than I ever imagined.

12

THE AFTERNOON AFTER ABE'S VISIT I FOUND MYSELF sitting at home, alone. Margo and Rosalie had gone out and I was catnapping on the sofa when the phone disturbed me.

The call was from Bob Marsh, who we called Swampy. He and his wife Penny ran the sly grog shop in Surry Hills. Swampy wanted some more beer and some plonk for the winos and I told him that I'd take care of it as soon as possible. I left a note letting Margo know where I was going and that I'd probably be an hour or so. Then I went to the Port Jackson, who supplied the grog to us in bulk, and headed off. I pulled up in Swampy's backyard and banged on the rear door. A little six-inch-square window opened.

'Gee, that was quick, Jimmy,' Swampy's missus said, and opened the door for me.

'Hi, Penny,' I said. 'Where's Swampy?'

'Gone out for a while. He didn't think you'd be here this quick. Would you like to come in and wait?'

'Nah! I'll get this stuff inside, love. I can handle it. I've been sittin' on my arse most of the day.'

There was a fair amount of grog in the car and in the boot. While I was carrying it inside, Penny said quite casually as I passed her . . .

'Has Margo gone into business with Bob Driscoll now?'

'Not that I know of, Penny. Why do you ask, love?'

Penny must have thought that she was out of line and tried to get out of the conversation.

'You should wait for Swampy to give you a hand with this.'

'Listen Penny! Don't beat around the bloody bush. What do you mean about Margo and Driscoll?' I said it quite firmly and she sensed my annoyance.

'Jesus, Jimmy! I don't want to make any trouble. But a couple of days ago Shirley Larkin and me were having a few drinks while we were in town. We slipped into the lounge at the King's and we saw Abe Stafford in the Saloon, talking to Bob Driscoll and Charlie Costanza.'

I nearly dropped the case of beer.

'What! You're joking aren't ya, Penny. That's gotta be bullshit.'

'No Jimmy. Don't get angry. It's true, we both seen him. Shit! I know Abe when I see him. And Driscoll. Charlie Costanza was with 'em. If you don't believe me you can ask Shirley. I suppose I shouldn't have said anything. It's just that I thought it was a bit queer seein' them three together.'

'Look, Penny, I want you to keep this to yourself, you hear? I appreciate you lettin' me know. But not a bloody word to anyone about this, okay? No one. Does Swampy know? Have you mentioned it to him?'

'Yeah, but all he said was I suppose we'll be seein' some changes around here. Jesus, Jimmy, you know Swamp. He wouldn't say anythin' to no one who wasn't in the know.'

'You tell him not a bloody word to anyone. In the fuckin' know or not. Not a bloody word, Penny.'

'Shit, Jimmy! Don't go crook. Margo knows we wouldn't let her down.'

'I know that, love.'

With the booze unloaded, I didn't hang around to have a word with Swampy. I smelt a rat, and a pretty rotten one at that, so I headed back home as quickly as I could. My mind was racing, full of suspicion. No, it couldn't be. Not Abe, surely? But I had a lot of questions and didn't have any answers.

Margo was home, listening to the wireless and reading while Rosalie was knocking something up for tea and having a talk to her budgerigar, that was screeching away as if it understood. I went over to the sideboard and fixed myself a good stiff drink. I hadn't been in the business long, but I knew that what I had just heard from Penny didn't tee up right. I sat down next to Margo, who put her magazine down and smiled at me.

'Everything go all right, love?' she asked.

'Well, yes and no, sweetheart. There was no problem with the grog, but I heard something that I don't think you'll like.'

'What do you mean?'

I took a good swig of my drink and repeated what Penny had told me. The more I said, the paler Margo's face became.

'The fuckin' bastard! The dirty fuckin' bastard! I'll kill him.'

'Hey hey hey, why are you yelling at me? Just settle down for a minute, sweetie.'

109

'Settle down! Jesus I'll settle down all right when I know that bastard's dead.'

'Just take it easy, Margo. Settle down and think. Here, have some of this.' And I passed her my drink.

She gulped it down and looked at me.

'I'm sorry love, you're right. But this could mean real big trouble.'

'Listen to me, Margo. I've never interfered before, but if there's going to be trouble I'm not just going to sit back and see it happen. For once I'm going to get involved, and try to help get to the bottom of this.'

She was about to open her mouth with her usual refusal.

'Ah ah,' I said to her. 'I'm in.'

She took my hand, raised it to her mouth and kissed it.

'I'm not mad at you, Jimmy, really I'm not. Okay, let's reverse roles. What would you do about it?'

'Well, I think I'd do what Penny suggested. Have a chat to Shirley Larkin. See if she's said anything to her old man. He works for Abe, after all. The second reason you need to see her is to find out that it really was Abe. One thing I do know is that it's not going to do any good going off half-cocked. Getting to see Shirley without tipping your hand is going to be the dicey bit, especially as I have a terrible feeling that Penny was right.'

'You're right, Jimmy. It's not going to be easy.'

It was a real dilemma. If we hauled in Shirley she would shit herself and squawk like mad to her old man. That in itself wasn't so bad, but if Garry Larkin then went to Abe he'd be alerted. If he'd already thrown his hand in with Driscoll and Costanza, then we were in real bad trouble.

Rosalie had been privy to most of the business conversations since moving in with us, and she was real staunch. That night, over dinner, she told us she'd always felt Abe was a rat.

'You never know, Rosalie. Maybe Penny and Shirley were mistaken.'

'How can you say that, Jimmy?' Rosalie said. 'They wouldn't have made a mistake like that. It's not like they don't know Abe that well. They see him nearly every day. It would have been him all right. You can bet your bottom dollar on that.'

'There's a few things going on at the moment, Jimmy, that you wouldn't be aware of,' Margo said. 'I think they got it right about Abe. And if so I've got to do something about it quick. I want you to call me a cab, love. You stay here with Rosalie. No arguments. I know what I'm doing.'

'Jesus Margo ... What are you going to do?'

There was a horrible feeling in me. Something ominous and dark. It must be that a little bit of primeval man has remained in us down through time ... from when our ancient forebears sensed danger lurking, afraid of the tiger.

'For God's sake don't argue, love. Just ring me a bloody cab.'

Like the obedient slave that I was to her, I went to the phone and rang the cab. Rosalie saw my distress.

'Don't you worry, Jimmy, she'll be all right. She's a tough little nut and she knows what she's doing.'

But I wasn't so sure. Something told me the tiger was

out tonight ... out and on the prowl. Margo came back and had a quick drink while she waited for the taxi. At the door she paused for a moment, looked up at me and smiled.

'Won't be long, Jimmy. We'll do something nice tomorrow.'

But there was to be no tomorrow for Margo and me.

13

THE PHONE CALL CAME AT 2.30 IN THE MORNING. IT WAS Frank Riordan, a copper of our acquaintance. He broke the news to me the only way he knew how.

'Jimmy . . . I'm sorry to have to be the one to break this to you, son, but Margo has been found dead. I'm sorry, boy. I really am.'

Shock and rage burned through me like a white heat. Then it was replaced with a cold, gelid feeling.

'How, Frank? What the fuck happened?'

'We don't know the whole story yet. We're still trying to find something to go on. A couple of winos found her. In Rushcutters Park. She'd been shot. Look, are you going to be okay? Can I do something? Do you want someone to come round?'

'No Frank, I don't want to see anyone. Fuckin' no one. Just find out all you can for me.'

I put the phone down and walked into the lounge, grabbed a bottle off the sideboard and took a long pull at it. I turned the room lights off and let the light from the hall wash in through the door. I put the bottle on the table and sat on the lounge. A violent tremor ran through me and I wept. Jesus! How I wept. She was gone. My beautiful Margo. That wonderful woman who had found me in a moment of need and recognised me for what I was. Who had accepted me for just what

I was. She could have had anybody, but she chose me. Took me in, showered me with love, comfort, devotion. She had given me pride, taught me all I knew about the hard side of life that she knew so well. She had taken me from boyhood and turned me into a man. Loved with me, shared with me, given me everything and more. No strings attached, no conditions. Live for today, fuck tomorrow, it'll take care of itself. I could see her beautiful face, swimming through the tears of my grief.

'Nooooooo!' I screamed.

I picked the bottle up off the table and hurled it against the wall with every ounce of my strength. It exploded in a thousand pieces and a violent spray of spirits. I stood and cursed God, defied him to strike me down too. And somewhere, I believe, God heard me and turned his back. I screamed for Lucifer to help me, to come to my aid and give me the power to smite down those who had taken my love. I promised my soul to the Devil as payment.

'Jimmy . . . Jimmy . . .' Rosalie's voice broke through to me as she turned on the lights. 'What's the matter . . . Jesus! What's going on? What's happened?'

I sat back down on the lounge, my head in my hands. Margo had gone. Something inside me had just died too. A part of me was gone forever. But a new part of me was born at that moment. It was a part that was dark and evil, that cried for vengeance. It gave me a knowledge that I had not possessed before, that I never knew I had. I had prayed to the Devil, asking Lucifer to protect me from my friends, because I knew who my enemies were.

114

'She's gone. Margo's gone. Dead.'

'You mean . . . ?'

'Yes! She's dead. Frank Riordan called me.'

'Oh you poor thing,' Rosalie said. Her tone was comforting, but she burst into tears as she spoke.

'I'm going to get them, Rosalie,' I said, but it was not my voice. 'I'm going to cut out their hearts. I am going to eat their livers. They are going to burn, and burn fuckin' slowly. I'm their damnation, I swear it. They're dead already, and they don't even know it.'

I grabbed another bottle of Scotch and a couple of glasses, and we drowned our sorrows.

For two days I wouldn't eat. I lived off alcohol and my thoughts of vengeance. The joys of vendetta. I thirsted for blood. Their blood was the only thing that would quench my thirst. I just drank and plotted death and retribution. Rosalie tried to bring me back to some sort of reality, but I was happy where I was. Lying in the dark in an alcoholic haze. Dreaming and plotting vengeance. But underneath, this new part of me was growing strong and resilient. Drooling for the chance to get even, to be Margo's avenger.

Two days later we buried Margo. I had never been to a funeral before, and I was amazed at the people who were there. Half the Cross was in attendance, but I never saw hide nor hair of Abe, or his newfound mates.

'She's gone to a better place,' the minister said. 'God has taken her.'

Fuck God! I yelled in a silent scream. Fuck the church.

Somewhere, Abe and his mates were laughing and

joking. They weren't worried about me. I was just a country bumpkin. What would I know? But I'd show them. Somehow. I would let them think I was a bumpkin, and no threat. However, the country bumpkin was about to become the tiger. Abe. Driscoll. Costanza. They would be my prey.

I drove Rosalie back to the house and we sat in silence for a while, just looking at each other across the room. Suddenly she stood up, crossed the room and sat down beside me. She put her arm around my shoulders and started talking to me in a soft, assuring tone.

I know what you're planning, Jimmy, and I don't blame you. If I was a man I'd do it myself. But what I'm about to say to you is to help you. So please, please listen carefully. You're strong, Jimmy, but you're no match for what you intend to take on. You need help. Not someone backing you up, but help for yourself. There are ways of achieving what you want to do, but you can't do it as you are now. You're inexperienced for this sort of thing, but I think I have the answer.'

What have you got in mind? I'm prepared to shoot the bastards and get it over with. Fuck the consequences.'

'Yes, well that's very gallant and all that, but what good is prison going to do you ... or Margo's memory? Do you think that's what Margo would want? Seeing you rot away in gaol? Wouldn't revenge be sweeter if you remained free?'

What Rosalie was saying was making sense. I didn't have a clue how I was going to extract my revenge and her calm voice bade me listen and learn.

'I want these bastards dead,' I said to her at last. 'And

116

if you can help me achieve this, then I appreciate it. What do you have in mind?'

'Well for starters, we've got to get out of here. Go and pack your things. We're far too vulnerable here. Empty the safe. Take everything. Don't leave anything that the coppers or any other bastards might want. Righto, let's get started.'

I went into our room, collected Margo's keys, opened the big wardrobe door that concealed the safe and unlocked it. It held bundles of bank notes, books, ledgers and other papers. Grabbing a leather case from the top of the wardrobe, I crammed everything from the safe into it. There was more cash, in neat bundles and in large denominations, in the drawer at the bottom of the safe. No one in Margo's business used banks in those days.

When I had filled the bag I loaded a big travelling case with my clothes. I went to the dressing table and took the framed photo of Margo and me and packed it also. There was a bottle with a thousand Purple Hearts and I took them too, along with Margo's jewellery box. Fuck 'em, I thought, no way anyone was getting anything belonging to her.

Down in the backyard there was a big incinerator. I grabbed as many of Margo's dresses as I could, piled them in, doused them with petrol and chucked in a match. Whooooomph! Off it went. I went back again and again until I'd taken every piece of Margo's gear from our room and I burnt it. No one would have, take, or wear anything that belonged to her. It was all that was left of my love, and I cremated it in a Viking inferno, watching as the smoke floated high up into the heavens.

Back in the bedroom I grabbed a chair and stood on it, checking the top of the big wardrobe. At the back, against the wall, was a wooden cigar box with a hinged lid. Inside was an automatic and a box of .38 calibre ammunition. I packed the box into one of the cases and carried them both to the car.

Rosalie came down the back stairs, carrying a case and her handbag.

'I've got a couple of more things, love,' she said. 'I won't be long.'

She went back inside and came back with a few string-handled bags, some books and a bundle tied in a sheet. She made one more trip and came back with a beer carton full of her special brew and one of her paintings that I had always admired.

'That's it for me,' she said.

'What about all that magic stuff in your room?'

'I can always make more. Let's leave it where it is, as a shrine. And a reminder to those bastards that a day of reckoning is at hand.'

I opened the boot of the car and we loaded it up. Some of the gear had to go onto the back seat.

'Righto, love,' Rosalie said when we'd finished. 'Fuck it, let's get moving.'

She walked up the side, unlatched the high gate and waved me forward. I drove through and waited as Rosalie came running up and hopped in.

'Head north, my light bearer,' she said. 'Destiny awaits.'

We drove in silence, and it wasn't until we were nearly at Hornsby that I asked her where we were going.

'Ever been to Nambucca Heads, Jimmy?'

'No. What's so good about Nambucca Heads?'

'That's where we're going. I'm going to introduce you to an old and dear friend of mine. I think he can help you in your plans. As a matter of fact I'm sure he will. He'll be your Warlock, your Sorcerer.'

We booked into a motel that night, where Rosalie treated me like a prince. She went to the car and got two bottles of her elixir, and we sat and talked and dreamt of Margo, saluting her with numerous toasts. Promising to be with her one day in Valhalla. I had a vision of her asking me to be happy and watch over Rosalie. I saw her. And I promised her I would. Rosalie ran me a bath and told me to take my drink and go and soak. I had no shame of nakedness with her. Christ knows, she'd seen Margo and me in the raw often enough, so I just stripped off and went into the bath.

Rosalie was not an unattractive girl in her own way. Her hair was jet black with a blue sheen to it and it looked unkempt, but she might have deliberately set and combed it that way. She had deep, dark almond-shaped eyes, like a cat, which she emphasised with heavy concentrations of mascara, giving them an even more slanted look. Her figure wasn't bad. She was slim, with long narrow limbs and small pointed breasts. It was more a teenage boy's structure than a woman's. And she had one fetish, if you could call it that. She couldn't stand body hair.

I hopped into the bath and lay there with my head back and my eyes closed, the elixir easing away the anger and hurt of the past week. Sensing a presence, I

119

opened my eyes and Rosalie was standing there. I hadn't heard her come in. She had nothing on. I smiled at her and she smiled back at me.

'I'm enjoying this,' I said, picking up some bathwater in my cupped hands and letting it run down my face.

She knelt on the bathmat and, reaching over, took the soap and started to slowly rub it into a lather on my chest and shoulders. Then taking my arms, she soaped them too before returning to my chest, rubbing the soap in with a slow circular rhythm. The soft circles moved further down my body until they reached my genitals. She used slow deliberate movements until I had an erection. Suddenly she pecked me on the cheek, took hold of a few hairs on my chest, not that I had that many, and gave them a light pull.

'Aaaah! Let's get rid of this.'

She looked into my eyes for assent. I just gave a nod. She took a couple of towels and left the room, but she was back in a moment.

'Hop out, my pet.' She held a hand out to me.

I got out of the bath and Rosalie led me to the bed, where the towels were unfolded on the middle of the maroon quilt. She had me lie on the towels, then went to one of her bags and took out a tube of lather, a safety razor and a packet of blades. She packed the pillows up behind my head, got me another drink and, while I was sipping away at that, she lathered my chest and then shaved every hair off. Next, she shaved the hair from under my arms, then moved to my legs and removed the hair from them before turning her attention to my pubic area. She lathered this with her hand and her movements soon had me hard and erect. It felt so good,

120

I didn't care what she did. Slowly, she removed every hair from my groin area, even from my testicles and right down to my anus. Every single hair. She kept running her fingers across her work, checking for stubble and I didn't have a hair on my body when she completed the operation.

Rosalie then asked me to hop back into the bath, and when I did so she hopped in with me and washed me all over again. I took the sponge from her and soaped and sponged her. I had another vision of Margo. She was smiling. 'Watch over Rosalie for me, Jimmy,' she whispered.

Rosalie got out of the bath and dried herself, then beckoned me to stand up. I obeyed and she dried me all over, just like a mother would a child, kneeling on the floor to do the lower half. She led me to the bed again and asked me to lie on the towels. Over she went to one of her bags and returned with a bottle of unusually perfumed oil. She massaged me all over and the oil sent a tingling sensation racing across my skin. Taking some more oil, she started rubbing it into herself. Then she poured a little oil into my palm and stood close beside the bed, offering herself to me. She spread her legs and pushed her pelvis forward. I reached out and started to rub her hairless vagina with the oil. When I let my middle finger slip into her she let her head fall back and moaned. She took my hand away, then lay beside me on the bed, her head on the pubic area she'd just shaved. She lifted a knee, spread herself apart and I went back to slowly rubbing her. She caressed my penis with her mouth, placing the tip of her tongue in its eye while stroking it gently with her hand. Then she took me into her mouth and gave a low moan. The warm wetness of her mouth wrapped around my penis and as she lay there, slowly sucking, I let my finger gently move in and out of her. Then she reached down and pushed my hand down further, until my finger was rubbing her anus. She gave a mewing sound and pushed against it. My finger was slippery with the oil and moisture of her vagina and slid into her bum a little way. She moaned and pushed back against my hand. She moved her head down further and licked my testicles and, sliding her finger down, she played with my anus, pushing her finger in a little at a time. Then she went back to sucking me again, with a slow, wet, deliberate up-and-down movement, her finger sliding in and out of me all the while. My come exploded into her mouth in a gushing spurt and she kept on sucking me, making the sensation unbelievable with her finger deeply in me . . . the climax even stronger. I had never experienced anything like it in my life.

Rosalie hopped off the bed, went to the bathroom and came back with a soapy sponge. She washed my hand, rubbed me down, dried me off again and poured us another drink. Then she lay beside me, propped on her elbow, gently rubbing more of the perfumed oil into my body. I didn't want to sleep. I wanted more. So I asked her to get some purple hearts out of my bag. We took two each, plus some more of her elixir, and she returned to her gentle rubbing. Her hand went back to my penis, just barely touching. The tingling effects of the oil and her gentle hand had me rigid again and she started sucking me, long and deep and slow. Suddenly she straddled me, lowering herself down onto me until I was deeply embedded in her. She sat there, squeezing herself. I could feel the pressure on my penis. She was hot and wet inside, and the squeezing effect made me feel wonderful. Bending forward slowly, she kissed me with a slow passionate kiss. Her tongue probed into my mouth and when it met mine a little spark seemed to jump between them. She moved her hips slowly at first, and then gradually increased in rhythm. I was almost ready to come again, but she seemed to sense this and stopped her movement. Lifting herself off me, she reached down, placed the head of my penis against her anus and slowly sat down on it until it entered her bum. She gave a little intake of breath, then breathed out in a soft purr and moaned with the joy of something recaptured that she had long been denied. Her hands came down and gently kneaded my nipples while her hips moved slowly up and down. She leant back, and arched her head, savouring the feeling . . . whispering . . . 'Oh, Jimmy, it's so beautiful.' I reached forward and slid my finger into her, gently massaging her clitoris. Her movements became faster, frenzied, she panted and breathed loudly until, as if by magic, someone flipped the switch and turned the current on and we exploded together. It was like an avalanche triggered by an eruption deep underground. Rosalie leant over me. She kissed my eyes. She bit my hair. Then, raising her face to the ceiling, she said . . .

'Oh beautiful and wondrous Lucifer! At last I've found my Warlock.'

She kissed me again deeply. I was about to speak, but she placed her hand over my mouth.

'Ssssh my darling,' and, taking me by the hand, she led me back into the bath and we washed each other again.

The next morning we showered and dressed and ate our breakfast without saying much. Then we drove further north towards Nambucca Heads.

As we drove along my thoughts were on the night before. It was strange. I had no guilt, or shame. I had tasted the forbidden fruits and I wanted more. I turned to Rosalie, whose silence I put down to the fact that she didn't know how I was feeling about the episode. She was staring straight ahead, smoking a cigarette.

'I enjoyed last night,' I said. 'In fact I enjoyed it more than I can tell you. I want more of it, Rosalie.'

Her face brightened and she turned and faced me, smiling for the first time that day.

'Oh Jimmy, I'm glad ... I've waited so long.'

She moved across the seat a little and started to rub my penis through the material of my trousers. As I got bigger, she undid my fly, stroking me until I was erect and then, leaning down, she took me into her mouth and sucked me, letting her head move slowly up and down. I pulled off the highway and parked under some trees at the edge of the road. I leant back as far as I could, lifting myself up to her. It didn't take very long, and as I came into her mouth she stayed there until she had every last drop out of me. I lit a cigarette and slumped back against the seat. Rosalie gently put my penis away and did up my fly.

'Was that nice, Jimmy?' she said, giving my crotch a final soft pat.

'It was beautiful Rosalie, beautiful ... Would you like me to do something nice to you?'

'Tonight my pet ... Let's wait till tonight.'

For the rest of the way to Nambucca Heads, Rosalie

sat close beside me. Offering me biscuits and drink. Lighting my cigarettes. And caressing my leg.

From that moment on I had no inhibitions with Rosalie. No shame, no hang-ups. We weren't in love, we both knew that. What we had was something different. We enjoyed the forbidden fruits that we could offer each other. And there were no lines of demarcation.

14

WE REACHED NAMBUCCA HEADS LATER THAT AFTER-
noon. Rosalie explained to me on the way that we were
going to meet a friend of her late mother's, whose name
was Rosalie also and who had been even more infamous
around the Cross. The man's name was Kurt Wester-
ling. During the Second World War he had been a
member of a famous group of men known only as Z
Force. They didn't even have a recognisable uniform
and not a lot was known about them, everything being
on a need-to-know basis only. But they'd received
special commando-type training for covert operations
and intelligence gathering behind enemy lines. They had
been used in the islands of Borneo and New Guinea and
also in Malaya, Burma and Sicily. At the end of the war
Kurt had become an army instructor, training men in
the arts he knew so well. With the outbreak of the
Korean campaign he had been active again with the military. He had numerous decorations for the work he
had performed and in later years he had done work for
MI6.

We had to ask directions to his place at a local shop.
It was about two miles down a dusty unsealed road
bordered by trees and heavy undergrowth. The house
and outbuildings were in a large clearing. As we drove
up to the front of the house, two large dogs came

bounding around the side of it and, mounting the four front steps, stood there snarling and defying us to leave the car.

'Lie down ya mongrels!' a stentorian voice bellowed out from inside. 'Lie down!'

The dogs looked over their shoulders as a tall heavy-set man walked out through the screen door onto the verandah behind them. He didn't seem to be able to get a good look at us through the windscreen, so he walked down the steps towards us.

'Sit! . . . And stay!' he yelled at the dogs. Which they did.

Rosalie poked her head and arm out the window and gave a little wave. 'It's me, Uncle Kurt,' she yelled. 'Rosalie.'

The bloody dogs started barking and growling again.

'Lie down ya bastards,' Kurt roared. 'Go on . . . Get around the back.' And, picking up a stick, hurled it in their direction.

As the dogs left the verandah and trotted away the big man walked to the car, stooped down and looked at Rosalie, throwing a quick glance at me and then bellowed again.

'Well I'll be stuffed! It's Rosalie. How the hell are ya, love?'

He grabbed the door handle and almost tore the door off as he opened it. Rosalie climbed out and he picked her up effortlessly, hugging her and saying 'Well I'll be stuffed.'

Up close like this, he seemed even bigger. He had a thick barrel chest and huge arms. His gingery hair was shot through in places with white streaks, his eyes were the bluest I had ever seen, and he had a great smile.

'And who's this you've got with ya?' he asked, still hugging Rosalie. 'Hop out mate and stretch the legs.'

I climbed out of the car and he put Rosalie down.

'Uncle Kurt, this is Jimmy Diamond, a very close friend of mine.'

Kurt stuck his paw out and it engulfed mine.

'How ya doin'?' I said to him, trying not to show the discomfort his grip was causing me.

'Good, good, mate. Jimmy, eh! Jesus . . . must be five or six years since I've seen you, Rosalie. I got ya letters and cards and things. Shit! Come on, let's go inside. It's too bloody hot out here. We'll have a cold beer.'

He opened the screen door and beckoned us in. It was a large rambling place, with a verandah all the way round and French doors, which opened inwards, to all the rooms. Insect screens covered the windows and doors.

It was cooler in the spacious living room, in the centre of which was a huge dining table.

'Sit down, sit down,' he said, dragging out a couple of chairs.

He walked to the kitchen, and amidst the noises of glasses clinking and the hiss of bottles being opened he chuckled and called out: 'Rosalie! . . . Jesus! Never thought I'd see you down this way.'

Kurt came back into the room with three bottles of beer held between the fingers of his left hand, and three glasses in his right. He plonked a bottle down in front of us, with a glass alongside it.

'Righto. Well, let's get a bit of this into us. This'll put hairs on ya chest,' he said, looking at me.

Rosalie glanced at me, and a sly smile spread on her face. I bumped her with my knee under the table.

After a mile of questions, directed at Rosalie, Kurt was silent for a moment. Then, with a note of sorrow in his voice, he said how much he still missed her mother. He then turned his attention to me.

'And what are you doin' with yourself Jimmy? You've got a bloody good girl there, you know.'

Rosalie saved me from answering. She told him the story from beginning to end, leaving nothing out. Kurt sat there, taking it all in, with an occasional nod of the head. He left the room only once, for more beers.

'Bloody dry argument, eh?' he said, patting me on the back.

After Rosalie's account of the events that had led us to his door, he sat quietly, nodding his head.

'She's right, you know,' Kurt said at last. 'Those bastards are like a pack of bloody wolves, they'd eat you alive, Jimmy. You've got a hell of a lot to learn ... Are you prepared to knuckle down? I'm telling you now, it isn't going to be easy. You've got a good frame, but there's not enough muscle on it. We've got to work on that, as well as other things. But if you can see it through ... then by the time I'm finished with you no bastard'll be your equal, unless he's had some of the same training. I've seen 'em all, you know. Some make it, some don't, but I've got a funny feeling about you. I think—and I said think—there's something there that'll keep you going. Are you willing to give it a go?'

'You can bet on one thing,' I said. 'I'll give it the best that I've got.'

'Oh you can count on that, Jimmy. In fact you'll give it your best and then some.'

After saying that, he rose from the table.

'Right, let's get some grub into us. But before we do that I'll show you where you can doss down. I suppose you buggers don't mind sleepin' together,' he said with a chuckle.

Rosalie and I moved our things from the car. The dogs must have sensed that we were friend and not foe and they just sniffed around us, wagging their tails and pissing on the wheels of the car. As we passed the kitchen on our to-and-fro trips we heard Kurt whistling and the smell of cooking wafted out to us. On the last trip he stuck his head out the door as we were going by.

'Everything okay?' he asked. 'Just yell if you want anything.'

Rosalie and I unpacked, sliding the case with the money and records from Margo's safe under the bed. We opened the French doors to the bedroom and we were sitting on the verandah having a smoke when Kurt poked his head around the corner.

'Tea'll be a little while yet. If you'd like to clean up, bathroom's just across the hall.'

'Thanks Uncle Kurt.'

Rosalie went to the closet in the hall and came back with some towels.

I feathered the taps till the temperature was okay and we climbed under the shower together. Our hairlessness had a stimulating effect on us both and I became hard as we soaped each other. Rosalie bent down and started sucking me, then stopped.

'Mmmmmm,' she said, 'I'll have some more of that later.'

Well, two can play at this game, I thought, and started soaping her vagina. Then I laid a towel on the top of a low cupboard.

'Come here,' I said.

Rosalie didn't even hesitate, but hopped straight up. I lifted her legs and, stooping under them, put one on each shoulder. Kneeling down in front of her, I looked right into her vagina. It was pink and wet, with not a single hair to be seen. I placed my mouth against it and kissed it, probing with my tongue. It was sensational. I touched the outside of her bum with my finger and she gave a little moan. Then I dropped her legs down, grabbed a towel and started to wipe up the water that had dripped onto the floor. She was still sitting there when I finished, smiling at me in a mischievous way.

'You just wait till later,' she said. And ran her tongue over her lips.

Showered and cleaned up, and randy as a pair of rattlesnakes, we shared tea with Kurt. It was a huge meal he had prepared. Steaks about an inch thick, potatoes, greens and a brown thin sauce that tasted superb. We washed it down with a bottle of red that Kurt said was made by one of the local Dagoes. After the meal he took Rosalie into the kitchen, showing her where everything was, and told her that he would appreciate it if she did the cooking . . . that he would be tied up with me most of the time.

The three of us were sitting around the table when Kurt announced that he was going to turn in. Rosalie and I decided to call it a day and do the same. With the door to our room closed and bolted, we stripped off.

‘What about we go through Margo's papers and things first?’ I said.

Rosalie nodded and I dragged the leather case out from under the bed and opened it. With the case between us, we started to sort the contents. We removed all the cash first, and counted it. There was nearly £19,000, which was a small fortune in those days, but Rosalie didn't even turn a hair. She hopped up, grabbed one of the bags with the string handles and packed the money away neatly. The only other thing of value that we came across was a black leather-bound ledger. It was Margo's diary as well, but along with personal entries were the dates, times, places, and amounts paid in various bribes. And who they went to. There was a complete list of all the coppers who were on the take.

‘Put it with the money,’ I told Rosalie.

The rest of the stuff we decided to burn.

With that out of the way, we lay on the bed. It was one of the earliest nights I'd had in the last two years. We lay there, playing with each other and talking quietly for a while. Suddenly, Rosalie turned and kissed me, long and lingering.

‘Now we've got some other business to take care of,’ she said.

Later that night, we drifted off to sleep, both exhausted from our lovemaking.

15

FOR THE NEXT EIGHT MONTHS KURT PUT ME THROUGH an intensive training program. I ran and jogged carrying weights. Cut down timber and firewood with a heavy axe. Did special exercises. Learnt how to survive in the bush and to blend into the environment. You were there but invisible. He taught me unarmed combat and how to use a knife. I mastered the use of rifle and handgun. I showed him the automatic in the cigar box and he went to work on it, making a silencer in his garage. Then he made me master it. With the silencer on the gun it gave only a muffled cough instead of an ear-shattering bang.

I learnt intelligence techniques. What drugs and injections can be used for purposes ranging from unconsciousness to death. How to use the cover at hand to one's best advantage. How to put together and detonate explosives without blowing myself up in the process. It was lucky we were so far from town, because the number of shots that were fired and explosive devices detonated during this time must have sounded like a mini-war.

I also learnt to pick locks and enter a building through glass in a silent manner. How to tail a vehicle, from in front as well as from behind. How to use camouflage. Types of clothing that were best for the job, whatever that job may be. How to handle dogs, trained to attack and kill. I learned how to secure a prisoner. How to interrogate him without leaving a mark, yet causing him excruciating agony in the process.

Under Kurt's guidance and training I had packed on the muscle he wanted. I looked good and felt good. I also felt confident. But one of the best lessons he taught me was patience.

Then, one night at the tea table, Kurt turned to Rosalie.

'Well ... He's ready. I can't teach him anything more.'

'Are you sure, Uncle Kurt?'

'Too bloody right I'm sure. The bugger could teach me a thing or two now. That's how sure I am.' His voice had a ring of pride in it and he turned to me and smiled. 'You've done real good, Jimmy. Real good, boy. Funny thing is, I always knew you would. There's one last piece of advice I'd like to give you, though. Never underestimate an enemy. Even a rat will fight if cornered. If you're not sure of an enemy and you've got him in the sights ... eliminate him. Give yourself nothing to worry about.'

With that last little speech, my training was complete.

We stayed with Kurt for another two weeks after that. Winding down physically but doing mental exercises to keep me sharp and alert. We offered Kurt some of the money we had but he refused, saying he didn't need it. No amount of enticement would persuade him to accept a penny.

On the morning of the day we planned to leave, Kurt asked me to go for one last walk with him. We walked for 20 minutes until we reached the bank of a nearby river. There we sat down and Kurt did all the talking. I listened to every word he said, and committed to memory all that he asked me.

At the last minute, when we were finally packed and already in the car, Kurt leant down and looked me right in the eye.

'Now you're sure you've got the name and address, right?' he asked. 'And the telephone number?'

'Like it's tattooed on my brain, Kurt. Once again, thanks for everything.'

'Don't mention it, son. My pleasure. Just remember what I told you this morning. Good luck . . . And don't forget to pop back some time, eh!'

When we were bumping our way down the track to the gate Rosalie asked what all the secrecy that morning was about.

'Just man talk, Rosalie. It's about an insurance policy Kurt wants me take.'

Rosalie gave a shrug. 'Seems pretty bloody mysterious to me. How long have you been interested in insurance?'

'Since this morning, love, I'm real interested.'

As we left Kurt's place, I took one last long look from the gate, then headed south for Sydney. We took our time, there was no hurry now. I was the hunter, not them. They were the quarry and I was the Tiger, and a hungry one at that.

The closer we got to Sydney the keener my senses got. We stopped at Parramatta and booked into a motel under assumed names. The next day we got rid of the Holden. It had been a gift from Margo and might be recognised, so we traded it in on a Plymouth, making up the difference in cash. Rosalie bought a couple of wigs, wore ordinary make-up and generally tidied up her appearance. I bought some close-fitting black cotton clothing, binoculars, a 12-gauge shotgun that I cut down, then test fired to examine the shot pattern, and all the other equipment that I needed. I got Rosalie to buy a box of surgical rubber gloves, which she dyed for me with Indian ink. I purchased a pair of black suede boots, with a rubber sole that was non-slip on wet or dry surfaces. Each and every thing we bought was chosen with care. We never left a correct address at the pubs and motels we stayed at and we moved constantly. When the time came to move in closer and start sur-veillance, we rented a house that was furnished with a lock-up garage and stocked it full of everything. By the time we were finished we had enough supplies to last for six months without ever having to leave.

The Tiger was on the prowl . . . Hunting!

PART

2

The
Tiger

16

THERE IS A CAR PARK, AVAILABLE TO PATRONS, AT THE rear of the Manhattan Club. The club itself is a gambling den, which, according to certain police and politicians, does not exist. However, it remained open and operational with the full knowledge of the local constabulary. Money speaks in all languages.

A shadow flitted across the parking area, then blended into the dark space at the rear of a parked vehicle. The silence was broken for a split second by a ripping sound as some adhesive material was peeled from a roll. A blackened hand moved across the rear bumper of a Chevrolet sedan parked in the lot. When the hand came away, a yellow textured piece of tape remained, about a foot long, on what was once a continuous chrome surface. The shadow moved again, to the edge of the allotment, and vanished into the night. The time was 1 a.m. and, apart from the distant barking of a dog and the occasional sound of a passing car on the main street, nothing else stirred.

The rear door of the club opened, spilling light down the stairs that led to the parking lot.

Joseph Flood emerged, called something over his shoulder and, accompanied by a female companion and another man, made his way down the stairs. Laughter broke out within the group as they chatted and made their way to Flood's Chevrolet.

The car moved out of the parking lot and drove up the alley at the side of the building. It paused momentarily at the kerb on Bayswater Road, then swung out and drove off. Further up the street, a vehicle parked on the left came to life and moved off also. Sitting well back, it followed Flood's vehicle. As the lights of the tail car lit up the rear of the Chevrolet, the reflective tape glowed brightly.

When the lead car entered the city proper, other vehicles got between the Chevy and the tail, but every now and then the tape would flash up ahead, enabling the trailing vehicle to follow and turn with ease. The Chevy wended its way through the city and finally pulled up in a side street at Redfern. The second vehicle didn't even turn into the street as the driver noticed a 'Dead End' traffic sign. It passed the street, did a U-turn and, with lights off, rolled to a halt on the far side of the intersection, giving the driver a clear view—with the aid of high-powered binoculars—as Flood's male passenger got out of the car, waved everybody goodnight, and made his way to a nearby house.

As the Chevy turned back onto the main street and drove away, the driver of the surveillance vehicle ducked down below window level. A moment later he appeared once more and flashed a quick glance down the side street, as if taking an instant mental photograph to be stored for future use. Then the vehicle fired to life again and moved off, picking up the flashing trail of the Chevrolet as it swung into Abercrombie Street. Twenty minutes later the Chevy pulled into the driveway of a house down by the harbour. The driver of the second car made mental notes of the address and details of the surrounding area as he continued on without stopping.

Inside the house, some time later, Joseph Flood unlocked the glass doors that opened onto a high balcony and walked out to look out over the harbour. He yawned, stretched, and breathed in the clean salt air that was carried to him on a gentle breeze. Down below, a soft growl was quietened by Flood as he leant over the railing and gave reassurances to a dog, unaware as he did so that a pair of eyes watched his every movement from the concealment of the jumbled and piled rock wall that separated the rear of the property from the harbour. Flood then walked back into the house, closing and locking the doors behind him. Ten minutes later, the lights inside were extinguished. The dog gave a low growl as, down on the rocks, a ghostly shadow moved, then dissolved into the surrounding darkness.

Along with the animals of the jungle, man is a creature of habit and pattern. Just as the lower species of life in the jungle follow the same game trails to the waterhole at the same times, so too does man, without being consciously or constantly aware of it, follow the same paths. Oh, he may vary his routine slightly in his day-to-day search to relieve boredom, just as the animals do as they forage wider in search of a tasty morsel or a new mate. However, he always returns and uses the same game trail that leads to the security of his den. But it betrays a false security in man, based on times when the lord of the manor lived in a castle with moats and drawbridges, with sentries posted through the night on the high abutments and parapets.

Some who need security could do no better than read back in history and learn that some of the strongest fortresses were breached, and the lord assassinated, not by an army, but by a solitary intruder with a single purpose.

For four consecutive nights, the surveillance of Joseph Flood continued. The pattern remained the same, with only slight variations of time and detail. To a shop here, a different restaurant for a meal, or a different pub for a drink. But, just like the animal that he was, Joseph Flood always returned to the waterhole, to his house on the harbour. And when he had done so he strolled out onto the balcony to breathe in some sea air before retiring to bed.

At 10.15 p.m. on the fifth night, on the rock formation at the rear of Flood's residence, a shadow moved with complete silence. The gentle, continuous, soft soothing music of the water was the only sound as it lapped and rippled at the base of the rocks. Then the continuity was punctuated by a gentle *plop* as something soft and wet landed on the lawn down below the balcony. The dog, who had been dozing, sprang to his feet and, with a growl, trotted over in the direction of the noise, where it picked up a pleasant scent. A sudden tearing sound of paper could be heard, and the sounds of the animal wolfing down the culprit responsible for disturbing its rest. A moment later there was a whimper, followed by a thrashing about on the lawn, then everything lapsed once more back into the steady rhythm of the water as it played its music against the rocky shore.

A minute or two elapsed. Then the top of the wall

swelled and momentarily changed its silhouette against the night sky. A dark figure appeared on the lawn, then silently moved over to where the dog lay on its side. The man squatted and checked the animal, like a doctor examining an accident victim. But there were no signs of life. Satisfied that the cyanide had done its job, he stood, then quickly moved over below the balcony, unwrapping a soft dark rope that had been coiled around his waist and removing a padded hook from his belt. He tied the hook to the end of the rope, along which he fashioned a series of knots about a yard apart. The hook, wrapped in surgical dressing, was thrown up and over the balcony rail, landing on the decking with a soft thud. The knotted rope was gradually reeled in until the hook snagged itself on the railing. Satisfied that the line was secure after testing his weight on it, he scaled hand over hand, locking his feet against the lower knots and lessening the weight on his arms. A hand clamped around the rail and the man climbed silently over it onto the balcony, removed the hook and retrieved the rope. Both ends of the balcony were closed in, giving it privacy from neighbours. The intruder moved to a chair in the corner and, sitting down, removed the padded hook from the rope and proceeded to unfasten the knots. He coiled the rope as he worked, placing it down alongside the chair.

The patience of an animal that waits in ambush is determined by its hunger. The greater the hunger, the greater the patience. The hunter reclining in the chair in the darkness of the Flood balcony was hungry, very hungry. He was ravenous, and prepared to wait for as long as it took. Only the occasional guarded flash of a lighter flame and the glow of a cigarette held in a cupped hand broke the darkened corner of his concealment. No ash was left on the balcony but was carefully placed in a paper bag. The butt was extinguished with saliva in the centre of the dark gloved hand, placed in the bag with the ash and then stowed away in a pocket of the black clothing.

As Joseph Flood unlocked the glass doors and walked out onto his balcony later that evening, the darkened figure moved swiftly and silently out of the corner. Flood was hit from behind with a paralysing blow with the edge of a hardened hand. The blow switched off all Flood's sensory powers, and his ability to call or scream for assistance. As he crumpled, two arms arrested his fall, then lowered him gently onto the decking without a sound. A noose was fashioned expertly and quickly, placed over Flood's head and pulled up firmly around his neck, the knot resting below the left ear. The inert body was dragged to the railing. Deft hands played out a little over six feet of rope, like a tailor measuring cloth, and then tied it onto the railing. Returning quickly to the chair, the hunter picked up the hook and secured it in his belt. Then he moved back to his victim. Picking up Flood, he laid him over the railing with his legs dangling into space and held him there, balanced. Flood gave signs that he was regaining consciousness and groaned softly. In two more seconds he became aware of his position. But so did his nemesis who was supporting him, who bent quickly to Flood's ear.

'Remember Margo? You fuckin' piece of shit,' he whispered, and heaved Flood over the rail.

The last thing that Joseph Flood saw, before he went to Hell, was a bright flash of light that exploded somewhere deep in his brain as the spinal cord in his neck snapped. With the nervous system of his lower body now cut off and unable to receive messages from his brain, the muscles that had previously controlled his bowel movements relaxed and voided themselves of the faeces they held, which ran down his legs, fouling his body in death and dripping onto the grass beneath his slowly turning and swaying body.

Flood's assassin moved to the rail and climbed over. Then, holding onto the edge of the decking, he let himself drop with a knees-bend fall to absorb the shock, rolled and sprang lightly to his feet. Moving over to the body of the dog, he retrieved the torn paper that had covered the deadly bait, picked up the dead animal and carried it to the edge of the rocks, where he stopped and looked back for a second at the hanging victim.

'That's one, Margo!' he said softly. Then, loaded with the burden of the dog, he melted into the shadows.

Neighbours of the Flood residence were rudely awakened that morning around 7 o'clock by hysterical female screams. And shortly after came the sounds of sirens wailing. The evening papers carried headlines ... 'UNDERWORLD IDENTITY SUICIDES.'

And, in Valhalla, Margo smiled. The vendetta had begun.

17

CHARLIE COSTANZA HAD A WEAKNESS FOR BOATS. EVERY spare moment he got he would either be out on his boat, deep-sea fishing or just sailing around the harbour, big-noting himself and giving those he was trying to impress 'a gooda time.' His boat, a 35-foot diesel-powered cruiser, had at one time been used to hunt marlin and yellowfin tuna off Cairns in North Queensland.

Costanza was big in stature, but not tall. He was obese, with a huge gut from the diet he liked most. *Italian.* Too much *vino rosso* and pasta dishes with rich sauces, coupled with his constant intake of pistachio nuts and salami, washed down with gallons of beer. He had a perpetual blotchy red complexion, stank of garlic, and sweated profusely at the slightest physical exercise.

It was his gluttony and entertaining on the boat that led to the predicament that he was in now. Lying on his side, trussed up on the floor in the cabin of his boat. His hands fastened behind his back, his ankles lashed together, a running non-slip noose was around his neck, the rope passing underneath his bound wrists and tied to the bindings on his ankles. His knees were bent back so any attempt he made to straighten, or stand, would tighten the noose around his neck and slowly strangle him. The final humiliation was a wide piece of adhesive tape across his mouth.

His captor, piloting the boat out through Sydney Heads, was muscular in build, and just a fraction under six feet in height. Dark-haired and tanned, he looked healthy and he was just that. Very healthy and extremely fit.

It had taken a month of patient surveillance and stalking to capture Costanza, the hunter waiting sometimes for hours for his quarry to reappear from sea or some other activity. Now his patience was rewarded.

Costanza had taken a party of three women and two men out to sea the previous afternoon for an all-night romp. The hunter spent that night in a vehicle parked up the road from the dock area, from which he had a clear view of the jetty. It wasn't till 8 a.m. that the boat returned. Then, wearing casual clothes, a cap and dark glasses, with a newspaper rolled in one hand, the hunter had strolled along the dock like a sightseer or a boating enthusiast. He halted just past Costanza's boat, feigning interest in a big two-masted schooner tied up to the pier. Costanza's party were on deck, all chatting away.

'Hey Charlie!' a voice said. 'What about all the fuckin' mess and garbage? We'd better stay and give ya a hand to clean this shit up.'

'No no no,' said Charlie. 'I'm a goa too. I goa home now and be backa later to clean him up. You noa worry, isa okay.'

Further offers were also made but Costanza refused all of them. He wouldn't hear of such a thing. Finally, the party left the boat, walked up to the street and went their various ways.

It was almost dark when Costanza made it back to his boat, climbing on board carrying a large plastic bin and some garbage bags. The hunter's senses quickened when he noted that Costanza was alone. Dressed in dark clothing and carrying a small canvas overnight bag in his left hand, the hunter walked purposefully onto the dock. It was deserted. A bit too early yet for the night watchman, who usually arrived around 7 o'clock. Walking quickly to Costanza's boat, he silently moved on board. He could see Charlie through a porthole alongside the open cabin door. He was chewing and drinking wine from the bottle. Reaching under the dark reefer jacket, the hunter took out a silenced pistol and stepped straight into the cabin, aiming the gun at Costanza's head

'If you move you're dead now, you bastard . . . *Capisce?*'

Costanza's mouth flew open, not to yell, but in fright and shock. The bottle in his hand dropped to the floor and wine gurgled onto the carpet.

'Not one fuckin' sound, Charlie. You understand?'

Costanza nodded his head. Still shocked at the suddenness of the intrusion.

'Move! . . . Get on the fuckin' floor right now . . . Move.'

With frightened movements, Costanza sat down on the floor, trying to avoid sitting in the spilt wine.

'Not like that. Get on your belly, you fat pig.'

The tone of the hunter's voice told Costanza his only chance of remaining alive was to obey. He looked at the silenced gun, then rolled onto his side and over onto his stomach.

'What cha doa here? What cha wanta from me?'

'Shut up! Not one fuckin' sound. Put your hands behind your head.'

Then, with one knee in the middle of Costanza's back, and the muzzle of the gun pressed hard into the back of his neck, the hunter reached one-handed into the open canvas bag and took out a length of rope.

'Put your hands down behind your back.'

As Costanza complied with the order, the looped end of the rope was pulled tight around his wrists and tied quickly and expertly. More rope was produced and used to secure Charlie's ankles. There was one more rope, which the hunter tied in a special knot, pulling it into a noose that he slipped over Costanza's head and tightened until it was a snug fit around his neck. Then he passed the loose end under the Italian's wrists and, pulling up his victim's legs, he tied it to the trussed ankles. Reaching back into the bag, he took out a roll of surgical tape which he stuck onto Costanza's cheek and wrapped it twice around his head. This done, he turned his victim onto his side.

'Understand this, you piece of filth. You move and that fuckin' rope around your neck tightens and you choke you bastard. Now fuckin' nod if you understand.'

Costanza nodded feebly, then his head fell back onto the carpet.

Moving out of the cabin the hunter inspected the dock area. It was still deserted. Slipping the front and rear moorings, he returned to the cabin, bent to recheck his captive's bindings and, satisfied, walked forward to the controls. He moved astern gently, away from the dock, and then engaged forward gear, opening the throttle a little as he headed towards the entrance of the harbour.

The boat moved out to sea on an easterly course. There was little wind, just a slight nor'-westerly breeze, and no swell. As night began its swift descent, the hunter spun the dial on the auto-pilot, threw the switch and engaged it. Checking the horizon, and then the radar, he turned on the navigation lights and left the helm.

Not a word was spoken as the boat ploughed through the calm sea. The hunter moved into the galley area across from Costanza and, opening the fridge, took out a bottle of beer and removed the cap. He sat down and smoked a cigarette. The frightened eyes of Costanza never left his face.

Hopping up from time to time, the hunter checked the radar and the horizon. The lights of Sydney had disappeared and become just a dull brightness in the western sky when he stopped the boat. Glancing at the fathometer but being unsure of the anchor cable length, he decided to let the boat drift in the calm conditions.

Walking back to his victim, he reached under his jacket and produced a hunting knife. Costanza's eyes widened as his captor bent down and severed the rope on the noose at the point where it was tied onto the ankles. Checking the bindings on the wrists once more, he jerked Costanza up into a sitting position and leant him back against a bunk. Then, reaching behind Charlie's ear, he located the end of the tape and ripped it off Costanza's face with a winding motion. A yelp of pain followed the final rip as the tape came away from the captive's mouth. The hunter sat across from his victim and, looking at him, said . . .

'Now we're going to have a little talk, you greasy bastard, and if I even suspect that you're feeding me bullshit I'll cut you to pieces, a bit at a time. You can scream as much as you like you treacherous fuckin' toad, but no one will hear you out here. We're over twenty miles off shore, so think hard, bucko, before you answer. Where's Abe Stafford living?'

'I don'ta know whoa you talk about.'

'You prick,' his captor shouted and, leaning forward, placed the knife between Costanza's ear and his head, pulling it back with some downward pressure. Costanza screamed and the question was repeated.

'Ina the big house ina Roslyn Street.' The voice was just a croak now. 'Please. . . don'ta cuta me a no more. I tella you whata you need.'

'Who lives there with him?'

'Heesa have his woman Mandy there. I'ma bleed bad.'

Blood was running down Costanza's cheek and dripped onto the collar of his shirt.

'You'll bleed a fuckin' sight worse if you don't keep the answers straight. Where's Bob Driscoll living now?'

'Ina his samea place ata Manly. Why a you wanna know alla this?'

'Now get this right, bastard. How did Margo end up in Rushcutters Park?'

'She is coming in to a the club and a yell at a Abe heesa doing the wrong thing. Heesa say no, I canna prove a to you. Heesa ring up Bob, and a then tell a her to come with a him and a he prove it.'

Costanza held nothing back. He explained that Abe had been told to get rid of her. Then he related to his captor that—after telling Margo that he was bona fide and that he could prove it—she had left the club with Abe and Mandy. Stafford had said they were going to meet with Driscoll, Flood and himself. Costanza admitted he knew that she'd never make it to the meeting. At Rushcutters Bay Abe had stopped the car and shot her, dumping her body in the park. When the other three were finally contacted, they celebrated the takeover with a party at Driscoll's home. The plan to take over Margo's business had been in operation for a long time, and Bernie Walker hadn't been hit for doing the wrong thing by the *Famiglia*, as Abe had suggested. He was shot because he'd found out what was going on and had tackled them about it before going to Margo. He'd died for his trouble and loyalty to her. Abe and Mandy were to take over the brothels. Driscoll and Flood were to get the gambling and drugs. And Costanza's piece of the action was the sly grog and SP bookie bag.

Costanza's captor acted swiftly after he'd listened to the information. Cutting the rope on his victim's ankles he ordered him to stand. Then, holding onto the rope still around his neck, he pushed Costanza onto the deck against the starboard railing and shot him in the back of the head. The impact of the .38 round knocked Costanza forward and his knees buckled, leaving the body half-draped over the rail. His assassin went further aft to three lobster pots and, cutting a large flat lead weight from one of them, he carried it back, tied it to the body with the rope still attached to the neck and threw it overboard. Then, grabbing his victim's legs he let

Charlie Costanza's body plunge into the shark-infested waters.

'That's two, Margo,' the assassin said, looking upwards, 'and I'll get them all. Every last one of them.'

Moving back inside the cabin, all signs of activity were erased. The rope and surgical tape placed in the canvas bag. The cabin given a general clean-up. Rubbish and food scraps were thrown overboard. Then the boat was fired to life and a course set for the harbour.

Arriving back at the dock in the early hours of the morning, the boat was moored in its place. Peering up the pier, the hunter noticed the lights in the night watchman's office at the far end of the jetty. He could see the man through a large glass window, reading at his table. Taking a big duffel coat and a cap from a cupboard in the cabin, and stuffing a cushion under his shirt, the assassin left the boat.

Stooped over a little and letting his shoulders sag in an endeavour to lose an inch or two in height, he walked onto the dock. When he was side-on to the office he glanced towards it. The night watchman looked up and gave a wave, as if in recognition. The hunter casually waved back and strolled off into the night.

After three weeks, by which time even the most optimistic started to suspect foul play in the disappearance of Charlie Costanza, the night watchman swore on all that was holy that he'd seen the man leave his boat in the early hours of the morning and that an entry he'd made in his log at the time supported it. This made him the last person to see Costanza alive, and inquiries concerning the missing man's whereabouts moved away from the marina.

Costanza's disappearance became the focus of the evening press, who treated Sydney's leading underworld figures as though they were movie stars. 'WHERE'S CHARLIE?' the headlines screamed repeatedly. But Charlie's whereabouts remained a mystery to all— except, that is, to a beautiful soul in Valhalla and the avenging hungry Tiger.

18

AS MARGO COLENZO HAD DIED INTESTATE AND, by careful manoeuvring, Abe Stafford and Mandy Palmer had taken over her house in Roslyn Street. With the assistance of documents that they'd procured, they manufactured a case that was put before the Public Trustee and they ended up buying the house for a paltry sum. That must have given them a special thrill. It made those who had been close to Margo feel sick to the stomach. There was very little the Public Trustee could do but accept what was before him and give his blessing to the silver-tongued lawyer who represented Stafford and Palmer.

A little more than three weeks after the disappearance of Charlie Costanza, a night-time meeting was taking place in this house. There were five people present: Abe Stafford, Mandy Palmer, Bob Driscoll, Georgio Bendini (Driscoll's chauffeur and bodyguard) and Freddie Kincaid, who had taken Joe Flood's place. The five people sat around a big oval table in the living room. Bottles of liquor, glasses, cigarettes and ashtrays littered the top, and a haze of smoke hung in lazy clouds under a big lamp on a high stand in the corner. It was 9 p.m., and to say that concern showed on the faces of all present would be an understatement.

'Will somebody tell me what the fuck is going on

155

round here?' Abe Stafford asked. 'Joe is found hanging by the bloody neck from his balcony . . . and before anybody says anything, I never bought that fuckin' suicide thing from the start. We all knew the guy. I spoke to him that fuckin' night. He had as much intention of committing suicide as I have of divin' off the fuckin' Harbour Bridge. But he's found hangin' with a broken fuckin' neck, while his sheila's in bed just twenty bloody feet away. Now Charlie's disappeared . . . Apparently he took the boat out before he vanished, but what fuckin' for? What do you reckon, Bob?'

'Jesus Abe, I told you before. I haven't got a clue and that's the truth. There's one thing I do know, though. The Eyeties know as much about Charlie's disappearance as we do. And they're as pissed off about it as we are. I wouldn't mind putting a wager on the guy Margo fell for's got something to do with this.'

'What? Oh, bullshit, Bob. This thing's got a bloody professional ring to it. Just think for a moment will ya. How the hell could whoever it fuckin' is get inside Joe's joint to do the job on him? You mean to tell me you believe that hillbilly did it? For Christ's sake Bob, act your age.'

'You're missing it, Abe. Margo's safe had been emptied and there must have been a decent haul there . . . What I'm trying to say is that he could have hired someone.'

'Hired my arse . . . Fuck me, Bob, hire who? You just don't go into the fuckin' phone box and ring some cunt and say, Hey! I want you to hit a couple of jokers for me.'

'What about Rosalie?' Mandy piped in. 'She's

nowhere to be seen. She knows a lot of people, Abe, and the three of them were pretty close, you know that.'

Abe gave a snort of disgust. 'Something to do with it my arse. You're as bad as Bob. What the fuck do you think she could do? They pissed off because they thought they might be next ... Nah! she'd be sitting somewhere talking mumbo-bloody-jumbo and holding those little black masses of hers.'

'What've the cops got to say?' Kincaid asked. 'Have they got any theories?'

'Freddie, those pricks wouldn't know if their arses were bored or sleeved. They believe Joe committed fuckin' suicide, for Christ's sake. When Joe's bird told us that the dog was missing I passed it on, and do you know what those brainless bastards came up with? ... That the fuckin' thing just up and ran away. You ever hear of a guard dog doing that?'

'Well what happened when you asked them to look for Jimmy and Rosalie?'

'It's the same story there. Look, our blokes are doin' what they can as a favour to me. And for them too. They know she had records somewhere, but it's not in their best interests to make too big a song and dance out of this in case that fuckin' book of Margo's turns up and tips the shit on everyone. Some of the names in it go right to the fuckin' top. So we can forget a bloody nationwide search for 'em.'

'Look Abe,' said Driscoll. 'I know you don't take it seriously, but I feel it all comes back to that Jimmy guy.'

'Christ, here you go again. Try and get it through

157

your bloody head, will ya? I haven't been sittin' on my arse when it comes to that cowboy. I sent a couple of blokes up to Lismore. He'd been back there all right, but it was while he was with fuckin' Margo. He hasn't been up there since. He'd know we were lookin' for him all right so, unless he was completely fuckin' crazy, that would be the last place he'd go to. He'll be livin' it up somewhere all right, and we'll find the bastard . . . But Joe and Charlie? No way, Bob, he wouldn't know shit from clay if it had fuckin' labels on it. Next you'll be talkin' fuckin' little green men.'

'Well what are we going to do about it then? Let's assume we've got a common enemy. How do we go about taking him out?'

'Now ya startin' to talk sense, Bob. I'll tell ya what we fuckin' do about it. We have a bloke on us all the time, in the house, the club, everywhere, even when we take a shit, do you get the picture? When we're goin' somewhere we have someone tailin' us. And if this bastard, whoever he is, pokes his head up . . . Whammo! We'll hit him that hard and fast he'll think he's fuckin' surrounded. So enough of this chickenshit we've been goin' on with. We keep constantly in touch. Anything, anything at all, no matter what. If it's unusual . . . let's know about it. We're gonna need a few extra blokes we can rely on, Bob. That's where you can help. Can you get us a couple of Don Luigi's boys? Just till we can clean this thing up.'

'Yeah. I think I can fix that. When do you want them to start?'

'Right fuckin' now. So get on it. Okay, let's break this up. I've got a few other things to take care of. But remember this bastard is good, whoever he is. So don't take any fuckin' chances. Keep in touch.'

The meeting broke up and the arrangements were made, but their problems were far from being solved. In fact, they had scarcely begun.

19

AS THE MEETING AT ROSLYN STREET WAS TAKING PLACE,
so too was another plan taking shape at the rear of Bob
Driscoll's seaside home. They were big houses in this
part of town, most of them on large blocks. The rear
section of Driscoll's home was completely enclosed by
a tall manicured hedge. Nothing at that time of night
seemed to be out of place or unusual. Nothing moved,
and there were only the normal sounds of the evening.
An occasional car as it passed on the street, and the
sound of the surf as it rolled onto the beach on the far
side of the esplanade. But there was something not quite
right. The wandering cat on its nocturnal prowl sensed
it as it came slinking through the bottom of the hedge
at the end of the yard. Moving with feline grace it suddenly froze in mid-stride, then streaked away down the
side of the house as a figure seemed to appear out of
the ground alongside the garden shed, gliding and
blending with the shadows in the yard as it moved
silently up to the house.

A rear window was the intruder's target. He had
studied the layout for the past half-hour. A black-
gloved hand reached into a pocket of the dark com-
mando-style overall and came out again with a thin
tool. It was slipped up between the timberwork of the
two windows, where they joined. A quick movement of

the wrist was followed by a dull metallic 'clack' as the locking mechanism sprang open. With the window open, the man looked like a fluid black mass as he entered the building over the sill and melted once more into the gloom. Once he was inside the window was re-locked and a small powerful flashlight was turned on, showing the intruder that he was in a games room. There was a large billiard and snooker table, a bar along one wall and an assortment of casual tables and chairs. Moving to a door on the right of him he came across a flight of stairs that ran to the storey above. Mounting these he came out in a small vestibule that led to a dining area, then to a lounge. Light from the well-lit esplanade filtered through partly closed venetian blinds. The torch was extinguished and the figure remained motionless for a few seconds to allow his eyes to become accustomed to the meagre light. He moved quickly then. Into a hallway which led to four large bedrooms and out onto a glassed-in section. At the end of this area was a door and a stairway that ran down to the garage. Quickly descending the stairs a flash of the torch revealed two car spaces, with an MG sports parked in one bay. Dust on the paintwork showed that it hadn't been used for some time. Further examination of the garage revealed what he was looking for.

Below the stairway was a large angular storage cupboard. There was not a lot inside. Towards the narrow end was a bundle of sails that had been tossed in untidily, while shelves running along the back wall held a variety of tools, boxes of nails and screws and car maintenance equipment. Along the other wall were two casement windows with standard securing latches on them.

The hunter's plan was now taking final shape. All that was required was the patience of the waiting game. Settling himself into a comfortable position with one of the sails under him and the others bundled loosely over him, he waited.

The luminous dial of his watch showed 11.55 p.m. when the sound of the garage door opening announced the arrival of the enemy. A car entered and the ignition was switched off. Then came the sound of car doors opening and closing, and of feet moving on the concrete floor.

'The other car's arrived, Bob,' Georgio Bendini said. 'It's across the street.'

'Thanks George,' said Driscoll. 'Jesus! What a bloody day.'

Sounds of the garage door closing and of a bolt being driven home came to the hunter.

'I'd better duck upstairs and take a look first, Bob. Then check out the back.'

'Let's call it a day, George, I'm really buggered. You get your head down too. The blokes out front can keep watch. Personally, I think Abe is being a bit paranoid over this business.'

Footsteps passing the cupboard storage area, then climbing the stairs.

'Gee! I dunno, Bob. I don't know about Joe Flood, but it's not like Charlie Costanza to just up and off.'

'Let's worry about it tomorrow. I'm stuffed.'

The door at the top of the stairs being closed and locked. Footsteps upstairs, muffled voices, doors opening, the sounds of running water. A toilet being flushed. More muffled voices, and finally silence.

The luminous dial showed the time was 1.45 a.m. before the hunter moved again. Slowly, he extricated himself from the soft sail cloth and, silently opening the door, he stepped out into the garage. Light from a narrow gap at the bottom of the doors gave a dim light. The burring noise of someone snoring came to the hunter, muffled by distance. Then, moving on the soft cushions of special rubber soles, he glided silently over to the two-door Chrysler sedan. It was a large vehicle, with big flashy tail fins. Just the fraction of a thank-you smile flickered on the camouflaged face, streaked with dark military make-up, as he noticed the driver's-side window was still wound down. Placing a leg over the door, and holding onto the hood with his gloved fingers, he leant back and lifted the other leg up, over, and into the vehicle and slid inside. Lying motionless for a moment or two, he then reached inside his overall and from a deep pocket produced a flat packet. Ten inches long, four inches wide, and an inch and a half thick. Unfolding the soft waxed covering paper, he screwed it up and placed it in his pocket. The tangy smell of nitroglycerine drifted into his nostrils from the AN90 gelignite resting on his chest. Taking the explosive in his right hand, and sliding further under the dash, he grabbed the bottom of the steering wheel with his left hand and carefully lowered himself down until his back was resting on the floor in front of the driver's seat. Reaching up he pressed the soft explosive in and behind the centre of the dashboard, moulding it around the cable controls that operated the vehicle's heater and several electrical leads till there was no hope of it falling down. Reaching back into a zip-closing pocket, he produced a detonator. He took out the pen-sized flash-light and, turning it on, held it between his teeth as he uncoiled the electrical leads of the detonator. The ends of the leads had small alligator clips that had been previously attached. Pressing the two-inch detonator into the explosive, he froze.

He quickly extinguished the torch. Footsteps sounded upstairs and his right hand moved in under his overall and took hold of the haft of a hunting knife. He felt his heart quicken slightly, but a moment later a toilet flushed far above him and the footsteps sounded again. Then silence. Waiting ten minutes more, he took his hand off the knife and switched the torch on again. Then, taking the clip on the black wire from the detonator, he earthed it on a supporting bracket on the back of the dash. Reaching once more into a pocket he produced a one-sided razorblade, a piece of electrical tape guarding the cutting edge. Peeling this off he stuck it to the steering column. With the blade he pared the plastic insulation off the lead that carries power to the solenoid when the ignition is switched on. Then, taking the red lead of the detonator he clipped it onto the exposed copper of the lead. He removed the insulation tape, stuck it back on the blade and put it away in a pocket. Taking the flashlight in his hand he inspected the work. Satisfied, he swung himself back up onto the seat and checked the floor for telltale signs of his handiwork. He picked up three small pieces of red plastic and placed them in his pocket. Turning off the torch once again, he lay there for a few minutes, letting his eyes become accustomed to the dark.

Moving quietly over to the casement windows, he

lifted back the dark curtain and cautiously looked out. To the left of the windows, a leafy bush was large enough to obscure the vision of the sentries on the far side of the road as he made his withdrawal. Gradually he inched the latch securing the window and snaked over the sill to the ground outside. He crouched there for a moment in the shadows before standing and, reaching through the window, he pulled the curtain back across before pushing the window closed. Using the bush as natural cover he looked across the street at the car with its two sentries. Light coming from the esplanade illuminated the inside of the vehicle, showing the occupants slouched down, their heads lying on the back of the seat, fast asleep. The hunter moved silently up the side of the house into the backyard, then disappeared into the shadows of the hedge.

Bob Driscoll had just about completed his breakfast when the phone rang.

'I'll get it,' he called out.

It was Abe Stafford, asking if he had anything to report.

'Not a thing, Abe. Quiet as a church around here.'

Stafford asked him to get over to Roslyn Street as soon as he could.

'See you in about forty-five,' said Driscoll, and hung up the phone. 'Come on, George, His Majesty demands an audience.'

Bendini led the way to the garage, followed by Driscoll, who climbed into the passenger seat while Bendini opened the garage door, waved to the car across the street and walked to the Chrysler. He fished the ignition keys from his pocket and climbed in behind the wheel. Placing the keys in the lock, he checked the gear lever, then turned the key . . .

Across the street the two sentries had already started up their car and were gazing up the driveway. As they watched and waited, there was a shattering roar. Flame and dust spewed from the garage and glass sprayed out in a deadly hail from the house, peppering the side of their car, which rocked with the shock wave. The front of the upper storey of Driscoll's house bounced up and then collapsed as the fractured walls of the garage refused to support it. Pieces of debris rained down into the street, and rattled on the roof of their vehicle.

As people ran into the street to see what on earth had happened, the driver of the sentry vehicle turned to his companion.

'Oh shit!' he screamed in panic. 'Let's get outta here. We're dead.'

He was already driving as he spoke.

The house by this time was engulfed in flames, fuelled to greater intensity by the Chrysler's ruptured petrol tank.

A quarter of a mile up the beach, a tourist in shorts, floral shirt and panama hat watched the scene through a pair of powerful binoculars

'Margo,' he said. Nothing more.

Back at Roslyn Street, a demented man raved and screamed. Too afraid to report personally, the sentries had rung their message through. Abe Stafford had turned ashen as he listened to the babbled message. Then, slamming the phone down, he screamed at

Mandy Palmer and the two extra men he had with him.

'I told him . . . I fuckin' told him, the stupid bastard. And now he's dead. They're both fuckin' dead.'

'Who are you talking about,' one of the bodyguards asked. 'Who's dead, Abe?'

'Who's dead? . . . I'll tell ya who the fuck's dead. Bob Driscoll and George Bendini, that's who's fuckin' dead. They drive home, park the car and lock the garage. There's two cunts in a car outside, supposed to be keepin' a bloody watch on things, and nothin' happens all fuckin' night they reckon. I rang him a while ago, for Christ's sake. Everything's okay Abe, he tells me, quiet as a fuckin' church. Then they get into the fuckin' car and . . . Whammo! The whole fuckin' joint explodes.'

He collapsed down into a lounge chair, head in hands. The others stood there shocked. Mandy Palmer walked over and placed her hand on his shoulder. No one spoke. Abe looked up at them.

'What the fuck are we dealin' with here—the fuckin' Phantom?'

WHEN ONE HAS BEEN IN PURSUIT OF AN ENEMY AND used guerilla warfare tactics, and the enemy is unaware that he is being stalked or about to be attacked, it makes the task of the hunter a lot easier. But things become more difficult when the enemy knows that he is in jeopardy. He may not know the size or the strength of his attacker, or even his identity, but the prey will close ranks and reinforce his perimeters and defences. If the hunter makes the slightest slip-up he can soon become the hunted. This leaves the attacker, who is taking on a superior force, with two options, and he can use either or both.

One course of action is to lull his enemy into a sense of false security ... somehow give the impression that the campaign is over. And, given time, the enemy will expose a flank, leaving itself vulnerable to the dogs of war, who will tear in, rip and wound and make the enemy bleed. And as it haemorrhages, it weakens and becomes wide open for the coup de grâce, the final shot.

The other manoeuvre is to force the enemy to fight on two or more fronts. This tactic has proved the undoing of some of the greatest leaders in military history. And history does not repeat itself by accident, but as the result of planning.

Don Luigi Luciano paced up and down the big room

while his four lieutenants sat in silence, showing respect. It would be considered an outrage to interrupt the Don while he was deep in thought. Earlier in the day he had received a most unusual phone call. Two things puzzled him concerning this.

The first was that the call had been on his private line, the number of which was known only to a few trusted confidants and was used only for business. It was a secure line which he had checked regularly to make sure it wasn't tapped. The second frustrating matter was the call was made by a woman. It is not the way of the *Famiglia* for women to enter the business. And it was an unfamiliar voice, a voice he had never heard before.

The caller explained the deaths of Flood, Costanza, Driscoll, Bendini, and Margo Colenzo in detailed terms, then went on to discuss sensitive business dealings of his that she should not have been aware of. The call ended abruptly after the old Don asked her where she had received her information and who was responsible for the spate of recent deaths. She said one word only—'Stafford!'—and then hung up.

Fifteen minutes passed before the Don spoke. During this time he had given careful consideration to the facts, and one thing alone remained to be done. He had to talk to the man. Two men were dispatched to carry the Don's request that Abe Stafford and he should meet to discuss certain business matters that were causing concern. *Pronto!*

The messengers received a more than casual inspection on their arrival. Stafford had turned his house into a fortress. He had men posted everywhere, and no one came or left unless he okayed it personally. After being satisfied that the men were indeed messengers from the Don, and nothing else, he had them ushered in. But after listening to them he point-blank refused to go anywhere to meet anyone.

'You can go back and tell him that I'm stayin' right where I am. There's a fuckin' maniac runnin' around out there, and if anyone thinks I'm goin' to leave here and let this lunatic have a fuckin' crack at me, just to sit down and discuss bloody business, he's out of his mind. I'm not budgin' till I know that whoever it is who's runnin' around wallopin' our people is fuckin' dead. You tell him that.'

'Don Luigi is not going to like that,' said one of the messengers. 'He has made a friendly gesture and you have turned it down. Would you reconsider for the sake of peace?'

Stafford all but exploded.

'Peace, my arse! Are you fuckin' deaf or somethin'? I don't give two shits what he fuckin' likes or dislikes. He doesn't tell me what to fuckin' do. Get it? . . . Now fuckin' piss off and tell him. I've got more to do than sit around here yakking to you cunts.'

Stafford's words were conveyed to the Don, who was infuriated by them. Plans and details were discussed at length, phone calls made to important people. And as a result of this, over the next nine months a second front appeared that Stafford was forced to defend. His collectors were robbed. His brothels and gaming houses were raided by police not on the take. These raids and attacks were carried out in an efficient manner, and at times when they did the most damage. There were numerous fines and court costs to be paid, and Stafford himself had to face the indignity of being hauled in for questioning by the police on four occasions. A hefty fine was dished out for running houses of ill-repute and living off the earnings of prostitution and gambling. Dissension set in with his own people, many of whom deserted him and took up less harrowing options. Every loss Stafford suffered became the Don's gain. It was harassment at its best and, little by little, the world around Abe Stafford started to crumble and fall apart. Heavy drinking and drug abuse began to take their toll on Stafford and Mandy Palmer.

All the while they remained cooped up in Roslyn Street, but the place was no longer a hive of activity. The battle was lost and the war was over. His soldiers were gone, deserting their general in his hour of need. He lost his air of confidence and he could no longer intimidate those around him. People who once feared him did so no longer. They were now in greener pastures under the protective umbrella of the old Don himself, whose protection was not to be trifled with. It was based on a centuries-old code of Sicilian honour. The word was out that Stafford was out. Abe and Mandy found themselves defenceless and alone with not only the flank wide open but the jugular exposed and vulnerable.

It was around this time that Don Luigi Luciano received another unusual call on his private line. This time it was a male voice, but one the Don did not recognise. Shortly after the conversation began a name was dropped to the Don of a person from his past. The mention of this name immediately quelled any doubts or fears that had started to build. The caller said the vendetta would soon be over, thanked Don Luigi for his assistance in making the path clear and, as was the custom, promised to one day repay him in full for that assistance. The caller could be reached by contacting the person he had mentioned.

As Don Luigi replaced the phone, he smiled as his thoughts flashed back to his younger days ... to the Second World War ... and an explanation for some of the mysteries that had eluded him in recent months became happily clear. He picked up the phone again and made a long-distance call which lasted for ten minutes and was full of laughter and warm nostalgia. The call ended with the old Don saying, '*Bene fortuna, Kurt.*'

With the way clear and the blessing given, the enemy was alone, unprotected. And the scent of the exposed flank had attracted one of the dogs of war. He was testing the air in the lane that ran behind the old house in Roslyn Street where Stafford and Palmer slept, unaware in their alcoholic and drugged slumber that their nemesis was poised, ready to exact final retribution.

In Valhalla, a soul stirred in anticipation, looked down through the darkness with a smile and blew a kiss in a breath of midnight air. It touched the cheek of her Paladin with a loving caress ...

21

THE HUNTER'S GLOVED HANDS TOOK HOLD OF THE top of the eight-foot-high back fence and he scaled it, balancing like a large black cat for a fraction of a second before dropping to the ground in a fluid motion. It was the witching hour. Nothing moved except for a hand that had removed a small leather wallet from the hunter's soft black overall. He removed two small metal objects from the case and, placing them in the back-door lock, manipulated them until they moved its mechanism and the door swung open slightly. Returning the small picks to the wallet, he quickly stepped inside on soft rubber soles, moving swiftly through the darkened house as if he had done it a million times before.

He stopped outside the big bedroom, taking out an automatic pistol with a silencer attached. Sounds of deep slow breathing came to his ears as he moved into the room. A hand moved to a switch on the wall and flooded the room with light. The two sleeping figures remained oblivious to the intrusion. The intruder moved to the foot of the bed and, taking a handful of bed coverings, ripped them off and away, exposing the sleepers' naked bodies. Mandy Palmer was the first to respond, slowly at first, then suddenly sitting upright. In a display of female dignity, she folded her arms to cover her breasts and moved her legs to a more ladylike position.

'Abe ... Abe!' She called in a voice that quavered with terror. Removing an arm from her breasts, she reached down and shook her sleeping partner. 'Aaaabe!'

Stafford awoke with a growl of displeasure. Then, realising his predicament, sat bolt upright, his eyes wide with shock.

'What the fuck ... ?' The rest of the sentence froze in his throat, as if he had been struck dumb.

They both looked at the armed figure standing before them. Dressed in flat black from head to toe. A balaclava covering the head. Only the menacing eyes and the mouth, which had been smeared with dark camouflage paint, were visible.

'Put your hands on top of your heads ... Now!' The tone matched the eyes and left no room for negotiation.

Stafford and Palmer obeyed, but not before Stafford tried some bluster.

'You won't fuckin' get away with this,' he yelled.

As Mandy Palmer placed her hands on her head, the figure at the end of the bed motioned towards her with the gun.

'Take a good look at her, Abe, you stinking piece of shit.'

As Stafford slowly turned his head to look at Mandy Palmer, the silenced gun coughed and bucked in the gloved hand. The bullet struck her between the breasts and its impact slammed her back with a thud as her head struck the bed's high backboard. Then she collapsed, with her chin lying on her chest.

'Oooooh! you bastard.' Stafford's voice was all agony as he leant over towards his lover. 'Mandy!' he wailed. 'Maaandy.'

He looked back to the end of the bed, but the hooded figure had moved and was standing at his side. The gun was extended and placed against Stafford's left temple.

Abe's eyes opened wide and he screamed.

'No please. Noooooo.'

The gunman reached up with his left hand and pulled the balaclava from his face. Stafford's eyes opened wide in shock. His mouth moved, but no words emerged . . . only a gasp of utter disbelief.

'Yoooou!' he croaked at last.

The dark hand pressed the gun harder into Stafford's temple.

'Remember Margo, you stinking bastard.' And he shot Stafford. The force of the shot at so close a range almost blew the eyes out of Stafford's head. Blood, bone and ruptured brain matter sprayed over Palmer's dead body beside him as the bullet exited. Then his body slumped over hers.

The executioner removed the silencer from the weapon and placed it in the side pocket of the matt black overall. Then, reaching down, he picked up Abe Stafford's dead right hand and pressed the gun into it. This done, he let the hand fall.

'You'll burn in Hell now you lump of shit, Abe. And that treacherous bitch can burn with you.'

He took one last look at the bodies. Then, walking quickly down the long hall, he left the house through the back door, hearing the satisfying clack as it relocked. Looking up into the dark sky he whispered . . .

'Rest in peace, Margo. Rest in peace. It's over.'

Once again a gentle breeze touched and caressed his exposed cheek and left a tingling sensation on his skin. He raised a hand and placed it over the spot, as if to hold the sensation there forever. Then, moving quickly across the yard, he went over the fence in a fast, agile movement.

The darkness of the lane engulfed him and he disappeared from view.

PART 3

3

Family matters

22

ROSALIE AND I RENTED A HOUSE IN BAYSWATER ROAD at the Cross. It was a nice large place and Rosalie went to a good deal of trouble to decorate it and make it as comfortable as possible. Once we had settled in we made a visit back to Roslyn Street. We parked outside Margo's old house letting memories flood back through us. Then we had a grand headstone made for Margo's final resting place.

Rosalie turned one of the upstairs rooms into a private witches' den. She had quite a few female friends who were equally interested in the occult, and many a night I could hear the incantations as five or more of them got together in a coven and practised the dark arts. While they spoke in a language that was completely foreign to me, they used me on numerous occasions for their Warlock in their love rituals. With all of us naked and drinking the magic elixir, I just lay there while they had their wicked way with me, and with each other, and I with them.

We also kept in touch with Kurt and he would stay with us whenever he came to Sydney.

It was on the last of these visits, and thanks to Kurt, that a new chapter in my life began.

Don Luigi Luciano had died and Kurt was down to pay his last respects. I remember well the conversation we

179

had the night before the funeral. Kurt had gone to Sicily with a Commando unit, and it was during this time that he had met Luigi Luciano, who was a member of a Partisan band. A bond developed between them, and it was Kurt who had sponsored Luigi and pulled the strings that finally got him to Australia after the war. He knew that Luigi had ties with the *Cosa Nostra*, but, as he explained to me . . .

'Jimmy, you must always treat a friend like a friend. Never put labels on them, son. And if he's a good close friend? Hang onto him. A man never has so many good friends he can start chuckin' them out the door and look around for more. You see, son, situations don't make a man. They only reveal him.'

I have never forgotten those words of Kurt's. And they certainly came to mean something to me later on. I could understand how those two men had become such close friends. Kurt was a good friend to me, and Rosalie and I thought of him as one of the family. He never asked me to keep anything he told me to myself, since he knew I would. That night he explained to me the workings of the *Cosa Nostra* . . . of the *Famiglia*. 'Cosa Nostra' means literally 'our affair' and is also referred to as the Family. And that's exactly what it is, I recall him telling me.

'One thing you can count on. They never forget a favour, and you can depend on their loyalty with your life. They won't let you down when you're down. They're a bloody sight better than some of the bastards around this town who were bloody born and bred here. They stick to themselves and their friends 100 per cent.'

We stayed in the background at the funeral, but even so, after the grave-side ceremony, someone approached Kurt and spoke quietly in his ear. As we were leaving the cemetery, Kurt told me we'd been invited to a 'do' they were having.

The wake was held at a huge house at Vaucluse. It was full to overflowing, some of the guests having travelled from Italy and Sicily to pay their last respects. Most of them babbled away in Italian and I couldn't understand a word of it, but these blokes certainly knew how to throw a spread.

Kurt and I remained outside, where a big marquee had been erected. There were tables set up with every conceivable type of food and drink. The guests were scattered from the back of the house right down to the boatshed and jetty at the end of the property. It was while we were standing there, admiring the view, that we were asked to come up to the house. We were ushered inside, with people nodding as if they had known us forever. I didn't recognise anyone, but smiled and nodded back as we were taken through the mansion. The silent joker who led us up knocked on the door.

'Come,' I heard from inside and our guide opened the door and, placing his hand on Kurt's back, ushered him in. He nodded at me and with a wave of his hand indicated that I should wait in one of the chairs in the hall. I didn't think it was strange. After all, I didn't know anyone there. But I was starting to get a bit pissed off after I had been sitting there for nearly half an hour.

Then the door finally opened and the chaperon who had escorted Kurt in nodded to me again, with a backward sweep of his head, indicating that my presence was required. He hadn't spoken a word since he'd invited us up to the house.

It was a beautiful room. It had personality and you could feel a strength and power in it the moment you entered. You also got the feeling that the person who owned such a room was not someone to be fucked about with. You could almost see your reflection in the polished wood panelling on the walls, which were decorated with paintings that reeked of wealth. A long sideboard on one wall was made from the same timber as the panelling and was covered with crystal decanters of spirits on silver trays. At the far end of the room was a huge desk. Two upholstered chairs sat in front of it, and Kurt was sitting in one of them. Behind the desk a bloke in his late thirties to early forties lounged in a deep leather-padded swivel chair with side wings and armrests. As I approached the desk, Kurt got to his feet.

'Jimmy, I would like to introduce you to Paolo Agostini.'

The guy behind the desk got to his feet and came around, offering his hand. He was average size, but quite lean compared to some of the heavyweights I'd been rubbing shoulders with earlier. You could see he took care of himself. When he spoke it was without any trace of an accent.

'Pleased to meet you, Jimmy,' and he gripped my hand warmly. 'Won't you please sit down?'

Kurt stood up and placed a hand on my shoulder.

'See you back outside,' he said, then nodded to Paolo. 'Thanks a million.'

The two shook hands. Then Kurt and our speechless guide left the room.

Paolo smiled. 'What about a drink?' He moved over to the sideboard. 'Scotch?'

I nodded my head. He came back, placing two glasses on the desk.

'Smoke if you like,' he said, pushing a large glass ashtray towards me.

He pulled up the chair Kurt had been sitting in, sat down and smiled at me.

'You've given some people a few headaches over the last year haven't you?' he said.

'I'm not sure I follow you,' I replied, lighting a cigarette.

'Let me put it another way then. It appears that we have a couple of things in common. You respect loyalty, and you detest treachery. Would that be a fair definition?'

'Yes, I suppose you could put it like that. But I've just met you. So I can't really tell what you're like or give an opinion one way or another.'

'Well yes,' he said, smiling again. 'I suppose I asked for that. You'll just have to accept my word that I feel exactly as you do. I am also pleased that you speak your mind.' He paused and took a small drink. 'I have just had an interesting conversation with your benefactor and friend. Kurt was also a close friend of my uncle, who is now no longer with us. Even though they went their own ways they remained loyal friends to the end. Which brings us to the reason for this conversation. There is a certain problem we feel that you could assist us in solving.'

'What problem is that?'

'Let me put it this way. We know more about you than you think or, for that matter, than you'd like us to know. Kurt has informed us that you possess the talents needed for what we have in mind. And as far as not knowing each other ... this lack of association makes you perfect for the job.'

'What fuckin' job? I wish you'd just come straight out and say what's on your mind.'

He winced a little at my language but the smile returned and he carried on.

'There is a building that houses some material we are most interested in acquiring.'

'Why don't you get one of your own people to do the job?'

'We could do, but we also feel you owe us this. However, it's up to you. But one way or another I must have your answer in forty-eight hours. If you decide that you will assist us then I can assure you that you will get our utmost cooperation, not to mention that we would also be greatly indebted to you. I can also guarantee that you'll be generously remunerated for your time and effort. Talk it over with Kurt. He has more details, but forty-eight hours is the maximum for your answer.'

He went behind the desk, took a pen from a holder and wrote on a scratch pad, ripped the page off and passed it to me. 'That's my unlisted number here. Memorise it. Then destroy it. I hope I'll be hearing from you soon.'

We shook hands and Paolo escorted me back to where the festivities were in full swing. A band was playing Italian music and some couples were dancing

184

on a wooden dance floor. We spotted Kurt and went over to him. Paolo and Kurt shook hands and, after a bit of light banter, Paolo left us. We had a couple more drinks, but my curiosity was getting the better of me.

'Let's piss off, mate,' I said after a while. 'I've had enough of this.'

Kurt nodded in agreement and we made our way out to the car.

It was late at night before Kurt and I finished our discussion. The job Paolo wanted done wouldn't be easy, but in Kurt's words ... 'A bloody cakewalk if you do it right.' The more he spoke the surer I became that it could be done. My only wish was that he was a bit younger and could have come along with me. But he was leaving for Nambucca in the morning.

'Bloody Abos'll have the place cleaned out,' he kept mumbling. 'Pinch Christ off the cross if he wasn't nailed down. Bloody dogs and animals have to be fed. Hate fuckin' cities.'

The building in question was a pharmaceutical supply warehouse. A security guard remained inside the premises at all times when no staff were present. There were no exterior or interior alarms, but one that the guard could activate would bring every law enforcement and security guard for miles around. Two things made the job difficult. The guard had to be put out of action, and the goods were in a strongroom. The 'material', as Paolo had called it, happened to be base morphine and an amphetamine used in speed. The guard didn't have keys to the strongroom, so it would have to be blown. The general layout of the building was known and a complete floor plan had been drawn up.

In the morning I hopped in the car and did a complete outside case of the joint, taking mental photographs. The plan we had been given was accurate, as far as the exterior of the building was concerned, and satisfied that the information on the plan tallied with what I could see, I was confident that entry could be gained reasonably easily. The only major problem was the fuckin' security guard.

Drugs were becoming fashionable in Sydney, even back in the very early '60s, and I didn't have a problem with them, mentally or physically. To me they were just the same as booze and cigarettes. They were there if you wanted them. Some did, some didn't. So what? Some became alcoholics and some didn't. It just depended on how much of the stuff you took. Nobody forced anybody to become an addict. That was voluntary. So I didn't have a big hang-up on the drug thing.

The job also had a bit of a challenge to it. And when I had the full details I wanted to give it a go. As Kurt would say, *When in doubt, attack!* Fuck society and their rules. Rules were made to be broken or there wouldn't be any in the first place. There was some kind of a rebelliousness built into me that wanted to break out. I can't make any excuses. I just wasn't at all interested in conforming to what was supposed to be the right thing. If society said it's wrong, I said, 'Let's get it on.' I got a kick out of being different and a kind of pleasure at seeing others, whom I didn't know, or had no feeling for, squirm when I voiced certain opinions. Yet I felt deeply for those who I held close to me and would have laid my life on the line to protect them.

All there was left to do was to catalogue what I would need to do the job and then phone Paolo.

I rang later that morning but he was out. He called me about an hour later and, giving me no chance to speak at all, said he'd send someone around to pick me up.

Half an hour later there was a knock on the door.

'You Jimmy?' said a well-built guy.

I nodded.

'You have to come with me. Paolo wants to see you.'

We ended up in the city at an Italian restaurant called Domino's. I walked in and saw Paolo seated towards the back. He was eating and had a small carafe of wine and a couple of glasses alongside it. He looked up and gestured with his hand, inviting me to join him.

'Pull up a chair. Would you like something to eat?' He pushed a glass towards me and poured me some red wine. 'Try the veal. It's delicious.'

I nodded and the head waiter appeared at once, as if he had anticipated the request. Paolo spoke to him in Italian. I tasted the wine and it wasn't bad.

'It's a good chianti,' Paolo said, 'one of my favourites. Now what have you got for me?'

'The job's on, but it'll have to be tonight and I need to get some gear before then. Can you organise that?'

'What are you going to need?'

'First of all, it's not a one-man show. I want one of your people as driver and back-up. We're going to need a car. Not a hot one, but one that can't be traced back to you or me.'

'No problem. What else?'

'There's a fair bit. Do you want me to write it down?'

'Tell me first, and we'll take it from there.'

'A good quality glass-cutter, a stick of AN90 gelig-nite, or even higher grade. An Armco electric detonator and about twenty feet of cable. A small wrecking bar, about two foot long. A roll of one-inch electric tape. Thirty feet of three-quarter soft marine rope. And I want a gun, equipped with a silencer. It has to be small but have stopping power. Nothing under 7 mm. The gun's for insurance.'

Paolo started to speak, but paused as my meal was delivered.

'There shouldn't be any trouble with the gear.'

'There's one more thing,' I said to him. 'Now that I know what we're after, what's in it for me?'

He didn't even bat an eye. 'Ten thousand. As soon as we have the merchandise. You satisfied with that?'

I nodded my agreement and we finished the meal in near silence. Putting down his knife and fork, he looked at me and asked how confident I was.

'As much as I can be. Only I don't want to take out the night watchman.'

'Would you if you had to?'

'If it comes to me or him, or the completion of the job, yes.'

Paolo stood up. 'You'll have everything you need by eight,' he said. 'Stay here a while. We can't be seen together just yet. Take your time ... have another drink. The meal and drinks are on me. I'll leave word on the way out.'

He gave me a light tap on the shoulder and left.

True to his word a car turned up just before eight that night. Rosalie and the girls had pissed off some-

188

where and I was by myself. I let the guy in. Angelo was his name. He looked hard and fit and had an air of confidence.

'Where's the gear?' I asked him.

'Ina the car.'

'Right, let's have it in here mate. But take the car round the back.'

He nodded and did as I requested. We brought the gear inside and put it on the kitchen table.

'You might as well make yourself comfortable, mate. We won't be leavin' for a while yet.'

Angelo had patience, I'll give him that. He just sat and smoked while I checked the gear. Everything I had asked for was there, right down to the gun. It was a flat 9 mm Beretta, equipped with a one-twist on-off silencer. It had enough stopping power to put a bull elephant down. I examined the explosive and the detonator, went and got dressed in some dark gear and put a balaclava in my back pocket. It was 10.30 p.m.

I thought it might be wise to reconnoitre the building and surroundings one last time. Everything was quiet. The only thing I didn't like was the light burning on that second-floor landing I had planned to use as an entry point. The light had a glass and wire dome on it, so getting rid of it meant more than just removing a bulb. It was far too risky to be up that high and illuminated. I got Angelo to drive down the back lane and let me off a building away, then to return to the front street and keep his head down. I'd signal with the torch when I needed him.

Waiting in the shadows to let my eyes become accustomed to the darkness, I took out the balaclava and slipped it on. All the rear windows of the building were barred on the inside, making a silent entry impossible. I moved around to the dark side of the building, where there was a sewerage pipe running up the side. About a foot away from where it entered the building was a louvred window. I scaled up the pipe, using the wall clamps as footholds.

Coming up level with the window, I was able to keep a reasonable footing on the pipe and grab onto the edge of the sill. I was about to reach for the glass-cutter when I saw that it wouldn't be needed. The metal ends holding the panes in place could be prised open. I took the hunting knife out of the scabbard under the overall and, using the tip of it, levered the metal ends up. When I had done both sides, I slid the bottom louvre down and out and placed it on top of the sill. This left a six-inch gap between the next louvre and the sill. I put my arm through to get a better grip and went to work on the rest of the louvres. Taking out the penlight I leant in a little, being careful not to knock the glass off the sill, and quickly played it around the room. The toilet was a little to the left of the window. I put the flashlight in my mouth and reached in and laid the louvres on top of the cistern, one at a time. This done, I slid over the sill, headfirst. Standing still for a moment, I listened carefully, but heard nothing.

I moved quietly to the toilet door and opened it an inch or two. I was on a mezzanine floor, looking down to the floor below, which was covered with rows of pallets and drums and large cartons. The end office to my right was lit up, with the door open and light spilling out.

The guard must have been in that office and I was about to step out and move towards it when I suddenly froze ... Downstairs a tap had been turned on, followed by the sounds of some sort of container being filled. My mind flashed to the plan I had seen. Smoko room. I moved silently along the landing and to the top of the stairs. When I was halfway down I could see another row of offices and the canteen. I had found my night watchman.

I took the remaining stairs quickly and moved underneath them, pressing myself up against the wall of the canteen, listening to the watchman moving about. A minute or so later he walked slowly by, not three feet away, with a mug of steaming tea in his right hand, concentrating on not spilling any. He was just past me when I stepped in behind him and hit him hard with the edge of my hand where the skull joins the neck, just down and behind the left ear. An *uga giri*.

The watchman went down like a bag of shit, his mug of tea spilling everywhere. I gagged him with adhesive tape and bound him hand and foot with the rope that I had wound around my waist. He was trussed up and going nowhere. I checked his pulse with my fingers on his carotid artery. It was fluttery, but he'd be okay.

The strongroom was in the end far office. Since there was no fear of anyone seeing me I moved into it and turned on the light. There was a desk to the right of the door and I used this to prepare the job. The strongroom itself was no Fort Knox, but it would have proved difficult for those who didn't know what they were about.

A big brass shield covered the keyhole. I slid this to one side and took out the AN90. Teasing it out like plasticine, I fed it into the keyhole. The Armco detonator is a slim one and I slid it into the keyhole, pushing it into the explosive. I unwound the two electric leads from the detonator and, taking the extensions, bared the ends and twisted them onto the other leads. I got a lump of pre-pared putty out of a pocket and pressed it over the keyhole so it covered everything but the wires. I then took the small wrecking bar and bound it strongly onto the handle on the door. The arrows on the handle showed that it turned clockwise to open, so most of the bar was sticking out the right-hand side. I had three inch-wide rings of rubber that I'd cut earlier that day from a tyre tube and linked together end to end. Lashing one end of it to the bar with more tape, I took out a flat metal hook I'd also made, placed it in the end of the rubber and stretched it across and onto the lower hinge of the door. I switched on the penlight and turned off the main light. Taking the chair from behind the desk, I stood on it and with the aid of the penlight in my mouth removed the light bulb. Hopping down off the chair, I broke the bulb on the edge of the desk, picked up the two extension wires to the detonator and joined them onto the terminals in the globe. I climbed back up on the chair and replaced the modified bulb.

All ready now. I slipped out of the office and, with the wall between me and the strongroom, reached around the door and flicked the switch. There was a solid bang and a slight tremor ran through the building. I moved back inside and was rewarded with the sight of the door handle and the bar that I had taped to it in a vertical position . . . meaning that the locking bars were open. It's important to have a weight on the handle as it is sometimes possible to blow the lock, jamming everything.

I turned the handle a little more and the door swung

open. It didn't take long to find what I was looking for and I stacked the four boxes outside the room. Then went back for a further inspection. There was a tray that held a bank bag with cash and cheques. No reason for the cops to have this, I thought, as they usually grab something of value after a break-in. There was a carton of Benzedrine as well and, lo and behold, another one full of the old purple hearts. None of these were bottled, but in bulk, in plastic bags. There was also a box with three trays of glass ampoules of morphine, which I added to the boxes outside the door. That's that, I thought.

A quick check of the security guard revealed a very angry one, but he was still held securely in his bonds. There was Buckley's hope of him recognising me with the balaclava on. He was an innocent bystander and I held no grudge against him. He was doing a job. So was I.

I moved to the front of the warehouse, opened the door and peered out into the street. Quiet as a church mouse. I could see the car, but not much of Angelo. He was doing a bloody good job. I flashed the torch in the prearranged signal and the car fired up. He drove straight to the door with the lights off and I stood guard, just inside the door with the gun out, while Angelo loaded up. Then we pissed off out of it, laughing. The whole operation had gone smoothly. Nothing was hurt except the security guard's pride, though his neck might be a little stiff for a few days.

'Jees christ!' Angelo said to me. 'Don Paolo, he be very happy eh?'

Back home, I showered and changed and checked the

bag out. I burnt the cheques in the fireplace and pulverised the ashes. There was nearly fourteen hundred in cash. I considered this my bonus.

I had just completed this when Rosalie and a couple of her mates arrived home, pissed and happy. We sat down and had a few drinks together. Rosalie had no idea I'd been out on a job when the phone rang. It was Paolo.

'How are you feeling? Are you tired?'

'Shit no. I'm fine. Why?'

'Oh, we're just having a little celebration and I thought you might like to come along.'

'Yeah sure, but I've got my girl here with me.'

'No problem. Bring her along. But listen, Jimmy, catch a taxi. Don't bring your car.'

'No worries.'

He was a careful man, Paolo, and he didn't want any prick recording numberplates. State or federal police.

Shortly after Rosalie and I arrived at the party. It was also my baptism into *Cosa Nostra*.

23

THE PARTY WAS IN FULL SWING WHEN WE ARRIVED AT
2 a.m. and showed no signs of winding down. Rosalie and
I were standing in a small group when Paolo came up.

'I'd like to have a talk with Jimmy,' he said to
Rosalie. 'Would you mind?'

We ended back in that beautiful office. There was
someone sitting in one of the chairs in front of the desk.
Well-dressed and wearing some flashy expensive jewellery, with a drink in one hand.

'Jimmy,' Paolo said, 'this is Carlo Bellari from Brisbane and a good friend of the family.'

Carlo stood up and offered me his hand. I shook it.
Paolo indicated the other chair to me, went over to the
sideboard and came back with a couple of drinks. I had
a sip and looked at it.

'Campari,' said Paolo. 'It's good for you.'

I took another couple of sips. It wasn't all that bad
but I put it on my list of drinks to be avoided if possible.

'We're very happy with the way things went tonight,'
Paolo said to me. 'In fact we are more than pleased,
and most grateful. The family doesn't use people
outside the circle all that often. But if we do and they
measure up, as you have, we take care of them as if
they were our own.'

Carlo raised his glass and said 'Salute!' Paolo lifted

his glass in my direction and repeated the toast.

'Here's lookin' at ya!' I said.

As we took a sip, Carlo gave a snort into his drink and we all burst into laughter. You could feel the formality that had been there just a moment ago disappear, replaced with a warmth and camaraderie.

'By the way,' I said 'I want some of those fuckin' purple hearts.' Which started a new outburst of leg-slapping laughter.

The three of us sat talking for a while longer, with Paolo telling me I would receive payment for the job before I left, and that there would be a bonus for the extra merchandise I'd grabbed. We returned to the party and had a great time. I ran into Paolo's silent concierge a couple of times and learnt that his name was Frank Trimboli. Paolo took me back to the office and handed me a brown manilla envelope. A cab was called for us and we fell into bed, pissed and exhausted.

I was awakened later that day to the sensation of Rosalie's warm soft wet mouth gently sucking me into consciousness.

My association with Paolo and the Agostini family grew. I took care of a few problems for him, burying them in a hole and forgetting the map reference. It was this association that kept me from going to gaol for the rest of my life when I went and did a freelance.

Rosalie's following of women had grown in number since we moved to Bayswater Road. And now that Stafford and company had left the planet, some of her old acquaintances drifted back. One of her new friends was an 18-year-old named Helen, who came along when the coven were upstairs doing their thing. This relationship grew into a lesbian affair and, finally, to a three-way thing with Helen often sleeping in the big bed with us. Helen had been adopted by a childless Greek couple, but she expressed an intense dislike for her adoptive father, because of his advances. Rosalie and Helen's affair became common knowledge around the Cross, though it meant nothing in the bohemian circles we moved in. It was just accepted. But when it became known outside the area, tongues started wagging. Helen came to live with us. We went along in case there was trouble during the move, but no one was home and nothing eventuated. Helen's adopted father ran a cafe and delicatessen in Woolloomooloo, not far from The Bells, a pub owned by ex-Bantamweight World Champion Jimmy Carruthers.

A month or so after Helen moved in, she and Rosalie went out to the Cashmere. I was at home just taking it easy when the front door opened and I heard crying and Helen's hysterical voice calling my name.

I flew downstairs. Helen was trying to get Rosalie inside. She'd collapsed in the doorway, and shit she was a mess.

'What the fuck happened?' I yelled as I grabbed Rosalie and carried her into the lounge room.

Through her sobs Helen relayed what had happened to Rosalie.

'That fucking bastard of an old man of mine bailed us up coming down the street. He spat on me, called me a slut. Then he turned on Rosalie, calling her a dirty bitch and started punching her. Rosalie fell down and he started kicking into her. He took off when someone came running over. I hate the bastard, Jimmy. I hate him.'

I bent over Rosalie and was shocked by the damage that the Greek had done to her. My anger was savage but controlled. The bastard who'd done this to Rosalie was dead.

Rosalie was hurting so badly I had to ring for an ambulance. Then, bending low, I kissed her softly on the cheek.

'Don't say a word to anyone,' I whispered, 'but I promise you I'll kill this sonofabitch. Do you hear me, I'll kill him.'

She tried to smile at me and nodded her head weakly.

Helen and I followed the ambulance to the hospital. On the way, I told Helen not to say a word. Nothing. That I would fix this up. Helen gave me her word.

Rosalie had a broken jaw, a fractured cheek bone, four fractured ribs, a ruptured spleen, with possible other internal injuries. The police didn't use any heavy-handed tactics on us. What we had said was near enough to the truth, apart from Helen saying she couldn't recognise the guy who'd attacked them.

I asked Helen to stay at the hospital with Rosalie. To ring and keep me informed after she came out of the theatre. On the drive home I thought and planned. It's hard to describe the emotions I felt, but one thing stayed at the front of my mind. I was going to kill this Greek bastard.

I rang Paolo. 'I've got to see you. It's urgent.'

'Come straight out,' he said.

I got a cab out to Vaucluse and Paolo and I sat in his big study. We talked things through. He wanted to use someone else to take care of it but I said no.

'I want to take care of this personally,' I told him. 'All I want from you is an alibi if I need it, and a driver.'

We discussed what I had in mind and came up with a plan. We went over it again to see if we'd missed anything and, when we were satisfied, decided it was a go.

When I got back home I rang the hospital. Rosalie was out of theatre but still in poor shape. Her condition had stabilised and they'd ring if there were any more developments. Helen phoned not long after. She couldn't stay with Rosalie in intensive care so I drove to the hospital and picked her up.

Back home we hopped into bed, but it was a sleepless night, what was left of it. We lay there, saying the odd word to each other. An attempt at sex, to take our minds off things and ease the tension, was given away as a bad joke.

I packed Helen off to a friend's place early in the morning and told her to stay there until she heard from me. With Helen gone, I went into the room where the coven gathered and, taking a wig with black hair that wasn't so long, I put it on and combed it into some sort of shape. Satisfied with this, I took one of the girls' eyebrow pencils and darkened my eyebrows. I placed two balls of cotton wool in each cheek and, after they'd dampened a little with saliva, I patted them into place. I put on three shirts, turning the collars of the first two under, then a dark blue wind-breaker. After I'd jammed a cap on, and a pair of sunglasses, an examination in the mirror said it all . . . It wasn't me.

I took the 9 mm automatic that I still had from the warehouse job, put on the silencer, removed the clip and checked the action. Smooth as silk. I dry-fired it, inserted the clip and, after cocking the gun, placing a round in the breech, I lowered the hammer and stuck the weapon down the front of my pants under my belt. I walked around to see how it felt. Satisfied that it wouldn't be a problem, I went into the bathroom, put a half-used cake of soap into my back pocket and walked downstairs.

At 6.45 a car drove down the side of the house, pulling up in the backyard. It was Angelo. I hurried out and climbed into the car.

'Jees Christ!' said Angelo. He could scarcely believe it was me.

'Come on son,' I said. 'Let's move it.'

The delicatessen opened at 7.30 and we were parked opposite it with five minutes to spare. Moments later the Greek turned up, put a key in the door and unlocked it.

'Now!' I said to Angelo, giving him a slap on the shoulder with my right hand. He quickly started the car and, with a glance into the rear-view mirror, pulled a little ahead then did a U-turn, pulling up right outside the shop.

'Keep it running,' I said as I stepped out of the car and moved quickly into the shop, taking the gun out and holding it down by my side.

The Greek was behind the counter taking some bills and coins out of a gladstone bag and putting them into the till. I moved straight along the counter and, as I got close to the end, he realised my intentions.

'Hey! You no come back here,' he shouted.

'Fuck you, wog,' I said to him, and stepped around

the end of the counter. There was nothing now between us. 'Remember last night, you fuckin' greasy bastard?'

Panic came into his eyes and they darted to a large wooden cutting board with a long-bladed knife resting on it. As he grabbed it I swept the gun up from my side. His mouth dropped open and he stepped back a pace.

'This is for Rosalie, you cunt.' And I shot him low down in the belly. The impact of the bullet knocked him backwards and he collapsed onto the floor behind the counter, holding his hands to his stomach and groaning. I stepped forward to him. He looked up.

'Goodbye bastard,' I said, and put two rounds into his brain. I turned, grabbed the bills out of the till, and those still lying on the counter, shoving them into a pocket to make it look like robbery.

I had just cleared the doorway when I charged straight into a lady who'd been walking past. She went down hard. Angelo was leaning over, pushing the door open.

'Go!' I said as I dived in.

The last thing we wanted was to be pulled up by a traffic cop so he took off quickly, but not fast enough to cause undue attention. We drove to Hyde Park and I got out. While Angelo circled in the car, I went downstairs to the toilets there. The place was empty. Moving into a cubicle I took off the wind-breaker, the two outside shirts and the cap, throwing them down behind the toilet bowl. Some wino would find them and put them to good use. I turned up the collar of the last shirt, took off the wig and stuffed it down the dunny until it went up over the bend and was out of sight. When I flushed the bowl it started to fill and I thought it was going to overflow, but as the water got close to the top the wig eventually gave way and was washed off into the sewerage system.

I walked over to the washbasins and, taking the soap out of my pocket, I washed and lathered my face until all traces of the eyebrow pencil disappeared. I dried my face with my handkerchief, then strolled casually out onto the street. Angelo came round the corner a minute or so later.

We drove straight to Vaucluse, Angelo letting me off near Paolo's place. As I was getting out of the car, I dropped the gun on the seat.

'You know what to do with this don't ya, son?' I said to him.

'No worry,' he said with a smile. 'An a the plate from the car too.'

'Good man. See you later.'

I stayed all that day at Paolo's. Near midday I rang Helen and told her I'd pick her up at five. I then rang the hospital and asked to speak to the doctor looking after Rosalie. He was too busy to come to the phone, so I gave them Paolo's listed number. The doctor called a couple of hours later. He said Rosalie wasn't much better, in fact she'd worsened a little, but that she'd pull through. Paolo and I were driven into town and had a meal at Domino's. After that I picked up Helen from her friend's place and we went back home to Bayswater Road.

The papers were full of the story. Front-page stuff. 'ROBBERY SHOOTING. MAN DIES.' Two days later I got a visit from the Homicide Squad. The first theory was robbery, but because of the connection through

202

Helen they became more interested in me. They didn't have anything to go on except suspicion but I was screamed at, threatened . . . told everything was going to happen to me at once. This time, however, I was prepared. Paolo had made arrangements for a top lawyer to watch over me and he did just that. And did the coppers hate that! They told me they had a witness and made a big thing about the line-up they were going to put me in. It was a joke. They went to the cells and brought up half a dozen prisoners, put me in amongst them and brought in the woman I'd flattened when fleeing the delicatessen. Her eyes didn't linger on me for even a second. She pointed to some portly individual who was half-pissed and not capable of pulling his prick, let alone the trigger on a gun. The cops weren't very impressed either. They had to let me go, but they harassed me every moment they got over the next few months.

After Rosalie recovered she decided she wanted to go to Europe. There was some occult movement over there she wanted to join.

'Where is this place?' I asked her. 'Transylvania?'

We had a great farewell party for her a few weeks later. Then we saw her safely aboard the *Mariposa*, and watched as she sailed away to Europe. I have never seen her since, but I've often thought about her, and always in kindly terms. Witch or not, she believed what she believed and was a free spirit, but someone I trusted completely.

Helen and I remained at the house, but there was no respite from the coppers. If we were out walking a plain car, with CIB jacks, would stop and we'd be questioned in the street. In the end I had a private meeting with Paolo, telling him I'd decided to go away. I'd keep in touch, I told him, but I needed a complete change. I was going to sell up and go to Brisbane. He gave me his blessing and offered help, but I let him know I'd be okay.

'Don't forget to say hello to Carlo,' was his parting remark. They say fate moves in funny patterns and travels to the strangest places. This was proved to me one night in Lennons Hotel shortly before I left for Brisbane. The other thing I learnt that night was that this is a very small world we live in. I was preparing to move, slowly selling all my stuff. Bugger the coppers, I thought, if I rush too quick they'll probably say I'm running away and only hound me more. So Helen and I decided to take our time. I had offered to set her up in her own place, but she said she liked it with me. And I had to admit she was good in bed.

Anyway, we were having a drink in Lennons one night and a guy I'd never seen in my life walked up to me.

'Your name wouldn't be Diamond would it? Jimmy Diamond?'

'Why?' I said. 'Who wants to know?'

'Look, mate, I don't want to pry. My name's John Hammel and I've just got out of the Bay. I worked in the carpenter shop there with a bloke called Ed Diamond who told me he had a son called Jimmy. And shit, mate, you sure look like him. If you were thirty years older, you'd be him.'

'My Dad's name was Edward Arthur Diamond,' I told him.

'Christ!' he said. 'That's his name. Why don't you go and see him?'

We chatted for a while and I thanked him for his information.

Later that night I talked it over with Helen and we decided that I had nothing to lose by going out and giving it a go. I had never seen my father and only had a couple of memories of my mother, one of them frightening. So why not, I thought.

The next day we drove out to Malabar to the infamous Long Bay gaol. There was an ominous feel about the place, which I suppose shouldn't have surprised me. Anyway, I pushed the button on the main gates and a loud jangle rang out somewhere inside. A small spy trap in the door opened and part of a face appeared.

'Yes, what's the problem?' The voice was cold, uninviting.

'I'd like to see my father,' I replied.

'What's his name?'

'Edward Arthur Diamond.'

'Hold on, I'll check.' And the small spy trap closed.

I lit a cigarette and had smoked it by the time there was a rattle behind the gates, and the small entry door opened.

'Move through,' we were ordered, 'and wait in there till you're called.'

We were in what could only be described as a giant monkey cage, a building inside the main gates. A few prisoners, in blue denim clothes with numbers stitched on them, moved around under the watchful eyes of armed guards in towers.

We entered the visitors' room and waited about twenty minutes. Then a door at the end opened and a guard called out to us.

'Visitors for Diamond. This way.'

We stood up and walked down a hall that was separated off into cubicles on the left. The warder pointed to a cubicle and, when we entered, he walked further up the hall and through a door. We were standing in front of a barred and wire-meshed grille, on the other side of which was another narrow corridor and another grille. The warder appeared in this narrow corridor and yelled to someone we couldn't see.

'Right! In here. Number 772.'

A moment later a man walked into the cubicle across from us. I looked through the two grilles at him and just knew that the man who was facing me was my father. The resemblance was uncanny.

'Gidday!' I said. 'I'm Jimmy . . . and this is Helen.'

'How come you know I was in here?'

'I ran into a guy in a pub last night. John Hammel.'

'What was your mother's name?'

'Gwenda,' I replied. 'Gwenda Maree.'

'Do you know her maiden name?'

'Flower,' I said. 'Her maiden name was Flower.'

After a few more questions only a relative could answer, Edward Diamond put his head down for a moment, then looked at me.

'That makes me your father all right. There couldn't be any mistake. I'm sorry you had to meet me in a joint like this.'

I went on to explain to him about the people in my past. How Aunty Freda always spoke well of him. But the meeting was very formal, with the warder listening to every word.

'Time's up!' The guard said after half an hour.

'Could I just give him his sister's address?' asked my father.

'Make it quick,' said the guard.

Helen rummaged in her bag and came out with a little book and a pen which she handed to me. My father gave me an address.

'Can he have anything, or am I allowed to get something for him?' I asked the guard.

'You can leave money for prisoners. You'll be issued with a receipt. He can use it for purchases.'

My father had his head down when I looked across.

'I'll leave you twenty quid to get some things.'

My father looked up. His eyes were wet with shame or emotion, I wasn't sure which. He nodded his head in thanks and appreciation.

Helen started to sob gently beside me. I put my arm around her. My father had been called by another guard and was turning to leave.

'I'll come and see you again soon,' I called to him.

'Thanks Jimmy. Take care, boy. I'm truly sorry.'

He turned and smiled in a sad sort of way, then walked away.

As we were being led out I told the warder that I'd like to leave some money for my dad. He led us into an office, sat at a desk and pulled out a large receipt book.

'Right. Prisoner's name?'

'Edward Arthur Diamond.'

He printed the name on the receipt and asked how much I wanted to leave.

I pulled a wad of bills out of my pocket and peeled off a couple of tens.

He looked quite shocked . . . Twenty quid was probably as much as the warder made in a week. What I'd put back in my pocket was more than he'd earn in a bloody year. I was given a receipt for the money and we were escorted to the little door in the big gates. I never saw my father again. He died of a heart attack in Nowra not long after he was released.

That afternoon Helen and I drove to Summer Hill to meet my sister Pauline. She was living in a flat, but a neighbour told us she was out. I left a brief note, with our address and phone number.

About an hour after we got home, the phone rang. I answered it.

'My name's Pauline. I believe you've been looking for me?'

I told her who I was and that I'd been out to see our father that morning. I was sorry, I said, if I'd caused any embarrassment, that I'd understand if she didn't want to meet me. After all it had been more than twenty years. What could we have in common? But she was keen to come and see us right there and then.

'Shit!' I said to Helen after I'd hung up. 'She's coming right over now!'

'I wish I knew if I had any brothers or sisters,' Helen said.

It was about 6 p.m. when Pauline arrived. She was an attractive girl with fair hair and blue eyes. Helen left us alone and went into the kitchen to prepare a meal for us. We talked through dinner, then we retired to the lounge and the three of us got pissed as rats. Pauline was so legless she had to stay the night and we packed her off to bed. In the morning she had a king-size hangover, rang her work and reported sick.

We had several more visits from Pauline and she tried to talk me out of moving away. But I'd made up my mind that Sydney was not for me. I felt like I'd been there all my life. A lot had happened in a short while and there was a lot I'd remember about the place, including things I would prefer to forget. Still, I didn't want for anything. Financially I was well off compared to a lot of people. I owned the Plymouth and I had a sweet companion and friend sitting beside me who was willing to please my every whim. What else could a man want out of life?

I don't think I was happier than when we bumped our way up the old dirt road to Kurt's place and pulled up in front of the house. The dogs barking. That friendly face coming out onto the verandah, roaring. 'Lie down ya mongrels.' And with a big smile on his wrinkled face, hugging us both. 'Ya took ya bloody time gettin' here ya buggers. What have you been up to?'

'Good to see ya again you old coot,' I said. 'What about a drink?'

'Why not?' He roared laughing.

We joined in with Kurt and did a little jig in the front yard.

24

WE STAYED WITH KURT FOR A MONTH. SOAKING UP THE sun, hunting, fishing, getting pissed, the usual things one does in the country. But I had itchy feet and didn't want to be tied down.

On the way north I visited Mum and Dad Gee. Only this time I didn't get the third degree and the big lecture. They even wanted us to stay longer. And I got reacquainted with my brother, too. He was married, trying to settle down and we didn't have a lot in common. He was a bit of a wimp and I reckoned he couldn't have been my brother. Someone must have swapped him at the hospital. After a few weeks I was glad to move on. The whole area gave me the creeps.

We finally arrived in Brisbane. And from the word go, I liked the place. We booked into a motel and stayed there for a week until we could find a place to live, picking up the *Courier Mail* every morning and going over the places for rent. Some were good and some were complete shithouses. Then one morning we came across one down in New Farm, close to the water.

The moment we saw it we both knew that this was what we were looking for. It was an older style Queenslander house, set back off the road, with a long drive. There were trees everywhere, from gums to shrubs, with fruit trees around the back. It was like a fruit-salad orchard. There was a big walk-through trellis with grapes in abundance, and a passionfruit vine completely covered the back fence. You name it, it was there. There was a fowl run too, empty of course, but I'd soon fix that.

We pretty well broke the land speed record driving to the real estate office, where we signed the necessary papers, and were given a rent book and the keys. The house was semi-furnished and we moved in at once. That night, with the power still not connected, we ran naked through our house playing a kind of hide and seek, we called it. Find me catch me fuck me.

A few weeks later, once we'd settled in, we had just finished our meal and were drinking some wine and chatting. We didn't know a soul in Brisbane, the only company we had was each other, but I loved the peace and quiet. However, I also realised that we couldn't keep this up for ever. I was far from being broke, but we couldn't just vegetate under the trees and down by the water forever.

'Stuff this,' I said. 'I'm going to get a bloody job.'

Helen gave a bit of a giggle.

'Well I'll let you into a secret. There's not going to be any more of that other stuff up here. I've had a gutful of it. I'm going to get an ordinary job,'

'Well,' she said, 'if you can get a job so can I.'

Helen actually got a job before I did, at the New Farm Hotel. It was just a hop skip and a jump away from the house. A month later I landed a job as a fitter in the shipyard at Kangaroo Point, building new vessels and doing running repairs on others.

For two years we stuck to our jobs. But unionism was becoming militant in the shipyard and it seemed that we'd no sooner get to work than someone would breach the lines of demarcation. A meeting would be held post haste, then it was 'Everybody out.'

One morning we'd been working for about two hours and out we went again. On strike. I'd got used to going to work and didn't want to go back to the life I'd left. I'd got used to not having to look over my shoulder all the time. But the endless strikes were giving me the shits.

We were standing around outside the shipyard when one of the guys said he was going to the pub.

Three of us decided to go. Jack Coleman, John Quiggley and me. We went to the Storey Bridge Hotel and, boy! Did we rip into the piss. By lunchtime we were rotten. There was a poster on the wall about the Army.

'That's what we ought'a do,' John Quiggley said. 'Join the fuckin' Army.'

It was a hell of a joke we all thought, but we were pissed and fed up with the strikes so at 1 o'clock we caught a cab into Eagle Street to the Army Recruiting Office, walked over to the counter and said we wanted to join up.

We were given forms and told to fill them out. When we got to the space that asked sex we wrote 'Yes please.' Generally, we gave everybody a hard time. When we had to do our medical they gave us these little bottles to piss in. We'd been on the bloody booze all morning so we told the medical guy they won't be fuckin' big enough, you'd better go and get three buckets. They thought in general that we were a real bunch of smarties. And the Army hates smarties.

Still, we were told we'd be required to come back the next day. We had a talk out on the street and decided that we'd only be on strike anyway, so why not. The next morning the three of us turned up again. Not so full of cheek this time. We did tests and everything that they poked at us for two days. Then we had an interview and we were told that we'd be notified by mail if we had been successful.

Two weeks went by and I was starting to think I must have failed. Then one afternoon I came home from work, walked into the dining room and there it was, sitting on the table . . . an envelope stamped *AUSTRALIAN MILITARY FORCES*. I ripped the flap open and pulled out the papers inside. The top one said, 'You are required to report' to such and such a place in Sydney on such a date. On the bottom there was a legal bit in darker letters explaining that it was an offence not to report under some statute, blah blah. There was a voucher for a rail pass and a brochure telling me what a great time I was going to have.

I broke the news to Helen. She was upset at first but she soon calmed down.

'Where will I stay when you go away?' she asked me.

'Right here. It's as much your home as mine. I won't be away forever.'

A few days later, with Helen and half of Brisbane waving to one and all, a whole bunch of us took the train to Sydney. The Army picked us up in buses and took us to Victoria Barracks. That night we were all addressed as gentlemen. Next morning, we were driven to Wagga Wagga. Kapooka. The Army Basic Training camp. Still gentlemen, we were fed and bedded down for the evening.

In the morning we were called out of the barracks and milled around like Brown's cows. After breakfast we were taken to the big hall and in we went as gentlemen. As we walked in we signed an Assertation and then, in unison, repeating after the major up on stage with a microphone, we took the Oath. At that point we went from hero to zero in one move. No sooner had we said 'So help me God' when this voice roared . . .

'Riiiight! Outside on the double moooove!'

We weren't gentlemen any more and they treated us like a bunch of cunts. And we had another bunch of cunts training us. Shit! Did they bore it into us. We were outfitted. Medically inspected. Shots in the arm. PT every morning. Marching everywhere. They were going to train us, or kill us in the process.

'No talking in the ranks!' was roared at us continually, whether anyone spoke or not. There were inspections for everything. We didn't have rifles or guns. They were 'weapons'. Woe betide those who called them anything else.

We were going on a forced march one day and one of the guys yelled out . . .

'Hey! Sarge, do we take our guns?'

The sergeant looked like he was suffering from apoplexy. His face went red, streaked with blue, veins stood out on his forehead and neck, and when he finally found his voice he did so with spittle flying and nearly foaming at the mouth.

'I want that man,' he roared. 'I want him out here now. I want that man.'

The twit that had said it walked out, the silly bastard. The sergeant had him out in the middle of the parade ground for hours. Kneeling down on all fours, with his *weapon* lying in front of him, bobbing his head down like a bloody Muslim on a prayer mat and kissing it, saying 'I love my weapon. I love my weapon.'

The days went by and the training continued. Three long months later, Basic was over. We had a passing-out parade, with the bands and all that jazz. As you marched, weapon in position, right arm swinging to just that right height, chin in chest out, to the beat of military brass, you felt proud. You felt good. You had accomplished something. But training was far from being over.

When I arrived back at Brisbane on a short leave Helen made a big fuss that I was back. Then she told me that Judy, who worked with her in the pub, had been tossed out of her flat and had moved in. They could keep each other company while I was away. I didn't mind, but after a couple of days I realised that they were on together. The little looks, the quick peck on the cheek when they thought I couldn't see, the little touches. Then, one night I came home from the pub earlier than I'd said I would. I wasn't trying to sneak up on them, I'd just had enough piss. Anyway, they were either oblivious to the fact that I was back or they just didn't care, but they were in bed together, getting it off. It actually made me a bit horny, so I stripped and climbed in with them, just as I'd done when Rosalie was around. They didn't seem to mind and we romped away till we were exhausted.

Infantry training at Singleton was far different from Kapooka, and it was here that I started to shine. With

215

all the training that Kurt had given me I could have instructed the instructors. I'd forgotten more than they even knew. After only the second week I realised that if we stuck to what some of them were advising, someone was going to get their bloody heads blown off in the real thing. Either they knew fuck-all about bushcraft or, if they did, they weren't showing us.

One evening we were being given natural camouflage instructions. We all painted ourselves up and stuck leaves out of everything we wore and were standing around waiting when this WO2 came up.

'Right men,' he said. 'Four of your instructors have concealed themselves. And your job is to see if you can spot them or detect their whereabouts.'

We were marched over to the top of a short rise that fell away on the far side. There was long grass and undergrowth about two feet high, with trees and small bushes everywhere. We were told to study the terrain and locate the enemy if we could. It wasn't a dark night, there was a full moon. The main bunch of blokes were standing around and everything looked normal to them, but I moved off to one side and let Kurt's words flood back through me . . .

'Silhouette, shape and shadow, son. Look for the break in conformity. If there's cover and a light breeze, watch for the bush or branch not moving like the rest.'

That's how I found the first guy. About twenty yards away and straight in front of us I noticed this patch of shadow. There was a gusty breeze and all the other shadows were changing shape as the undergrowth moved. I moved forward, then rushed to the spot and put my boot down hard. Wooooooph! The air exploded out of the instructor and he rolled around in agony for a minute, then got to his feet and slunk away like a mongrel dog.

A babble of voices started.

'How did he know he was there?' someone said. 'Fucked if I saw anything.'

The CSM came down to me.

'Good work,' he said, then turning to the others. 'Cut the chatter. Let's get back to the exercise.'

I located the other three over the next few minutes. The rest of the guys thought it was great, even though they hadn't done the actual spotting. The platoon had put one over on the instructors and I was a kind of hero in their eyes. But the instructors were different. They hated me.

Things came to a head for me one morning when we were being given fixed-bayonet combat instruction. One of the instructors, whom we'd nicknamed 'Guts and Gaiters,' singled me out to teach me a lesson in front of the rest of the boys. There were guards on the bayonets so no one could do any real injury with them. Pointing to me he yelled out.

'Right you. Out here, move!'

I moved towards him. 'On guard!' he roared, and assumed the classical stance for bayonet engagement in close combat.

Kurt's words raced through my brain, pictures flashed. I heard his voice whispering urgently . . . 'That's it . . . that's it . . . Get inside the thrust lad . . . Parry . . . thrust . . . then hit . . . Go . . . Go in for the kill . . . Good . . . Good boy.'

Because he was trying to make an example of me, and

217

do it quickly in front of the men, Guts and Gaiters moved in fast and made a thrust towards my midriff. I moved, stepped inside, deflected his thrust with my weapon and, carrying the deflection on in the natural forward motion, thrust my bayonet hard into his solar plexus. Then I let the butt of the weapon come around in a natural arc with all my weight behind it. He was totally unprepared.

'Oooooomph,' he went as the air whooshed out of him. Crack as the butt of my SLR hit him hard along-side the jaw. He went down hard, his weapon clattering onto the parade ground. As he landed on his back, I put my boot down hard on his chest and placed the end of the bayonet into the hollow of his throat. But he wasn't going to be doing anything more that day. He was out cold.

'Shit!' someone said in the ranks.

'Jesus!' another voice exclaimed. 'Did you fuckin' see that?'

'Silence in the ranks!' roared the CSM.

He bent down and examined the sergeant instructor, got up and ordered the platoon commander to get a stretcher on the double.

Orders started to fly all around the place. The CO and the major who was his 2IC had been watching the session and they came over and went into a discussion with the CSM. I'm still standing there when the CSM approached me and placed his hand gently on my weapon.

'I'll take that . . . Let me have it, son,' he said quietly.

'We're not supposed to surrender our weapons, Sir', I replied, taking a firm grip on my SLR.

The CSM lowered his hand and stepped back half a pace.

The 2IC approached me.

'This is not a theatre of war, Private,' he said quietly. 'This is a parade ground. Surrender your weapon, that's an order.'

He reached out with his palm up, so I reluctantly gave him my weapon.

The CO walked over to me.

'Fall out to the edge of the parade ground, Private.'

'Sir,' I said, and saluted him.

I marched off to the edge of the parade ground. You never strolled or walked on that hallowed ground. You marched. All the guys in the company were looking at me. Two guys came on the double with a stretcher and loaded Guts and Gaiters onto it. The brass were having a pow-wow and I'm standing on the edge of the parade ground like a shag on a bloody rock. It looked all very solemn. I thought the next thing that'll happen is the firing squad will march on and I'll be shot in front of the men without a court martial. But instead of the firing squad the 'Old Man' and the major came over and said to me, without stopping . . .

'Follow us, Private.'

I saluted with a 'Yes Sir' and fell in behind them.

I was ordered to wait outside the CO's office, even being permitted to sit. The CO and the major were inside behind closed doors. Five minutes went by and in marched the RSM, stiff as a ramrod, with his baton firmly under one arm. He marched up to the office door and came to a halt, slamming down his right boot so hard it shook the office. He knocked on the door, then looked down at me without the slightest bit of emotion, and after receiving a summons from inside, he entered.

Fifteen minutes passed before the door opened again and the RSM called me.

'Right! On your feet Private ... Remove your hat ... On parade inside. March!'

I marched to the colonel's desk.

'Halt!' yelled the RSM, just about shattering everyone's eardrums.

'Stand at ease, Private,' the colonel said in a voice about 80 decibels lower than the RSM's. He gazed at me for a moment or two and then spoke.

'It is quite obvious to us, Private, and to all and sundry around the camp, that you possess some remarkable talents. Talents that are not what one would describe as being natural ones. In other words, Private, what you have displayed here over the last couple of months in the course of your training—or, as the major so aptly put it, "Who's training who?"—are advanced combat, infiltration and guerilla techniques ... that one is not gifted with, so to speak, at birth. Am I making myself perfectly clear to you?'

'Yes Sir.'

'Good,' he said. 'These skills make it quite apparent, in fact glaringly obvious, that you have received prior military training. I think you owe us an explanation, Private?'

'If you say so, Sir.'

'Right!' said the colonel. 'Let's start at the beginning, shall we. Just explain, in your own time, where you received this training.'

We were in the office a long time. I explained that I had a friend, the name of whom they continually tried to prise out of me, who had trained me in military and covert action techniques. I then told them about Kurt's involvement in Z Force and his other activities. They were impressed, to say the least. I explained every detail of training that I had received and answered a barrage of questions. I even bordered close to insubordination.

'If we have to go into combat, Sir, armed only with the knowledge and things that we are being taught here, then someone better take along a good supply of body bags.'

A hint of a smile appeared on the colonel's face.

More questions followed—about small arms, incendiaries, military and home-made, explosives, demolition, hand-to-hand with and without knife, the piano wire with two wooden toggles on each end that, when placed over the head of an enemy from behind with a right over left hand technique, causing the loop to cross, would sever the head from the body soundlessly, like a cheese cutter through soft cheddar. Infiltration and intelligence gathering. I was given a pen and paper to illustrate booby traps and explosive devices, some created with everyday household supplies.

'That's just about it, Sir,' I said at last.

'Just about it,' the colonel sputtered. 'Christ almighty man, I hope you haven't used any of this . . . this training for clandestine purposes have you?'

A few pictures flashed across my mind but I couldn't very well admit why I had learnt and what I'd used it for. 'No Sir, not at all,' I said.

'Thank God for that!' The Old Man said, leaning back in his chair, shaking his head from side to side.

I was dismissed shortly after that and returned to the barracks . . . No, I wasn't under arrest . . . Yes, I had the freedom of the camp . . . Yes, leave would be permitted that evening after mess. But I was not to join the men who at the moment were doing exercise and classes.

At lunch, all the blokes asked me if I was in the shit. I said I didn't know. They whispered that Guts and Gaiters had a broken jaw. I had to admit that things didn't look good from where I was sitting, and I was actually waiting for the provost marshal to cart me off to Holsworthy Military Detention Centre. When we were fallen in after lunch I was *told*, not *roared at*, to stand fast and, when the other men were deployed to whatever it was they were doing I returned to barracks. After mess that night I went on leave, where my mates asked me as many questions as the colonel had.

Reveille sounded at 0600 hours. I fell out and lined up with the men.

'You may go straight to the mess, Private,' the platoon commander told me. 'You're excused from PT.'

After breakfast we were making our way from the mess hall when the CSM approached me and told me to follow him. This is it, I thought.

I was taken back to the CO's office and told to wait in the outer office. Less than a minute later the door opened and the 2IC beckoned.

There were only the three of us in the room this time. The colonel, the major and me.

'You may sit down, Private,' the Old Man said. I did so. 'To be frank, your actions here have placed us in a rather embarrassing position. However, after careful consideration and recommendations to GHQ, the major and I have come up with what we believe is a solution. Would you be willing to undergo special training, where these talents of yours could be put to a better use?'

I was about to reply but the colonel raised his hands and bored on.

'You see what we have here is an invidious situation which can only cause further embarrassment. It would be unfair to ask you to back off, so to speak, because that's not what military training is all about. Do you follow me?'

'Yes Sir.'

'Good . . . It is my recommendation, then, that you be transferred to the Special Operations Group unit in Queensland where I'm sure, as is the major, that you'll fit in splendidly. Now, would you like to give it a go?'

As I listened, I realised what the true facts were. I had made the instructors look pretty ordinary, I was a pain in the neck, and they needed to save a bit of face. At the same time, I could put what Kurt had taught me to better advantage.

'Yes Sir. I'll give it a go.'

It was as if I'd lifted a heavy weight from them. They broke into smiles and looked at each other with that 'aren't we clever' look. Then the Colonel picked up a manilla folder and opened it, taking out some paperwork.

'You have been granted special leave, effective immediately. There's a clearance that you can present at the paymaster's for your pay and your transfer to the Canungra Jungle Training Centre effective from . . . ' He glanced at the document a moment and read out a date, about three weeks away.

I looked at the Colonel. 'I'm sorry, Sir, about old Guts and Gaiters,' I said. I'd meant to say Sergeant Moody.

'Who?' he asked. 'Oh! Oh yes, Sergeant Moody . . . Well I'm sure the sergeant will be all right. Now you'd better go and pack your kit.'

At 0800 hours the next morning I was back in Brisbane. There was no one at home but the place was all neat and tidy. I lounged on the big sofa and I wondered just what the future held, then drifted off to sleep.

I woke late in the afternoon, starving hungry, and opened the fridge. There was bugger all in there. After I'd showered and shaved and was putting some civvy mocca on I noticed that the dressing table looked pretty bare. I went to Helen's wardrobe and opened it. It was empty.

I really didn't feel disappointment. We'd been together for over two years but I always knew that things wouldn't last. I drove down to the Valley, had a meal and decided I'd go to the New Farm Hotel and at least say good luck and goodbye. I went into the saloon, then the lounge, but there was no sign of her, so I went back out to the bar and ordered a beer.

'What's happened to Helen?' I asked the barmaid.

'She and Judy quit a month ago and took off for Melbourne. Why?'

'Ah nothin',' I said. 'Just wanted to say hello.'

We dropped the conversation, I finished my beer, and when I arrived home I checked the letterbox. Power bill. Telephone bill. A letter I'd written to Helen from Singleton. And a letter to me from Melbourne.

Dear Jimmy,

I'm sorry that I've left like this. We've gone to Melbourne to live. Please don't feel that I'm doing this to hurt you because that's the last thing that I'd want to do. We've had some good times together and shared a lot of laughs. You stood by me when I was in trouble and helped me back on my feet. I will never forget that.

You have found a new life now that doesn't leave much room for the way it used to be. And I have decided to make a change too. Please keep in touch and let me know how things go with you.

Please don't feel badly about me, I'm only doing what I feel is best for both of us. I'll always be there if I can help.

Love Helen, XX

She was right. We were two different people, living in two different worlds. But she was a good girl and I will always think kindly of her.

25

CANUNGRA JUNGLE TRAINING CENTRE. AND THAT'S just what it was. A great tangled jungle, and the law of the jungle prevailed—only the fittest and best survived. If you didn't have what it took, it soon stood out. Formality was down to a minimum, spit and polish a thing of the past. They didn't even care if you shaved. What they cared about was turning you into an automatic killing machine that would react instantly. No matter what, no matter where, no matter when. SOAD—Seek Out And Destroy—was the only game they played. Nothing else was allowed to matter. Nothing else was tolerated.

We learnt to live like animals. Sleeping and living off the jungle with the barest of essentials, which in most cases was what you stood in and a combat knife. We learnt to make weapons with whatever was at hand. Became skilled at detecting booby traps and making them out of the natural surroundings. Learnt to eat things that would have made a billygoat puke. All the stuff Kurt had so patiently taught me came in handy and saved the day on many an occasion. But times had changed, and so had tactics. Ideas and techniques that were once thought to have been the best were shown to have flaws. We were being trained and made ready to fight a new type of enemy—the Viet Cong—in a war of attrition. Sure there were some things that never change, but I had to learn quite a bit more than Kurt had taught me.

We stalked and hunted each other through swamps and mangroves, over hills and through creeks, up rivers, into jungles, and over open ground. We learnt to become familiar with various Russian and Chinese weapons such as the Kalashnikov assault rifle and the Tokarev automatic, the AK47 and the Chinese ARM 50 heavy machine-gun, Chinese and Russian mortars and recoilless rocket launchers, grenades and flame-throwers. Not to mention numerous varieties of American weaponry. It became second nature to handle all the new plastique explosives. We became experts in ambush and the silent kill.

After nine months of this intensive training we were honed and sharpened into a military blade that could cut deeply. So, as a test, we were sent to the Shoalwater Bay training area near Rockhampton to act as the enemy against ordinary-trained, everyday-type servicemen. The CMF were there too. Weekend warriors and cut-lunch commandos we called them. There was a whole regiment of everybody in all shapes and sizes. Infantry, engineers, signals, assault pioneers, transport, medical corps, armour and artillery. The bloody lot. We acted as a guerilla enemy unit. Christ! It was a massacre. And I knew then just how good our training had been. The poor bastards didn't know what hit them. They made more noise than a herd of elephants when they moved through the bush. Talking, laughing, their gear clanking and crashing about in the undergrowth. They thought it was all over once night fell, but did we have news for them. We took out the forward scouts and sentries first. Then we went to work on the main bunch, pulling them out of their weapon pits, choking off their cries and tying them up with their own toggle ropes. Then we drew a big red mark across their throats with an indelible marker.

There was this one lieutenant, Donaldson, who was a real prig in every sense of the word. The silly bastard tried pulling rank when we captured him. We took him out right under the noses of his own bloody platoon, and when clear of the camp we stripped him bollocky naked and tied him to a tree. Did he perform.

'I am giving you a direct order to release me now.'

We told him to go and get fucked.

This bloke had just come out of Officer Training School at Duntroon.

'I demand to know your names and regimental numbers now. I intend to bring you three up on charges of insubordination.'

'Insubordination my arse,' we said. And for good measure we gave him a couple of heavy punches where they'd do most good and a kick in the balls, then pissed on him. The snotty bastard needed an attitude adjustment, and if this poor silly prick thought the bastards he was going to fight in Vietnam were going to observe the Geneva convention then he was in for the shock of his life.

However, as it turned out the mongrel had the last laugh. Blood is thicker than water when it comes to family, and the old school tie carries weight amongst brother officers, even if the bastards are only junior ones. They're a queer breed I can tell you, but Lieutenant Donaldson's daddy was a retired brigadier. After an investigation was held it wasn't too long before we were named as the parties responsible for the incident. The Raspberry Creek Cock-Up it became known as. We were pulled in onto the mat and, Holy Hell, did they lay it on.

No respect for authority, you lot, they said ... Not one iota of respect. Didn't we understand that an order was an order in the field. That to disobey a superior officer in the field can result in being summarily shot. Lucky not to be court-martialled. Blah blah blah.

It didn't matter that we got the job done. Oh! no. The brother officer had been humiliated. His feelings were hurt and he had to be defended at all costs. It was the Breaker Morant syndrome all over again. Bugger all the training that had been drummed into us. I thought we were supposed to be the enemy.

'Your treatment of the prisoner, and an officer to boot, was a blatant and flagrant disregard of the Geneva Convention on the treatment of prisoners of war.'

Then they turned their attention to me, bringing up the incidents at Singleton, saying I'd struck an NCO instructor ... Which was a load of bullshit. The truth is that the instructors thought their bloody shit didn't stink, and that they knew it all.

We couldn't take the still-wet-behind-the-bloody-ears piddling little pansy of the junior officer like we had. And treat him like the fuckin' Viet Cong would ... show him what sort of an enemy he was going to be up against. Knowledge is something the Army doles out on a need-to-know basis, but if this officious little junior officer was ever captured by the Viet Cong, they'd do a bloody sight worse to him than we had. They'd chop his dick off and shove it down his throat. Or shove a piece of garden hose up his arse, poke barbed wire up inside, then pull the garden hose out and hook the wire up to an electrical current.

So, the end result was we were kicked out of the Special Operations Group, forthwith, immediately, and split up.

I was transferred to 6 Battalion RAR, at Enoggera Camp at Ashgrove in Brisbane. It was a different scene and ball game from the start. You could feel the camaraderie and pride in the men. The battalion was made up of regulars and nashos, and called the baby battalion because of this. The guys in charge had all come up through the ranks and the CO, Lieutenant-Colonel Townsend, was a top man. He had respect for all the men and in all my time with them I never heard a bad word spoken about him. George Chinn was our RSM. You knew exactly where you stood with George. I finished up in 11 Platoon, Delta Company, and our company commander was Major Harry Smith, who was a man's man and never asked anyone to do anything that he couldn't or wouldn't do himself. Jack Kirby was the CSM and another top bloke. Our platoon commander was Lieutenant Geoff Sharp, who got the best from us because he deserved the best.

Boy oh boy. The nights we'd have when we'd go into town on leave. Our favourite watering hole was the Treasury Hotel. We loved it and they loved us. There was a huge basement bar called the Cellar that featured top bands and on our leave nights the place was packed out. There were wall-to-wall women, most of them eager to please and very free with their favours. After all, this was the mid-'60s, the age of enlightenment.

But like all good things, it had to come to an end. And for some of the guys who shared a beer with us, called each other mate, trained, lived and laughed together, it ended forever on the bloody battlefield of Long Tan in Phuoc Tuy province in South Vietnam.

We received our orders that we were going to Vietnam—The Farm, we called it. But none of us were really shocked. We'd known for some time that we were the next lot to go. Some of the guys dreaded it, but accepted it. And some of us looked forward to it. What was the good of being a soldier sitting on your arse safe and sound, or running around the bush like bloody maniacs in your own country, pretending all the time? If we had a real enemy, a genuine foe, then let's engage the bastards in mortal combat. Let's get it on! We're ready to give a good account of ourselves.

We arrived in Vietnam towards the end of winter, 1966. And the first thing I remember about the place and the Task Force Headquarters at Nui Dat was the mud. The monsoon season had come early and set in with a vengeance. The lines that had been allocated to us to set up and establish were a real shithouse. There was rain and mud everywhere and we all squelched about in it. But we took it in our stride. We had been sent to do a job, so let's do it without the traditional whingeing. Fuck the weather, we said, and went about the business the best way we could. In fact morale lifted. Nancy Sinatra had a big hit out then called 'These Boots

Are Made for Walkin',' so a pair of Sad Sack boots were painted and became the battalion emblem.

The shit really hit the fan about 3 p.m. on 18 August. There was going to be a big concert that arvo at the Bowl, as we named the open-air theatre. Little Pattie and the Joy Boys, the Rajahs and a couple of others were going to put on a show for us. It nearly turned out to be their last.

Apparently intelligence reports had come in that suggested an enemy force was headed in our direction. For once they got it right. Prior to that we had been out on a few clearing patrols based on intelligence reports which turned out to be nothing more than one of the local natives straying a bit too close for comfort. The only clandestine action he was engaged in was taking a crap. But in fairness, Charlie played hide and seek with us to gather information regarding our strengths, weaknesses and numbers ... and took the odd snipe at us from cover. This worried the top brass and all the scrub and trees were cut down to ground level for a good distance around the camp. It gave us a good open killing field if the Viet Cong or NVA decided to attack.

Some enemy had actually been spotted that morning, and it was thought that 6 RAR was their target. We were the new kids, the baby battalion, and fair game as far as the 'rice burners' were concerned. One of the things that has always amazed me about the Army was that a lot of the men in 6 RAR hadn't finished their training before we left Australia. The mental giants who make the decisions reckoned they could complete their training over in Vietnam, based I suppose on the Napoleonic philosophy that 'The best way to blood a soldier is to send him into battle.' There was another piece of Napoleonic logic I felt like telling these mental giants ... 'There's no such thing as bad soldiers only bad officers.' He got that right.

Charlie sent a few mortar rounds into the lines that afternoon. A couple of guys ended up with superficial wounds but, miraculously, no one was killed. So Delta Company was made ready to search and engage. We knew that Charlie was out there somewhere, but we didn't know their numbers or their position. After receiving extra ammo, and thank Christ for once they were pretty generous with it, the D Company Platoons were ready and we left camp in search of Charlie.

We crossed the river and moved into a rubber plantation. The place was Long Tan. You wouldn't have believed the rain. I had never seen it that heavy in all my life. It was bucketing and pissing down and was to affect the direction the APCs were forced to take later. Delta Company split up and 11 Platoon was sent ahead.

We moved forward stealthily. It is difficult to describe what followed with complete clarity. It's something like one of those old machines you put money in, then turn the handle and the pictures flick over at a fast rate. You get the picture, but it comes to you in flashes, some of which stay clear in your mind forever. They can never be erased. I have asked others who I served with on that day and, just like me, they see the same vivid flashes.

The first thing I remember about the battle was that the visibility was so poor. Then, suddenly! ... The bushes in front of me seemed to be sparkling with a

233

million winking lights. And then came the noise. Jesus! The noise was horrendous. The firing and the VC screaming, our guys yelling, and the volume of incoming fire was unimaginable. How the Platoon wasn't cut to ribbons in that opening moment I will never know. We hit the ground, rolled and returned fire. The air above and around us was full of a million hot lead and steel hornets that hissed and buzzed. You could taste it, see tracer everywhere, you could feel bullets in the air as they passed over and smacked into everything around us. You could actually smell the fuckin' stuff. Cordite fumes hung low and wafted in swirling clouds. And the rain pouring relentlessly. It just kept on pissing down.

I had positioned myself behind a rubber tree. The incoming fire was tearing it to shreds. Bark and latex sap flew and sprayed out of it. The bloke alongside me was Freddie Topp. He took one through the head. I heard the bullet strike him. Phwock! He just slumped down with his face towards me. Blood ran like a flood from his nostrils onto the ground. Christ! I could smell it, coppery. The Viet Cong bastards kept charging forward. Bugle sounds, then a scream from them and a human wave would crash towards you spewing lead and flame and death right at you. At times we fired at point-blank range. Bam bam bam. I tried to keep count of the rounds that were gone from the clip so there'd still be one up the spout and I wouldn't have to re-cock my weapon when I shoved a new magazine into it. Steam was hissing off it. If it hadn't been raining the barrel would have turned red hot. Mortars were exploding now, the incoming shit was unbelievable.

Their mortar rockets were landing in the trees above and all around us, tearing branches and foliage away and exploding in roars of mud and greasy slush.

Major Harry Smith had set up company HQ somewhere behind us, and they were taking it too. We were fuckin' surrounded. But, somehow, some way, with all this going on, the noise ... the rain ... and the firing ... the mortars, and the constant jack-hammering of the enemy machine-guns and tracer ... some of us survived.

Company HQ got through to base at Nui Dat, and the artillery started to send in some of our own. I could see the incoming landing, exploding. They gradually decreased the range until it was dropping practically in front of us. It landed in and among the enemy, ripping them to shreds, blasting chunks out of bodies and blowing the pieces everywhere. But the bastards still kept charging over the dead and mangled remains of what had once been their comrades, bugles blaring, screaming, wave after wave of the bastards. A slight lull, perhaps a second or two, and our platoon commander Geoff Sharp looked around the tree he was using for cover to check his men. Another scream went up and the next wave came forward. A round took him through the neck and Geoff saw his life blood spurt out of him as he died against that tree.

It was getting darker and we were running critically short on ammo, real short. This is it, son, I remember thinking. The dirty bastards have got us. There was a dead VC just a little to the right of the tree I was using as cover. He had ammo pouches and an AK47 still gripped in his dead hand. I made a wild dive towards him, arm outstretched and grabbing for the weapon. Something hit me hard on the inside of my right leg between my hip and knee as the ground around me erupted and sprayed mud, but I had the weapon in my hand. I rolled a little and squeezed off a burst into the four or five who ran towards me. Three were hit hard, reeling back, and the other one or two dropped. I pushed myself back, flicking the trigger, bam bam bam bam. As I moved I grabbed the leg of the dead VC and, pushing myself back behind the tree, I wrenched back on the dead leg with every bit of strength I had. The dead Charlie slid across the mud, the blood and the slush. I ripped the ammo pouches from his body, knocked another magazine into the AK and let a burst go into another wave. I swung away as return fire ripped the tree and the ground around me. I lay on my back for a moment, trying to let the rain wash over my face and into my mouth. Christ I was dry. There was an explosion in the treetop above me and I felt the impact of a handful of mortar shrapnel as it slapped into my left leg. I put my hand down quickly and could actually feel the little cuts in the cloth of my JG trousers. Blood welled out between my fingers. If I didn't do something I was going to die. I swung back over on my belly and into the tree in the prone position. 'Fuck you Charlie!' I screamed out and fired again. I don't know where the fuck sergeant Bob Buick came from, but he came slithering up from behind somewhere.

'Ammo mate,' he shouted.

He dropped it and was gone again, slithering away. I grabbed up the SLR, shoved in a fresh magazine and tore into the bastards again. It was starting to get really

236

dark. The artillery was practically on top of us by now, and through the flashes when the shells burst I could see the dirty bastards silhouetted like shadows in a sunset, trying to drag their dead and wounded back. I fired into them and waited for another shell burst to fire again. The tracer was still coming like racing fireflies.

It just didn't stop. Everything I did from that point on I did like an automaton. The next thing I remember was the sound of the APCs behind us growling their way towards us. It was the sweetest sound I'd ever heard. But in their rush to get up and assist us the bastards nearly ran over the top of us. The next thing, someone yelled close behind us.

'Pull back eleven . . . Pull back.'

So we slowly pulled back, still firing as we did. Then our artillery really opened up. Where we'd been a few moments before was like Armageddon. The firing from Charlie gradually died down. I couldn't walk. My legs were numb and I'd lost a lot of blood. I was sitting with my back against a blown-off stump of a rubber tree, my chin on my chest. Then Pom Rencher grabbed me.

'Come on cobber,' he said. He hauled me up and got me back.

The armoured personnel carriers had formed a defensive ring and we harboured inside these as a perimeter. I saw Colonel Townsend moving about. He must have come down from the base. Our medic Phil Dobson came over, took a look at me, tore open a couple of field dressings and applied pressure bandages on my legs. Major Harry Smith was everywhere.

'Good work men,' he said as he went by. 'I'm bloody

proud of you.' And moved on to check others.

They loaded the wounded into an APC and took us to Nui Dat. The artillery was still blazing away when we got back. They knew Charlie was pulling back and they were trying to follow him up to inflict more casualties.

The badly wounded were evacuated to 1 Military Hospital at Vung Tau, where they put me under and took an AK47 round out of my right leg and five pieces of deeply embedded shrapnel out of my left leg. I had these long pieces of gauze soaked in some antibiotic ointment plugging up the holes and they'd change these 'drains', they called them, every day. Pull them out and poke new ones in. It was torture.

'Can't you just sew the bloody things up?' I kept asking.

'No,' I was informed. 'They have to heal from inside. There was that much muck in the wounds that infection would have started.'

Shit it was painful, I can tell you.

While I was in the hospital I learnt that the enemy force that had engaged us was the 445 Mobile Regiment, made up of NVA Regulars and Viet Cong. We also lost our CSM Jack Kirby while I was in hospital, but in a separate engagement. We had 18 killed and 22 wounded in the company at the Battle of Long Tan, which raged without let-up for three solid hours. I've never forgotten it and I never will. None of us will. There is a monument there now, and those who took part were flown over for a commemoration service. Good-bye to our fallen comrades, and brothers in arms.

Decorations were handed out. The CO Australian Task Force Brigadier Jackson and our CO Colonel Townsend received the DSO. Major Harry Smith the MC. CSM Jack Kirby and Corporal Jack Carter got the DCM. Sergeant Bob Buick and Private Ray Eglinton were awarded the MM. Bob Buick should have got the Victoria Cross. And eight of us including yours truly were given the MID. The US General Officer Commanding, General Bill Westmorland, wrote us up and we were awarded the PUC (Presidential Unit Citation) which read:

D Company, Sixth Battalion Royal Australian Regiment, distinguished itself by extraordinary heroism while engaged in military operations against an opposing armed force in Vietnam 18 August 1966. While searching for Viet Cong in a rubber plantation northeast of Ba Ria, Phuoc Tuy Province, Republic of Vietnam, D Company met and immediately became engaged in heavy contact. As the battle developed, it became apparent that the men of D Company were facing a numerically superior force. The platoons of D Company were surrounded and attacked on all sides by an estimated reinforced enemy battalion using automatic weapons, small arms, and mortars. Fighting courageously against a well-armed and determined foe, D Company maintained their formations in a common perimeter defence and inflicted heavy casualties upon the Viet Cong. The enemy maintained a continuous, intense volume of fire and attacked repeatedly from all directions. Each successive assault was repulsed by the courageous Australians. Heavy rainfall and low ceiling prevented any friendly close air support during the battle. After three hours of savage attacks, having failed to penetrate the Australian lines, the enemy withdrew from the battlefield carrying many dead and wounded, and leaving 245 Viet Cong dead forward of the defence position of D Company. The conspicuous gallantry, intrepidity and indomitable courage of D Company were in the highest tradition of military valour and reflect great credit upon D Company, Sixth Battalion, The Royal Australian Regiment and The Australian Army.

We were presented with a ribbon and insignia to wear, patted on the backs and told well done.

The South Vietnamese government wanted to decorate us too. They had all the medals and ribbons prepared, but at the last moment headquarters back in Australia wouldn't allow the award. We were not to receive a medal from a foreign power, they said. It had me and everybody else over there fucked. We were protecting them, after all. However, the South Vietnamese government didn't want to lose face so we had a parade and we were all presented with a little *Chinese* doll.

At the end of the tour we returned to Australia, were given extended leave and were presented with the Key to the City of Brisbane. Parties were thrown in our honour. I couldn't work out what all the fuss was about. We had done what we were supposed to do. We received a hero's welcome but that sort of reception wasn't to last. After Jim Cairns spearheaded the Moratorium to end the war in Vietnam, open hostility set in and the mob that returned after us were greeted with rotten eggs, tomatoes and any other shit that people could throw. The press loved it. In fact, they aided and abetted it. The opposition politicians got on the band-wagon and made us out to be a bunch of homicidal maniacs whose main pastime was the slaughter of defenceless women and children.

I would have liked to have taken the political pricks and dropped them into the middle of the Phuoc Tuy Province as we had been, and told them to go ahead and use the bullshit here that you're using at home. See if you can talk these bastards out of cutting your dicks off and blowing your fuckin' brains out.

Like a lot of my mates, I became disgusted. We had pride in going over and doing the job. Now politics was giving us a dirty name and we felt like a bunch of pariahs. We became disillusioned and turned to drugs to ease the humiliation and shame that was being heaped on us by politicians using us as a tool to win an election.

Our leave over and, back at camp again, we went about our duties in a different frame of mind. When we went on leave we went in civilian dress. And when we were huddled together in the corner of some pub, smoking a joint or two, we'd pour the piss into us and silently think, and then say aloud, 'Fuck the army. Fuck the politicians. Fuck the press. Fuck everybody.' It was this resentment that took me down a path I didn't even dream I'd travel on again.

I remembered I had a friend who I could trust in Brisbane and—for understanding and comfort—I went and knocked on the door of Carlo Bellari.

26

THREE AND A HALF YEARS HAD PASSED SINCE I HAD had any contact with the family, and one doesn't go around asking people how to get in contact with Carlo Bellari. You could find yourself with your head sticking up your arse before you even reached first base.

One evening when I was on duty in the orderly office at Enoggera I rang the directory assistance and got the number of Domino's. I rang them and was asked if I wanted to make a reservation.

'I would like to make a reservation for the *Famiglia*,' I said.

'Hold the line please.'

A moment went by.

'How may I help you?' a different voice asked.

'Write this number down,' I said, giving the orderly office extension number. 'Now ring Don Paolo and ask him to call me here tonight.'

'May I ask who's calling?' I was asked.

'Tell him it's Jimmy . . . Jimmy Diamond. And let Paolo know I'll only be at this number tonight.'

'I will pass the message on. Good night.'

Fifteen minutes later the phone rang.

'Six Battalion Orderly Office. Diamond speaking.'

'Jimmy! Paolo. Is that really you? . . . What the hell are you up to? . . . You just disappeared.'

'Yeah it's me all right, Paolo ... Look it's a long story. And not one I can talk a lot about, especially on this phone. I'm in the Army, mate. Been back in the country for five months. I was over in Vietnam for over a year. I was wondering if you could let Carlo know I'm at this number. I've had a gutful.'

'Jesus Christ, Jimmy. Vietnam! What made you join the Army?'

'Fucked if I know, Paolo. If you can figure it out then you'd better explain it to me.'

'Why didn't you come back here? I told you there's always something for you.'

'Like I told you, it's a long story. But what about Carlo? Could you speak to him about me?'

'Sure, but there's not much I can do tonight. Look, write this number down.' I did as Paolo asked.

'Righto, now memorise it. It's right here at home. I've moved from Vaucluse. Ring me tomorrow around ten. In the army ... ' and he gave a chuckle. 'Unbelievable.'

'Thanks Paolo. I'll call you tomorrow.'

'*Bene Jimmy. Bene fortuna.*'

I sat there, in deep thought. What is life all about? What had I achieved so far? Was I born to be a soldier to fight other people's battles? Why had fate dealt me the hand that it had? Had I played it fair, by the book, by the rules? We're born free, yet the moment we enter the world we're everywhere in chains. You can't do this, you mustn't do that. We all suffer from this fatal disease called life, yet society does everything to make us forget that, sooner or later, we come to an end. But none of us are ready for that end. We are cowards and we thrust it out of our consciousness. One of the most tragic things about funerals that I experienced with the death of Margo, and the death and destruction I witnessed in Vietnam, is not just the sense of shock at the Grim Reaper reminding everyone of their mortality, but also the sense of lost time, of missed opportunities. We live as if we are immortal, but we aren't, and by the time the funeral comes it's too late to say *if only* . . . But the real problem about life and death as I see it concerns not sadness or a sense of loss, not even our own mortality. It seems to me that it is to do with the question that mortality asks us . . . what, after all, is all this rigmarole about? Are we born just to die, and does our inevitable death make all our achievements, our dreams, hopes, love and longing worth as much as an empty cigarette packet? All that night I tossed these concepts around and near dawn I made a decision.

We all only have so much life from alpha to omega, from birth till death. Some will go through this time being led like sheep. Others will rebel and society will try to stop them. You must conform, you must obey, or we'll punish you. You are allowed to be free but we'll govern that freedom. You must kiss society's arse. Well, *I* was alive. I had seen death, tons of it, and I know my own life has to finish that way. But the bit before that belonged to me. Society could kiss *my* arse.

Then the night shift was over and the camp came to life for another day. I was living on the base now and I went to my quarters, set the alarm for 9 a.m., just three hours away, and fell asleep.

The jangling of the alarm woke me. I showered, shaved and dressed, jumped into the car and drove to Ashgrove post office. I rang the number Paolo had given me. The phone was answered almost immediately.

'Hi Paolo. It's me. What's happening?'

'Ah, Jimmy. Good. Listen, can you remember an address?'

'Sure.'

He gave me the address in St Lucia.

'I spoke to Carlo this morning. He's a bit surprised, you know, but he wants you to go there for lunch. Where are you ringing from?'

'Jesus mate. I'm in a bloody phone box. Old habits die hard you know.'

He laughed then, and we had a long conversation. Discussing what I'd done and where I'd been. The bullshit I'd put up with. Paolo breaking in and asking questions.

'Why don't you leave and come back down here?' he said at last.

'Shit! They'd love that, Paolo. Me go AWOL. I'd be in fuckin' Sydney all right. In the bloody stockade at Holsworthy.' This gave him a good laugh. 'Listen Paolo, I'm running out of coins here. Thanks. I'll let you know how I go.'

'Okay, Jimmy. Keep in touch.'

I had a bit of time to kill and I didn't know what I was going to say to Carlo. What I did know was that the Army had nothing more to offer me. I was disillusioned with the whole kit and caboodle, a warrior without a war. Ever since the night I'd lost Margo, there'd been an empty space in my life. But what could I do to fill that hollow? She was one of a kind. No one would ever take her place. Nothing I'd done since then had given me a sense of purpose. Only helped pass the time. I had a hunger inside me, for what I didn't know. Like an explorer who didn't know just what he was looking for, I craved achievement, but I didn't know what I wanted to achieve.

I drove to St Lucia and decided to have a couple of beers before going to see Carlo. Then I got a cab.

The taxi pulled up in front of a pretty impressive piece of real estate.

'This is it!' said the driver.

I paid the cabbie, walked to a gate set into a high wall topped with broken glass and jabbed the intercom button.

'Yes,' a voice said.

'Jimmy Diamond to see Mr Bellari.'

There was a clack as an electric lock snapped back. 'Come on through,' the voice said. 'And please close the gate after you.'

I walked up a long drive that was paved Roman-style. The house was a real beauty, two-storyed with a large columned patio in the front. It had great landscaping.

A moment or two later the door was opened by Carlo himself. He was a bit heavier now, but hadn't changed a great deal.

'How ya doin', Jimmy? It's been a while,' he said, pumping my hand. 'Come on in. Hungry?'

'Yeah. I am a bit. It's good to see you again, Carlo. I hope I haven't upset the applecart or anything getting in touch like this.'

'No no no. I was surprised when Paolo rang, but no worries. Come on through and say hello to the missus.'

Cupping his hand alongside his mouth he gave a yell. 'Connie . . . Hey! Connie look who's here?'

Connie came in, from the kitchen I guess. She was wearing an apron and as she entered the room she brushed back a wisp of hair that was annoying her. As she walked towards us she wore that smile tinged with a little sadness, like the *Mona Lisa*, that all married Italian women seemed to possess.

'It's a good to see you again, Jeemy,' she said. 'I go fix the dinner for us.'

Carlo walked over to a drinks cabinet and poured a couple of glasses of vino.

'*Salute!*' he said.

I picked up my glass and returned the toast. Then we lapsed into silence for a moment.

'Well Jimmy,' he said at last, 'what have you been doing with yourself? What's all this about the Army?'

For the next five minutes I spoke to Carlo, answering all his questions until Connie came in with the food, placing bowls of everything on the table. There was heaps of it. We ate mostly in silence with just the occasional remark. With the meal over, Carlo rose.

'Let's go out the back to the pool, it's good there. I'll just grab us a couple of drinks.'

One thing that I'd learnt from my past association with the family was that business was never discussed at the home meal table. Never. I followed Carlo outside to the well-appointed pool and we sat in a couple of easy chairs in the shade.

'Okay Jimmy, what do you want me to do for you?'

'I was hoping you might have a place for me. I've still got seven months to serve with the Army. But I'm not

247

going to re-enlist. I've had enough. It's run on bullshit and brass bands. I guess I'm looking for what I once had with Paolo and the Agostini family. People that respect loyalty and accept you for what you are. Paolo wants me to come back to Sydney, but I can't desert, Carlo. I hate it, but I'm built of better stuff than that. I suppose I'm asking a lot of you to try and find a place for me, but I do so because I know I can trust you and Paolo.'

When he heard these words—of respect, trust, and loyalty—his face took on a proud look. These are three of the four ingredients of the code. The fourth is *omerta*, or silence. He sat there for a pensive moment, then nodded his head.

'Jimmy, we don't forget our friends. I've had a long talk with Paolo and he has asked me to take you in and give you something . . . I know you do good work and we just might have something that will suit you. You can't do anything yet, but don't worry, we'll take care of you. All right? Now do you have enough money?'

'I've got a bit put away. I'm right.'

'Well, are you allowed to live away from the camp?'

'Sure. It's just that I don't have any need to.'

'Righto. Well let's get you away from there first. I'll get my man to organise a few things for you. Sam Bacco's his name. We'll get you into a unit, eh? It'll be better than where you are.'

'Thanks Carlo.'

'Paolo deserves the first thanks. He's got a lot of time for you, and so have I. Just move into the unit and get yourself comfortable. I'll get Sam to bring you down to the club and introduce you to the right people, *capisce*?'

'Sure Carlo.'

We spoke a little more, then we rose from the table and he took me in the traditional family embrace and kissed me on both cheeks. 'Welcome home *paisan*,' he said quietly in my ear. 'Now just relax, eh? Get things sorted out.'

Carlo gave me a lift to my car and I returned to the base. I had two more nights on the dog watch to go and thought I'd get them out of the way before I made any changes.

I rang Sam Bacco around 10 on my first day off, and I liked the guy from the moment I heard his voice. You just knew from the sound of it that he must be all right.

'Hey! I've been waitin' two bloody days for a call from you, what ya been doin'? Sticking it to some bloody sheila or somethin'?'

'No mate I've been jammin' it up the arse of one of these cunts out here who calls himself a fuckin' officer. He loves it.'

Sam erupted in real laughter. 'Hey! do you know how to get to Kings Road in Taringa. It's not ... ' he broke into laughter again ... 'Oh shit!'

It was an infectious laugh and it started me off too.

'Oh Christ!' he said. 'You must be a crazy bastard ... Look it's not far from Carlo's place. We got a nice place for you at number 34. I'll meet you there in an hour, okay? ... jammin' it up ... ' And he broke into more rib-splitting guffaws.

'Yeah sure Sam, I'll see you there.'

About an hour later I pulled up in front of a ten-storey place on the river. There was a near-new dark blue Ford Fairlane parked to the left of the entrance. I pulled up behind it, lit a cigarette and sat there. There was a guy in the Fairlane, and he kept looking back through the rear-view mirror. We eyeballed each other for a while, then the guy in front climbed out. He was only about five-seven and round as a beach ball. He waddled up to the window of the old Plymouth.

'Hey! You wouldn't be Jimmy would you?'

'Yeah,' I said. 'I'm the bastard who's been stickin' it up a pig.'

'Oh shit! We're going to get along just fine.' He stuck his hand through the window. 'Sam Bacco.'

'Pleased to meet ya, mate.'

'Whata ya doin' drivin' round in a heap of shit like this for?'

'I haven't had much need for a car the last couple years.'

'Well back it up and drive it down that fuckin' ramp there.'

We went down into the basement garage.

'Park it over there, Jimmy. Spot number 9. That's if the bastard will fit. Jesus, you want to give this the arse as soon as possible. Stands out like fuckin' dogs' balls.'

I followed Sam over to a locked tenants-only lift and we rode up to the ninth floor and walked out into a small foyer. Sam took the keys again and opened the unit door.

To say it was an impressive place is an understatement. It was fully furnished and there was deep cream pile carpet right through the place. As we walked through we opened windows to let in fresh air. Big sliding glass doors opened onto balconies from the lounge and the main bedroom, giving a fabulous view of the river and city. There were three bedrooms and the place had everything. All I needed was my clothes and a toothbrush.

Sam sat down and threw the keys onto a glass-topped coffee table.

'Now,' he said, 'let's have a talk. The power's on, the phone's hooked up and there's an extension in the main bedroom. You've got the whole floor. If someone's at the downstairs foyer and wants to come up, you can talk to 'em on that phone over there.' He pointed to another phone on the wall. 'If ya want the bastards to come up, press that button and that'll unlock the front door. Well, that's about it.'

'Jesus, Sam, I can't afford this joint. I've got a few bob saved up, but what's this place worth a month?'

'Don't be bloody silly. Carlo said to let you have it. It belongs to the business. Tax deductible you know, phantom rent. So enjoy, eh! It's gotta be better than the fuckin' Army. Now I got to get to the club.'

He took out a card and handed it to me.

'That's the number of the 21 Club if you have to reach me. And I've written my home number on the back.'

Sam threw the keys over to me and we left the unit.

Back out at Enoggera, I filled out the form to let the Army know where I was moving to. It was no big deal, quite a lot of the guys lived off the base. I went to the guard room and looked at the duty roster. Shit! I didn't believe it. I'd drawn the dog watch again after my leave. But that was three days away.

I'd just got my stuff packed away in my new home

251

when the door phone started buzzing. It was Sam.

'Hey! what ya doin' up there, *paisan?* Come down here a minute. I need a hand.'

When I got down Sam had propped the front door open with a carton and was placing another one alongside it.

'Couple more out in the car, Jimmy. Give us a hand.'

With the five boxes stacked outside the lift I asked him what it all was.

'We just thought that you'd need a few things till ya got on ya feet. My old girl went to the supermarket and Giovani's Deli and we picked ya up a bit of *mongari*.'

'Well what do I owe you for this, mate? There's enough tucker here to feed the fuckin' Army.'

'Don't worry about it. We'll work it out later. Anyway the boxes from Giovani's are a gift.'

'Thanks a million, Sam.'

'Yeah, well settle in a bit, then come down the club about nine. It's in the Valley.'

No wonder Sam's overweight I thought when I'd finished unpacking. There was even a complete smoked ham.

There was a nice drinks cabinet in the lounge so I went to the local bottle shop and came away a few hundred dollars lighter in pocket. Then I sat around my new home for the rest of the afternoon, listening to the stereo, enjoying a few drinks and admiring the view. A nice breeze was wafting in through the open glass doors, cool and refreshing. Life couldn't have been better or kinder to me at that moment.

For the rest of my days off I went down to the 21 Club each night, had a laugh and a few cold ones with

Sam, who introduced me to a few people including a hostess, Julie, who I invited back that first evening. We screwed our bloody brains out. In the daytime I went to the beach, did some shopping, sunbaked on the high balcony and generally lazed about. I actually returned to duty in a better frame of mind.

It was 2340 hours on my watch when I noticed a Falcon, not an Army car, illegally parked outside the enlisted women's quarters, which were out of bounds at that hour. If the provos spotted it I'd be in the shit. The Army was pretty strict about non-military vehicles on the base, so to save my own arse I put a ticket under the wiper blade, returned to the office and rang the regimental police, who were as bored as I was and just itching to do something. They came and towed the vehicle away, putting it in the locked impounding area. I wrote a report and had just finished it when the phone rang.

'Six Battalion Orderly Office. Diamond.'

'It's John Duffield, Jimmy.' John was the senior man on duty that night at the RP station. 'Listen, have you logged a report yet on that vehicle we impounded?'

'Yeah John, it's all done and I've signed it into the book.'

'Shit! Do you know whose vehicle it was?'

'Wouldn't have a clue. Why? What's the problem?'

'It belongs to a major from Victoria Barracks. He's out front now and he's kicking up blue murder.'

'He knows the rules. If it was you or me we'd be in the shit and on the carpet in the morning. Who's the major, do we know him?'

'You know him better than we do, mate. It's Donaldson. He's the one you blokes gave the treatment up at Shoalwater Bay.'

Surprise surprise, I thought.

'Look, an illegally parked car isn't serious enough to wake up the night duty officer. You tell that peanut that the matter's already logged and can't be erased. To do so would be an offence. He knows that. He's going to have to wait for the morning and apply to the provost marshal's office and face the music.'

'Jesus Jimmy!' was all John Duffield said.

I was sitting back in my chair with the radio playing softly in the background when a vehicle pulled up outside. Just as I was about to get up and investigate the phone rang. I picked it up and went through the usual formal dialogue.

'Sergeant Norm Blackburn here from the provost marshal's station, Indooroopilly. I believe you've impounded a vehicle down there?'

'That's correct, Sergeant. I've logged it and the report's been sent over the printer to HQ. There's nothing I can do about it.'

'You could override the printer message with a recall, and note in the log that a statutory warning was given. That would clear it up.'

'Yes I could do that, Sergeant. But I'd know that it was improper, just as it is improper for you to suggest it.'

'Christ almighty, man! The vehicle belongs to a Major Donaldson, 2IC Signals. What are you trying to do?'

'Just my job, Sergeant?'

'You're making an awful lot of trouble for yourself, but I can't argue with the book. Good luck.' And he hung up.

Two figures marched into the orderly office. John Duffield and Donaldson. Instead of the two pips he used to wear he now had a crown on his shoulder bars. Still thinking his shit didn't stink. I stood up and saluted, but not in a way that said I respected him.

'Oh yes,' he said. 'I remember you. Trouble-maker from way back. Still haven't got any respect for authority have you? Well I'm giving you a direct order. You are to give Private Duffield a release for my vehicle.'

'I'm sorry, Sir. I don't consider that order to be lawful. And it is my duty to disregard an order if I know it isn't lawful.'

'Get your duty officer here immediately.'

'As this matter is not one of grave importance, Sir, I'm afraid that under standing orders I am not obliged to disturb the captain. And I'm sure he'd agree with me.'

Donaldson spun on John Duffield. 'Take me back and release my vehicle. And I'll deal with you later,' he said, pointing at me.

I stood a little taller and looked right at Donaldson.

'With all due respect, Sir, when military personnel return to, or enter, a closed camp they are supposed to report here at the orderly office, irrespective of rank. That is standing orders. Even the CO himself would do that. I have to ask you what you were doing down around the enlisted women's quarters at this time of night, when under standing orders they are out of bounds, and why this office has no knowledge of your visit or its purpose. And as far as Private Duffield is concerned, if he releases a vehicle without a clearance from this office, I'll have no alternative than to ring the provost marshals and have him arrested for a blatant disregard of AARMO. I shall also be asking for a report from the sentry or sentries who permitted your entrance without informing this office so it could be logged, Sir.'

Donaldson looked as though he was going to explode. He knew I had him by the balls, and I was squeezing pretty hard.

'Just call me a cab,' he hissed.

'Very good, Sir, but I'm afraid Private Duffield will have to drive you up to the main gate.'

As Donaldson spun on his heel and stormed out, John Duffield looked back over his shoulder.

'Jesus Jimmy!' he said in a whisper. 'There'll be fuckin' hell to pay over this in the morning.'

'Fuck him, John,' I said just as quietly.

I walked out quickly, jumped into the duty vehicle and drove to the main gate, where I parked in front of the incoming boom arm. Billy Parsons, the sentry there, opened the glass door and let me in. I picked up the clipboard and saw the yellow pass on it. Donaldson had signed it himself but it wasn't dated, had no time on it, and the designation stated signals office business. Not down at the enlisted women's lines, pulling rank and screwing one of the WACs. Got you, you bastard, I thought. I took the yellow pass and climbed back into the duty vehicle, passing the RP's car on the way back to the orderly office.

I placed the pass in the locked security drawer, went

256

to the log and made a further entry underneath the parking matter.

To wit: that it had been established by the watch that Major Donaldson, 2 I/C Signals, Victoria Barracks, was discovered in the Ordinary Ranks Enlisted Women's Lines at 2340 hours The Major did not report to the Orderly Office on entering the base. The pass, see attached, was not valid, in as much as it wasn't dated, and no time thereon appears.

It is also my duty to report that the said Major Donaldson gave me an unlawful command, and knowing it to be so I refused. To wit: release his impounded vehicle. Without the proper authorisation. I also report for your information that on my refusal to comply with the said Major Donaldson's unlawful order, that he threatened me by using the words 'I'll deal with you later.' All the above was duly witnessed by Private John Duffield, Regimental Police.

Signed Corporal J. Diamond. Watch Orderly.

I then typed the report onto the printer and sent it off to headquarters. Shit, I could just see Donaldson's face when he was matted and confronted with it . . . and his CO dressing him down. (Not done old boy. Officers consorting with the ordinary ranks. Tut tut. Bad show, old chap.) I asked Billy Parsons to submit a report on Donaldson's entry to the base. The phone rang and John Duffield informed me that Donaldson had left the base by taxi. I asked John to submit a report also, and just to tell it like it was.

Until the end of the shift I was expecting blue lights to come sweeping up to the orderly office door and to be carted off to the stockade, but all was quiet.

It wasn't until three nights later, on my last night shift, that I heard anything about the matter at all. When I got to the office that night the duty officer, Captain Phillip Lang, handed me an order and informed me that I was to report to Northern Command HQ, Victoria Barracks, at 1400 hours the next day. I couldn't have given a tinker's cuss. I'd done things by the book and the fact that a field-rank officer was involved meant nothing to me. Fuck 'em, I thought.

I turned up at HQ and after a ten-minute wait was let into an office where three officers were seated behind a large table. In the centre was Brigadier Scanlon, CO Northern Command. To his right was Colonel Stretton his 2IC and on his left my CO, Lieutenant-Colonel Townsend.

'Sit down please,' Scanlon said.

'Now what's all this mess about a car the other night?'

I explained to them exactly what had happened, from first to last.

'Yes but you weren't exactly behaving in a manner that is expected,' said Scanlon. 'You were insubordinate to Major Donaldson.'

Here we go again, I thought. The old school tie. But bugger it, I'm going to stick up for myself.

'I strongly deny, Sir, that I was insubordinate to the major. He was the one who breached the rules, not me. It seems to me that the wrong person is being interrogated.'

I thought Scanlon was going to have a stroke.

'You're being insubordinate now, Corporal, and this is not the first occasion that you have been seen on matters such as this. There was quite a serious one concerning this same officer at Shoalwater Bay during the Kangaroo Hop exercises. And you were turfed out of Special Operations weren't you?'

'Be that as it may, Sir, I was only doing my job as I had been instructed to, but the major didn't like it. I was only doing the same thing the other night. I can remember, Sir, when I did my carter course that I was told if you're not sure, go by the book. Well it appears that every time I do things by the book I end up on the carpet.'

'By God!' he exploded. 'Fifty years ago you'd have been shot for something like this.'

'For doing my job, Sir. Didn't they get a fair go then either?'

Scanlon was so angry he spun his chair around and turned his back to me.

'Look here, Corporal,' Colonel Stretton said, 'no one is questioning that you haven't done your job. I've just finished going through your file. It's how you react to authority that concerns us. You seem to have a hostility to the fact that someone has to be in charge. If we don't have discipline we end up with chaos. It's because you've done your job that you're sitting here now, and not in the stockade at Indooroopilly. You were decorated in Vietnam, at Long Tan too. That stands to your credit. But your file shows that you have at times exhibited a complete disregard to those senior to you. Do you understand what I'm saying?'

'No, Sir, I don't. It seems to me that there is a set of rules for some and a different set for others. The inci-

259

dent at Kapooka came about because I'd had some previous training. I wasn't insubordinate then, just a bit better than the instructor. As for Shoalwater Bay, before we left Canungra we were told—sorry, ordered—to get in and hit 'em hard. Give them a taste of what they could expect over on the Farm. Donaldson was captured fair and square, and from word one he tried to pull rank. That's the truth, Sir.'

Scanlon swung around in his chair.

'Rubbish,' he yelled. 'Do you hear me? Rubbish. This Army observes the Geneva Convention. We don't strike and kick and then urinate on captured officers. We treat them in a humane fashion and afford them the dignity that is due to them. Understand?'

'Yes Sir, I do, and I would have treated him differently if we'd been on the same side. But we were the enemy and told to act as such. We captured a lot of other blokes and they got the treatment too, but nothing was said about it, then or now. I did what I was ordered to do, Sir, just as I was supposed to the other night. And once more we have the same officer making the complaints. I feel that I'm being made the scapegoat for this officer's inadequacies. And if that is being insubordinate, then I apologise.'

Scanlon dropped his head down into his hands and shook it from side to side.

'Just wait outside,' he said at last. 'You'll be called back in a moment.'

I stood and saluted and let myself out. A couple of guys in the outer office looked up at me. They must have heard Scanlon yelling. In fact the whole building probably heard him.

Five minutes later I was called back in. My file was all neat and tidy now and Scanlon had his hands on top of it. He looked at me and then looked down at my file. The bastard couldn't look me in the eye.

'It is my opinion,' he said, 'that you have something wrong with your reasoning. And have a disposition that could only be described as hostile. It is not to the interest of the other people you serve with and has the ability to create unrest in the ranks. It is therefore my recommendation that you will be medically and psychologically examined by the Medical Corps immediately. You are suspended on leave with pay, pending the result of the medical report. You may remain at large. I have noted that you live off the base and you are not to return to the base pending the outcome of this report. You will report immediately down to the medical officers, and after their examination you are on indefinite leave. You are dismissed.'

I saluted and left the office for the last time. Somehow I couldn't help but feel that it wouldn't have mattered what I said. The result would have turned out the same.

27

I HAD MY MEDICAL AND WAS TOLD TO RETURN AT 1100 hours the next day to see the psychiatric officer and take some tests. The visits continued for three more days but I didn't give a damn. At least I was on pay and didn't have to report for monotonous duty. I didn't even have to convince anybody that I was sane or otherwise. This was just a formality, something to put on my record and keep that fuckin' Donaldson in the clear. My Army days were over.

It was five weeks later that I received the letter, which was full of military terminology and gobbledegook. Translated, it meant that I had been discharged from the Army. The reasons stated that, as a result of mental strain and duress in the course of battle, I had developed a belligerent personality complex common to those who have been under heavy fire. The condition making me totally unfit for further military service.

It was bullshit. I knew it and they knew it. But I didn't mind. Veterans' Affairs had been sent a report on the matter and I was to be granted a pension. There was a cheque enclosed for $1,200 for back pay and allowances, and I would receive another lump-sum payment as compensation in the near future.

So that was that. I was a free man again and I didn't have a care in the world. I went out that night to the

21 Club, pulled Sam aside and told him the news and we really tied one on. We just about drank the place dry and we both woke up in the back office the next morning. My mouth tasted like the bottom of a parrot's cage and I had a hangover and a headache that was so bad I could hear it. I got a cab home, had a shower and fell into bed.

During the next nine months I did various jobs for the Bellari Family, mostly pick-up and courier work. It didn't take me long to fathom that nothing had changed that much. There was a lot of shut-up money going to the coppers, only now it was on a bigger scale. I was making a lot of these payments and got to know who was on the take, from the lowliest sergeant to the superintendents. The Bellari organisation was a large one and its activities ranged from just below the Queensland border to the tip of Cape York Peninsula.

One night I went to the usual drop spot to make a payout to a copper who was a particularly nasty bastard—not because he was on the police force but because he was on the make all the time. Glen Callaghan was his name, and he was always making some shitty comment. This time he tapped me on the chest with the envelope I'd just given him.

'You go on back to your wog mates and let them know that things better improve in this department or things are going to get a little sticky ... You get the picture? Now piss off and tell them.'

I'd have liked to have blown the bastard's head off right there and then. I had nothing personal against bent cops. They had always been there and they always will be. I looked upon them as doing the organisation a favour. They knew that prostitution, gambling, and now drugs, would always be around. So our giving them a little sugar from time to time kept the peace. But this fuckin' Callaghan came on like he was in charge of everything. That we had to do better, bigger, more, so that his dirty money would increase.

I told Callaghan I would pass the message on, and nothing more, and went back to the club.

Sam was talking to a high-ranking copper named Owen. I sidled up behind them and, leaning over Sam's shoulder, said, '*Prego Sam, mi scusi per il disturbo, noi avere una problema.*' [Pardon me Sam, I'm sorry to trouble you, but we have a problem.] I had gathered a little working knowledge of the language from my Sydney days but I was learning more Italian all the time now. And when the cops were around it sure came in handy.

'*Va bene*, Jimmy,' he said. '*Il minuto.*' [Okay Jimmy. Just a minute.]

I got myself a drink, took it to the back office and waited. A minute later Sam came in.

'What's the matter, Jimmy?'

'It's that bastard Callaghan. He wants more money, and he says things are going to get sticky if we don't lay a little bit more sugar his way.'

'How much more does he want? Did you ask him?'

'Shit Sam, that's not my job. I'd be right out of line asking that.'

'Good boy, Jimmy. Don't you worry, we'll fix this prick up properly.'

'I'll fix the cunt for good if you'll give me a fuckin' gun. I'll put his lights right out.'

Sam started to laugh. 'You don't like him much, eh?'

'Never did. He's a real cunt and you know it. Christ Almighty, man, ask Carlo to give the nod.'

'Take it easy. He'll keep. Have another drink, get something to eat. I'll talk to Carlo in the morning.'

I didn't get to bed till 4.30 a.m. It was the sound of the door phone buzzing that woke me five hours later.

'*Jimmy, Sam. Potere entrate noi sopra per il minuto Amico favore?*' [Jimmy, Sam here. Can we come up for a minute please mate?]

'Sure Sam,' I said, a little surprised, and pressed the buzzer to let them in.

I was pulling on a dressing gown when the doorbell chimed. I opened the door and Carlo and Sam were standing there, smiling.

'*Buon giorno Jimmy Come sta?*' Carlo said.

'Good thanks mate. Gidday Sam. *Entri prego, Si metta a sedere.*' [Come in, take a seat.]

Sam poked his thumb up the hall in the direction of the bedrooms.

'You on your own?'

'No worries,' I said. 'We've got the place to ourselves.'

'Jesus Christ! This bloke lives like a fuckin' priest,' Carlo said to Sam. We all laughed.

I made us all a coffee, then we got down to business.

'We want you to help us to set this fuckin' Callaghan up once and for all,' Carlo said.

'Best fuckin' news I've heard this week,' I replied. 'Am I the lucky one who gets to shoot the mongrel?'

'Hey,' said Sam. 'We just can't go round shootin' the fuckin' coppers, Jimmy, as much as we'd like to you

265

know. What we want to do is set this bastard up so it will stick. So his own kind will get rid of him. We've been talkin' to Owen. He and his mates think Callaghan's a fuckin' arsehole too, and they're prepared to help us get rid of the fuckin' *carne*. We're gonna give this prick some more *denaro*. But when he grabs it, he's goin' to have a million fuckin' cameras takin' pictures. Now look Jimmy, we've got to use you on this one. If we send someone else he's gonna smell a fuckin' rat. We'll guarantee that you walk clean, but you're goin' to have to go down in the bust. All you got to do is say that he threatened to set you up and verbal you on a hoist. *Capisce amico?*'

' 'Course I understand. Christ Almighty. You don't have to ask me to help out with your hat in your hand. It'll be a fuckin' pleasure. What's the deal?'

'First of all,' Carlo said, 'Sam and me have to stay right out of the picture. You'll have to ring him. All we gotta know is where the drop is and what time. Ring the prick now. Tell him you've got another five hundred. That'll make him bite.'

I dialled Callaghan's number at the City CIB.

'Glen Callaghan. What can I do for you?'

'Jimmy Diamond. I've got something for you.'

'How much?'

'Five hundred. It's all they'll come across with.'

'Yeah, well that's a bit better. You know where the Osborne Hotel is?'

'In the Valley.'

'That's the one. Be in the car park 3.30. You'd better not be fucking me around with this. See you then.' He hung up.

I replaced the phone. '*Non mi piace*,' I said. 'I don't like it. He came on too quick.'

'Don't worry about him, Jimmy. He thinks he's got us rattled. But believe me, he's a *stronzo*.'

'Okay,' I said. '*Cosa desidera debbo fare?*' [What do you want me to do?]

'*Buono Ragazzo!*' said Carlo. 'Come on down the club in a couple of hours.'

A little after 1 p.m. the three of us were sitting around a table in the dining room of 21 Club having lunch. And it was a beauty. I loved the aromas that wafted through the club. Italian cooking intermingled with coffee and the mouth-watering smells of delicatessen smallgoods all rolled into one.

After lunch we sat smoking and Sam pushed an envelope across the table to me.

'That's the dough. Just be sure that he takes it off you. Maybe he'll have that fuckin' stooge who gets around with him. Peterson. Don't give it to him. And listen, no rough stuff for Christ's sake. No matter what he says, keep your hands in ya fuckin' pockets. *Capisce?* We hate this *stronzo papigallo* just as much as you do, but believe me when I tell you. This is the best way. We'll fuck him at his own game. And don't forget, everything's been taken care of. Okay? *A domani Jimmy, buona fortuna.*' [See you tomorrow, good luck.]

I took a cab to the Osborne Hotel with half an hour to spare. I wanted the advantage of being there before Callaghan.

As I sat in the Saloon bar nursing my drink I gave the car park the once-over. A movement caught my eye and I noticed a head appear quickly and then disappear behind the windscreen in a Holden parked way out in the corner. Also there were two guys in the bar who had copper written all over them. They were sitting near the window trying to look nonchalant, but not doing a very good job of it. The back wall was lined with mirror squares, so I turned my back to the bar and looked straight ahead at them to check out what was happening.

I looked at my watch and it was nearly time. I'd no sooner turned to look out the window than Callaghan drove in in an unmarked Falcon. I tipped the rest of my beer down and walked outside.

Callaghan saw me coming and the driver's door of his car opened. He got halfway out of the car and stood with his arms leaning on the top of the opened door.

'Come on,' he said. 'I haven't got all fucking day.'

I reached inside my jacket and touched the envelope. If only this was a gun, I thought, you'd be dead right now. I took out the envelope and handed it to him. I'll give him this, the bastard was confident. He took it off me and opened it right there, looked inside and ran his thumb across the bills, counting them.

A car came tearing into the car park and pulled up alongside us. The two guys who'd been playing hide and seek in the Holden jumped out and came over on the gallop, one holding a camera. A tall, grey-headed guy in uniform with a superintendent's insignia got out of the passenger side.

'I'll take that envelope, Glen,' the superintendent called out.

Callaghan slumped back into the seat of his car. He was fucked and he knew it.

The bloke with the camera snapped more shots. Then another uniformed copper walked up and snapped handcuffs on me.

'Let's go,' he said, leading me by the arm to the back seat of an unmarked car. Then he opened the other door and got in beside me.

Not one word was spoken as the convoy of cars made its way to Roma Street Police Headquarters. Just the sound of the radio squawking intermittently in police jargon. On arrival, I was taken to an office marked Superintendent Operations. The handcuffs were removed and I was told to sit down. The copper with me leant back against the desk and placed his arse on it.

After five minutes the superintendent came in.

'I want a record of interview,' he said to the uniformed guy.

The cop went around the desk, pulled out three sheets of paper, placed carbon between them and rolled them into a typewriter. The superintendent dragged a chair away from the wall and sat close to me.

'What is your full name?' he asked.

'James Francis Diamond,' I replied.

Clackety clackety went the typewriter.

'What is your present address?'

'Thirty-four Kings Road, Taringa.'

Up went his eyebrows.

'Why did you give five hundred dollars to Detective Senior Constable Callaghan?'

'Callaghan told me that if I didn't come up with it

he was going to fit me up with a hoist. I've been told he's fitted up a few other people like that so I didn't have much option, did I?'

Clack clack from the typewriter.

'Why didn't you report the matter when you were first asked for the money? If you had nothing to hide.'

'Come on, be serious will ya. If I'd of come and reported it, all Callaghan had to do was deny it. Then I'd be charged with making a false complaint. Not to mention what Callaghan would have done.'

'Have you ever been involved in or committed a criminal offence that Detective Callaghan has knowledge of?'

'I was medically discharged from the Army nine months ago, and I have friends that Callaghan doesn't like.'

'I didn't ask you that. I asked you have you ever committed any criminal offence that Detective Callaghan has knowledge of?'

'No.'

'Have you committed an offence in the company of others, and does Detective Callaghan know that these others have committed a criminal offence?'

'No.'

'Are you currently employed?'

'No. I receive a Veterans' Affairs pension and was discharged with a lump-sum payout.'

'Do you associate with any known criminals, or do you consort with any known criminals who are committing criminal offences?'

'No.'

'Is this the only occasion that you have given money to Callaghan?'

'No, I've given him three other payments, but he kept saying it wasn't enough.'

'What were the amounts of the other three payments?'

'Two hundred dollars each time.'

'So you've actually given Detective Callaghan eleven hundred dollars, all told?'

'That's correct.'

'Were these payments made to him in the same car park?'

'No. In the toilet at the George Hotel.'

'Do you know of any other payments being made to Callaghan?'

'Only hearsay.'

'Did Callaghan tell which job he was going to fit you up with?'

'No. He said he had a drawer full of unsolved jobs, that I could take my pick.'

'Do you honestly feel that if you hadn't made these payments to Callaghan that he would have carried out his threat?'

'Like I said before, I've been told he's fitted blokes up. His nickname is "Verbal".'

'Do you feel that you have been treated in a reasonable manner since your arrest at the Osborne Hotel car park?'

'Yes I have.'

'Are you prepared to sign this record of interview without threat or favour from the police?'

'Yes I will.'

'Has any threat been made towards you in any way to force you to have this record of interview?'

'No there hasn't been.'

'Have you made this record of interview of your own free will?'

'Yes I have.'

'Have you got all that down, Constable?'

'Yes Sir. Got it all.'

'Right,' said the superintendent. 'I would like you to sign the record of interview on all three pages, and the constable will witness your signature. Then you will be free to go, but we may have need to speak to you again. Is that understood?'

'Yes, I understand.'

I signed their record of interview, my signature was witnessed and the superintendent took the three copies.

'Right, well we'll get you run home then. But a word of advice before you go. It would be wise not to discuss this matter with anyone outside those in this room, unless you are asked to do so by me. Do you understand that?'

'Yeah I do.'

'Good. My name is Superintendent Ronald Casey. Can you remember that?' I nodded to him. 'Right, well if you are approached by anyone on this matter you may feel free to contact me here. If I'm not here leave a message where I can contact you. Is that clear?'

'No worries,' I said.

'Okay, I'll arrange to get you home then.' He turned to the other copper. 'Will you look after that, Constable?'

'Yes Sir, right away.'

The superintendent slapped his leg with the three rolled-up sheets of interview and left the room.

'Come on,' said the constable, 'I'll run you back home.'

After I'd been home for a while and had a couple of drinks the phone rang. I picked it up and heard the rattle of a coin.

'Yes,' I said.

'*Bravo amico.*' It was Sam. '*Mille grazie noi dovere to molto ... Ciao.*' [Well done mate ... we owe you a lot. Bye]

I kept a pretty low profile for a couple of days, didn't go near the club or ring the boys. But they sure as shit looked after me. I got a delivery from Giovani's, and wine. But the best surprise came in the form of the door buzzer going.

'Yes, what can I do for you?' I said.

'I've got something here for you from Sam,' a woman's voice said. 'Are you going to let me in?'

'Hang on,' I said, and punched the buzzer.

A few moments later the doorbell chimed. I looked through the spy-hole. There was a girl standing outside, on her own. I opened the door.

The view I had of her through the spy-hole hadn't done her justice at all. She was five foot three or four, blonde, with a great figure. Her hair reminded me for a second of Margo's and I wondered if the cuffs and collar matched. She came in and rummaged through the large carry-all she had slung over her shoulder, then handed me an envelope.

'From Sam,' she said, smiling at me.

We walked through into the lounge.

'Take a seat. What's your name?'

'Carmel. And I know yours is Jimmy. This is a nice place you've got here.'

Jesus! Her perfume was unbelievable. She sat down on the lounge and crossed her legs.

'Mind if I smoke?' she asked me.

'No, go for it.'

I opened the glass door onto the balcony, walked out and read Sam's note.

Jimmy,

Posso presentar Le Carmelita. Fermare come una fungulo Priesti vivere . . . mi piace favore. Sam.

[Jimmy this is Carmel. Stop living like a fuckin' priest. Enjoy. Sam]

I smiled to myself and walked back inside.

'Would you like a drink?' I asked.

'Why don't you sit down?' Carmel said. 'Let me get it.'

'Yeah, a beer will do fine. The kitchen's through there.' I pointed the way. 'I'm going to take a quick shower. Be back in a minute.'

I went into the main bedroom and turned the shower on in the en-suite. I was lathering away, humming a tune to myself, when the glass door slid back and Carmel stood there. She had nothing on and she was beautiful, even more so naked. Her boobs stood out without any support. And yes, the cuffs and collar did match. She was a natural blonde.

She stepped into the shower, slid the door closed behind her and put her arms around my waist, pulling

herself in close until our stomachs joined and her
boobs were resting just under my chest. She leant her
head back and closed her eyes, letting the water run
onto her face. As it ran down her neck it formed a
pool between her breasts. I bent down and kissed her
half-open mouth and she reached up and placed her
left hand behind my neck, pulling me down a little
more as she returned the kiss, her tongue sliding and
darting in and out of my mouth. When I became hard
she stood back, took the soap from me and rubbed it
over my swollen penis, then softly massaged it with
her hands. She pushed me back a little and let the
water rinse the soap away. Then she lathered me all
over. When she'd done that she handed me the soap
and I did the same for her, lathering her gorgeous
boobs. When the water washed the suds away I bent
and kissed the pink nipples. Then I slid my hand down
between her legs and soaped her vagina, letting my
finger slide over the downy pubic hair and into her
soft crevice. I turned the water off and we stepped
out, not bothering to dry ourselves.

I picked Carmel up, laid her across the bed and,
kneeling on the floor, I placed her legs over my shoulders and bent down, looking into her exposed woman-
hood. I opened her vagina further with my thumbs and
let my tongue slide into the soft pink sweet orifice. She
moaned softly and pushed up a little with her hips. I
licked and kissed and sucked her till she climaxed, grabbing my head when she did and pushing me harder
against herself. She gave a little cry and a shiver ran
through her body as she arched her hips up further.
Then she grabbed at me and, moving up and onto the

bed proper, pulled me up alongside her. I slid onto the bed on my side but she pushed me over onto my back, taking my penis in her small hand, bending over it and sliding her warm mouth down over it, then lifting up rolling her tongue around the head of it. She let her other hand gently lift my balls and played with them as if they were delicate and precious jewels that would break with too much pressure. Then she stopped, turned on her back and pulled me over on top of her, reaching down with her hand and guiding me into her. She was wet and warm, soft and slippery, and I sank into her slowly all the way and pushed a little more. She was firm and soft and wonderful. I thrust in and out till I couldn't stand it any longer and came into her in a hot wet explosion that didn't want to stop. She cried out and pulled my head down and kissed me, letting a soft moan of ecstasy escape into my mouth as we kissed and she exploded into climax again.

We lay there for a while, breathing deeply, then I got up and went into the shower. Carmel went into the toilet, then came and joined me. When we'd finished our shower I donned a pair of briefs and Carmel wrapped a towel around herself. We walked out onto the balcony and drank a couple of fresh beers. The first two were still sitting there getting warm. She hadn't even lifted the tops off them.

Out in the sun on the balcony she suddenly asked me how long I wanted her to stay.

'Shit, I don't know. Why? Is there somewhere you have to go?'

'Sam told me I was to look after you,' she said. 'I will if you want me to.'

'What, be here all the time you mean?'

'If you want me to. But if you want to be by yourself that's okay with me.'

'How old are you Carmel?'

'Nearly nineteen.'

She picked up my empty glass and asked if I wanted another beer. I nodded.

'Look, I don't want to pry into your affairs,' I said when she returned, 'but how do you know Sam? I've been to all the brothels and escort joints with him and I've never seen you.'

'I've never been in them, that's why. I came down from Charleville six months ago and met this guy and we got on pretty well. After two months I moved in with him. He'd been doing break-ins but the cops caught him and he got three and a half years. Somehow he knew Sam. Anyway I visited him yesterday at Boggo Road and he told me to go and see Sam and that he'd take care of me. It wasn't any good me waiting around till he got out. I've been given notice in the flat and I don't want to go back to Charleville, so I didn't have much option. Sam offered me a place in an escort agency, but I didn't want to do that sort of thing. Then he said he had a friend who was on his own and might appreciate some company. I'm sorry if I've come on too strong, but I don't want to work in the escort agency.'

She put her head down and started to cry. I felt like a heap of shit . . . as if I'd used her to satisfy my own needs. And what she'd done for me wasn't phoney, she was for real. She needed someone and somewhere and was desperate. Jesus, did I know that feeling! The ugly memories flooded back and I pushed them away.

'Just hang on here for a moment, love. I won't be long.'

I went to the bedroom and phoned Sam.

'What's the story with Carmel?'

'Hey, isn't she a nice lookin' kid? Look mate, she was hangin' out with this arsehole, Billy Grant, who used to be one of our drivers, but he never looked after the girl and she's a nice kid. I offered her something with the agency but she don't want that kinda work. So I thought of you. Why? Don'tcha like her?'

'No it's not that, mate. I feel a bit sorry for her. She's too nice to chuck to the bloody wolves.'

'Well what's the fuckin' matter with you? Take care of her, *paisan*.'

'Thanks Sam. I just might do that. *A presto. Ciao.*'

'*Va benissimo a presto amico.*' [That's all right mate] '*Ciao.*'

I went back onto the balcony, lit a cigarette and thought for a moment or two. Carmel had replaced her beer and was looking out over the balcony rail.

'Are your mum and dad up in Charleville, Carmel?'

'No, they died when I was little. I was raised by a family who knew them.'

There it is again, I thought. Every woman I become close to has a problem way back in the past with the loss of their family. I looked across at Carmel. She was a lovely-looking girl but had this sadness about her. She had depth and didn't talk a lot, as if she was in constant thought. Christ knows, I didn't have anyone around, and I had sort of taken to her.

'Where is this flat you're in, love?' I asked.

'Gresham Street, West End.'

'Well we better put some bloody clothes on and pick up your gear.'

It's hard for me to describe the look that came onto her face. The sudden radiance, like the sun suddenly appearing from behind clouds. She stood up, letting the towel fall away, walked over naked and sat on my lap. She kissed me and it was different from the ones we'd shared a while back. It was soft and electric, as if her mouth melted into mine. After a long while she looked up into my face.

'You'll never regret this,' she said. 'I promise you.'

I knew at that moment that Carmel had fallen in love.

We got dressed and went over to her flat, which was a real dump, loaded up her things and took them back to the unit. I showed her all over the place then and I told her to make it into a home for us.

'Where do you want to sleep?' I asked her. 'You can have any room you like.'

'Can't I sleep with you, Jimmy?'

' 'Course you can love, 'course you can,' I said, giving her a hug.

Things sure changed around home after that. It was as if we'd been together forever, and she was unbelievable around the home. There was never anything dirty on the sink. Clothes that I shoved in drawers suddenly appeared ironed and hanging up in the big walk-in wardrobe. And I had to confess there was something special about opening the big mirrored doors and seeing her dresses hanging there too. And her make-up and things on the big dressing table.

Life got back to normal with the organisation. The papers had a field day over Callaghan's dismissal from the force on corruption charges. He pleaded guilty. I was never called again about it. And I went back to doing the things that I'd done before, plus a few more.

I also made a fuss over Carmel. Taking her out to places she'd never been before. Going down to the Gold Coast on the weekends, eating freshly cooked prawns and washing them down with a nice fruity wine. We went dancing and dining. I have always believed that we live by encouragement and die without it—slowly, sadly and angrily—so I treated her like she'd never been treated before, and it was all worth it. I gave her money to go shopping for us and for her, and I gave her presents and flowers. When I gave her words of praise and encouragement I filled that deepest principle of human nature . . . the craving to be appreciated.

It was a craving she had never had answered before, and she turned out to be one hell of a girl.

PART

4

A little
more
persuasion

28

THE DRUG SCENE WAS STARTING TO TAKE OFF IN A BIG way now. Gone were the days when it was mainly the hippies and the knockabouts who wanted them. Everybody wanted to get into the scene and grab a piece of the action. I had the occasional bit of speed, and smoked grass when I wanted to wind down or was at a party.

But drugs create problems for those in the business of marketing them. Knowing I would never break *omerta*, the family made good use of those talents learned with Kurt and the Army. Mouths started wagging at times and had to be stopped. What upset the applecart most was opposition. There were huge sums of money involved, but what the opposition didn't know was that it wasn't in the police interest to have others fucking around indiscreetly in this side of things. They caused trouble, publicity, and it became all too obvious that the drug world existed and in no small way.

Do-gooders jumped on the bandwagon and drugs were the subject of media stories, where you didn't have to be a genius to read between the lines that the police weren't doing their job. If the police hate anything it's bad press. It makes them nervous and the powerful ones get pissed off. 'Get off your arses,' they say, 'and stop this bad publicity with a few arrests.'

To overcome this problem the police who were getting regular payments let us know who and where the opposition was. So places and people had to be shut down, and shut down quick. This was usually done with a subtle hint, like 'If you don't shut down I'll blow your fuckin' head off.' And, most took the suggestion for the sound advice it was. A couple needed a little more persuasion. But there was one particular person who put himself right out of reach and just wouldn't take no for an answer.

Charlie Davenport. Not only did he make it hard on us by taking away business, but he decided to use his own methods to finish us. He had been in our employ once, so he started to inform to the untouchables within the police about Carlo and Sam's role in the business—their outlets, suppliers and so forth. And he knew a lot about what we did.

The best way to stop a snake from wriggling and talking is to cut off its head, so we decided to make a real example of this particular pain in the arse who had betrayed us. No one was just going to pop him and leave him lie in his own shit and blood. He was going to disappear altogether. Nothing works better as a deterrent than the disappearance of a person without trace. People start wondering what has actually happened. Oh they know he's dead all right. But they speculate, try to guess what actually happened. And the longer the speculation goes on the wilder it gets, until it takes on sinister proportions that would make the Devil himself cower in fright.

Davenport was being looked after real well. It was hard to nail him down in one spot and he had the best protection in the world. He had straight police on his side ... police who would have liked to put Carlo's organisation right out of business. Davenport was their main hope of doing that and these coppers who were the untouchables to us sure took good care of him. We had nothing on them, they took no graft from us, and they also received no payments from him. He stayed in business and retained his own freedom, with the information he passed on to them. That was Davenport's thirty pieces of silver. The amount of business lost in itself wasn't that damaging, but the information he passed on about the family was.

Carlo and Sam got raided. Their homes turned upside down. Their womenfolk insulted, called sluts and molls by the raiding police. And to say that Carlo and Sam were pissed off was an understatement. Their children were scared to death as police raids erupted into their homes in the early hours. There is a law in the *Famiglia* that is common knowledge to all. Do what you will to the soldiers and so forth, but don't fuck about with their women and children. Cause them grief and you may as well sign your own death warrant.

Of course Davenport's actions were treacherous in themselves and made his removal from this planet a top priority. But when his actions and information brought disrespect to Carlo and Sam's wives and children, nothing or no one could save him.

It was early one morning when my turn came to enter the fray. Up to this point I'd kept a pretty low profile and no one from the police even gave me a second glance. The dealings that I had with them were very discreet. It had been my suggestion to Carlo and Sam that, instead of making several payments to several people, we should pay one man the lot and he could pay the rest. It was a good idea and the bent coppers got their own bagman, who was the only person I dealt with. To the family I was mainly the silent backstop. There but not there, working quietly and silently. No one outside a select few realised that I was lurking in the shadows as the silent Button man.

Carmel and I were asleep when the phone dragged us back to consciousness. I rolled over and picked it up.

It was Sam. '*Mi scusi il disturbo amico. Abbassi il ricevitore, ottenere la piu vicina cabina telefonica.*' [I'm sorry to disturb you mate. Hang up and go to the nearest public phone box.]

'*Va benissimo amico. Quale e il suo numero?*' [That's all right, mate. What's your number?]

'Paolo,' was all he said. Then he hung up.

'What's the matter?' Carmel asked.

'I've got to go out for a while, love. You go back to sleep.'

'God!' she said. 'Look at the time. It's one-thirty!'

I drove to a nearby phone box and rang the number of Paolo's Gold Coast unit.

'Is that you Paolo?' I said. '*Come sta?*'

'*Si Jimmy. Molto bene grazie.* [Yes it is Jimmy. I'm fine thanks.] Look, can you come straight down here. How long do you think you'll be?'

'I'll leave at once.'

An hour later I was sitting around the table in Paolo's unit in a high-rise block. There was a fourth guy there, Joe Petracci, Paolo's right-hand man. The problem under discussion was Charlie Bloody Davenport and his connections.The police had made a raid up north in one of Carlo and Paolo's interests and they'd lost such a bundle through it it looked like things up there would have to be closed down permanently. Ideas were being tossed back and forth and always it came back to the same old thing. Taking Davenport out was not a job that could be done by just anybody. It needed finesse, and with my background they felt I'd come up with something. Joe Petracci had volunteered to do the hit if it was viable.

'I don't know why everybody is fuckin' around with this clown,' I said. 'I could take him out without too much trouble. It just needs a little organisation.'

'He's got coppers keepin' an eye on him around the clock Jimmy,' Carlo said. 'He knows the business and seems to know every move we make. We don't even know where they've got him hidden.'

'Sure Carlo, but there's got to be a gap in the armour somewhere. Let's look at what we've got on our side of the fence. Who's the most senior cop we can use . . . the one we know can't say no?'

'Herb Jackson,' said Sam.

'Right, Herb Jackson,' I said. 'Christ, if he can't find out something for us no one can. He's also got strong political connections. He's got to be a fountain of knowledge.'

'Shit I hope you're right,' Carlo said. 'All we know about Davenport is that he's not in Brisbane and he's not down in Paolo's territory. The coppers whisked him away.'

'If we can locate him, Jimmy, what will you need?' Paolo asked.

'It's a little early to know that, mate, but you get me the information then you can sit back. Pumping Jackson is your job, though there's an element of risk there. If Davenport disappears and Jackson looks like coming under the spotlight he might just fold up and yell. The risk's slight but it's there. The thing we've got on our side is that he couldn't put the finger on you without implicating himself. So when Davenport goes it has to be a clean surgical operation. Total disappearance.'

'What's he talkin' about, Paolo?' Sam asked. 'I can't understand half of what he said.'

The discussion went on for a while longer. 'Sam will go back to Brisbane with you, Jimmy,' Carlo said. 'I'm going down to Sydney with Paolo. Sam will keep us all up to date. When we've got enough, get rid of this fuckin' cockroach. *Capisce amico presto!*'

'Loud and clear, Carlo,' I said, and Joe nodded his head.

On the way back to Brisbane Sam and I chatted about this and that.

'Hey,' he said when I dropped him off, 'When are you gonna get rid of this heap of shit? Christ, it's as big as a tank.'

'One of these days, Sam. You'll be the first to know.'

The 21 Club wasn't much to look at from the outside. There were no neon signs or anything to say that there was a sprawling club inside that catered to your every need, from gum-ball to gambling. You could actually walk past it and miss it. Just a door in a building on a main street in the Valley. The area it was in was not that spectacular either, a random mixture of shops and businesses and a couple of banks.

It was 11.30 in the morning when I arrived. I'd received a call from Sam, asking me quite casually to come down and have some lunch. Since we were pretty sure that the club plus Sam and Carlo's phones may be tapped, no business was discussed at all, no matter how innocent it may be.

I stuck my head into the restaurant and exchanged greetings with one of the waitresses, who smiled as though she was genuinely happy to see me, which was more than most of them did. The warmth of her smile and her looks and colouring reminded me of Margo and brought back a wistfulness for the old days. I sometimes found myself fantasising about this waitress, and sometimes if I needed a lift in spirits, I would go out and watch her working.

I walked into the office and Sam threw me a smile.

'We've found him, Jimmy. Put the finger on him. They've got the bastard up in Townsville.'

'Have we got an address?'

Sam told me and asked if I knew the area, but it meant nothing to me. I'd been up to Townsville a couple of times with the Army, but I wasn't all that familiar with it.

We went to the bar, which was empty except for Patsy the barmaid. She gave us a couple of Scotch and sodas and went back to her cleaning and polishing.

Sitting there in near darkness, with just the bar lights washing out over the area, Sam leant forward.

'What do you want to do now, Jimmy?'

I thought for a moment, letting a few things run through my mind.

'I'm going to have to go up there and do a bit of a recon. Sus the area out. I won't need Joe at the moment, he'll only get in the way. So I'll fly up and check it out personally.'

'We got people up there, if you need anything.'

'No, mate. I want the lowest profile I can manage. Look like a fuckin' tourist. How many coppers know he's up there?'

'Not many, according to Jackson. He reckons it was a fluke he managed to find out anything. They've really put the lid on this one.'

'How many people have they got on babysitting?'

'He's apparently got a copper with him at all times. They do it in shifts. And that fuckin' moll of his is with him too. That's all we've got.'

'Okay Sam, it should be enough. I'll get a plane up there today, if I can, and for Christ's sake don't even mention to our people up there that I'm coming up. I'll contact them if I need anything. How many here know we've got him tabbed?'

'Just me and you and Jackson. Even Carlo and Paolo don't even know yet. I'm waitin' for their call.'

'Good. Let's leave it like that, *paisan*.'

We ate lunch in silence. Gina, who was Sam's girl Friday, kept looking at him, and this made him really uncomfortable. In fact they were both jumpy. Sam sliced a pat of butter but dropped it on the table. Gina broke a match trying to start another cigarette and tossed it angrily into the ashtray. Little things. Sam was getting a bit on the side from Gina and it was apparent that they'd had a lovers' spat.

290

With lunch finished, Sam pulled me aside. 'You're gonna need some expense money, *amico*. Go and get a couple of drinks and I'll see you in a minute.'

I went into the bar, knowing Sam wanted to get Gina alone, tell her she was a bitch and thank her for fucking his lunch up.

'Same again Jimmy?' Patsy asked.

I just nodded.

'What's eating Sam? Shit, he's hardly said a damn thing all day?'

Most of the staff talked openly to me as I wasn't so strict on protocol. She was right about Sam. He was uptight, not his happy-go-lucky self.

'Gina's got the rags on,' I said. 'And she won't give him a suck because she's got a toothache.'

'You're crazy, Jimmy,' she sputtered.

Sam came up beside me and handed me a manilla envelope.

'There's a couple of grand in there. Just phone down if you need any more.' He looked at Patsy. 'What the fuck's got into her?'

I told him and Sam roared with laughter too. 'You know you're pretty uptight,' I said. 'Patsy has noticed it. What's biting at you, mate?'

'Christ, it's not just Gina. I've got the fuckin' coppers breathin' down my neck. The boss has pissed off to Sydney leavin' me holdin' the fuckin' baby, and at the same time wantin' this mess cleaned up, by yesterday. Why wouldn't I be pissed off.'

29

I DROVE HOME AND CALLED THE AIRPORT. THERE WAS A hop flight at 6 that evening and I booked a seat. I didn't have first-hand knowledge of the Townsville area, so it would be like going back to the Special Operations days of being dropped in the middle of nowhere and told to 'secure it ... do a surgical removal of the enemy ... then get yourself out in one piece undetected.

I sat down with Carmel and told her I had to go away for a while on business.

'Where to?' she asked.

'Melbourne, love. Might take a couple of days, could be a week.'

It wasn't that I didn't trust her. It was better for her sake if she didn't know.

'When will you be going?'

'Leaving here around 4.30,' I said. 'How about a drink for the road?'

We were about halfway through a beer when the bloody phone rang. It was Sam again.

'I've got something for you. Can we meet?'

'Give me twenty minutes.'

I apologised to Carmel, but it was unnecessary, and drove to the club. 'You get a plane?' Sam asked.

'Six o'clock, tonight.'

'Listen, Carlo rang. I had to go to the phone box and ring him back, but we got somethin' for you that might come in handy. There's a copper up there on the take, name of Collins.'

He told me everything he knew about Collins. We owned his arse, lock, stock and barrel.

'Might come in handy?' I said. 'Christ, Sam! It's great.'

'While I'm here, there's something else I'll need on this trip. I don't want to have to go to our people up there for anything but I'd hate to get close to this bastard and not have something to take him out. Can you arrange a gun and a silencer?'

'No problems. What do you want?' He asked it casually, as if he was asking me what sort of drink I wanted.

'Automatic something with a bit of stopping power.'

'What about a Beretta 9 mm. I can get you one with a silencer but I don't have it here.'

'Can you get it to the unit?'

'Consider it done. Probably be an hour.'

Back home I went into a spare bedroom and dragged out a couple of old duffel bags. I pulled out a Special Operations overall, camouflaged and almost black, a set of black pistol webbing, jungle combat knife, black-dyed surgical rubber gloves, balaclava and a pair of soft black suede boots with special rubber sole and built-in titanium toecaps. I packed them into a flight bag. Carmel was in our bedroom laying out some gear for me.

'Can we go to bed before you leave, Jimmy? There's still plenty of time.'

'Couldn't leave without it,' I said, kissing her quickly

on the cheek. 'But I'm expecting a parcel from work. Can you wait a tick?'

Not much later the downstairs buzzer went. It was Gina with my parcel. I checked the weapon, then put it straight into my case in between the clothes.

Time flew after that. Carmel and I made love, then I had a shower, dressed, rang a cab, and was at the airport at 5.35.

I felt myself tingling as we flew. I was the hunter again, and I had the scent of my prey. This animal had hurt my family and I was going to trap it in its lair. Paolo, Carlo and Sam had given me loyalty, trust and friendship. Now I was going to repay it. I developed a loathing for Davenport. With the plane hissing through the sky like a giant bird of prey homing in on its target, I sat there thinking of the coming mission.

In Townsville, I booked into the Allen Hotel Motel under a fictitious name and got some sleep. In the morning I rented a car, bought a cheap imitation leather briefcase and a road map. I checked the map out until I had a good idea of the direction and the site. The address was in an outlying town that had been swallowed up and become a suburb.

It took me about three-quarters of an hour to drive out to the address, and during the drive my mind flicked back to the last hit that I'd done for Paolo. Shit! What a mess it was. I started to get uptight. I could feel the nerves stretching and tightening. My hands gripped the wheel and went white. Then sanity and training came back. Steady, relax, you don't get uptight before a hit, or a mission. My mind racing. Penetrate quickly and silently, I recited to myself. Get in, hit, and get out. Still my mind kept flashing back to that botched job in Sydney years ago.

The man had a girl in the room with him. I hadn't done my homework. I was supposed to know that but I didn't. I can still see her standing there in the bathroom doorway with the red and white striped towel wrapped tightly around her, clutching at her throat with both hands as she begins to scream, then her hands dropping to her belly as I shot her. Blood pumping. And the man—the hit—coming out of the other room, warned, running into the hall. The lights so bright in the hallway of the apartment building, the bright yellow walls swaying around me, another man coming out of a door, mouth open, eyes wide, shouting 'Stop, stop. I'm calling the police.' That man's leering face distorting out of all humanity when I shoot it, the splatter of brains and blood on the wall. The hit was still ahead, running, running, now frantically punching buttons for the lift, then turning for the stairs and I shot him there. People screaming in the hall behind. I shot him again, and the man, the hit, looking down in horrified amazement at the fountain of red from his belly ... They never believe it's happening to them, they always look so surprised. Then I shot him again. *Die*, you bastard! Someone being sick in the hall behind me. Shouts for somebody to call the police. The hit finally falls, sliding down the wall, fighting it all the way, still surprised, but mad too, and scared, and maybe a lot of other things. I shot him then through the head. He slumps down and his head rolls to the side, eyes open.

The lift doors open. Nobody inside. It seems so small and bright and quiet going down. Nobody has seen my face, the black stocking prevents that, and I get away clean, running down an alley and through a little park.

Paolo talking to me.

'Jesus, Jimmy. When I say a clean hit, you know what I mean, Jimmy? You know what I mean?' He looks at me from under his dark eyebrows. 'I don't mean a massacre. I don't mean to waste him like a fuckin' rabid dog in front of everybody. But you've got balls boy, that's all I can say. Christ!'

Paolo is the *Capo di tutti*. Nobody messes with the Godfather. He runs everything and he's angry. Then he looks at me and the anger fades a little. He's waiting for me to speak.

There is nothing I can say to him, so I say nothing. He comes over and puts his arm around my shoulder.

'Jimmy, Jimmy . . . You know what you've done was stupid?'

Paolo looks into my eyes as though he can figure me out.

'I know,' I finally say, 'but you said to take him out no matter what. Before he spilled his guts to the coppers. That's what you said, Paolo. I figured if it was that important that I better do it before he got away from me.'

'You couldn'ta waited . . . at least until you got in the lift, or took him into the bushes or something? It doesn't make sense. What about all those witnesses in the hall?'

'They never saw my face.'

'You really believe that?'

'Sure as shit.'

Paolo doesn't know it, but he believes me.

'Christ, Jimmy, nobody will be able to say you never earned your bones.'

'I got away clean, Paolo. I guarantee it.'

He looked at me and smiled. 'Let's forget it, *paisan*. The job's done.'

My mind snaps back to the job at hand. Once again I'm in unfamiliar territory.

I drove right by the house, fairly slowly, and saw nobody around. There were no vehicles. It was a gut feeling, but the pigeons had flown, I knew it. I drove back and pulled into the drive, stopping a few feet away from opened garage doors. From the seat I took the neat little briefcase I had bought that morning, adjusted my tie and headed for the front door.

No one answered my knock. I tried twice more, giving plenty of time for an answer, then stepped off the verandah and walked around behind the house. The house was too isolated for me to worry about suspicious neighbours, but if someone was here and hadn't heard my knock, then the briefcase would give me cover.

I went back to the front and into the opened garage, then slipped silently into the house.

There was a clipboard on the kitchen wall loaded with notes and receipts and messages, all of them old.

There was an out-of-date calendar with a picture of a woman in a long silvery dress agonising into a microphone. *Lady Sings the Blues*, I read underneath it.

I glanced around and went through to the living

room, then checked out the rest of the house. The place was deserted. There was no one here and there hadn't been for some time. I wondered if it might be a set-up, some sort of a trap, but nothing happened. I was in a deserted house.

When I got back to town I called Sam and gave him the number of the hotel and my room.

Twenty minutes later Sam rang me.

'That address was a bodgie, Sam. The place is fuckin' deserted and has been for a while, so best have a word to that bloody Jackson. He's all bullshit. But don't worry, I'll find the prick if he's here.'

'No worries. There's somethin' else too. Our man has a friend up there who was also responsible for the loss of our business. Todd is the name. Frank and his missus Barbara.'

Sam gave me an address. 'We can be sure of this can we? It didn't come from Jackson did it?

'No no no, this one is guaranteed. Will you take care of it if you get a chance?'

'No worries. Scratch 'em off the ledger.'

I got a beer out of the bar fridge, turned the air-conditioner up a notch and looked up the number of the Townsville police. I dialled it and asked for Sergeant Collins. Eventually he came to the phone.

'Sergeant Collins.'

'I understand you know Carlo Bellari,' I said.

A long silence, then 'Who's this?' he asked cautiously.

All I knew about Collins was what Sam had told me. That he was paid something every month to see that Carlo knew whatever was necessary about police actions and other matters that might affect the business in North Queensland. Judging by the way that Collins was behaving, it seemed there wasn't much that Carlo cared to know.

'I work for Carlo,' I said, 'and I need information. I want to know where they've got Charlie Davenport. I can hold on or call again in ten minutes.'

Another long silence.

'Look, I don't know who the hell you think you are, but the Police Department doesn't give out that kind of information.'

I started to wonder if I had the right man.

'You are Sergeant William P. Collins?'

'Yes.'

'And you know Carlo Bellari? You're being paid a monthly retainer to keep him up to date. Carlo was supposed to get a message to you that I'd be in the area.'

This last bit was bullshit ... but anything to get Collins to show his hand.

'Listen,' Collins said in a lower voice, 'I can't talk here. Give me your number.'

'No,' I said, 'I'll phone you.'

We haggled for a while. Collins sounded out of his depth and more than a little scared. Either he was quite an actor or he was genuine and inexperienced. I decided to trust him. After all we did own the man.

'All right then,' I said at last and read the hotel number and the extension to him and hung up.

When the phone rang it was Collins.

'Who are you exactly?' he asked. 'You're not the man I usually talk to.'

'Never mind who the fuck I am. I want that information on Davenport. Can you get it for me?'

'I suppose so. Can I call you back at this same number?'

'Yes. One more thing. This information better be right or you're goin' to wake up one morning with your head right up your arse. How long do you think you'll be?'

'I don't know. Half an hour, maybe more. It all depends.'

'See it's no more than forty-five minutes.'

'I'll try but . . .'

'Collins, don't squirm on the hook. You're on now and you won't get off . . . Just do it.'

'Don't get all upset,' Collins returned. 'I'll get you your damned information.'

There was a truck stop across the street from the motel. I went over and had some coffee and a toasted sandwich, watching the big-boobed waitress move around the place on legs that were just a little too thick. I fantasised about throwing her down on the bed in my motel room.

I hadn't been back in my room more than two minutes when Collins called again.

'They've got him at a place called Crocodile Lake, about twenty miles north of here. It's off the main highway. There used to be a gold mine there, but now there's only a small settlement, pretty spread out. All that's really left is a sawmill.' He gave me a good description how to find the place. 'Look what's this all about?'

'You ought to know by now that we don't answer questions, we ask them. You get your whore money and life goes on.'

'I have a wife,' Collins protested with some attempt at dignity.

'Don't we all?' I said drily, thinking about the waitress with the big boobs.

'I'm faithful to mine,' Collins said firmly.

'What the hell has that got to do with it?'

'Huh?'

'Never mind. One last thing. I want you to call me here if anything happens with this Davenport. Anything I should know about.'

'There's not going to be any rough stuff is there . . . ?'

'What the hell did I just tell you? Keep your mouth shut except to spit out answers when we put money in and pull the lever.'

'Well if that's all then, I've got to get back. They'll wonder where I am.'

'Is your wife a good fuck?'

'What the hell business is it of yours?'

'Big tits? Gives you a good suck?'

'What are you, some kind of pervert?'

'Give your wife a good fuck for me Collins, will ya?' I hung up, smiling out the window at the truck stop across the street.

I left the motel just before dark and headed north at a leisurely pace. It was September and it was hot and sticky. Too late for winter and too early for summer. I had the radio on and the air-conditioner was blasting away. So, I thought, the bastards thought they'd be safe way the hell out in the country. Right out of sight, jungle and scrub both sides of the road for at least twenty miles. What do the bastards do all day? Watch the fish jump? Swat mosquitoes, watch the trees grow, Christ! I had to admit, though, we'd never have found him so quickly without Collins and the rat could have done more damage.

I saw the petrol station Collins had mentioned, and then the little town. Way out in the middle of nowhere. I passed the sawmill and a bunch of rickety old houses all queer-looking colours in the headlights.

The trees looked solid but I soon saw the notice-boards that Collins mentioned, supposed to lead to holiday camps. Then the Crocodile Lake sign. I killed the lights and turned in. The car bottomed on a rock and I banged my head into the roof. 'Shit!'

The road was bloody terrible, all washed out, and I drove as slowly as I could go without stalling. The car won't take this, I said to myself. If I knock a hole in the sump or the fuel tank I'll be stuffed. Collins had said the place was a mile off the road. When I'd gone about a third of the way I saw a place where I could conceal the car. I couldn't risk bogging the vehicle so I got out and tested the ground. It was solid underfoot. I drove the car into the gap and camouflaged it with branches and anything else I could find.

The only things I took with me were the Beretta and a spare clip, a pair of gloves and the balaclava. I already had my night gear and webbing on. The time was 8.07.

It was exactly 9.20 when I moved in for the kill. I had been watching them, heard every word that they said. I couldn't believe it when I heard the copper chaperoning Davenport and his sheila say they'd run out of beer.

'Go and get some more,' said Davenport.

'You're not supposed to be seen in town, Charlie. You know that.'

'I'm all right here. Who the fuck knows we're here? You go and get some.'

They spoke back and forth for a while, with Davenport promising he won't leave the house. In the end the copper agreed.

'I'm going too, Charlie,' Davenport's sheila said. 'Can I?'

'Yeah, suit yourself.'

Christ! Talk about falling on your feet. I couldn't believe my ears. I watched from the cover of the trees as the copper and Davenport's bird climbed into a Land Rover, slammed the doors and drove off.

I waited a few minutes in the quiet, then moved out onto the rutted roadway in front of the cottage, paused to check the Beretta and to settle the final details of my plan of action. Then I crossed silently to the door.

With the Beretta in my right hand, I opened the door with my left, throwing it wide quickly so it slammed back against the wall, shuddering. In the yellow light of the overhead lamp Davenport was caught in an awkward position. He was kneeling on the floor, back to the door and looking for something in a bottom cupboard. He spun around at once and started to rise to his feet.

'Stay where you are you piece of shit,' I said.

I had no wet palms, no nervousness. My training is taking over and I am in control. The way this man will die is completely in my hands. And to make up for what he's done he is going to die slow.

Davenport's face was white and he made a sudden lunge for the cupboard.

Goddamn you, you bastard, I thought.

I didn't have the silencer on the Beretta and I heard it loud. It shattered the tight little cottage quiet. Davenport stumbled. Blood spattered from his left wrist onto the floor bright glistening red.

Davenport lurched up and collapsed behind a bench in the middle of the room, where he probably has a gun. This won't do, I thought. I circled, gun out in front of me in the classical position, heart pumping regularly, teeth clamped together. Davenport was fumbling for something under the bench. Clever, very clever, Charlie was. If somebody came for him he thought he'd be ready.

Davenport's face is stark white now as he looks up. The cottage shudders again with the noise of the gun. Blood shoots out from Davenport's right shoulder. He screams this time.

'That's it you bastard,' I yelled. 'Scream. Carlo and Sam would love to hear it.'

Davenport stumbled and headed for the door. There is the stench of urine and shit. He's one scared cock.

I finished it from the door, taking my time.

Tcrack!

Davenport was screaming deafeningly now. He clutched his gut and pitched head-first into the dusty gravel driveway, kicking and writhing.

Tcrack!

Blood reddened Davenport's hip.

'Missed,' I said.

Davenport is twisting and struggling and bleeding like a dog.

There's the shot I want. *Tcrack!*

Davenport clutched his balls, screeching his lungs out.

'What's it feel like, Charlie?' I yelled at him.

Tcrack!

A hole appeared in Davenport's forehead above his right eye. He gave a shudder and went still, eyes wide open.

I stepped out of the doorway, walked carefully across the leaf-cushioned ground to the gravel and stood looking down at Davenport. The buzzing in my ears from the shots draining away into the quiet surroundings, leaving only a faint ringing. He was dead all right. There was no question about that.

I don't know why, but I had no desire to leave right away. It was almost like being in one of those big cathedrals out here. The light coming out the door and the windows caught the bottoms of the branches overhead and made them look like a vaulted ceiling. It was quiet and peaceful. Cool now, though.

A shiver ran through me. I went inside and closed the door. And found I'd yanked a hinge loose in slamming it open. I had a sudden urge to fix it. I wanted to clean the place up and leave everything neat and sparkling.

That's stupid, I told myself. It doesn't make sense.

But I did feel like hanging around and just listening to the quiet. This was a rare treat, being able to hang around like this, and not having to beat a hasty retreat.

In fact, I thought, why *not* fix the door?

Of course the main thing now was to get rid of the body. There was time enough before the copper and the girl returned. I looked around in the cottage and there was nothing useful there. I went quickly back outside.

Davenport lay on the road, a twisted huddle, like a pile of old clothes. I could smell his fouled clothes and backed off. The last thing I wanted to do was deal with his filthy body. I imagined myself at the sink trying to wash away the filth and it wouldn't come off.

I went back inside and searched the place quickly and methodically, pulling out drawers, yanking out the contents of the closet. There was a torch on top of one of the cupboards, and it worked.

Just as I was about to go out I pictured the copper coming to the door and then coming inside. If he saw this mess, blood on the table and the floor and the wall, bullet holes, he'd start an immediate wide sweep.

I cleaned up quickly and carefully, put back the contents of the drawers and closet. The bloodstains didn't come completely off, but with the dust and stuff around it'd take a while to recognise them. I hid the bullet hole near the baseboard with the end of the table and the one higher up the wall by moving a poster over it.

After a final check I turned off the lantern and I went back outside. There was a rowboat pulled up on the lake shore.

Perfect.

I went around the building, peering underneath it. There was rotten timber, old paint cans and a large piece of heavy plastic that looked like it was used to protect the firewood during the rainy season. I carried it around the front and unrolled it near the body.

Davenport was heavy. Corpses always seemed that way. But I dragged the body onto the plastic and with some effort rolled him up in it and tucked the ends in. I shovelled up the blood-soaked gravel with a spade and pitched it as far out into the lake as I could. Then I raked fresh dirt and gravel over the bloodied area.

I found some rope in a shed and a good-sized rock by the road. I wrapped the rock in the outer rolls of plastic and tied the whole thing up.

I was sweating by now and the flashlight was getting dim. There's not much kick left in these batteries I thought and had to wipe the sweat from my face with my sleeve. I stood up and listened hard for a few minutes, but all I heard was the wind in the trees and the sound of my own heart beating. I bent down and took hold of the bundle.

Getting the thing into the rowboat was the hardest part. And once that had been done I found it took up so much room I couldn't row properly. But I picked up one of the oars and pushed off until I had to reach a bit to touch bottom. I wasn't worried about the lake being dragged. It was far too big for a systematic search.

It was hard work after that and I paddled awkwardly, almost falling out a couple of times. I was unused to the tipsiness of the boat. My knees were starting to shake from having to squat awkwardly. I felt cold and my teeth began to chatter.

After paddling what seemed quite a distance, I decided to risk the torch to find out where I was.

The light didn't reach any trees on the shore, so I had to be a hundred yards away or even more.

Then I shone the light down into the water. Just a murky wind-spattered wave. I put the light out and tried to reach bottom with an oar, but I couldn't, even with my arm down in the water.

'Hell,' I said. 'That ought to be deep enough.'

I looked at the shore again for lights, thinking that I had heard engines. But there were no lights and I figured that it was the wind making the noise.

Still the copper and the bird would be back pretty damn soon.

Shoving the oar blade under the thwart, I stepped carefully over it and got hold of the body. It was slippery in the plastic, and when I rolled it to the side the boat nearly went over. Scared, and thinking about crocodiles, I gave a heave. The body splashed and was gone and the boat righted itself.

My teeth started chattering again and I was shaking all over, both from tension and from cold. I fumbled around for the rowlocks and fitted them in their sockets. Then I rowed like buggery back towards the shore, putting my back into it.

I landed the boat, pulled the bow up a bit, then peered into the wall of trees. I could see nothing. It was as black as a dog's guts. Moving to go into the trees I tripped over a gnarled root and fell hard onto my hands, which sent pain all the way up my arms. Bloody mangroves!

All of a sudden there was the sound of an engine. I froze in the darkness as the lights of the vehicle pitched wildly, heaving shadows through the thick scrub. I squatted behind a good-sized tree and watched the lights of the vehicle come towards the cottage. It was the Land Rover. It came past my cover, not fifty feet away, and stopped outside the cottage.

There were low voices and then the copper yelling.

'You gone to bed, Charlie? Why didn't you leave the light on?'

I was glad now that I'd turned the lamp off.

After a moment the door slammed and there's a woman's voice calling from inside the cottage.

'He's not here, Des.'

'What, what do you mean he's not here? Hey, where are you Charlie? Come on, stop the clowning around.'

The lights of the Land Rover were turned back on.

'Light that bloody lantern in there will ya,' yelled the copper.

Matches were being struck, and then the lamp came on.

'He must have gone for a walk,' the woman said. 'The torch is missing.'

It was at this point that I extracted myself from the area. Training again took over. The best time to effect an extraction is during confusion. When I was a safe enough distance from the cottage I stepped out onto the road and ran back to the hire car. I pulled away the camouflage, started up, reversed carefully out onto the track, bumped my way over the path to the main road, then stepped on the gas. About halfway back to town I stopped and changed my clothes, throwing the overall and the rest of the stuff into the flight bag in the boot. I was back in the Allen before midnight, but I was so hyped up it took some hours before I got to sleep.

I slept in till 11.30, but I didn't know what the aftermath of the hit had turned into and decided it was too risky to ring Brisbane yet. I dug out the address of the other squealers, the Todds, and studied the road map again. Shit, all these bastards go bush.

In the afternoon I drove out to do a reconnaissance

309

on the Todds' place, driving past a few times to take mental snapshots. When I was satisfied that I had a picture and a plan that was operative, I drove back to the motel. I used the rest of the day catching up on sleep, ringing Carmel and talking to her for fifteen minutes to bring her out of the doldrums. The only friend she had in the world at the moment was the TV.

At quarter to eight that night I was driving south again. I looked at my watch and took my foot off the accelerator. I had started out too early and I didn't want to get there until I could be reasonably sure that the Todds were in bed. In the end I reached their place at 10.20.

It was a double-storyed house on a T-junction, just off the main road. Moderately large, in need of some running repairs and a coat of paint. There was sugar-cane growing all around it. I drove on by slowly. There was a light on downstairs but no car in the drive.

I drove on for ten minutes, going fast as though it might speed up the passage of time, then turned round and drove back. Things had changed. The lights were still on downstairs, but a sedan was parked out the front. I parked in an unfenced paddock behind some bushes and cane, killed the lights and waited for a break in the traffic on the main highway before trotting back.

I was dressed in the black camouflage with nothing on me that was reflective. I checked the Beretta and cocked the action, letting the hammer down slowly with my thumb. Then I twisted the silencer in place and tucked the weapon into my belt.

I strode quickly towards the house, staying out wide in the shadows, before I hurriedly crossed the grass to a window.

Cautiously, I peered into the kitchen. I could hear voices but I couldn't quite make out what they were saying. A man and a woman were standing next to the refrigerator, glaring at each other. The woman was waving her arms as she spoke. She was taller than he was, and the way she was dressed made me a little bit excited. Fingering the gun, I watched her body move under the sheer negligee.

The man shouted at her and the woman slapped his face and left the room. The man looked after her for a moment, then poured himself a Scotch and drank it slowly, thoughtfully. Then he turned off the lights and left the room.

I waited for a few minutes, then tried the kitchen door. It wasn't locked. I moved into the kitchen, where I stopped and listened before I moved to the foot of the stairs and paused again. I could make out voices, still angry, interrupting each other or both going at once. I started up the stairs.

The door to their bedroom was closed but the hall outside reverberated with their argument. The woman was going to move out if he didn't quit chasing some other woman, and the man was denying it, saying it was all her imagination.

My excitement was gone by this stage. It was just another dirty hit on a pair of squealers . . . cleaning up the shit that was making a stink.

Fuck 'em, I thought. I was angry. I slammed the door open and stepped in, gun in hand.

The two stared at me with their mouths gaping wide open.

'You Frank Todd?' I asked with authority.

'I . . . yes what the . . . ?'

'This Barbara?'

'Who the hell . . . *what* the hell are you doing?'

'Is it?' I roared at her.

'Yes I'm Barbara. And this is our house. And you get out. Get *out!*'

A fist came out of nowhere and caught me on the jaw. My knees gave out for a fraction of a second and I had to fight to regain control. Pushing Frank aside, I was still shaking as I lifted the Beretta and put two bullets into the woman, slamming her back and down. 'You fuckin' bastard!' I said to Todd, and shot him straight in his open mouth just as he was coming around for another swing. Todd's momentum and the slam of the bullet through his mouth into his head spun him round before he dropped to the side onto his face hitting the floor. That was that, then. They were both dead, the bastards, bleeding big pools on the carpet.

I undid the silencer and slipped it into my pocket. Reaching down I picked up Todd's arm by the wrist, placed the gun in his hand and wrapped his fingers around it. I put his right index finger through the guard and onto the trigger, then let his hand fall to the floor with the gun in it.

'Try talkin' to the cops about this one,' I said. 'You've talked to 'em about everything else, you prick.'

I checked around the room. There was a phone by the bed and a black-covered address book which I slipped into my pocket. I went downstairs back out through the kitchen door, checked the perimeter and slipped into the night. I changed into fresh clothes behind the cane and drove back to the motel, where I freshened up a bit, splashed on some aftershave and then strolled across the street to the all-night cafe.

Bigtits was there again. I walked over to the counter and smiled at her. We had the place to ourselves. I ordered coffee and some bacon and eggs, then walked across to a table. She came over and put a silver coffee pot and cup and saucer down in front of me.

'You're up late,' she said.

'Yeah. Couldn't sleep and decided to take a walk.'

'You visiting, or do you live here?'

'Just visiting ... Staying at the Allen.'

'It's nice over there,' she said, then moved back behind the counter to put the bacon and eggs on the grill.

I sat drinking my coffee and she brought my meal over.

'I'd shout you a drink or two,' I said, 'but it'd be a bit hard while you're working.'

She looked up at the clock. 'I finish soon. I wouldn't mind a drink then. I find it hard to sleep when I go straight home ... I've worked too long now on night shift.'

'It's a date then. I'm in unit 44. Come on across when you're finished.'

'Okay I will,' she said with a smile.

Just then another sheila came in dressed in the same cafe uniform. I bolted the meal down, I was hungrier than I thought.

I walked up to the counter and paid the bill.

'See ya soon,' I said. 'What's your name?'

'Rosemary. Rosemary Wheeler. What's yours?'

'Jack Smith.'

'I won't be long now my relief's here.'

'Righto. I'll leave a light on for ya.'

I walked back across the street and nearly had a hard-on just thinking about those tits of hers.

I slipped into the unit, kicked off my shoes and lay back waiting, sipping a Scotch. The minutes dragged by, then there was a light tap on the door. I got up and opened it. It was bigtits, only she'd changed into a skirt and blouse that made those boobs seem even more inviting.

'Hi! Come on in.'

She moved into the unit looking around, taking it in, then walked over and sat on the sofa.

'What would you like to drink?' I asked her.

'I don't know. What have you got?'

I moved over to the mini-bar, and swung the fridge door open with a sweep of my arm.

'Take your pick,' I said.

She kicked her shoes off, came over and chose a vodka. I made the drink for her and lifted the cap off a bottle of Tooheys for myself. We chatted away and after she'd had a few more drinks I picked up her hand.

'You're beautiful you know,' I told her. 'I'd love to take you to bed.'

'I'm not very good at that sort of thing,' she said shyly.

'Says who?'

'A boyfriend I used to have.'

I put my arm around her and, lifting up her chin, kissed her softly on the mouth. She was a bit rigid but I kept kissing her and put my hand on a boob and gently squeezed it. A small tremble went through her, her mouth relaxed and she put her arm around my neck. I could feel her nipple getting hard. I undid a couple of buttons on her blouse and slipped my hand inside the cup of her bra. God she had gorgeous tits. She stopped kissing me.

'I've been working all night,' she said. 'I haven't had a shower.'

I didn't speak. I just took my hand out of her bra and coaxed her to her feet, kissed her again and led her into the bathroom. I undid her blouse and she let it come off while I was kissing her. I unhooked her bra and took it off her. I bent down and took one of her nipples in my mouth and teased and sucked it. She began to pull my shirt up from under my belt and rubbed my back. I put my hand up under her skirt and let it run up between her legs. She moved a leg to allow my hand to reach her. I gently pushed my finger in under the elastic of her panties. She was wet, and I was hard and throbbing.

'Jesus, I can't stand this,' I said.

And stopped. Then led her by the hand back into the room. I took off her skirt and panties and laid her on the bed. Threw off my clothes. I was standing up hard and erect. She was watching me and looking at my erection as I lay down beside her and kissed her. She let her hand move down and take hold of my penis.

'I haven't done it for a while,' she said, 'Don't hurt me.'

I moved on top of her and she spread her legs and lifted her knees. I kissed her, letting the tip of my tongue tease the tip of hers, and slowly pushed into her. She

315

gave a little mewing sound into my mouth and I pushed in a little more, pulled back a little and then pushed right into her. She gave a gasp and then pushed her head back into the pillow, and with her eyes closed and mouth open she started to work her hips. I came into her with a spurt and kept moving in and out. Her eyes opened and a bitter-sweet look came onto her face. I thought she was going to scream.

'Uh uh uh uh aaaaaaaaaaaah!' She pulled my head down and kissed me as she climaxed. 'That's never happened to me before,' she gasped.

I flew out of Townsville at 9.05 that day, and as I was winging it back to Brisbane I couldn't help smiling when I thought about Rosemary from the truck stop. She really was a bit of all right.

30

AS SOON AS I GOT BACK TO EAGLE FARM IN BRISBANE I
went to the public phones. I called the police station in
Townsville and I asked to speak to Sergeant Collins.

'Sergeant Collins. What is it?'

'It's me, Collins. Did you give your missus a good
fuck for me?' I said, just so there'd be no mistake who
was calling him. 'I want a number where I can call you.'

'I wish you wouldn't say things like that,' he whined.

'Cut the crap, Collins. Just give me a number.'

'I took the number of the phone box out in the street.
Do you want it now?'

'No I want it next bloody week you imbecile
... 'Course I want the fuckin' thing now. Now what
is it?'

He gave me the number and I wrote it down.

'I'll call you in ten minutes, Collins. You be there.'

'I will, I will,' he said. 'Don't get all upset again.'

I hung up, picked up my bags and smoked a cigarette
before calling Collins back. When he answered, I
demanded to know what was going on.

'Charlie Davenport has gone missing ... They know
he just didn't disappear all by himself ...'

'Yeah, yeah. What else, Collins?'

'I thought that Carlo Bellari and his people just
pushed drugs, ran the gambling and had the escort

317

agencies. I don't know if I like getting mixed up with killers,' Collins said. 'Is that what you are? A killer? A hit man for the Bellari organisation? Have you killed Davenport and got rid of his body? There are two more bodies up here, friends of Davenport's. The circumstances appear suspicious. I don't think I should get involved any more.'

'You signed on for life, Collins, when you took your first envelope. The only way out for you is the way the Todds' did. You understand me?'

I could hear street noises during the pause on the other end.

'Yeah, I understand. I'll keep you informed. I don't know if I'll be able to get much though. There's a special task force working on it. The federal blokes are here too.'

'All you've got to do now is keep this end informed through the usual channels. You got that?'

'I'll have to be careful. This is a CIB matter but I'll get something.'

'Do that,' I said.

As I made my way out to the taxi rank I wondered who'd win the race in the game of Let's find Charlie Davenport. The police or the crocodiles. My money was on the crocs.

I was back in our unit at Taringa, having some coffee. Carmel was all excited that I was back and fussing over me like a mother hen. I felt a twinge of guilt sitting there with her spoiling me and just hours before I had been screwing the arse off Rosemary Bigtits, but I swept it away. 'Any port in a storm,' they say. 'Ships that pass in the night.' And put it out of my mind. I told Carmel that I'd better slip down to work and see Sam, that he didn't know that I was back yet.

Gina looked up in surprise when she saw me. I made a motion with my head towards the door which she understood immediately. She left, closing the door behind her.

I walked across to Sam's office and gave a brief knock before turning the handle and pushing the door. He hadn't even finished saying '*Entri prego*' and I was standing there.

'Jesus Christ!' he said in surprise. 'What the fuck are you doin' back?'

I closed the door and sat down.

'It's over Sam, all clean and tidy.'

'You mean . . . ?'

'Yes Sam, they're all fuckin' dead.'

I then explained what had taken place at some length, with all the lurid details. When I told him how I'd taken Davenport out slowly with six rounds a slow snarl came into his voice.

'Jesus, I wish I'd fuckin' been there to hear the bastard squeal.'

'That Collins was starting to pack the shits too,' I said. 'But I've quietened him down. Told him the only way out is the same as the Todds.'

I then told Sam about my conversation with Collins. Asking what sort of fuck his missus was, and Collins' reaction. Sam slapped his leg and burst out laughing.

'Fuck me!' he chortled. 'Look, *paisan*, you'll have to hold the fort here. I've got to go and let the Old Man know about this. I'll be back soon as I can.'

We left the office together and I made my way to the bar, where I chatted with Patsy.

Sam was back soon, and with a happy look on his face. He got us a drink each and we moved to the end of the bar, away from the other drinkers.

'I'm going to have to watch my arse, and my job,' he said lightly. 'You're the golden-haired boy, I can tell you. They want to see you.'

'Where?' I said.

'They're coming up tomorrow. They had the news already. What did Paolo mean when he said they never stood a chance once we gave it to you ... that you'd do it clean after the last time?'

'It's a long story, Sam, and it happened a long time ago.'

'No no, come on, tell me what happened.'

Sam was a *capo*, a trusted lieutenant. He loved humour, especially the dirty variety, and he also loved anything macabre. So I told him.

'Holy shit! Oh Jesus! Shit,' he kept saying. 'Shit, you got away clean. Christ! you really made your bones.'

'I made them a long time before then, Sam, and that's something I won't talk about and neither will Paolo.'

'I always knew you two were close. Now I know why he'd like you back in Sydney.'

'Yeah Sam, but that thing in Sydney was unbelievable. It'll never happen again.'

'Jesus! Holy fuckin' hell,' was all Sam said. And gulped his drink down.

I returned to Taringa and spent the rest of the day with Carmel.

In the afternoon I took out the Todds' address book and as I was going through it I received a shock. I'd got to the Js and listed there as plain as you'd like was Herb Jackson's home and work numbers.

I got the phone directory and checked it out. There was no listing for Jackson. Thinking that he might have a new number, I rang information and asked the operator if she could give me the number of H. C. Jackson, Chermside.

'I'm sorry, sir,' I was told. 'The number you have requested is restricted.'

I thanked the operator and hung up. Thoughts were flying through my mind. Why would a couple of traitorous bastards like the Todds have Jackson's unlisted number? I filed the information away till I could talk to Carlo about it.

Later that evening Carmel and I went and painted the town, as I had promised her.

Paolo and Carlo came up from Sydney and stayed at the big unit at Surfers Paradise. Sam and I went down in his car. He refused point-blank to travel in my old Plymouth.

It was 7 p.m. and the four of us were sitting around the big dining-room table. We had gone over the events up north. I received a lot of verbal back-slapping and had been presented with a big fat envelope as a reward for a successful job. I'd also been through a special ritual and was told I was no longer to do any legwork. I'd been promoted. The conversation had sort of broken down to small talk and the occasional joke, Sam wanting to send out for more food and booze and it was shaping up as a long night. I put a spanner in the works when I fished into the pocket of my jacket and threw the Todd's address book into the middle of the table.

'What do you want me to do about this?' I said.

'What is it?' Carlo asked.

'I'll tell you what it is. It's a damning bit of evidence in two ways. One, it could link me to the Todds' place, 'cause I got it off their bedside table. And two, fuckin' Herb Jackson's private and work numbers are in it.'

'What! Where?' asked Carlo.

'Listed under the Js,' I said. 'But I think it should be under C for cunt. Why would they have Jackson's number? I rang Telecom and confirmed it's a silent one. He had to give it to them. They've even got his work number alongside it. I picked it up thinking it might give us a list of rats. What we've got is a fuckin' skunk. The address he supplied for Davenport was bullshit. Remember that.'

'Jesus Christ!' said Sam. 'Give us a look.'

'Good work, Jimmy,' Paolo said 'You're going to have to take care of this, Carlo.'

I looked at Carlo. He was so incensed he'd have cut Jackson's heart out right then if he could have.

The questions flew back and forth for a good while before things got back into the festive mood. We were all a bit pissed when Carlo asked me to tell them about Davenport one more time.

I really didn't want to but they kept at me, so I retold the story. Carlo roared with laughter.

'Shit,' he said. 'I'd give my fuckin' balls to have been there.'

'That's what I told Charlie,' I said.

And that had them rolling on the floor.

It was a good deal later when we broke it up and Sam and I went home.

What did come out of the meeting was that Herb Jackson was in a lot of trouble if he was playing both ends against the middle. He could have a perfectly good explanation for the whole thing, but I didn't like his chances.

A week passed and nothing more was spoken about the matter—to me, that is. But questions had been asked behind the scenes and things were warming up. Carmel and I went shopping during this time but we didn't buy the usual bits 'n' pieces. We drove home in a new car. It was a black V8 Holden Brougham, and did we run some miles up on it that week. I started to teach her to drive.

Carmel and I were down the club one night having a last drink when Gina came up and told me Carlo was on the phone. 'Hi Carlo,' I said. 'What can I do for you?'

'Can you come to my place on your way home? . . . No need to rush.'

I dropped Carmel at the unit and drove on to Carlo's, where we sat in his office with the door closed.

'This Jackson,' he said to me, 'he's been a bigger pain in the arse than we thought. I'd like to see the prick burn in Hell. Want to take care of it?'

'You got any time or place in mind?'

'Do what you gotta do. But make an example of this one, just in case someone else gets the idea they can fuck us about. He's a real sweetheart, this *stronzo*. He wants our money but he also wants the pat on the back if he can pull us down. Know what I mean? He's been stabbin' us in the back and we've been payin' the cockroach to do it. What a bunch of *testa le gutza* we've turned out to be!'

'I'll have to plan it myself, and it's in my time and I pick the place.'

'*No problema.*'

When I got home I sat down and thought about this hit. It was delicate all right. Then again, I knew where Jackson lived—I'd taken payola there to the mongrel— and he was totally unaware that he was in any danger. His wife had divorced him some years back and he lived on his own, but he often had one of the girls sent out to his place. It was Carlo's words to me that gave me an idea for what I'd do.

I went shopping the next day and bought some fruit cordial in a half-gallon plastic bottles, a container of concentrated liquid soap, a spark plug, a roll of heavy duty autoelectric cable, insulation tape and a quick-drying two-part-mix cement.

Back home I emptied the cordial down the sink and washed and dried the container. When this was done I took one of them and, lying it on its side, I used a soldering iron to make a hole in it that was just large enough for the threaded end of the spark plug to be pushed in and screwed up while the plastic was still soft, cutting its own thread. When it had cooled I screwed the plug back out, coated the thread with the cement and screwed it back in. I put a build-up of cement around the plug and the side of the container. Then, taking about two feet of the electrical cable, I stripped the insulation off both ends. Taking one of the bared ends I fashioned it into a small eye loop that would just fit over the threaded top of the plug before I screwed the lead connector back on. I cut another piece of cable and wrapped it around the metal base of the plug a couple of times, twisting it tight and wrapping some insulation tape around it.

Taking the liquid soap, I poured about two inches into the bottom of both containers. Then I completely filled one with petrol, and almost filled the container with the spark plug. I swirled the containers around to mix the liquid soap and petrol together, paying special attention to the container with the spark plug, examining it to make sure there were no leaks around the plug. Then I washed the outside of the containers to remove all telltale smells of gasoline and placed them in a black canvas carry-all in the boot of the car. Homemade napalm . . . Nasty stuff!

By 2 a.m. I was inside Jackson's garage and it didn't take long to set the whole thing in place. I had brought along a flat flexible steel strip to open the car door, but Jackson hadn't locked it. He probably thought that the Yale lock on the garage was security enough.

The stickiest part of the job was that I had to open the bonnet. I pulled the release . . . Clung! . . . I stood perfectly still, all senses alert, but the sound hadn't disturbed Jackson. I turned on a torch with a handkerchief around the end of it to break down the glow.

The first thing I did was take a prepared piece of cable and, taking one of the sparkleads out of the distributor cap, I pulled the insulator and metal end off and joined the prepared wire onto it and poked it back into the distributor. I taped it in place and let the other end of the wire fall down the side of the engine and fire wall to the floor of the garage. I then took another prepared piece of cable, twisted it onto the rear lifting bracket of the engine and let it fall to the floor also. Then, with my body half under the car, I removed the rubber grommet drain hole and poked the wires I'd secured to the engine up inside the car. I taped the wires up under the vehicle so that they wouldn't hang down.

Then I knelt on the garage floor and, lifting the car's floormat, I took hold of the wires coming up through the grommet hole and pulled them out the side of the carpet before I put the mat back in place. I pushed the containers full of petrol and liquid soap out of sight under the driver's seat. The one with the sparkplug in it was placed with the plug facing up, leaving a gap of about an inch between the volatile mixture and the firing terminals of the plug. Any petrol on the plug end would soon evaporate, leaving the terminals dry. Taking the wire from the distributor cap, I twisted it onto the wire on the top of the plug, then twisted the wire from the engine bracket onto its base. I insulated both joins with some tape and hid the wires out of sight under the seat. Checking that everything was in order, I closed the bonnet and the car door as gently as I could and left the garage.

It was the best bit of mechanical work I've ever done and I congratulated myself as I drove away, smiling when the words of the colonel at Kapooka came back to me . . . '*I hope you haven't used any of this . . . this training for clandestine purposes!*'

The driver would turn the key, the engine would turn

over, and when that plug's turn came to fire in the engine cylinder it would fire into the napalm containers under the seat. A sheet of flame would fry Jackson, and even if he managed to get out of the car he'd be soaked with napalm that would stick to him and—just as Carlo had wished—he would burn just as surely as he would in Hell.

It was early Saturday morning, and Jackson always went to the races. He was an addict. In fact it was this addiction that had him in the clutches of the family and indebted him to Carlo.

The other reason I used this method of removal was that the heat generated from a motor vehicle on fire is so intense that, except for the sparkplug, all the equipment used would melt. Even the copper wire.

I went home and climbed into bed. The last thing that flashed through my mind was a picture of a Ford Falcon, igniting into an inferno, when the rat behind the wheel, with a pocketful of dirty money, turned the ignition key.

'*Ciao ballo fuoco Herb!*' [Enjoy the fire dance Herb], I murmured, and went to sleep.

Sunday's papers were full of it. 'DRUG SQUAD BOSS DIES IN CAR INFERNO,' screamed one tabloid. 'NO COMMENT FROM POLICE ON JACKSON,' read another.

Carlo, Sam and I were sitting in the club as we read the papers. Then we charged our drinks and raised our glasses.

'*Salute!*'

PART

5

Our place

31

I PULLED BACK THE TENT FLAP AND WENT OUTSIDE INTO the coolness of the morning. I felt good. I flexed my biceps with a grunt of satisfaction and stretched my arms over my head, then let them fall by my sides. The four-wheel drive Carmel and I had bought stood alongside a huge ironbark tree. The back of the Toyota was a storehouse, filled with groceries, cigarettes, ammunition, a couple of rifles, shotgun, a medical kit and enough beer and liquor to start a bar on wheels.

Kicking at the embers of the fire we had made the previous night, I threw some more twigs and branches onto it. I walked a short distance to stretch my legs and had a piss against one of the many trees that surrounded the clearing.

We were in the Northern Territory, on the north-east coast. Carmel and I had decided to take a holiday and enjoy a different lifestyle. We were on our own, and God we were happy. I hawked and spat out some tobacco-induced phlegm, then filled a billy and put it on the fire.

Sitting down on a wooden box I lit the first of the two or three cigarettes Carmel told me I was not supposed to smoke before I had eaten, but are always 50 per cent better than those you smoke later.

The smoke of the cigarette hardly wavered as it

spiralled up, and it was going to be another stinker of a day. A scorcher, just like yesterday. Still, I thought, so what? It was a bloody sight better than that lung-rotting shit we were breathing back in Brisbane.

Three weeks of pleasant idleness had passed since we left Brisbane. It was the first real relaxation Carmel and I had shared since we got together. And since finding the camp site a week ago we had enjoyed roaming around in the early part of the day, and catching up on a bit of reading in the heat of the afternoon. We were miles from anywhere and spent most of the time naked. Babes in the woods, Carmel called us.

Late in the afternoons I used to take the shotgun or one of the rifles, and with Carmel in tow I would set off exploring and hunting.

There was an immense complexity and variety of flora and fauna. The first of the tree belts around the camp site were too open to be called forest, but there was heavily timbered scrub and jungle nearby that ran unbroken for miles. The jungly bush and timber were completely different from anything that I had seen before. Groves of wild plantain bananas stood beside near-impenetrable bamboo-like grass and palms, which in turn gave way to various twisted, stunted, stinging trees and towering redwoods, gums and ironbarks whose lower branches were festooned with drooping clusters of vines and staghorns and other parasitic plants. Orchids flourished in wild abundance.

It was steamy, but in the half-light the big trees brought to mind images of Roman temples, bounded by vast colonnades. The heavy stillness gave the illusion of being in consecrated halls, though broken from time

332

to time by an extraordinary range of birdcalls, screeching and chattering

Where the big timber joined overhead the light grew especially dim, but then you would suddenly emerge into a glade of green-gold, and as we walked along we often put up a bird or scared a huge goanna or frilled-neck lizard ... once a huge python that were either resting or in search of prey. A composty odour hung in the air, the musty smell of dying wood and dead foliage combined with the healthier scent of new growth and, in some places, the heavy and heady fragrance of the orchids.

When we went on these expeditions through the outer fringes of our camp site it always seemed to me to be a place of both charm and menace, light and darkness, deep silence and nerve-jangling screeches. A mixture of dark fears and bright fancies ...

I lifted the billy off the fire, ground out my cigarette, and as I walked back to the flap of the tent I looked back across the clearing. Old habits I suppose, just checking that no one was around. A faint waft of Carmel's perfume came to me. I looked in and she was on all fours, trying to straighten out our big air bed on the floor of the tent. She stood up as I approached her and noticed that I was becoming excited by her nakedness. A mischievous smile flickered on her lips and she stood there in an attitude of waiting.

In the soft light of the tent her tan looked warm and healthy, her large golden breasts and her flat stomach more desirable to me than ever before.

I beckoned her and as she came slowly towards me I reached out and took her wrist and pulled her close. I slid my arm around her waist and my fingers felt the satiny skin of her back. She leant into me and I put my hand down behind her back and let it cover one of the soft round cheeks of her buttocks, kneading it softly. She snuggled even closer, moaning, then reached down between us and took my penis and rubbed it and squeezed it gently.

Cupping her chin with one hand, I tilted her head back and kissed her. Then I bent down and kissed her in the hollow of her neck and along her soft rounded shoulders.

After more playing and kissing I lifted her up and laid her on the bed. I bent over her, kissing her stiffened nipples and fondling and caressing her body until she gave a slight tremble. Everything she did during our lovemaking became a signal to take another step and I lowered myself onto her. She lifted her knees and as I slowly pushed into her she raised herself, accepting me. We kissed and moved with each other in a practised rhythm, bringing us both to climax in a wonderful out-pouring of love and desire. We lay there for a while after that, just holding onto each other.

'How would you like a cup of tea?' I asked her. 'The billy's on?'

'Never thought you'd ask,' she said with a little giggle.

They were the first words we had spoken for the day.

There was a fair-sized billabong about half a mile from camp, a mixture of swamp and deep water, and I had forbidden Carmel to go near it. This was crocodile country. There were slides on the bank from where they entered the water, and on a few occasions we had seen them sunning themselves on the bank. I had also noticed that big bustards, or plains turkeys, came down to the billabong in the evening to drink and pick at the sweet green shoots around the edges. They were great eating, but flighty birds that would take off running as soon as you were near them. You had to approach them with stealth to get close enough to get a clean shot off, but I was determined to bag a couple.

I explained to Carmel what we had to do and pointed out where we would go. Explained to her the difference between upwind and downwind. She was very attentive and a fast learner and became quite excited about the adventure.

Late in the afternoon I told her to circle the waterhole to the right, stop downwind, wait for my signal, then scare the birds.

We had our clothes and boots on as we bellied forward through the thin spiky grass, Carmel working her way around to the right just like I'd shown her. We did this for perhaps five minutes until, rising up on my elbow, I could see the waterhole. We were nearer to it than I had estimated . . . about twenty yards away.

Here and there ibis waded in the shallows, and a number of ducks were swimming around further out. Beyond the reedbeds a variety of waterlilies made scattered splotches of vivid colour. There were perhaps a dozen or so galahs and twice as many finches and parakeets and some black cockatoos milling around and scooping up the occasional drink. And three bustards.

I slid the shotgun up in front of me through the grass, thumbed back the safety catch and then raised my right arm up above my head and waved it. Carmel immediately set up with a yell that had the bustards break into a run towards me. I raised the gun and fired with a single movement, getting one with the first barrel and another with the second.

It had all been accomplished in a matter of seconds. But as I stood up I noticed a danger that must have moved to the waterhole while we were crawling into position. A cow buffalo started snorting loudly in a flummox of indecision while her calf ploughed through the shallows and the oozing and sucking mud at the edges of the hole.

'Get down!' I yelled to Carmel.

I dropped back down and with just my head above the grass watched the agitated animal. It was plain that the cow had not caught our scent and I knew that, with her poor vision, she could not see us.

As soon as the youngster was out of the mire she nudged its backside with her nose and set off upwind at a fast trot, across the open ground around the billabong and into the scrub on the far side. When they were gone far enough I stood up, called out to Carmel to come back, then walked down and examined the two birds.

'Did you see the size of that thing?' Carmel said breathlessly. 'It was huge.'

'Yes and bloody nasty too, love, when they've got a calf like that. If she'd seen us or got wind of us she would've charged. I wouldn't have been able to drop her with the 12 gauge.'

I slung the shotgun over my shoulder and we picked up the birds and made our way back to camp, where we plucked and cleaned them. I thought that it would make Carmel squeamish, but she pulled a few faces and then waded in and helped me without complaint.

I cut the breast off one and she cooked it in the camp oven with some onions and potatoes. And made some nice gravy. I cut the rest into pieces and placed them in a bucket in which I had made up a strong brine solution and told her I'd show her in the morning how we could smoke it so it would keep. We sat at the camp table after we had eaten and drank half a flagon of sherry to wash the meal down. Half-pissed and happy, we fell into bed and slept like logs.

After breakfast we got the sections of poultry, threaded them onto some wire and hung them on a steel rod across the top of the fireplace. We collected some branches and built a roof over the meat and fireplace, closing it in like a tepee. Then we let the meat cook slowly over the coals, throwing in a handful of green twigs every now and then so the smoke would rise and cure the meat.

A few days later we came across a well-worn buffalo path. The amount of fresh dung and old droppings made it clear it was a regular one and that evening when we were sitting in the cool I asked Carmel if she'd like to go on a buffalo hunt.

She said she would, but I sensed her apprehension.

'You won't have to get close,' I told her. 'And you'll be able to see me. All you've got to do is stay behind some cover and you'll be right as rain.'

The next morning we found the trail again and moved cautiously along it through thick scrub which thinned out and eventually opened up into a large swampy tract about half a mile across. I stopped and lifted the binoculars, and there they were. It wasn't a big herd. There were seven animals all-told. One old bull, three cows, two with calves, and a young bull.

'Well there they are, love,' I said, handing Carmel the binoculars.

'Gee, don't they look close. Do you think they can see us?'

'Not a chance. The buggers have piss-weak eyesight. See those birds dancing all over their backs?'

'Yes. What are they doing?'

'They're feeding off the ticks and things on their hides. They also warn them of danger.'

I took the glasses back and examined the scene again. There was no breeze at all. Moving across and behind a good-sized blackbutt tree, I beckoned Carmel over and handed the glasses back to her.

'Listen, love, you'll be able to see me at all times with these. Okay?'

She nodded. 'Do you want me to stay here?'

'That's precisely what I want you to do.'

'Please be careful, Jimmy.'

I put my arms around her and gave her a hug and a kiss.

'Just wait here. I'll be okay.'

Every so often the buffalo stopped browsing and lifted their heads, scenting the air. When I had closed the distance I went down on my stomach but still had the animals in view.

I turned on my side, brought the Winchester around from my back and removed the magazine. Then I went through a bit of nonsense that I had picked up in Vietnam. I took a few loose rounds from my pocket,

338

picking out the one that looked the shiniest, and put the rest back in my pocket. Then I began to burnish the bullet against my shirt-front while I watched the target. After a while I drew the bolt and slid the round into the chamber, keeping the thumb of my left hand on the bullet and the front of the bolt until it was well forward to avoid even the smallest metallic click. Then I slid the bolt forward and locked it down for the first shot, the one that counted.

There were ten more rounds in the magazine, and now I'd completed the superstitious nonsense I quietly fitted it, pushing against the release with my finger so it wouldn't make a telltale sound. I had a good look at the buffalo again before I bellied towards them.

For ten minutes more I moved carefully forward in stretches of ten or fifteen yards. All the time now I watched the young bull buffalo in particular, but kept an eye on the others. Every time a lazily chewing muzzle was raised, I froze.

I lay still for a moment, resting, and watched a grass-hopper crawling through its immense private jungle of brown grass stalks. When I raised my head again I saw that the young bull had turned and moved a few yards closer to me. I was no more than twenty yards from the small herd and became aware of the beat of danger and excitement in my veins.

I memorised the position of a bit of low scrub I had selected, then bellied forward again, face-down and more slowly than before, only moving my face enough to see the heads and the backs of the buffalo. At least I'd have some sort of cover if they stampeded towards me.

The beast I had selected was at the right angle now

for the shot. I increased the pressure of the rifle stock against my shoulder, sighted, held my breath ... and applied the final squeeze to the trigger. *Wham!* roared the .30.06 round. The young buffalo became a statue, then a shudder ran through his body. He took two or three steps forward, went down on his knees and rolled over on his side. With a loud bellow of annoyance the old bull bolted away to the left with his harem and calves in hot pursuit.

I stood up and, remembering what I had been taught, drilled another shot in behind the downed animal's ear. Always give a *coup de grâce*. It's the dead ones that jump up off the ground and kill you.

I waved and whistled back to Carmel, who came trotting up, all excited and yelling with glee.

I took the best cuts off the young bull—the fillet, the sirloin and rumps—and we staggered our way back to camp. It was steaks for tea that night. Inch-thick fillet. We didn't have any sort of refrigeration, so we cut the rest of the meat into strips and packed it in salt overnight. In the morning we washed it in a solution of vinegar and pepper and hung it on a branch frame to dry, just as Kurt had shown me some years before. Biltong, he called it. When it was finally dried and cured it was fantastic. And the heat didn't affect it.

Carmel and I had found something special being together in isolation, but after another month in our camp we decided it was time to move on. Perth or Sydney? We flipped a coin. Carmel had always wanted to see Sydney, and she won the toss. When we had finally packed the Landcruiser we took a last look around and headed east.

It took us a week of unhurried driving to reach Sydney. We weren't in any rush and there were still plenty of funds in the bank.

I gave Paolo a ring when we arrived. He was in good spirits and wanted to know when I was going back to Brisbane. I told him I thought I'd cleaned all the shit up last time I was there. We laughed and joked on the phone and he invited us out to Double Bay for a meal. Afterwards we had a long private discussion. He didn't push me to get back in harness. In fact it was the other way. He wanted me to relax and unwind and return when I was ready.

He made a few phone calls and got us a nice place to stay in Bondi Beach for a week. Carmel wanted to see some of Sydney and we did, but chills went up my spine when on our second evening alone she asked me when I was going to take her to check out Kings Cross.

Memories and pictures flashed through my mind. I was full of reluctance, but I couldn't disappoint her. I thought of the time some years back, when I had been drawn to the Cross like a moth to a candle. How I had grown to manhood there, with Margo's love and assistance.

'Sure love,' I said. 'Why not?'

It hadn't really changed much from my time there with Margo. The signs and shops were gaudier and other things had been added here and there. But the atmosphere, the charisma and the smell were unchanged and would never change. It was still the same Cross.

As I stood in the main drag with Carmel, I watched a passing throng of dropouts ignore a girl drug addict in a filthy T-shirt as she sat huddled and shivering on a doorstep. There were sailors from the naval docks, there were glitter-eyed gays, there were the lonely old ladies going slowly to the fruit shops and delicatessens, there were snappy but frightened country boys living alone for the first time. And there were the strip-club bouncers and minders who bawled out to passers-by for their custom from the sex-stirring warmth of the tree-lined streets, where even the leaves rustled like skirts coming off.

We strolled into the air-conditioned comfort of a hotel for a drink. And, over the next hour I told Carmel all about the Cross and my early life here with Margo, Rosalie and Helen. She asked me would I show her all the places I'd mentioned and, deep down, I wanted to have a look again too.

We walked past the old haunts, many now with different names or totally different businesses, and finally arrived at the top of Roslyn Street. We walked down the footpath and stopped in front of the house where Margo and I used to live. It had been painted a different colour, but to me it was still the same. The memories as sweet and painful as ever and I had to turn my head and wipe tears from my eyes.

'Hi Margo!' I whispered as I finally walked away.

We decided it was time to move on not long after that. We'd head back north and live on the Gold Coast. I met with Paolo and told him of our plans. We could use his place in Surfers as long as we liked, he said. He would ring and make the arrangements. Then Paolo and I had another long and private discussion. I needed to straighten things out in myself, I told Paolo, which he understood. We promised to stay in touch. Then Carmel and I loaded up and headed off to Paolo's unit in The Sands.

On the outside, The Sands was gleaming white and modern, but in Paolo's unit the rooms were furnished in dark timbers and decorated with golden-tasselled drapes that made it look refined and old. There were reproductions of paintings by Gauguin and Van Gogh hanging on the walls. Thick pile carpet covered the floors throughout the whole place. And as well as air-conditioning there were ceiling fans in gilded metal with wood-grain paddles. We were up eighteen floors with a balcony view of the other high-rise towers, the swimming pool, the spray-hazed beach and surf. The day was sticky and hot when we arrived, so we turned on the air-conditioning, the fans, the stereo and the shower.

Carmel and I were lying in a couple of easy chairs on the balcony with a cool drink. I let my thoughts wander. I had started life as a simple country boy. I could have returned home to Mum and Dad Gee that day so many years back and told them I'd been fired. But I didn't, not because I had anything saintly in the way of a conscience but because I was still so green. Things had changed since then. In the last fifteen years I had seen death and destruction and war at first hand, had become part of an organisation where all I saw around me was affluence and corruption, dodgy politicians, gangsters, gambling club pay-offs, drug and prostitution pay-offs, rip-offs, square-ups, federal and state cops with their hands out, lawyers doing deals, real-estate scandals, thousands of acres of northern

New South Wales and south-east Queensland sown with marijuana from which the police took their percentage and then turned the other way. I was living in a great but lousy city, and I was here because I'd taken part in and helped organise all this corruption.

It was by my own choice. Perhaps my early years of hurt and maltreatment were the trigger, but it still boiled down to the fact that I was the one who wanted to be judge, jury and executioner to my own and other people's problems. I had developed an internal switch that I could turn on or off where conscience was concerned, and I made enough money to be able to take a holiday whenever I felt like it. The talents I possessed were worth money and the job was always there. As I lay here on the balcony, I had no regrets, and no illusions.

But when I am at a low ebb the whole thing sickens and disgusts me. I feel dirty. Who cares if the cops are on the take, that the politicians lie and cheat, that justice is not the same for all, that drugs are a roaring trade, as are gambling and sex? It's never going to stop, and my part in it won't matter one way or another. It's like I was a grain of sand in the desert. Apart from a giant cock-up, where I hadn't done my homework in Sydney, which I regret. I had never hurt anyone who didn't deserve it. It was they who had broken the code, and they knew the penalty. I like a laugh, and a drink, and a bet, and money in my pocket. But I still kept promising myself that one day I would really take off and be free, free of it all, and I'd go and find a spot with a beach of its own, somewhere way up north, pure and unspoilt ... right away from the corruption. Let the white sand and the blue water cleanse me, and I'll never see neon again or have to take care of the garbage.

Sometimes the frustration of my dream nagged at me like a toothache. Then I'd remember when, and how, the whole sordid business began. When, at the loss of Margo, in a rage so bitter and useless that I thought I'd go mad, I turned the key and opened another door and stepped through into a new life.

My mind flashed back to the days of Margo and her girls. How things had changed now. The girls back then made their money lying on their backs, but they had a code and they stuck to it. Now the organisation has changed all that. Hustlers and massage parlour girls are often hard-drug addicts. They lead lives these days that demand it, and have cash to pay. It follows that one of the steadiest sources of income for the organisation is the sale of drugs to its own girls. When they sign up the organisation may preach the benefits of big money and early retirement, but what their bosses actually seek is to control the women for years through feeding their habit.

Other users are of less interest, except for their money. The organisation actually despises them. All it wants is to make the women hustle to pay for their habit. When they get old or worn out or become too difficult, all it has to do is stop their supply of drugs. Women, or the gay men hustlers to whom this also happens, might find small flatettes, or serviced rooms in noisy rabbit-warren buildings. More often than not they literally work the streets, taking men in doorways and lavatories, and every so often the Vice Squad swoops and clears a few of them away to give the impression that they're doing their job. So far as the organisation is concerned these castaways and used-up chuck-outs must buy their drugs on the open market. Because they have ceased to be useful and finally proved that they're rubbish.

My reverie was broken by a couple of cleaning ladies. They were Poms, whingeing about the heat and saying that they were going back to England at the end of the month. They didn't like it here or Australia.

Fuck the Poms, I thought, and drifted off to sleep.

32

I WAS SITTING IN PAOLO'S UNIT WATCHING TELEVISION with Carmel when the phone rang. The first call that we had received.

It was Sam.

'Hey Jimmy, I need your help. Can you get here quick?' He gave me an address in Palm Beach, which I scribbled down.

'Got it Sam,' I said.

'*Bene amico*.' Then he said something that convinced me that it was urgent. '*Il guaio affrettarsi!*' [Get here quick. Trouble!]

I phoned for a cab and waited for it in the lobby.

'Visiting the dead are ya?' the driver asked when I gave him the address.

'Dead?'

'What's wrong with you mate?' he said. 'Can't you take a joke? The street's full of pissos, know what I mean?'

'Pissos?'

'Piss-head cases, mate. Winos.'

Music and commercials blasted from the transistor radio that hung from the rear-view mirror, and all the windows were down because the night was warm and steamy.

'A fit lookin' bloke like you has to want to get into

347

a bit of female company,' the cabbie said. 'I got some-thin'. If you say so I can take you to it. How long ya gonna be at Seventeenth Avenue?'

'Just fuckin' drive,' I said.

He screeched to a halt and turned in the seat to look at me. 'D'ya wanna get out?'

'I apologise,' I said sarcastically. 'I'm a New South Wales wanker. Now fuckin' drive on!'

He must have sensed something in my voice because he did so, and after that muttered about me in the third person. 'Fuckin' bloke's a real fuckin' bastard!' he said as he sped away from the towers and their shimmering reflections in the canals and marinas. We crossed the wide concrete bridge going south at Broadbeach, then slowed when we came to a sign that said Palm Beach.

At first there were substantial brick-and-tile homes with flash cars parked outside, but then the road surface deteriorated and the houses too, which were wood and fibro, many on short stumps, with overhanging trees brushing their corrugated-iron roofs. The telephone and electricity wires were overhead on poles. There were some cars parked on driveways but no people to be seen.

'Seventeenth Avenue,' said the driver. 'I've forgotten the number you wanted.'

I paid him off, not without a few muttered insults and obscenities on both sides, then quickly slipped into the shadows. The rear lights of the cab glided away from me. It was so quiet I could here the rustle of indi-vidual leaves as they moved in the warm evening breeze. Apart from that not even a cat moved.

I ducked through a yard a few houses before number 16 and circled around to the house. There were banana palms and the scent of frangipanni filled my nostrils, but it suddenly occurred to me that I made a perfect target and that I didn't have a gun on me . . . Shit! I'm slipping, Kurt would have hung his head in shame.

Something was wrong. In fact it was all wrong. I stood still in the shadows, but nothing moved. Staying where I was a few more minutes before I moved forward and banged on the door.

A light came on.

When the door opened I tripped on a broken step and almost fell in.

'Jesus!' said Sam, propping me up with a fist that held a can of beer.

He gave me a hug and then got wound up into a speech about how I should keep in touch even if I am having a break. He'd only just found out where I was.

'What the fuck's going on, Sam?'

'Some prick's been takin' potshots at us with a silencer. This is the second time in fuckin' two weeks.'

'Here?' I swayed back a little, poking just enough of my head round the door to look at the street. There were deep tropical shadows and an unbroken chorus of frogs, crickets and cicadas. I pushed past Sam, moved further into the house and nearly tripped arse over head again. There were paint and dust covers and old newspapers strewn everywhere and paint cans on the hall floor. Angelo grinned in recognition then pointed to the bright yellow paint that I'd just kicked over.

'Hi, mate,' I said, 'long time no see. What do you think of my work down there?' I pointed to the paint I'd just kicked over. Angelo just shrugged. Still can't speak I thought.

One of the girls who used the place and worked for a while as a hostess at the 21 Club came in, looking unexpectedly glamorous.

'Hi Jimmy!' she said as she dashed into the bathroom.

'Hi Jacqui,' I said to myself.

'I'm late for a client, love,' she shouted in the echo-like voice of someone looking into a mirror and doing her face.

I looked around, amazed by their normal, ignorant behaviour.

'Where's Eddy?' I asked Sam, referring to his right-hand man and driver. 'He should be bloody well here with you.'

'I sent him out to do the collections.'

'Christ, Sam! That wasn't real smart,' I said to him, *capo* or not.

Apart from Angelo's handiwork the house was shabby, as rented houses usually are, and had bizarre items of furniture including a dinner-gong, of all things, that must have once meant the world to someone.

'What the fuck are you doin' in this place, Sam?'

'We've been havin' a bit of trouble in Brisbane the last couple a days and we've only just got this joint, so I thought it was safe.'

'Where do you sleep?' I said.

'In there,' said Sam, pointing. 'What the fuck is goin' on Jimmy?'

'It's no good askin' me, Sam. You rang me. Remember? I can't believe you've got no back-up here or that Eddy's not with you.'

'He's doin' the collections, movin' from house to house. He's gonna get a couple of people for security too.'

350

I went through to the rear of the house. Old insect screen doors opened onto a verandah and the garden.

'Has he phoned in?' I asked.

'Why would he phone?' said Sam. 'He said he'd only be half an hour or so.'

'Well how long has he been gone now?'

A look of uncertainty swept across Sam's face and then he hung his head down. ' 'Bout two hours, Jimmy, so I made a couple of calls and found you.'

'Who did you tell that you'd be staying here?'

'No one. It was a spur of the moment thing, you know. Christ, you know me better than that.'

'Well I don't like it one little bit. It stinks.'

Jacqui appeared again, drawn by the confused tone of our voices.

'What's up?' she said.

'Just answer me one question,' I said. 'Did you tell anyone that Sam was staying here?'

'You bastard,' she said.

'Look, cut the crap and answer the fuckin' question, Jacqui. Did you say anything to anybody?'

'No!'

'Jacqui, don't fuckin' lie to me. This is vital. We could be in deep shit right here and now.'

They all stared at me. There was a beer commercial on the TV, a lot of men guffawed and leered at a scantily clad barmaid. Sam's desperate face swung this way and that.

'You'd better explain this!' he said to Jacqui. 'You better say right now what the story is!'

'Its fuckin' trouble,' I cut in. 'That's what the story is. You've been set up.'

Then the doorbell rang.

'Is that Eddy?' Sam asked. 'What's happening, Eddy?' he yelled.

'It's my taxi,' said Jacqui, running back to the bathroom. 'Tell him to wait for two minutes.'

'You can't go now!' Sam said.

'It's a client!' she yelled out.

Angelo opened the front door and we heard him grunt, then try to shout an alarm. Afterwards I swore to myself that I heard the sound of the shots fired through the silencer, but I'm not sure that I did. What I do know is that I saw Angelo collapse backwards, that I wondered why he'd fallen, and that as he tried to get up blood spattered loudly from his mouth onto the newspaper-covered floor. I knew then.

I know that Sam yelled something incoherent in the back of his throat and rummaged in his bag on the floor. I know that my training and instinct had my hand flick the lounge-room light off, and that as Jacqui came out of the bathroom she was too shocked to even scream at Angelo as he writhed like a landed fish.

Then the petrol bomb came through the window in a crash of glass and landed at Jacqui's feet. It was a milk bottle with a burning rag in it, and it didn't even break. It rolled with unbelievable slowness, and as it did so flaming liquid spilt everywhere and Jacqui's clothes caught fire.

She made gasping panicky noises and ran into the kitchen, where I heard her bang wildly and scream as she tried to open the door.

Sam tried to run through the inferno to help her, but a shot from the front door hit him in the head and sent him flying. He was dead before he hit the floor. I knew by the way he fell. God no, not my friend Sam. The gun he'd been holding flew from his hand and I grabbed it, feeling the pain of my movements as though they were in the distance, and my arm not a part of me.

Then the second petrol bomb crashed into the room and there was the stink of gasoline and a roar as it shattered and sent flames everywhere. I heard Jacqui's animal howls far away and there was fire all around me, even around the television picture as the old wooden cabinet burnt. I plunged towards the screen doors at the back, and as I opened them a bullet ripped through the gauze. In the light of the fire I saw the silhouette of a man and I ran at him, shooting as I went down the verandah steps. He staggered or maybe he didn't. I couldn't be sure.

Then I hurtled through bushes and across raggedy lawns, stumbling once and getting up again as thorns dragged at my clothes. I heard other branches whip and swish behind me and I knew that someone was in pursuit.

As I ducked along the wall of a wooden shed, bullets splintered into it with a slapping sound. On an impulse I dropped to my hands and knees, turned around and dog crawled for about ten yards or so, then got up and ran through the deep shadows. There was a sudden pain in my side. Bloody stitch, I thought. Then fences blocked my way and I ducked along them until I came to a house with the back door open.

I ran into a big kitchen where a family was watching television as they ate their evening meal out of foil containers. The TV set was tuned into the show I had just seen wreathed in flames, except the picture had been better there. The old man of the family stared at me, gravy dripping from his fork.

'You want to fix that fine-tuner mate,' I said, my chest snatching at breaths, and then trotted through the house and out the front door. I ran downhill along deserted streets, trying to keep on the grass verges to muffle my steps until I came to a deserted supermarket car park. Beyond it was a brightly lit bowling club lawn, and the main highway.

I was dizzy and soaked in sweat as I paused for breath. The white-clad evening bowlers moved about slowly as though nothing had happened and I thought I'll borrow their phone and call a cab. Then I saw a bus pulling up at a stop and I staggered towards it. The bus doors hissed open and I got in.

The driver looked at me strangely.

'No trouble is there, mate?' he said.

I shook my head, sat down and hid my face until the bus had travelled several blocks.

Then I sat up and looked at my reflection in the window. My sweatiness was disgusting, my sleeve was torn and I had some bumps and scratches. Then I panicked a little because of the gun. I should have it. I looked around wildly. My side hurt me. Bloody stitch. Relax. You threw the gun away. I did? Where? I couldn't remember.

Why won't this stitch go away? Why am I sticky there? Then I realised it wasn't a stitch. It was a bullet wound in my left side, and I was soaked in blood and hurting like buggery.

Oh Jesus, where am I? Where are we going?

I closed my eyes but I heard Jacqui's cries and saw her silly dress and shoes on fire. I smelt petrol, retched without anything coming up and clung to the chrome back of the seat in front of me. I pressed the side of my head against the cool of the window glass. The bus hit a bump and jogged me painfully.

I looked at the destination card on the bus and realised that I'd made a fool of myself. It was a Surfside service, and after the Broadbeach stop and a couple of set-downs it wasn't going anywhere except back around the circuit again.

The driver's eyes were watching me in his large mirror. He wore glasses and had a half-grown mousy beard. Had he seen the blood? Why hadn't I seen it? What did he think? Keep your wits, I thought. Find help, your own help. Keep your bloody self together.

But I couldn't. Shock was setting in. I was too shocked, and waves of pain and nausea swept over me and knocked me out. When I woke I was stiff and shivering, slumped down near the window, but clear enough in my head to realise I was the centre of attention. I looked up. Seven or eight people were staring at me.

From the bus driver's pale and apologetic face I worked out that he had stopped the vehicle when we reached the Broadbeach stop, gone to the police station and summoned the huge lantern-jawed sergeant whose big paw was on my shoulder. His grey eyes were about as friendly as a couple of dumdum bullets.

My next clear memory is of a cubicle in the Southport Hospital Casualty Department. I lay on a trolley and stared at the ceiling light. The screen curtain rustled and instruments rattled. I heard shuffling of rubber-soled shoes, a cough, and voices, but I had no idea of how long I'd been there. A doctor cut my clothes away with scissors and looked at my wound. She was slim and bronzed, a cheerful woman of about thirty with her hair tucked neatly under a surgical cap and a gold pendant on a chain round her neck.

'Christ!' she said as we all stared at the blood-caked bullet tear above my hipbone. 'However did you do this, mmmm, fall off a bar stool?'

I grinned weakly. The big sergeant sat the wrong way round on a tubular steel chair, his muscular arms folded along its back and his jaw resting on them.

The doctor took an alcohol swab and went to work.

'All joking aside,' the sergeant said. 'What would you say that was?'

'I'd say what we have here, Sergeant Harris, is a bullet wound. In fact I'd stake my career on it.'

'So would I, doctor,' Harris said. He picked my jacket up off the floor and poked a sausage-sized finger through the hole the bullet had left. He wiggled the finger at me. 'Now what's your story and opinion sir?' He gave the finger another wiggle for emphasis.

I pretended to be in pain and let forth with a low groan. They managed to draw a bit out of me, but it was anything but the truth.

I was shocked at what I'd seen happen to Sam and Angelo and Jacqui, and ashamed that I hadn't been able to save Sam. Weary, feverish and troubled, I knew I needed to confide. I needed to tell Paolo or Carlo what I had witnessed. Heads would roll, then.

But I couldn't talk. I realised that. How could I talk to the police about drug dealers and drug fights, about petrol bombs and my own shots at a man in the garden? And I couldn't tell them that a good percentage of everybody else in their position closed their bloody eyes to corruption. So why didn't they stop asking me questions? No one else was going to get excited about it.

They treated me and humoured me as if I was a child and tucked me into bed. The doctor slid a needle into me that relaxed me and jumbled my thoughts. Who's responsible for this hit? Why Sam? And I thought of a dark-headed hooker named Jacqui in flames. Why the fuck did I have to climb onto that fuckin' bus. Jesus, I'm getting too old for this shit. I'm not in good nick, must be slipping. If Kurt were still alive I could go to the farm. Got to get a message to Carmel. Can't tell the fuckin' cops. Fuck it, stop moaning.

When I woke up it was broad daylight but not late. I could feel the morning cool. I could hear traffic outside in the street and the sun made irregular patterns on the ceiling of the ward. The sheets were fresh and I felt clean and washed.

I moved my head. I was in some kind of side ward and the other two beds were empty. After making a few tentative movements I felt headachy and a little stiff but not bad. Then I heard a sniff and a throat being cleared and saw there was a policeman sitting in the corridor, next to the doorway. I got up out of bed and staggered slightly, but by holding onto the bed I kept myself upright. I took a deep breath and stepped out for the door.

The young constable stood up. 'Good day. Where do ya reckon you're off to?'

'Goin' to have a piss,' I said.

He walked me to the toilet, holding onto my elbow, and as I held my cock and the golden stream flowed out of me I felt bloody ridiculous. Then he walked me back to my bed, still holding my elbow.

'Thanks a lot Constable,' I said. 'Much obliged. Have you been on here all night?'

'No way. I've only been here since six.'

'What did they tell you? Have you got any orders?'

'Just to keep an eye on you,' he said, 'and not to answer any of your questions.'

He gave me a lopsided grin and went back to his chair.

'Hey, where are my clothes and things?' I yelled to him.

'Your shoes and socks and jacket are in the locker there. The rest had to be chucked out. They were covered in blood and shit weren't they?'

'Am I free to discharge myself?'

'Yeah sure. But leave the pyjamas behind . . . they're hospital property.'

'Fuckin' bastards,' I thought. Then a nurse came breezing in. She propped me up with pillows and gave me breakfast on a tray. There was also a newspaper there and the headline read: 'THREE DIE IN PALM BEACH BLAZE.'

According to the story, neighbours who called the fire brigade to 17th Avenue, Palm Beach, said that the occupants of number 16 had been painting and decorating recently. The tragic circumstances all pointed to an accident with turps and cleaning fluid. The house was completely gutted and contained the badly charred bodies of a young woman and two men.

Inquiries had revealed that the house was being rented for the holiday season by Jacqui Wallace, a hotel and bar hostess. Well that's one way of putting it, I thought. A vehicle outside the house was registered in New South Wales to a Mr Angelo Trimboli of Griffith and his body was thought to be one of those found in the living room of the house.

The second male body had so far still not been identified. Neighbours described him as being cheerful and friendly and probably of Mediterranean extraction. But he had only been at the address for a day or so.

The chief of the Gold Coast fire station was then credited with some stern words about the dangers of smoking while cleaning paint brushes, and that was it. Not a word or even a hint of gunshots or foul play.

I couldn't believe it. It was bullshit, crazy. Something was not quite right. There were other fingers in the pie here and I decided to get out. When the nurse next appeared to dress my wound I told her I wanted some clothes.

'Sure, okay!' she said.

'There's money in my wallet in my jacket.'

'I know,' she said and took some. She promised to be back in an hour or so.

That was 8 o'clock. Two hours later the young constable was relieved by a colleague and at 12 'Son of Kong' Harris appeared with a pair of cotton slacks, underpants and a white-sleeved shirt in a plastic shopping bag.

'Here,' he said, passing them to me. 'Do you want to put these on?'

'Fuckin' oath I do.'

He grunted and as I dressed he affected to ignore me and read the paper. Here it comes I said to myself.

'I don't suppose you know anything about this?' he said, tapping the front page.

'What am I supposed to have done ... burnt the fuckin' house down?'

'Two of the victims were known to the police and had criminal records.'

'So?'

'Well there is also the matter of a person who was detained not far from the premises with an unlicensed concealable firearm in his possession.'

'Look!' I said. 'I told you last night I heard a bang and something hit me in the side. I didn't see anybody. I can't be of any further use to you.'

'Do you know a person by the name of Terrence William Fraser?'

'Never heard of him.'

'Of course not,' Harris said. 'I suppose you think that this place being the backwater that it is and me only being a uniformed sergeant of police means I'm not up to an inquiry of this nature. Maybe you think defective brake lights are more my line of work?'

I just did up my fly and remained silent.

'What I mean is this,' he continued. 'I don't imagine for one moment that you'd wish to hinder or impede the inquiry, would you?'

I still said nothing.

'That's why if I was in your shoes I'd be tempted to

360

say my piece for my own safety. Know what I mean?'

'Thanks for the concern,' I said, tucking in my shirt carefully around my wound. 'I'm discharging myself.'

Harris nodded and I set off for the door. He stuck out a giant foot. I stumbled over it and banged against an empty bed. Gasping as pain knifed through my side, I dragged myself upright and sat on the edge of the bed. Harris grimaced and took out his notebook.

'Before you go,' he said, 'there's one or two questions I'd like to ask.'

I waited. He held his notebook at arm's length and scribbled something. Bastard needs glasses, I thought.

'Do you know a person by the name of Angelo Trimboli?'

'No, I do not.'

'Mmmmmmm,' he said and scribbled some more. 'Are you the licensed owner of a motor vehicle.'

It was no good denying that, so I told him the number and the make. Then he asked me where I was staying and I told him that too.

'And you are not prepared to give a written statement or make a formal complaint concerning the gunshot wound?'

'No I'm not. I don't know who did it, I couldn't identify them even if you put me face to face with them. I just want out of here.'

He closed his notebook and put it away, carefully buttoning the flap of his shirt pocket and deliberately pushing the pen in beside it, then looking up at me.

'I'd watch my step if I were you,' he said. 'These are nasty people you're dealing with.'

'I'm not dealing with any bloody body!'

'Okay. You can go. We'll probably want a word with you again.'

Not if I can help it, I thought.

I asked the reception desk to get me a cab, and as I sat in it on the way back to Surfers I thought of the name. Terrence William Fraser.

When Carmel found out that I had been wounded she really freaked.

'Please, Jimmy, give it up and let's go away again,' she pleaded. 'I don't care where we go or what we do. Just let's get away.'

I promised her that I would, but not just yet. One of my friends had been murdered and I had an obligation to avenge his death. I asked her to trust me and promised that we'd go away soon. She seemed to calm down a bit and looked at me.

'Promise?' she said.

I kissed her. 'Soon, I promise.'

I met Carlo and we walked along the beach at Surfers.

'Jimmy, you've got to find this fuckin' cocksucker for me. I don't care what it takes or what you got to do. I want his head. You understand? You can write your own ticket on this one. I know Sam was your friend too, but you'll be well looked after. Now, what do you need?'

I told Carlo what I needed.

'Right,' he said. 'You got it. You'll have it by tonight.'

Carlo was true to his word. The gun and silencer, lockpicks and stuff were delivered that night. Carmel and I drove up to Brisbane for Sam's funeral and after a short stay at the wake we returned to Surfers.

For the next two days I used all that I could to locate Eddy Molloy and my search paid off. I found out where he was living. He had apparently had the unit secretly for nearly six months. It was the police contact numbers that Carlo had sent down with the other stuff that did the job. All I had to do was sit back while they did the detection and legwork for me.

I parked at the end of the street and walked past the boatyard to the unit block. I looked around. All was quiet and magical in the city of lights and water.

According to the information I had received, Eddy was a poofter and had a few camp associates living in the same block. Remembering the unit number of one of these gay blokes, I pressed the entry-phone button.

'Yes?' a voice lisped.

'You don't know me,' I said, 'but I'm a Qantas steward and Bruce gave me your address.'

'Cheeky young devil!' said the voice. The buzzer went and I was in.

I rode up to Eddy's apartment and pressed the bell. No reply, not even the faint noise of a man placing himself on alert. I rang again. Still no reply, not even the sound of bare feet coming to the security eye in the door.

I opened the lock with a couple of picks and slammed it back hard and fast in case he was behind it. He wasn't. The place was empty, although I knew at once from the smells of habitation that he hadn't been gone long. I closed the door and looked around.

A quick search of the place revealed a large bundle of bank notes under the mattress. I broke the thick wad

363

into two and stuck them in my pockets. I noticed the soiled sheets, the tubs of ice-cream in the freezer, the filthy clothes soaking in the bottom of the shower, the drugs and the syringes and the confusion.

I checked all the light-switches and planned where I'd wait and make him sit, and I took up my position in the kitchen. I could not be seen from the front door and had my hand on the switch for the hall light.

My side was still sore and aching and I had a bad moment when I thought I might fall asleep or that Eddy might not return at all. Stop it, I said to myself, he's gotta come back. He's got no choice. The drugs and the money would guarantee that.

Suddenly I heard the lift. Then a key rattled and the door opened. There was light from the outside hall and, after a click, in the hallway of the unit. The front door closed and in that instant, hoping that his hand was not still on the lock, I flicked off the light.

'Don't move,' I said in the darkness. 'If you do I'll blow your fuckin' head off where you stand.'

'Who is it?' he said.

'The Tiger,' I said, stepping out so he knew that I could see him in silhouette. 'Go into the living room.'

'Okay, man,' he said. 'How are you? I've never heard of you.'

'Sit down in the upright chair.'

He did so, and the light from the street fell on him as I had planned. I stayed in the shadows of the hallway.

'What have I done? Are you sore at me or somethin'?'

'Why Sam, Eddy?'

'Shit! I know who you are. Long time no see, man.'

364

'Why Sam, Eddy?'

'I had to do it, man. I couldn't trust anyone who worked with him. He wouldn't listen. He wouldn't take Terry Fraser's deal. He kept saying nah, we'll stay with Trimboli, it's safer. I had too much to protect. They paid me real well to unload their stuff. I got hooked myself and Sam would have shot me if he'd found out. Christ, man, you know what they're like. They don't trust no one, man, that takes a shot with the needle. I suppose I'm not too late now to do a deal?'

'Maybe not,' I said, 'Where's Fraser, Eddy?'

'Christ, man, give me a chance and I'll help ya. He's down in Sydney.'

'Who's backing him?'

'Bobby Bradshaw.'

'Where is he now?'

'Singapore. Still in Singapore. Listen, is this visit for them or you?'

'Neither.'

'Neither?'

'It's for the Tiger.'

'Don't give me a lot of crap, man. Who's the Tiger?'

'You'll find out, Eddy.'

'Come on, man, what do you want? I've got a good stash of coke in the cupboard. It's yours.'

He was unshaven and lined, and he had lost a fair bit of weight. If he was shooting up as hard as it seemed he probably hadn't slept for a while. There were blotches on his face and his eyes glittered.

'I need a shot, man.'

He shifted in the chair. He was wearing a lightweight leather jacket and sneakers. Fantasy gear, I thought.

Tonight he's Brando in the movies. When he jams in the needle he's whoever he wants to be and everything's true.

'Have you really got a gun there?' he said.

I let him see it in the light.

'I don't need this,' he said.

'Yes you do. This is the last Big Dipper.'

He stood up but I jabbed the gun towards him and he sat down again, snarling.

'Look, if there's a deal, say what it is.'

'Seventeenth Avenue, Eddy. It was you who rang the doorbell, you who set up Sam. When Angelo answered you shot him and threw the bombs in. I was there, Eddy. I'd gone to see what the trouble was about and I saw Jacqui burn. I saw Sam and Angelo die, and I've got a bullet wound in my side that you gave me.'

He laughed an addict's pitying laugh.

'It wasn't just me. Terry was there, he did most of the shootin'. I just rang the bell and took care of Angelo and chucked the Molotovs in.'

'Yeah, Eddy, but the Tiger hasn't forgotten.'

He gave me a twisted smile. 'Tell me one more thing . . . smartarse.'

'What, Eddy?'

'Who is this Tiger?'

'The Tiger's the killer,' I said and pulled the trigger.

Four weeks later I was down in Sydney. Information had been received, plans made. Paolo had seen to all that. He got hold of the information, the weapons I said would be needed and a uniform. 'Who do you want to ride with you on this one?' he asked me.

'Joe Petracci and Bart Olivera,' I said to him, his best men.

He looked at me for a moment and then said, 'You've got them.'

Joe, Bart and I sat down that night and went over the plans with a fine tooth comb. We left at 4 the next morning, heading for Berowra.

I was watching the steel and glass checking station that stands alone on a side road where the tollway comes through the cuttings and across the forest-banked arms of the Hawkesbury River. It is where you first get a hint that you're getting close to the city . . . a suburban railway station, aluminium streetlights, service station petrol pumps and a house or two.

On each side of the tollway scrubby ridges roll towards the horizon . . . and the tops were touched with brightness by the newly rising sun. As I waited with Joe Petracci, grasshoppers whirred, light glared and reflected off the rocky outcrops, and even at that time there was the irritating sweat-prickling heat that I hated.

Heat makes men snap, even when they look as cool in their shirtsleeves as Bart Olivera did as he carried a clipboard that looked absurd in his street-fighter's fists. I was standing concealed with Joe among the gum trees behind the parking area. We both had high-velocity weapons, L2Als 7.62 calibre, an automatic version of the SLR but with the bipods removed and replaced by conventional SLR front stocks. The two transport officials were tied and gagged inside the station. Bart lifted the clipboard in a prearranged signal, and when the truck came into sight things happened very quickly.

With much diesel roaring and hissing of vacuum brakes, the truck slowed down and came to the strip road, turned off the tollway to the right and headed for the checking station. Bart strolled out casually so he could command the driver's-side door. The truck halted under the checking station's canopy. Bart looked up at the driver's brown complexioned face and realised it was the man he had been warned to expect, the petty drug dealer and part-time gunman Terrence William Fraser.

In the same instant Fraser recognised Bart, slammed the truck into gear and stood on the gas.

The truck began to pull away. Bart shouted and waved his arms as he ran towards the front in a brave effort of bluff, hoping to stop it. Fraser made no attempt to avoid him and the 16-wheeler rolled over him and began to pull away.

'Now!' I shouted to Joe, and we opened up from behind the gum trees.

Bullets slammed into the truck's tyres and they blew. Wheel rims screamed as they came into contact with the road. The truck swerved and skidded, with Fraser still trying to accelerate and control it, plunging away from the checking station, through the metal barriers and across all four lanes of the highway. It smashed into the far barrier, rolled on its side and came to a rest among the trees.

We kept firing. Bullets clanged into metal and ripped through branches. Then we stopped.

Almost at once Fraser stumbled out of the undamaged side of the cab, clutching a case under his arm. He was wearing jeans and a white T-shirt and ducked into the scrub and trees on our side.

Joe fired another burst. The bullets hit the gas tank and the truck exploded into flames that danced across the highway following the spilt liquid.

Fraser was running a little to the right of me, still carrying his briefcase. I put the scope on him, let it drop to his buttocks area and touched the trigger in a five-round burst.

The 7.62s slammed into Fraser's pelvic area, pushing him violently forward onto his face. I tapped Joe on the shoulder and we raced over. Fraser was lying where he had fallen with his head on one side, his piggy eyes watching as we approached. His hips and pelvis were smashed. Joe and I stood there looking at him.

'For Sam, Angelo and Jacqui you fuckin' dog,' I said, and spat on him.

Joe and I fired together and ripped him apart. One more score was settled.

Bradshaw was still to come, but not long afterwards he was found with his throat cut in a back alley in Singapore.

33

TWO DAYS AFTER WE'D DISPOSED OF FRASER WE WERE back at The Sands. Carmel was out shopping and I was watching the news on the television. A picture came on to show a wrecked and burnt-out truck and, much to my amusement, there were police officers and firemen standing around with their hands on their hips. There were close-ups of bullet holes and of blood on the road.

'Berowra Heavy Vehicle Checking Station, New South Wales,' hammered the voice, 'where, two days ago, two men who were known to the police as drug smugglers died. The vehicle inspection officers were overpowered shortly before by three armed men in balaclavas, who drove up in a stolen vehicle. The inspectors were tied up and placed in the storeroom of the office over there in the inspection station.' A close-up of the office and storeroom. 'It has been established that one of the attackers, dressed in the uniform of a vehicle inspector, was crushed to death under the truck.' Another shot of the truck. 'Did the killers have a Queensland connection? Who tipped them off that cocaine was being carried? Could it be, as this program was informed by phone today by an anonymous caller, that police tipped them off. Could it have been established dealers eager to use the law to wipe out competition?'

The picture changed and the reporter was now in the picture . . . a brash young man in shirtsleeves. He was standing outside what must have been a government office block. As the camera pulled back he thrust a hand mike towards a smartly suited, quick-blinking man of about forty-five. John Fadden, Minister for Justice.

'Could this happen, Minister?' barked the reporter. 'Could one criminal gang use police information to wipe out another?'

Fadden listened politely, but with a smile that implied that the young man was an impetuous fuckwit.

'I'd say that the police would act on any information that they received, but not as you suggest,' he said.

'What was the source of the Sydney tollway information?'

'You'd have to ask the officers concerned.'

'I have. They won't tell me.'

'Quite right too. You journalists won't reveal your sources either.'

Fadden flicked an eye at the camera, as if to say that's shown the young whippersnapper. But all it did was make the reporter more indignant.

'Could a police source be corrupt?' he said.

'Corrupt?' said Fadden, as though he didn't understand the word.

'Could corrupt officers, themselves, be a party to drug smuggling?'

'No. Categorically no. That's a disgusting allegation.'

Fadden looked the reporter full in the eye. The young man swallowed but battled on.

'Have politicians and police never been involved with organised crime in this country?'

'Would you like to name names?' asked Fadden.

'There are surely many instances of gambling casinos operating in flagrant defiance of the law?'

'Not to my knowledge.'

'Would you say that big-time criminals who buy protection for gambling and prostitution might also seek it for drug operations?'

'I've no evidence of protection for anything,' Fadden said. 'Have you?'

The reporter opened his mouth but did not speak.

'Because if you have,' Fadden said a bit prissily, like a headmaster at a P & C meeting, 'it's your duty to give it to me, since I am one of the Crown's law officers.'

'In other words,' the reporter ground on, 'your department has no worries at all that criminal organisations might be able to buy themselves protection?'

So far both men had entered into the spirit of the hammer-and-tongs ritual that every viewer expects. But Fadden decided to break the mood.

'Robert,' he said, as though the reporter was his favourite pupil, 'I've always respected you and we've had some fair and square tussles in the past, but this is sheer sensational journalism.'

The reporter tried to speak but Fadden held up his hand.

'Last week,' he said, 'your program criticised my department for being too eager to prosecute hippies who grow drugs for what they allege to be their own religious use. Today you want me to admit to softness towards drug criminals. Come on, Robert. Where's you consistency?'

'Same as everybody's, mate!' I shouted, 'It's where his money is!'

A new Commissioner of Police was appointed in Queensland and things started to change. The papers were full of it. A few heads rolled and a few coppers pulled their heads in. From the word go the new commissioner made it perfectly clear that he intended to crack down on crime, especially the organised variety. He wasn't a local, he'd been pulled in from the outside, he was a disciplinarian and he wanted action.

About a month after his appointment, at about 12.30 one afternoon there was a loud banging on the door. It was four hard-arsed coppers, uniform boys.

'Is your name James Diamond?' the leader of the pack asked.

It was useless denying it. 'Yeah, you've got it right.'

'We have a warrant here to search this apartment.' He produced it and gave it to me.

They found a 9 mm Beretta, ammunition and a silencer. The leader of the pack, Barnes was his name, came on real strong telling me what a bastard I was and accusing me of every single unsolved crime he could bring to mind. I remained silent throughout his tirade. Just watching him weigh the Beretta in his hand.

After he had shown his nasty streak Barnes became quite pally, as some of them often do. He and his off-sider drove me to the police station, where I was allowed to phone a solicitor who was known to me. Then we sat in an office with a cup of tea and chatted. The gist of his conversation was that a lot of outsiders criticise the Queensland Police, but to him it seemed to clean up a darn sight more crime than the New South Wales Police did. They were going to be given wider powers to crack down on organised crime, and there lay my problem. At the same time, he confided, it was my one great advantage.

'I mean, what are these firearm charges, Jimmy? If you ask me, I'd say it was a bargaining position you're in. You talk and put them in a position to clean up a few things and they'll drop the charges.'

'Is that strictly official?' I asked.

'Official . . . what do you mean?'

'I mean, is that what they told you to say?'

'Look, Jimmy, all I'm doing here is having a friendly chat, mate. You know what I mean?'

I knew what he meant all right. He sniffed and cleared his throat, then made circles with his thumbs as he leant on the table with his fingers knitted together. He threw me what was meant to be a subtle glance as he changed the subject to the holidays he'd taken up in Cairns. Then we heard the sound of voices in the outer offices, and heavy feet on the lino-covered floor.

'That'll be them now!' said Barnes, and stood up to greet the two detectives from Brisbane. One was tall, flabby and had a huge beer gut; the other was wiry and wearing tailored slacks and a floral shirt. Both sweated a lot and smelt strongly of beer.

'How are you, Peter, you old bastard?' said the flabby one. 'Is this the famous Mister Jimmy Diamond we've been hearing so much about? How ya doin'. I'm a Sergeant O'Reilly and this is Senior Constable Sid Baker.'

'Good day,' said Baker.

I just nodded and said 'Yeah.'

'The way that Sid and I see this, we don't reckon we'll have too much trouble, do you? What's your defence? That this gun's a set-up I suppose? In that case who do you reckon put it there? Little Red Riding Hood? That's about where we should start, don't you reckon? And, of course, we've also got the silencer, know what I mean?'

'No I don't,' I said. 'What are you on about?'

'You'll soon see what we mean. No trouble at all. She'll be right, mate. No sweat.'

'Got a beer around somewhere, Peter?' asked Baker. 'Christ it's hot.'

'Jesus, no. Not in here, Sid,' Barnes said, 'Not with the new super snooping around doing snap inspections.'

'Fuck it then!' said O'Reilly. 'We'll just stroll across to the pub, what d'you reckon?'

'Yeah, that's the move,' Baker said.

'Sound all right to you, Jimmy?'

I thought I'd seen a few class acts in my time, but these two really took the cake. They're both fuckin' mental and dangerous.

'I said does that sound all right to you, Diamond?'

'No it doesn't,' I said. 'I'm staying put.'

'What?' said Baker. 'What did he say?'

'Tell you the truth, Sid, I didn't catch every word. But I think he's askin' for a smack in the kidneys.'

'Kidneys?'

'Kidneys,' repeated O'Reilly. 'Your famous old steak and kidney.'

'My old steak and kidney, oh yeah!' Baker said, half-laughing and shaking his head.

'Not a mark to show as evidence in the courtroom.' O'Reilly started chuckling. 'But you'll be fuckin' pissin' blood for a week.'

Old steak and kidney. Piss blood for a fuckin' week.

'Bullshit,' I said, 'Who are you guys tryin' to con? You're a couple of Rhodes Scholars spruiking prose.'

O'Reilly lifted his left leg, stood for a moment like a circus elephant, and farted.

Baker sniffed. 'I still prefer them with the right leg in the air.'

Barnes stared at them. They unnerved and worried him and I saw in his deadpan sternness the reason why they were in plain-clothes attached to the CIB but he would always remain in uniform.

'If you appreciate prose, Jimmy, I reckon you should be game to knock back a couple of quick ones. What do you say?' said Baker.

'Just a friendly chat over a couple of beers,' O'Reilly chipped in.

They were shooting me smiles but their eyes weren't smiling, they looked cold. I felt that if they got me outside the station and away from the uniform boys who were witnesses, there was no telling what this pair of bastards might do.

'I appreciate the offer,' I told them, 'but the fact is that I'm waiting for my lawyer to turn up.'

'We reckon we could save you all that expense you know,' O'Reilly said. 'Don't you, Sid? Couldn't we?'

'Yep we certainly could,' Baker said.

'We might not have to proceed with these charges at all,' O'Reilly added.

'I'm still going to stay put,' I said. 'Out of politeness

and self-preservation, and wait for my barrister. Know what I mean?'

They stared at me. Barnes cleared his throat.

'Politeness?' O'Reilly asked.

'Self-preservation? What bloody barrister?' echoed Baker.

'It's Jeffrey Ballard.'

'Ballard . . . the fucking QC?'

O'Reilly was so angry he walked into the corridor and kicked the wall.

'Fuckin' Ballard,' he said as he came back. 'This is right out of our bloody league now, Diamond. This is Detective Chief Inspector crap right from day one.'

Baker stepped up to me and cuffed me around the back of the head.

'Bastard!' he said. 'We could have had a quiet chat and pulled you out of all this shit. All ya had to do was give us a couple of names and something to go on.'

'No,' I said. 'I don't think you could have done anything except attend the funeral.'

There was a moment of complete silence.

'So what are you going to do boys?' Barnes asked. 'You going to charge him?'

I noticed for the first time how blotchy and puffy O'Reilly's face was, how small and close together were his eyes . . . and yet quick and cunning as they glinted and computed the odds for and against bail against a signed statement, guilty pleas against reduced charges and a fine, him up against his superiors, and their need to have more knowledge about organised crime against what knowledge I possessed and could use as a bargaining point to save my skin.

'Sid,' he said, 'we've got no option, I think we'll just charge him.'

Which they did in a rapid and perfunctory manner. I felt as though I had just got married. My status had changed, but I didn't know how disastrously.

'If I get the constable to keep his eye on our friend Diamond here,' Barnes said, 'maybe we could slip across and have a couple before you take your prisoner away.'

'We'd better take it easy, I reckon,' said Baker.

'Yeah, you hit that right on the button, Sid. What's Ballard doing, driving down from Brisbane now is he?'

I nodded and said 'Yep.'

O'Reilly looked at his watch. 'Shit, if it's Ballard it'll be a bail and negotiate a deal job. We'd better hang on here till he arrives.'

'No sense in standing around here though like a stale bottle of piss. We can wait across the road,' said Baker.

And that's just what they did, O'Reilly rolling and wide-arsed and Baker neat and tidy in his slacks and floral shirt. Barnes joined them shortly afterwards when he had locked me away in a cell with serious and grim thoughts, and my urgent need to see Jeffrey Ballard.

The cells weren't air-conditioned and were steamy and hot. They weren't that modern either, constructed from concrete and stuck on the back of the old stone police building. They smelt of piss and disinfectant and dead hopes. There was a bench to sit on and a bucket for a lavatory, and some graffiti that had resisted all efforts to remove it. I LOVE JENNY and FUCK THE COPS and GEORGE 15-2-73. I was buggered and tired and aching and I must have dozed off a little, so the constable had to bang on the door to let me know that Ballard had arrived. Lurid tropical twilight poured in through the window.

Jeffrey Ballard was a Queensland legend—a stubborn civil rights battler as well as a famous heavy operator in criminal cases and early plea deals. I had only seen him a couple of times to nod at, and wasn't prepared for his confidence or his impatience as we summed each other up over the interview table.

He was of medium height and a bit thin, about fifty years old, with slender hands that had nicks and scars from gardening or some other hobby, short grey hair, and piercing dark eyes with black brows.

'Hello,' he said, 'I'm Jeffrey Ballard. Carlo tells me that you're hot shit and don't come unstuck too easy.'

'How is he?' I said.

'Great. He sends his regards.' As Ballard spoke I realised that his hands were moving about under the table top as he searched for electrical bugs.

'Seems clear,' he said. He put his gold-rimmed glasses on and took a large pad out of his case. 'My knowledge of the matter is cursory. I haven't got all the facts. Why don't you fill me in, starting at the beginning?'

So I did. I told him the cops, as he must have known, were coming down hard on the organisations. How they had me in their sights I had no ideas. It was probably a case of loose lips sink ships . . . that my name had been dropped by someone. How they'd banged on the door with a warrant, found the gun, ammo and silencer and here I was. How the coppers had hinted that I could walk if I gave them names and something to go on. How they gave me the impression that they knew a lot more about me than they were letting on. Somebody must have done a lot of blabbing, because I hadn't rung and invited them around.

When I had finished Ballard took off his glasses. 'If you want my opinion, and it is Carlo's also, somebody *has* given your name to the police as a swap for something else. What do you want me to do?'

'I'd have thought that was pretty obvious. Get me out.'

'Bail?'

'Sure.'

'So you and your people can chase around and find the party responsible for putting you in here? That would really give the police something to go on, wouldn't it?'

I said nothing.

'Jimmy, do you realise what strife you're in? You're charged with having in your possession an unregistered, concealable firearm and a silencer that fits it. In this state that's a mandatory minimum twelve-month sentence. That's what it's all about. Your complete co-operation or gaol.'

'Can't we say that it was planted during the search? That's what I've already stated.'

'We can't take that to court unless we can prove it. Look, I can tell you this, it has come to my knowledge that there are some police in Brisbane who think you're right for quite a number of other matters, and not only in this state. I think you know what I'm implying.'

'We could produce witnesses to say otherwise.'

He stabbed a finger at me, then waved it magician-like in the air.

'That's how you think we get out of it do you? Produce witnesses. Easy! No sweat. All we have to do is march into court, tell our side of the story and call as our corroborative witnesses some of the most powerful criminals in the Commonwealth of Australia. As proof of our total innocence we invite them to throw discretion to the winds and tell the jury how they've corrupted half the police force in two states, dominated and controlled prostitution, gambling and the drugs market, and invested the huge profits they've made into legitimate businesses. To which all I can say is that they'll have you shot dead before you even reach the hearing.'

'I know that,' I said. 'That's why Carlo engaged you.'

For a second I thought he'd slap me but he didn't. He sat back in his chair and sighed and studied me. Then he leant forward.

'How much do you know about the Premier's pet boy on the job?' he asked me quickly.

'Everything. Why?'

'What about his unusual sex preferences?'

'I know where he goes and who takes him. I've even seen a movie of him in the saddle.'

For a full ten seconds Ballard's black eyes burnt holes in mine. Then the corners of his mouth moved a fraction and there was an almost contemptuous little twitch of a smile. Without saying another word, he gathered up his things, placed them in his briefcase and rapped on the door for the constable to let him out.

What I expected to happen, I guess, was that Ballard would join O'Reilly and Baker over at the pub, that the right words would be spoken and that I would be ushered into court the next day and everything would flow smoothly on a much reduced offence. I'd be fined and free to go.

But when Barnes brought me an evening meal, which was a counter lunch from the pub, I was shaken by his news. Far from coming to terms with O'Reilly and Baker, Ballard had made it perfectly clear that he was unwilling to discuss or negotiate any deal of any kind at any stage whatsoever.

In the morning Ballard arrived too late to speak to me in the interview room and barely glanced at me as I was led into the dock. The courtroom looked as if it had only recently been built and it reminded me a bit of a crematorium chapel. O'Reilly and Baker were lounging in a couple of chairs, at the ready in case they were called to give evidence. The press seats were occupied by two sharp-faced young reporters and a woman with a camera. The magistrate was a sad-looking, deeply-lined man wearing tinted spectacles.

We were the first case on after the drunks, the druggies, the traffic infringements and the break and enter of a shop. Everyone stared at me when I rose. The charges were read and my occupation was given as a Veterans' Affairs pensioner. The police prosecutor, dressed in a shabby suit, asked at once for a stand-down and two-week adjournment since further investigations were being carried out which, when completed, would almost certainly lead to further charges being laid.

'Mr Ballard?' said the magistrate.

'No objections, Your Worship,' said Ballard. 'May I make an application for bail for my client?'

The police prosecutor jumped to his feet again. 'May it please Your Worship, in view of the nature of this case and the possibilities of it leading to further charges of a more serious nature, plus the ramifications involved, and the fact that the police have reason to believe the defendant could be possibly linked to organised crime, I must stress that in our view bail would be extremely prejudicial to our investigations.'

Ballard rose and leant on the table. 'I beg Your Worship's pardon but I fail to understand how bail could possibly prejudice investigations. It has always been my understanding of the law that bail was intended to assist the defence rather than the prosecution. The prosecution has the entire might of the state's Police Force at its disposal. My client is on his own. His liberty is essential to his defence.'

The police prosecutor was still standing. 'Your Worship. If the accused in this matter is granted bail we have two fears. Firstly that he may leave the country altogether, and secondly that his life may be in grave danger.'

At this there was an audible stir through the courtroom. The clerk of the court swivelled around to look up at the magistrate and the press reporters scribbled away. O'Reilly shifted in his seat and cleared his throat.

'Please, Your Worship,' said Ballard. 'Permit me to submit that the statements made by the prosecution are wild and completely unfounded, and demand substantiation.' He gave a nod and a look which said, bullshit, prove it.

'I must beg the favour of Your Worship's discretion,' said the police prosecutor. 'I am quite sure that my learned friend knows the dangers I am alluding to.'

'I would like to assure Your Worship that I don't have any idea of what the police are referring to,' said Ballard. 'And furthermore, Your Worship, I am certainly not accustomed to melodramatics in a court of law.'

He leant back and stared up into the air as if to say, you'd better get it right amongst yourselves, and if you come up wrong I'll take you all the way to the Privy Council.

The magistrate flushed and cleared his throat. He had been forewarned of what to expect, I had no doubt, in some quick offhand conversation in his rooms and seemed determined that his courtroom would not be another place in which Jeffrey Ballard, QC, abused the police and pulled some smartarsed trick that other lawyers would talk about for years. He glanced at the police prosecutor, received a sternly supportive look and steeled himself for a moment before speaking.

'Mr Ballard,' he said, 'we will adjourn the proceedings for ten minutes, and I would like to speak with yourself and the prosecutor in my chambers. If you are agreeable, that is.'

'As Your Worship pleases,' said Ballard with a bob of his head.

The constable sitting beside me nudged me with his elbow to stand up as the magistrate left, followed by the prosecutor and Ballard. Then we went out into the corridor, where I lit a cigarette.

'I reckon you've got it made, mate,' said the

constable. 'You'll make front page on this one.'

'Bullshit,' I said. 'Lay off will ya.'

We were called back into the courtroom fifteen minutes later. 'Mr Ballard,' the magistrate said, 'having listened to the arguments from counsel and the prosecution I've decided to fix bail at twenty-five thousand dollars.'

Christ, I thought, they're determined to hang to me. I was taken back to the police station, and in the interview room Ballard spoke quietly and told me not to worry, that he was on his way back to Brisbane and he'd see that everything was taken care of. He would be seeing Mr Bellari and using the goods we had on certain high-ranking police officials as a lever. Things would work out. But be patient for a couple of days. That's all he asked.

Two more days I waited in that grotty cell. I grew sick and tired of the graffiti and the stink and the overnight drunks and druggies who filled the place each evening, and the heat and the food and the sanctimonious demonstrations of friendliness from Barnes. I just wanted out.

On the third day I was just about out of my mind when Barnes brought me my breakfast and informed me that I would be going to court again at 10 o'clock. A young solicitor came to see me and told me that Ballard had done what was necessary, that I was to plead guilty to a lesser charge and that I would receive a fine. The police would not be proceeding with other charges. And his parting words to me were: 'Jeffrey said to tell you not to rock the boat. I suppose you know what that means, because I have no idea.'

The magistrate was the same gloomy person but the prosecutor gave a half-smile as I was led in. Ballard wasn't there.

When I was called the police prosecutor stood and said: 'If it would please Your Worship the police do not wish to proceed with matters relating to the defendant numbers 225 and 226. And as a result they will not be submitting evidence in these related matters which the police wish to withdraw. But they wish to proceed with matter 271 if it so please Your Worship.'

The magistrate looked up and bobbed his head. 'Proceed,' he said.

The charge was read out but it wasn't the original one. I had been charged with having an offensive weapon in my possession, and the clerk asked how I pleaded.

'Guilty,' I said

'Fined $750 and $120 court costs,' said the magistrate. He looked at me as if he had never laid eyes on me before and asked if I wished to apply for time to pay.

'Yes, I do.'

'Granted fourteen days,' said the magistrate. 'You are free to go. Next.'

And it was over that quickly.

I went home and climbed under the shower and scrubbed for an hour to get the stink of the cells out of my system. Then pouring a good stiff drink I sat back and closed my eyes. Thinking of the promise I had made Carmel, I let my life run through the corridors of my mind, placing ticks and pluses and minuses, then evaluated the equation. I'd cleaned up the last mess and I wanted peace. Peace with God and peace with myself. I made up my mind and called a taxi.

'Where to, mate?' said the driver.

'St Patrick's in the Valley.'

Sunbeams speared through the clerestory windows, illuminating the central portion of the church. A scattering of people knelt in their pews, their eyes fixed on the altar's golden tabernacle.

I stood on the threshold and my gaze fell on the massive bronze-covered doors that depicted Christ in his majesty and Abraham leaving the Sepulchre. I debated with myself whether or not to enter the Eternal One's house. I put my foot through the door, then withdrew it. Perhaps He would give me a sign, perhaps He would listen to my pleas. And before I could argue myself out of the earlier decision I sucked in a mouthful of air and entered the church.

In the marble vestibule, I looked down at the benitier and, scarcely realising what I was doing, plunged my hand into the holy water. A soothing sensation flowed into my fingers and up my arms, engulfing my body. It was like being washed over by a sea of tranquillity. I held my dripping fingers up and shook the drops of water off them, then slid into the last pew without genuflecting. The bench extended under one of the ambulatory's arches and was bathed in shadows. Sitting in the darkness, I was perfectly still, hidden from the world and yet filled with a rage at the injustices I had suffered, and the ones that I had committed. Why have you forsaken me? Why did you desert me as a child when I needed strength? Why did you take away my

387

love? I have sought vengeance on others for your deeds. Vengeance may be yours but I was your instrument. I beg you no more, don't take any more. Please not again.

I sat for a long time staring at the altar, aware of the pain gnawing at my insides. An aching cold had invaded my body, numbing my bones. I hunched my shoulders and crossed my arms to preserve warmth.

Give me some sign, I prayed. I was close to despair.

Movement off to the right made me turn. Three Sisters of the Church were walking down the aisle. The one in front was young and very beautiful. My mouth fell open and my eyes grew wide in astonishment. It was Margo. It was her face that turned and looked at me and smiled and then walked on. Rising up out of my seat, I watched as she genuflected at the foot of the altar, pushing open the brass gate, and walked up the carpeted steps towards the altar. She turned and her face had changed but the Eternal One had sent me a message. Margo belonged to Him now and her smile had said all is forgiven, go and sin no more. On my past life I could kiss tomorrow goodbye.

Carmel was behind the wheel as we drove out of Surfers. We had said all our goodbyes. I had been given the message. And I thought, am I just one of those men who aren't so bad because they do dirty jobs cleanly? Not any more you're not, a soft voice inside me said.

'What's best,' I said, 'to love or be the witness?'

'Don't ask me,' Carmel said. 'I'm only the driver. Ask the Tiger.'

'Thanks,' I said as she put her foot down and headed

north on the expressway. 'You're as subtle as a train smash.'

'You're not so bad yourself, you know!'

Then we grinned at each other. She really can keep me together, I thought, and this is the day we're really doing it. We're taking off up north to find that place that no one has discovered. We'll call it our place, yeah, that's it, Our place.

We can stay there forever and be cleansed in the white sand and the blue water.

J.R. Carroll

No Way Back

VIOLENT . . . SEXY . . . CHILLING

His fellow cops say he's trigger-happy.

His ex-wife says he's unstable.

His new lover says he's obsessive.

His superiors say he's off the case and under investigation.

His world is coming apart. . .

He's a cop on the trail of a killer the law can't touch.

He has his own brand of justice.

He's got nothing to lose. Except his life.

When you've been pushed to the edge, there's no way back. . .

J.R. Carroll

Out of the Blue

SEARING . . . RELENTLESS . . .
THE ULTIMATE REVENGE

The shockingly violent death of his wife was no accident.
And Dennis Gatz knows it.

But the cops aren't interested. Gatz is a loose cannon
who couldn't handle the force. No longer one of them.
Not worth the trouble.

But trouble's on the way. Someone's out to get Dennis
Gatz and he can't wait to meet them. Head on.

This time it's personal. This time he'll do anything for
revenge.

And the best revenge comes out of the blue.

J.R. Carroll

Stingray

'You reckon you've seen everything, but you never have, have you? There's always something really shitful up ahead. Waiting for you . . . '

The bodies of eight women are uncovered in the scrub at Kinglake. For Kerry Byrne, head of the task force investigating the murders, it's a problem he doesn't need.

It's enough that his wife is slipping away from him. Enough that he has to put loyalty to a mate above loyalty to the force. Enough that he might become a target of investigation himself . . .

An uncompromising thriller from the author of *No Way Back* and *Out of the Blue*.

'Carroll gets better and better . . . not for the squeamish.' *The Sun-Herald*